SELECTED WRITINGS

The Library of Liberal Arts
OSKAR PIEST, FOUNDER

The Library of Liberal Arts

SELECTED WRITINGS

GEORGE HERBERT MEAD

Edited, with an Introduction, by
ANDREW J. RECK
Professor of Philosophy, Tulane University

• •

The Library of Liberal Arts

published by

THE BOBBS-MERRILL COMPANY, INC.
A Subsidiary of Howard W. Sams & Co., Inc.
Publishers • Indianapolis • New York • Kansas City

George Herbert Mead: 1863-1931

. . . .

For My Mother and Father

·191
M479

PREFACE

George Herbert Mead (1863–1931) was, after John Dewey, America's most creative pragmatist philosopher in the period between World War I and the Great Depression. This volume furnishes a selective collection of those writings which he himself published during his lifetime. In the summer of 1962, while preparing a study of Mead's philosophy for publication in *Tulane Studies in Philosophy*, XII (1963), in commemoration of the centennial of his birth, I discovered that, although five posthumously published volumes based on his lectures and notes presented his thought and were in print, his own publications, which number over sixty items and consist of reviews, journal articles, and chapters in books, had never been collected and were scattered in journals and out-of-print books. A critical review of these writings convinced me of their philosophical and historical value. The present volume makes available for the first time a selective collection of Mead's published essays, touching on every major feature of his thought.

The essays are arranged in the chronological order of their first appearance. Historically, they are important for revealing the intellectual breadth and development of Mead and, incidentally, for representing the characteristic currents of thought and topics investigated during a period now referred to as the "golden age" or "classic period" of American philosophy. Each essay, in addition to its historical value, is philosophically noteworthy. In originality of thought Mead was second to none. Both John Dewey and Alfred North Whitehead have praised him as a seminal mind of the first rank.

Although Mead was neither a prolific nor a graceful writer, he had the means to make his ideas as clear as their complexity, novelty, and incompleteness would allow. Like Charles

Peirce, he was haunted by the dream of stating his thought in a system, and unfortunately, like Peirce, he never lived to achieve his dream. He published each essay as a separate piece, with only occasional cross references, and so each can be read separately today. But within the ensemble a developing system may be discerned. The Introduction is devised to provide the historical and systematic context which unifies and illuminates the chronologically arranged essays. My aim in the Introduction is to articulate the genesis and structure of Mead's thought, and to do so, as far as possible, by reference to his own publications.

I owe whatever understanding and appreciation of Mead's philosophy I possess to many persons. Two deserve special mention. Harold N. Lee first introduced me to Mead by assigning *Movements of Thought in the Nineteenth Century* as a text for his course in Kant and German Idealism, which I elected in 1947, and by discussing Mead's philosophy with me on many occasions thereafter up to the present. Recently, Paul Weiss, knowing of my intention to pursue studies in recent American philosophy, urged me in several letters to look to Mead, and finally he persuaded me. I acknowledge gratefully my indebtedness to the George A. and Eliza Gardner Howard Foundation, affiliated with Brown University, for the award of a fellowship for 1962–1963 which, along with the supplemental generosity of the Tulane Research Council, afforded me the leisure to do studies on American thought, of which the present volume is a part.

ANDREW J. RECK

New Orleans, Louisiana
August 1963

ACKNOWLEDGMENTS

For permission to use the selections in the present volume, the editor and the publisher make grateful acknowledgment to the following:

The American Psychological Association, for "Concerning Animal Perception," *The Psychological Review,* XIV (1907); "Social Psychology as Counterpart to Physiological Psychology," *Psychological Bulletin,* VI (1909); and "Social Consciousness and the Consciousness of Meaning," *ibid.,* VII (1910).

Holt, Rinehart and Winston, Inc., for "Scientific Method and Individual Thinker," from *Creative Intelligence: Essays in the Pragmatic Attitude* (1917); and "The Nature of the Past," from *Essays in Honor of John Dewey,* edited by John Coss. Copyright 1929, copyright renewed © 1957 by Holt, Rinehart and Winston, Inc.

The Editors of *The Journal of Philosophy,* for "What Social Objects Must Psychology Presuppose?" *The Journal of Philosophy, Psychology, and Scientific Methods,* VII (1910); "The Mechanism of Social Consciousness," *ibid.,* IX (1912); "The Social Self," *ibid.,* X (1913); "Natural Rights and the Theory of the Political Institution," *ibid.,* XII (1915); and "A Behavioristic Account of the Significant Symbol," *The Journal of Philosophy,* XIX (1922).

The Open Court Publishing Co., for "The Objective Reality of Perspectives," from *The Philosophy of the Present.*

The Editors of *The Philosophical Review,* for "Suggestions toward a Theory of the Philosophical Disciplines," *The Philosophical Review,* IX (1900).

The Editors of *Science,* for "The Teaching of Science in College," *Science,* XXIV (1906); and "The Psychology of Social Consciousness Implied in Instruction," *ibid.,* XXXI (1910).

The University of California Press, for "A Pragmatic Theory of Truth," *Studies in the Nature of Truth,* "University of California Publications in Philosophy," XI (1929).

The University of Chicago Press, for "Philanthropy from the Point of View of Ethics," from *Intelligent Philanthropy* (1930).

CONTENTS
. . . .

SELECTED WRITINGS

INTRODUCTION

I. LIFE AND WORKS

Among the group of thinkers who gathered at the University of Chicago at the turn of the century and who soon came to be known as the "Chicago School," George Herbert Mead, after John Dewey, stands out most prominently. The son of a New England clergyman, Mead was born on February 27, 1863, in South Hadley, Massachusetts. In 1870 Mead's family moved to Oberlin, Ohio, where in 1879 Mead enrolled in college, graduating in 1883. From 1887 to 1888 Mead did graduate work in philosophy and psychology at Harvard University, when the department of philosophy was on the eve of greatness, with Josiah Royce, William James, and George Herbert Palmer the guiding spirits. In 1891, after a period of study at Berlin, Mead returned to the United States to join the department of philosophy at the University of Michigan, where John Dewey, James H. Tufts, and Charles Horton Cooley were teaching. At Michigan, Mead pressed his investigations into physiological psychology, and it is this specialty for which he was best known for the next decade. While Dewey offered a teleological theory of the emotions, Mead offered a parallel physiological theory.[1] Following Dewey to the new University of Chicago in 1893, he remained there until his death on April 26, 1931, and played a major role in the formation of the "Chicago School."

Mead is widely recognized as the thinker who, next to Dewey, contributed most to the development of pragmatism during the period immediately after World War I. Like Peirce before him, Mead won his place despite scanty publications. During his life, he published articles addressed only

[1] Mead, "A Theory of Emotions from the Physiological Standpoint," *The Psychological Review*, II (1895), 162–164.

to a small group of professional readers. Add to this his tendency (observed by John Dewey) to understate the originality
of his thought by linking it "to ideas and movements already
current" [2] and Mead's contributions risked oblivion. After
his death, however, his achievement became known to a wider
audience through the publication of four books based upon
his lectures and papers: (1) his Carus lectures published as
The Philosophy of the Present (1932); (2) notes from his lectures in his course in Social Psychology published as *Mind,
Self and Society* (1934); [3] (3) notes from his lectures in his
course in "Movements of Thought in the Nineteenth Century" published under the same title (1936); [4] and (4) unpublished papers, supplemented by notes from lectures, published
as *The Philosophy of the Act* (1938).[5] In 1956 Anselm Strauss
edited a fifth volume, *The Social Psychology of George Herbert Mead,*[6] based upon selections from the three earlier volumes published by the University of Chicago Press.

Yet those chapters, articles, and book reviews which Mead
himself had published during his life, though numbering over
sixty items, were not collected. Occasionally a paper would
appear in an anthology or would close such a volume as *The
Philosophy of the Present,* but otherwise these works have

[2] Mead, *The Philosophy of the Present,* edited, with an Introduction,
by Arthur E. Murphy, with prefatory remarks by John Dewey (La Salle,
Ill.: Open Court Publishing Company, 1932), p. xxxv. Hereafter *PP.*

[3] Mead, *Mind, Self and Society; from the Standpoint of a Social Behaviorist,* edited, with an Introduction, by Charles W. Morris (Chicago:
University of Chicago Press, 1934). Hereafter *MSS.*

[4] Mead, *Movements of Thought in the Nineteenth Century,* edited, with
an Introduction, by Merritt H. Moore (Chicago: University of Chicago
Press, 1936). Hereafter *MT.*

[5] Mead, *The Philosophy of the Act,* edited, with an Introduction, by
Charles W. Morris, in collaboration with John M. Brewster, Albert M.
Dunham, and David L. Miller (Chicago: University of Chicago Press,
1938). Hereafter *PA.*

[6] *The Social Psychology of George Herbert Mead,* edited by Anselm
Strauss, "Phoenix Books" (Chicago: University of Chicago Press, 1956).
At present the University of Chicago Press is planning another edition
of Mead's works.

been out of print, most of them in dusty journals at least thirty years old, and some dating back to the last years of the nineteenth century and the first years of the present one. A review of these items discloses that individually many of them are worthy of republication and that a selective collection of these works would compose an important volume. Such a collection touches on the full range of Mead's multifaceted thought, reveals the chronological course of its development, and furnishes the student and the scholar that optimum textual security which only the writings an author has himself published may guarantee. The primary aim of the present volume, therefore, is to provide a selective collection of Mead's own publications.

Because Mead scattered his theories in reviews, articles, lectures, and incomplete fragments, the justification of a selective collection is self-evident. Because amidst these dispersed publications a major unfinished system of thought is discernible, it is the aim of this introduction to recover its significance and to sketch its structure.

II. THE MEANING OF PRAGMATISM

The Historical Context of Pragmatism

As one of the most perceptive historians of ideas of his generation, Mead grasped the meaning of pragmatism within its historical setting and social milieu. Impressed by the fact that philosophy since the Renaissance has been preoccupied with interpreting the results of science (*MT*, p. 343), Mead traced the rise of pragmatism to the conjunction of two scientific developments—behavioristic psychology and scientific methodology (*MT*, p. 351). The behavioristic foundation of pragmatism stems from Darwin's theory of biological evolution. Viewing the living organism as engaged in a vital struggle for control over its environment, Darwin's theory entails a naturalistic conception of mind which radically redefines thinking or intelligence. An elaborate process instrumental to the organism's survival and success, thinking gropes to depict "the world so that it will be favorable for conduct. . . . The test of intelligence is found in action" (*MT*, p. 345). The methodological foundation of pragmatism is rooted in research science, which is "only the evolutionary process grown self-conscious" (*MT*, p. 364). For it, too, is essentially a problem-solving activity. And the problematic situations with which scientific method copes are similar to the obstacles with which animals struggle. Both sets of problems obstruct activity, whether it be the activity of intelligence or the muscular-motor activities of organisms, and the aim of the scientist in his laboratory, like that of the beast in the jungle, is to cope with the environment, so as to keep up the ongoing activity. As Mead said, "The animal is doing the same thing the scientist is doing" (*MT*, p. 346).

Pragmatism concentrates both upon behavior or conduct and upon the verification of ideas by means of experience. The concern with conduct implies a theory of action, but until Mead, no pragmatist attempted to advance a philosophy of act on a comprehensive scale. As regards the empirical demand of pragmatism that ideas be subjected to the tests of experience, it is important to note that the pragmatic conception of experience by Peirce, Dewey, and Mead is not the sort of subjectivism usually associated with traditional empiricism. Not only is experience conceived in terms of verbs, in terms of doing rather than of passively receiving, but also it is understood to be a social process.

Functionalism

Mead's pragmatism as a "philosophy of act" was originally an offshoot of functional psychology. Historically, the birth of "functionalism," suggested by William James in his *Principles of Psychology* (1890), is ascribed to the publication in 1896 of John Dewey's revolutionary article, "The Reflex Arc Concept."[1] An outgrowth of the impact of evolution on psychology, functionalism was within a few years an established school, associated with the University of Chicago, where it was advanced through the works of James Rowland Angell, Harvey Carr, and others. Mead carried functionalism into the field of social psychology, and in consequence, he discovered the merits of behaviorism, although he retained the functionalist conception of the evolution, character, and utility of mind.

Functionalism continued the attack on psychological atomism begun by William James. John Dewey had, in fact, pressed the attack against the very concept which had supposedly replaced the old atomism—namely, the concept of the reflex arc of stimulus and response. Dewey alleged that the reflex concept concealed the former atomism, but imperfectly since the distinctions between stimulus and response, sensation and movement, were atomistically conceived. Activity, Dewey argued, is a continuous whole, not a compound of discrete elements. The distinctions between stimulus and response, sensation and movement, are functional, being based on what the processes do. Dewey had further suggested that the stimulus provided by the environment, in order to be a stimulus, requires the attention and the responsiveness of the organism. Thus he placed attention at the center of consciousness.

Mead's earliest publications in philosophy and psychology were significant contributions to functionalist psychology. Two essays stand out: "Suggestions toward a Theory of the Philosophical Disciplines" (1900),[2] and "The Definition of the Psychical" (1903).[3]

Despite its obscurity, "The Definition of the Psychical"

[1] Dewey, "The Reflex Arc Concept in Psychology," *The Psychological Review*, III (1896), 357–370.

[2] Mead, "Suggestions toward a Theory of the Philosophical Disciplines," *The Philosophical Review*, IX (1900), 1–17. See below, p. 6.

[3] Mead, "The Definition of the Psychical," *The Decennial Publications of the University of Chicago*, "First Series," III (1903), 77–112. See below, p. 25.

argues two theses favored by the functionalists. First, by a thorough examination of the definitions of the subject-matter of psychology furnished by other psychologists, Mead sought to show how their methodological assumptions determine their definitions. Thus the subject-matter of psychology, instead of being given to the investigator, is rather defined or constructed by the investigator according to his assumptions and aims. A concept is valid when functional—when, in other words, it facilitates the successful realization of the purposes of the investigation. Secondly, Mead's proposed definition of the psychical, branching out from Dewey's treatment of the reflex arc, stresses the genesis and utility of mind and consciousness in activity. The psychical is itself a particular phase in the evolutionary development of reality. Mind or consciousness comes into existence when an intelligent organism has its ongoing activity interrupted by a problem. It is a special kind of instrument for the intelligent organism to deal with its problem and find the appropriate solution in order to resume its ongoing activity.

"Suggestions toward a Theory of the Philosophical Disciplines" also sets out from Dewey's treatment of the reflex arc, ambitiously sketching a general theory of all the philosophical disciplines based upon a "dialectic within the act." James Rowland Angell has cited the article as a superb example of the functionalist program of offering a "reasonable and cogent account of the 'rise of reflective consciousness and its significance as manifested in various philosophical disciplines." [4] Since reflective consciousness is a special kind of instrument by which the intelligent organism can meet problems that obstruct its ongoing activity, enabling it to find those solutions that make possible the continuance of its activity, the various philosophical disciplines, arenas of reflective consciousness, are defined in relation to the act and its problems. Metaphysics is the discipline which makes the "statement of the problem." When, by recognizing the problem, the intelligent organism

4 Angell, "The Province of Functional Psychology," *The Psychological Review*, XIV (1907), 89.

becomes conscious of the pertinent meanings of past experience, it grasps universals; and the systematic use of these universals is deductive logic. If, instead of attending to the old universals, it focuses on the immediate experience which presents the problem, then this immediate experience, with only subjective validity, is the subject of psychology. Inductive logic is the procedure of employing the subjective material of immediate experience to obtain new universals. Ethics is the application of both deductive and inductive procedures to conduct, and aesthetics is the artistic representation of objects either as ideals or as phases in the development of experience. Thus all the philosophical disciplines are explained in terms of the act and its problems. The neo-Hegelianism of Mead's conception is apparent not only in his phraseology, so characteristic of the period, but also in his systematic intention to embrace all the philosophical disciplines in a general dialectic.

Theory of the Act

In his early appreciation and exploitation of the philosophical potentialities of the functionalist concept of the dynamic relation between stimulus and response, organism and environment, Mead surpassed Dewey. The act is Mead's term for this relation, and he called the act the "unit of existence" (*PA,* p. 65). As early as 1894, two years before the publication of Dewey's famous article on "The Reflex Arc Concept," Mead had reached the conclusion that the attention of the organism is the crux of consciousness and that this attention is the domination of one activity over other activities issuing in a unified act. He explicitly cited James Mark Baldwin's equation of the Kantian unity of apperception with the act of attention, and in a discussion of the neo-Kantian philosophy of science, he proceeded to construe attention and its objects by reference to the activities of the organism in respect to its environment. Whereas the neo-Kantian theory of objects stressed their construction solely by means of conceptual categories, Mead insisted that all objects, in common sense, in physics, and in psychology, are the evolved products of the acts of organisms in respect to their environments.[5]

Mead defined the act as an "ongoing event that consists in the stimulation and response and the results of the response" (*PA*, p. 364). In 1907, in a short article, "Concerning Animal Perception," Mead had come to distinguish three stages in the act.[6] In terminology he used later, these stages are: perception, manipulation, and consummation. The discrimination of these stages must not obscure the concrete wholeness of the act, for the act, as the "unit of existence," is not a thin moment but rather "stretches beyond the stimulus to the response" (*PA*, p. 65). The act is an event going on in the present, but it has a past reference and a future reference, and so is qualified both by the past and the future.

Perception. Perception is defined as a "relation between a highly developed physiological organism and an object, or an environment in which selection emphasizes certain elements" (*PA*, p. 8). Perception is a temporal process pervaded by activity. There is the action through the media which stimulate the senses, there is the action of the organism selecting this stimulus, and there is the total perceptual response to this interaction.

The process of perceiving is subjectively experienced as sensing. Sensing is no passive presentation of content; rather, it is an activity or complex of processes and activities. Each type of sensing requires specific bodily acts on the part of the organism—for example, the focusing of eyes. The activity of sensing, furthermore, proceeds according to the sensitivity and the selectivity of the organism: without eyes capable of perceiving colors, there are no colors.

Before the perceiving organism stands the perceptual object. This object, while in part originating in the world in-

[5] See Mead's review of K. Lasswitz, *Die moderne Energetik in ihrer Bedeutung für Erkenntniskritik*, in *The Psychological Review*, I (1894), 210–213; and also "Herr Lasswitz on Energy and Epistemology," *ibid.*, 172–175.

[6] Mead, "Concerning Animal Perception," *The Psychological Review*, XIV (1907), 383–390. See below, p. 73.

dependent of this particular organism, is also in part a product of the physiological structure, responsiveness, and selectivity of the organism. It is perceived to be colored, to emit
sounds, odors, etc. Furthermore, it is perceived to be out there,
at a distance from the perceiving organism. "The object in
perception is a distant object" (*PA*, p. 12). As a distant object,
it invites not only action, but questions as to whether or not
it actually possesses the properties it is perceived to have.
Such questions, of course, arise "only when the conduct which
the characters of the object call out does or does not reach a
successful conclusion" (*PA*, p. 11).

Manipulation. Perception leads directly to the next stage
of the act—manipulation. An outgrowth of the behavior by
which organisms relate themselves to what is spatiotemporally
away from them, sense perception is a form of conduct that
leads the organism toward or farther away from the object
according as the act predicates contact or the absence of contact (*PA*, p. 141). Contact calls forth manipulation. As a physical thing, describable in terms of physical mechanisms that
condition its act, such as the muscular contractions, the nervous irritations connected with these contractions, the nervous
centers affected thereby, and the motor paths traversed (*PA*,
p. 451), the organism engages in a line of conduct which
brings it in contact with the object or which avoids such contact. "Contact is the test of the success of the act" and also the
test of the reality of the object of perception (*PA*, p. 141).

Consummation. As perception presents at a distance an
object which stimulates the organism, and as manipulation is
a mediate activity which brings the exterior of the organism
into contact with the object, consummation is final: it completes the act. Though Mead described the perceptual and
manipulatory phases of the act behavioristically and physiologically, he employed the language of values to depict the
consummatory stage. "Within the field of consummation all
the adjectives of value obtain immediately. There objects are
possessed, are good, bad, and indifferent, beautiful or ugly,

and lovely or noxious" (*PA,* p. 25). The consummatory phase of the act has the immediate qualitative character of aesthetic experience.

Reflection

Frustrated action is the cause of thought. "Reflective thinking arises in testing the means which are presented for carrying out some hypothetical way of continuing action which has been checked" (*PA,* p. 79). At one with the other pragmatists and heavily influenced by Dewey, Mead has outlined the experimental method of inquiry in five steps: (1) the presence of a problem; (2) the statement of the problem in terms of the conditions of its possible solutions; (3) the getting of ideas, or the forming of hypotheses; (4) the mental testing of the hypotheses; and (5) the experimental testing of the hypotheses (*PA,* p. 82).

In 1917 a group of prominent pragmatists, under the leadership of John Dewey, cooperated to state their common outlook on the major topics of philosophy in a textbook, aptly titled, *Creative Intelligence.* In a long essay, "Scientific Method and Individual Thinker," Mead treated the philosophy of science, and illustrating his arguments by examples drawn from the history of science, he contended that science is a method men devise to cope with problems which, arising in immediate experience, conflict with their inherited conceptions and usual expectations. Because these problems render the world unsettled, they disrupt action, and so, if conduct is to continue, they must be resolved. It is not that the entire world becomes problematic for the intelligent organism. On the contrary, only specific regions of the world are problematic at any one time. Thus the scientific mentality, while taking the rest of the world for granted, concentrates exclusively on problematic situations. Just as these problems are felt first within the immediate experiences of the individual thinkers, so too, as Mead suggested, it is individual thinkers who create or invent the hypotheses which solve these problems. In this sense, intelligence is creative. It reconstructs those regions of the world which have broken down, and in doing so, it reconstructs to varying extents and degrees the world of which the problematic situations are parts.[7]

The pragmatist conception of reflective consciousness as essentially problem-solving implies a special doctrine of truth and of judgment. In 1929 Mead stated his conception of truth and of judgment in an essay which appeared in the *University of California Publications in Philosophy* under the title "A Pragmatic Theory of Truth." He wrote, "Truth is . . . synonymous with the solution of the problem." Such solution involves reconstruction of the situation to allow action to go on. Into the problematic situation in which action has been checked, "the judgment comes with healing in its wings." [8]

Although it might at first seem that the pragmatic conception of knowledge is too restrictive and practical to allow investigations into general problems of a purely theoretical nature, Mead was careful to point out how philosophy rightly conducts investigations into the most general topics. Within the context of pragmatic philosophy, therefore, is found a place for the disinterested pursuit of knowledge for its own sake. As Mead declared in his 1917 essay:

> The conception of a world of existence . . . is the result of the determination at the moment of the conditions of the solution of the given problems. These problems constitute the conditions of conduct, and the ends of conduct can only be determined as we realize the possibilities which changing conditions carry with them. Our world of reality thus becomes independent of any special ends or purposes and we reach an entirely disinterested knowledge. And yet the value and import of this knowledge is found in our conduct and in our continually changing conditions. Knowledge for

[7] Mead, "Scientific Method and Individual Thinker," *Creative Intelligence: Essays in the Pragmatic Attitude* (New York: Henry Holt and Co., 1917), pp. 176–227. See below, p. 171.

[8] Mead, "A Pragmatic Theory of Truth," in *Studies in the Nature of Truth*, "University of California Publications in Philosophy," XI (Berkeley and Los Angeles: The University of California Press, 1929), 73, 82. See below, pp. 328, 338.

its own sake is the slogan of freedom, for it alone makes possible the continual reconstruction and enlargement of the ends of conduct.[9]

III. SOCIAL PSYCHOLOGY

As a functionalist, absorbing the impact of Darwinian evolution upon psychology, Mead undertook to find "such a place for mind in nature that nature could appear in experience."[1] Although Mead's early work was in the area of physiological psychology, he came to see that physiological psychology alone could not furnish an adequate account of mind. In 1900 he had introduced his famous course in social psychology at the University of Chicago. While functionalism in psychology was hostile to the structuralism favored by Wilhelm Max Wundt in Europe and by Edward Bradford Titchener in America, Mead was a close and sympathetic student of Wundt's broad cultural approach to the questions of psychology, and early in the century he published penetrating and comprehensive critiques of Wundt's theories.[2] By 1909 he was prepared to argue in print that in order to obtain a correct and comprehensive theory of mind, social psychology is the indispensable counterpart of physiological psychology.[3] The fundamental datum for psychology, according to Mead, is not the tract but the act (*MSS*, p. 8). In a capsule he summed up the history of psychology thus: "Psychology became in turn associational, motor, functional, and finally behavioristic" (*MSS*, p. 21). Outgrowing exclusively physiologi-

[9] Mead, "Scientific Method and Individual Thinker." See below, pp. 209–210.

[1] Mead, "The Objective Reality of Perspectives," *Proceedings of the Sixth International Congress of Philosophy* (New York: Longmans, Green and Company, 1927), p. 75. See below, p. 306.

[2] Mead, "The Relations of Psychology and Philology," *Psychological Bulletin*, I (1904), 375–391, and also "The Imagination in Wundt's Treatment of Myth and Religion," *ibid.*, III (1906), 393–399.

[3] Mead, "Social Psychology as Counterpart to Physiological Psychology," *ibid.*, VI (1909), 401–408. See below, p. 94.

cal psychology and also, in due time, functional psychology, Mead arrived at a position which is known as social behaviorism.

Social Behaviorism

Social behaviorism studies "the experience of the individual from the point of view of his conduct, particularly, but not exclusively, the conduct as it is observable by others" *(MSS,* p. 2). It may be defined by contrast with the social psychology of Charles Horton Cooley and with the psychological behaviorism of John Watson. From Cooley, his colleague at the University of Michigan from 1891 to 1893, Mead learned that in consciousness there is "a social process going on, within which the self and others arise." [4] And Watson, who received the first Ph. D. in psychology awarded by the University of Chicago, invented the behaviorism that served Mead as the foil to which he opposed his own theory.

Watson, Mead conceded, was essentially right when he sought to make psychology the science of overt behavior. In taking the act as the crucial fact in the origin and function of consciousness, Mead himself had, prior to the advent of Watson, concluded that the study of conduct, of overt behavior, is essential to psychology as a science. Favorably impressed with behaviorism, Mead nonetheless deemed Watson's approach wrong on two major counts: first, its restriction of psychology to the study of the behavior of individuals; and secondly, its denial of the existence of individual consciousness as a result of its inveterate distrust and repudiation of introspection. Individual behavior exists and can be understood only in the social process, in terms of social acts that go beyond the individual and aim at social objects that call forth the activities of other individuals. In 1909, in a paper delivered before the Psychological Association, Mead maintained that psychology as the study of individual experience

[4] Mead, "Cooley's Contribution to American Social Thought," *The American Journal of Sociology,* XXXV (1930), 700.

presupposes social experience, since the individual comes to
exist only in the field of social experience involving the recognition of other selves.[5] A fully developed psychology must,
therefore, proceed to the study of social behavior.

On the point of subjective consciousness, Mead had been
too much of a functionalist in psychology to embrace the identity materialism implicit in Watsonian behaviorism. According to functionalism, mind, or consciousness, emerging at a
late stage in the history of biological evolution, performs a
distinctive function in the life of the organism. There is,
then, a private irreducible side to mind—individual subjectivity—although, instead of dwelling in another world apart from
nature, it is a function of the physical organism, integral to
this natural world. As Mead put it: "The experience of the
individual in its exceptional character is the growing-point
of science, first of all in the recognition of data upon which
the older theories break, and second in the hypothesis which
arises in the individual and is tested by the experiment which
reconstructs the world." [6] Recognizing the creative role of
subjectivity in knowledge, Mead insisted that subjectivity is
the inner counterpart and, indeed, the source of overt behavior (MSS, p. 5). Thus, unlike Watson's behaviorism, which
neglects the inner side of behavior, that "part of the act"
which lies within the organism and only comes to expression
later, Mead's social behaviorism acknowledges the existence of
the inside, the inner, the private.

Mind

Mead traced the genesis of mind back to private situations
constituted by social acts. The fundamental concept, denoting
the simplest unit of social behavior as well as the historical

[5] Mead, "What Social Objects Must Psychology Presuppose?" *The Journal of Philosophy, Psychology, and Scientific Methods*, VII (1910), 174–180.
See below, p. 105.

[6] Mead, "Scientific Method and Individual Thinker." See below, p. 207.

origin of mind, is the concept of the gesture, which Mead derived from Wundt.

Essentially social, a gesture is the act of one organism operating as the stimulus to another organism for his response. At the level of animal conduct, gestures are merely stimuli to performed reaction, as in the case of "two growling dogs walking around each other, with tense limbs, bristly hair, and uncovered teeth." Human conduct, controlled by inhibition and voluntary attention, increases in gesture "the signs of activities which are not carried out." [7] When an image of anticipated consequences accompanies the gesture, meaning arises, and reflective consciousness dawns. Consciousness of meaning, rooted to gesture, is the essence of mind. Consciousness of meaning, Mead has said, "consists mainly in a consciousness of attitude, on the part of the individual, over against the object to which he is about to react. . . . The feelings of readiness to take up or read a book, to spring over a ditch, to hurl a stone, are the stuff out of which arises a sense of the meaning of the book, the ditch, the stone." [8]

The gesture marks the origin of mind, and as Mead was quick to note, it is social. Every gesture presupposes that there is another to react to it. In the development of mind Mead granted special status to the vocal gesture. Even in the case of lower animals some gestures are vocal, as, for example, the growls of the fighting dogs, but in the case of man vocal gestures are the very stuff from which language is constructed. "The vocal gesture is of peculiar importance because it reacts upon the individual who makes it in the same fashion that it reacts upon another." [9] A man hears his own voice. By means of the vocal gesture the individual is able to place

[7] Mead, "What Social Objects Must Psychology Presuppose?" See below, pp. 111, 110.

[8] Mead, "Social Consciousness and the Consciousness of Meaning," *Psychological Bulletin*, VII (1910), 399. See below, p. 123.

[9] Mead, "A Behavioristic Account of the Significant Symbol," *The Journal of Philosophy*, XIX (1922), 160. See below, p. 243.

himself in the position of the other, to assume the role of the other.

The significant symbol, or word, is the fundamental element of which language is composed. It is the product of the vocal gesture that acts as stimulus to both the agent and the respondent organisms. Mead defined the significant symbol as "the gesture, the sign, the word which is addressed to the self when it is addressed to another individual, and is addressed to another, in form to all other individuals, when it is addressed to the self." [10] It refers, on the one hand, to the thing indicated, which it denotes, and on the other hand, to the meaning or idea which it connotes. This meaning as noted above consists in the responsiveness of individual selves. Universals, while indispensable to the meaning process, are pinned to behavioral dispositions. Mead's social behavioristic theory of meaning is based upon the significant symbol interpreted in terms of a triadic relation between the individual organism as the agent of gesture, the object denoted, and the individual organism to whom the gesture is directed. Its operancy depends upon the universality of meaning rooted in the responsiveness of agent as well as patient organisms. "Our symbols are all universal" (*MSS*, p. 146).

Language for Mead is the field from which mind emerges and in which it dwells. This does not mean that mind and language are the same. Mead did not equate mind with linguistic behavior, since he recognized the presence of subjective content, such as imagery. Yet Mead's recognition of language as the social habitat of mind precluded the equation of mind to sets of mental processes locked up in the brains of separate individuals. Rather, for Mead, mind is a social process, and as a social process it is relational and involves terms, objects and other selves. "Mind," he said, "lies in a field of conduct between a specific individual and the environment, in which the individual is able, through the generalized atti-

10 *Ibid*. See below, p. 246.

tude he assumes, to make use of symbolic gestures, i.e., terms, which are significant to all including himself." [11]

The Self

John Dewey has suggested that the "nature of conscious-ness as personal and private" was for Mead the "original haunting question" that dominated all his inquiries and prob-lems (*PP*, pp. xxxvi–xxxvii). While Mead conceived mind as a social process, he also recognized the individual self, although itself the product of the social process, as a source of privacy, uniqueness, and creativity. Individual selfhood depends upon reflexiveness—the ability of the subject to be an object to it-self. A crucial problem in psychology is to explain how a nat-ural organism can attain reflexiveness, that is, the self-con-sciousness upon which selfhood depends.

The original mechanism of reflexive consciousness, of self-hood, is the vocal gesture. Aware of his own vocal gestures, the individual makes himself an object to himself. So Mead has confessed "every reason to doubt" that a "consciousness of a self as an object would ever have arisen in man if he had not the mechanism of talking to himself." [12] In the use of sig-nificant symbols the individual assumes the attitude of the other; he is both subject and object. "The mechanism of thought," said Mead, "is but an inner conversation." [13] The weight of Mead's theory of the self falls on the side of re-flexiveness in a social process, and the essence of this reflex-iveness, incarnate in internalized linguistic behavior, is cogni-tive.

Vocal gestures, significant symbols, internalized conversa-

[11] *Ibid*. See below, p. 247.

[12] Mead, "The Mechanism of Social Consciousness," *The Journal of Philosophy, Psychology, and Scientific Methods*, IX (1912), 405. See be-low, p. 140.

[13] Mead, "The Social Self," *The Journal of Philosophy, Psychology, and Scientific Methods*, X (1913), 377. See below, p. 146.

tion—in a word, language—refer to the fundamental causal factors in the genesis of the individual self. There are, however, other facts. In his mature essay, "The Genesis of the Self and Social Control," Mead cited both play and games as contributing to the development of selfhood. Mead's theory of education, conspicuously progressive, recognized the values of play and games in the school.[14] Selfhood depends upon the capacity of the individual to assume the attitudes and the roles of others. In "The Genesis of the Self and Social Control," he enlarged on how play and games develop selfhood. In play the child assumes the role of another, as, for example, when playing with a doll, he "responds in tone of voice and in attitude as his parents respond to his own cries and chortles." The organized game, with its regulated procedure and rules, marks a still more advanced form of self-integration. In the organized game the individual acts according to rules that require him to regard his conduct and that of each other participant from the standpoint of all others. Mead said:

> The child must not only take the role of the other, as he does in the play, but he must assume the various roles of all the participants in the game, and govern his action accordingly. If he plays first base, it is as the one to whom the ball will be thrown from the field or from the catcher. Their organized reactions to him he has embedded in his own playing of the different positions, and this organized reaction becomes what I have called the "generalized other" that accompanies and controls his conduct. And it is this generalized other in his experience which provides him with a self.[15]

A social structure that emerges from the social process, the self is also individual. Its individuality is paradoxically im-

[14] Mead, "The Relation of Play to Education," *The University Record* (Chicago), I (1896–1897), 140–145, and also "The Psychology of Social Consciousness Implied in Instruction," *Science,* XXXI (1910), 688–693. For the latter, see below, p. 114.

[15] Mead, "The Genesis of the Self and Social Control," *International Journal of Ethics,* XXXV (1924–1925), 269. See below, p. 285.

plicated in its sociality.[16] The individual self is individual only because of its relation to others. The essence of the self is reflexiveness—its ability to take itself as an object from the standpoint of others. Because this reflexiveness hinges on internalized conversation, the self is basically cognitive.

In an early paper (1903), in which Mead placed himself on the side of Kant against such empirical theories of the self as that of William James, he distinguished two aspects of the self—the "I" and the "me"—and commented on the "loss of dignity" suffered by the "I" in modern positivistic psychology.[17] A decade later, in his paper on "The Social Self" (1913), Mead approached the task of defining the self by means of introspection. The self, he reported, cannot appear in consciousness as an "I." What appears in consciousness is always an object, that is, a "me." The "me," however, is inconceivable without an "I," a subject for which it can be an object. But since this "I" cannot be a presentation of consciousness, it must be a presupposition.[18]

Despite noticeable alterations of phraseology in later years, Mead's distinction between the "I" and the "me" crops up in all of his subsequent discussions of the self. Recently it has spurred considerable comment. Mead's conceptions of the "I" and the "me" have been compared with Henri Bergson's conceptions of the dynamic self and the static self, with Freud's conceptions of the ego and superego, or with Sartre's conceptions of the self and the situation. Mead himself wished to avert a metaphysical explanation of the distinction and to elucidate its significance strictly from the point of view of conduct itself. For while the "me" exists as an object of consciousness, the "I" cannot be such an object. It, therefore, is a kind of fiction lying always beyond the borders of consciousness, al-

[16] Grace Chin Lee, *George Herbert Mead: Philosopher of the Social Individual* (New York: King's Crown Press, 1945), pp. 35, 50, 77.
[17] Mead, "The Definition of the Psychical." See below, p. 47.
[18] Mead, "The Social Self." See below, p. 142.

though "the very process of replying to one's own talk, implies an 'I' behind the scenes who answers to the gestures, the symbols, that arise in consciousness." [19]

Inasmuch as Mead's distinction between "I" and "me" is meant to be functional rather than metaphysical, memory illustrates the interchangeable roles of these two phases of the self. For in memory the "I" is constantly present in experience as that which remembers, while the self it remembers is always a "me." Whereas what is remembered is drained off into the "me" from a past "I" and is remembered by another "I" now, the present "I" possesses a measure of free responsiveness toward the "me" and hence toward its past. Consisting, moreover, of the internalized attitudes of the others, of others' conceptions of one's self, the "me" represents the social situation of the self; and so the "I," free in its responsiveness to the "me," is to that extent independent of social situation. As Mead said, "The 'I' is the response of the organism to the attitudes of the others which one himself assumes. The attitudes of the others constitute the organized 'me,' and then one reacts toward that as an 'I' " (MSS, p. 175).

Hence the "me" is both the past and the social situation to which the "I" responds, and its response may be an action which is more than an adjustment to the "me," since the "me" may internalize conflicts in the social situation which are disintegrative and since the "I" attends to ends which promise a consummatory harmony in the future. Thus it is the "me" that is conservative. "The 'me' is a conventional, habitual individual" (MSS, p. 197). And while this conservatism is invaluable to the social self and to society, guaranteeing integration and stability, its equally invaluable complement is novelty and progress. This the "I" supplies. Ideally both "I" and "me" are functions of a single self. Such a self is, in Charles Morris' phrase, an "open self." The disintegration of the "me" in the presence of the free, responsive, creative "I" would be but a prelude to a higher integration in which

[19] Mead, "The Mechanism of Social Consciousness." See below, p. 141.

the contents of the former "me," reconstructed, would be preserved while the "I" would still fix its gaze on yet higher ends that lie in the future.

IV. MORAL AND SOCIAL PHILOSOPHY

From the turn of the century to World War I, the clamor for social reform was a cardinal feature of the American scene, particularly in the field of municipal affairs. During this period pragmatism came into its own, and by its emphasis upon social reconstruction and the application of scientific methods to moral problems, it imparted intelligent direction to the general movement toward better government and social justice. The members of the "Chicago School" joined to make of pragmatism the social philosophy of democracy, adapted to its industrial, urban setting. Dewey himself had called upon philosophers to grapple with the "problems of men." Thus pragmatism, with its stress upon resolving immediate problems to gain or maintain cherished values in shared experience, came to be regarded as the philosophy of intelligent and democratic practice. Assigning conduct or action the place of central importance in philosophy, pragmatism is intrinsically a moral philosophy, for morality is the study of human conduct in quest of the standards to criticize and to guide it. As Mead's essay, "The Philosophical Basis of Ethics," suggests, the morality of the individual exists and evolves within an embracing social evolution.[1] Thus moral philosophy is indissolubly linked to a social philosophy. Pragmatism becomes a social philosophy par excellence.

Social Reform

The achievement of the "Chicago School" under Dewey that had the deepest and widest effect on American life, is

[1] Mead, "The Philosophical Basis of Ethics," *International Journal of Ethics*, XVIII (1908), 312–313. See below, p. 82.

progressive education. However, the moral influence of pragmatism was not limited to education, but spread to other
areas of practical affairs. Not only sound education but also
good government and social justice were among the most
pressing social needs at the turn of the century. Then, with
the advent of World War I, another problem engrossed the
minds of men—the problem of international peace. Along with
Dewey and uncounted others, Mead forged the pragmatic philosophy into a viable social instrument with which to grapple
with these "problems of men."

At the University of Chicago, Mead was active in the Experimental School, having attended its inception. A reform
movement in American education, progressive education
sought to change curricula. The existing curricula were inherited from a bygone time and were dominated by an out-
dated atomistic Herbartian psychology. When their interest
could be won, a condition which was rare, pupils were more
often than not prepared for a kind of life and mentality
out of step with the actual culture to which they belonged.
Curricula were needed which would bring into play the native impulses and interests of the pupils, stimulating them to
intellectual and moral growth, and which would be adjusted
to the realities of the American community. The progressive
educationist favored vocational schools, not only to develop
the skills needed in an expanding domestic economy, but also
because pupils would drop out of school when the curricula
were merely academic. Mead participated unstintingly in the
educational activities of the "Chicago School." In 1902–1903
he served as president of the School of Education Parents' Association.[2] He occasionally contributed editorial notes to *School
Review* [3] and served in 1907–1909 as an editor of one of the
University's major journals, *The Elementary School Teacher*.[4]
He spoke out as critic, as observer, and as advocate of new

  [2] See Mead's presidential address, "The Basis for a Parents' Association," *The Elementary School Teacher*, IV (1903–1904), 337–346.

  [3] Mead's "Editorial Notes," *School Review*, XV (1907), 160–165.

  [4] Mead's "Editorial Notes," *The Elementary School Teacher*, VIII (1907–
1908), 281–284.

policies, individually or in his role as member or as chairman of various committees, on the conduct of educational affairs at all levels in the city of Chicago and elsewhere.[5] Meanwhile, Mead published essays on educational theory. Half a century ago he apprehended the competition and the impending split between the humanities and the sciences. But appreciating the new social sciences, soon flourishing in American higher education, he saw in the scientific methodology that they employed the bridge between the humanities and the natural sciences.[6]

Education did not hold a monopoly on Mead's readiness to contribute to social philosophy and practical affairs. Social justice and governmental reforms were also close to his heart. He wrote articles on such topics as settlement houses,[7] criminal justice,[8] philanthropy, and what later became recognized as "social security." [9] Sensitive to the sorry condition of aesthetic values in a mechanized, industrial civilization, he even ventured to comment on the motion picture as a form of artistic expression and aesthetic satisfaction.[10]

[5] Noteworthy publications by Mead on practical educational matters are: "On the Educational Situation in the Chicago Public Schools," *City Club Bulletin* (Chicago), I (1907–1908), 131–138; *A Report on Vocational Training in Chicago and in Other Cities,* by a committee of the City Club, George H. Mead, Chairman (Chicago: City Club of Chicago, 1912); "A Heckling School Board and an Educational Stateswoman," *Survey,* XXXI (1913–1914), 443–444, and "Madison—The Passage of the University through the State Political Agitation of 1914; the Survey by Wm. H. Allen and His Staff and the Legislative Fight of 1915, with Indications these offer of the Place the State University Holds in the Community," *ibid.,* XXXV (1915–1916), 349–351, 354–361.

[6] Mead, "The Teaching of Science in College," *Science,* XXIV (1906), 390–397. See below, p. 60.

[7] Mead, "The Social Settlement: Its Basis and Function," *University of Chicago Record,* XII (1908), 108–110.

[8] Mead, "The Psychology of Punitive Justice," *The American Journal of Sociology,* XXIII (1917–1918), 577–602. See below, p. 212.

[9] Mead, "Philanthropy from the Point of View of Ethics," *Intelligent Philanthropy,* edited by Faris, Laune, and Todd (Chicago: University of Chicago Press, 1930), pp. 133–148. See below, p. 392.

[10] Mead, "The Nature of Aesthetic Experience," *International Journal of Ethics,* XXXVI (1925–1926), 382–392. See below, p. 294.

Mead's involvement in the practical life of his community is perhaps most conspicuous in his association with the City Club of Chicago. The contributions of city clubs to the improvement of municipal government have been considerable. Presumably voting allows individuals the opportunity to express their interests and so generates a public policy which suits these interests. But in view of the corrupt political machines, Mead was well aware how the voting mechanism was prone to fail. To overcome failure and to augment the likelihood of a public policy in accord with the interests of the citizenry, Mead, along with other pragmatists, not only stressed the role of better education in the formation of civic consciousness, but he also favored the establishment of independent committees to study civic affairs, inform the public and arouse its sentiment, and he welcomed the advent of the managerial form of municipal government. Mead's participation in the activities of the City Club of Chicago is accentuated by the fact that he served as president, retiring in 1920.[11]

Scientific Method and Morality

Since pragmatism rules out the divorce of thought from action, Mead's activities as a citizen performing duties meshed with his work as a philosopher. Accordingly, his first important article (1899) appeared not in a philosophical but in a sociological journal, *The American Journal of Sociology,* founded and edited by Albion Small and published at the University of Chicago; this article is entitled "The Working Hypothesis in Social Reform." Mead maintained that the proper method for social reform is the method of science. He cautioned against the adoption of full-blown ideologies, of utopian programs, since such programs are usually unrelated to the immediate problems that cry for solution, and consequently accomplish little or nothing. The social reformer facing a problem is like the scientist. What he proposes as

11 Mead, "Retiring President's Address," *City Club Bulletin,* XIII (1920), 94–95, 97–99.

a policy for action is a working hypothesis, and this policy is true to the extent that it solves the problem that has necessitated it. A policy for social reform is, therefore, not offered as an absolute panacea, but is subject to revision in the light of further experience; indeed, it may be abandoned whenever its failures exceed its successes. To be doctrinaire in social reform, to uphold as axiomatic a set of principles which are not testable by the realities of immediate social problems and crises, is to obstruct the processes of intelligent social reform and to worsen a broken-down social situation that needs reconstruction.[12]

As a pragmatist devoted to the task of social reconstruction, Mead, like Dewey, recommended the application of scientific method to the problems of men, the conflicts of social and moral values. The scientific method, broadly conceived in connection with the life-sciences, is the model of sound reflective consciousness, the paradigm of all properly conducted inquiry. In calling for the adoption of scientific method in the field of values, the pragmatists were aiming neither to strait-jacket moral and social issues to a narrow methodology, nor to reduce values to physical facts. Scientific method cannot force a choice of basic values, because these values grow out of the impulses, instincts, and habits of men in social interaction. In his crucial essay, "Scientific Method and the Moral Sciences" (1923), Mead contended that, just as in the study of nature, scientific method requires that all the facts be considered when a hypothesis is advanced to solve a problem, so when dealing with social and moral problems scientific method demands the consideration of all the values that stem from all the interests of all the individuals in the problematic situation. As the working hypothesis of a natural investigation must fit all the facts, so a moral rule or social policy must fit all the values. The outcome in both cases is a recon-

[12] Mead, "The Working Hypothesis in Social Reform," *The American Journal of Sociology*, V (1899), 367–371. See below, p. 3. See also Mead's review of Gustave Le Bon, *The Psychology of Socialism, ibid.*, V (1899), 404–412.

structed situation which comprehends the maximum of facts
or values from the antecedent, problematic situation. If there
is a fundamental conflict between values—say, of religion
versus public health—science does not legislate in favor of one
side or the other, but once a decision is made, the scientific
method may be utilized, relentlessly though experimentally,
to attain the values so elected.[13] Furthermore, the operation
of the scientific method in the field of values coincides with
the democratic procedure, for it is the intent of democracy to
give equal weight to the values and the interests of all individuals, and to strike upon a policy that furnishes the maximal
satisfaction of these interests. In this sense the philosophy of
democracy is at one with the pragmatist theory of the application of scientific method to the field of values.

Human Nature and Social Order

Whereas Mead viewed intelligence as a central element in
valuation and found in the scientific method the method for
the treatment of all value problems, he knew that noncognitive factors, impulses, instincts, and habits determine men in
the choice and pursuit of values. The task of intelligence is
not to replace the noncognitive factors, but to reorganize
them, to mold them together in such a way as to maximize the
possibility of their satisfaction. In some instances the noncognitive elements in human nature have to be modified or
rechanneled, if other basic human interests are to be gratified. Mead focused in particular on the hostile instinct, for
while this instinct is violently displayed in the pugnacity,
aggressiveness, and cruelty of men toward other men whom
they regard as outside the group, it is also the cement of social cohesiveness. In his paper, "The Psychology of Punitive
Justice" (1918), Mead delineated the interplay between the
instinct of hostility, operative in promoting the social cohesiveness of the group, and the judicial process in criminal

[13] Mead, "Scientific Method and the Moral Sciences," *International
Journal of Ethics*, XXXIII (1923), 229–247. See below, p. 248.

law.[14] What the criminal court is devised to ascertain is whether the accused is to remain in the group or be cast outside, and if cast outside, to what extent the instinct of hostility against him is to be vented in the infliction of penalties. The judiciary, as presently operating in criminal cases, institutionalizes the human instinct of hostility, and while this may enhance the cohesiveness of society, the vindictiveness of criminal law, Mead held, is far from the most effective technique of dealing with crime. Proper scientific method in the solution of criminal problems would never merely sanction the punishment of the convicted without consideration of the total situation of which he is but one component; it would seek that judgment which would rehabilitate the criminal and remove the causes of crime—in a word, reconstruct the social situation that breeds crime and produces criminals. More than judicial precedent and legal forensics, sociology and psychology would be relevant to legal science and practice. The procedures followed in juvenile courts, where the aim was not so much to punish the delinquent as to re-educate him and to alter the social circumstances that led him astray, were, in Mead's eyes, a forecast of the reconstruction of the judiciary in the area of criminal law. Mead was implicitly committed to the thesis that the moral function of the judiciary is not to sentence men to punishment in accordance with the hostile instinct of the group, but rather to promote intelligent amelioration of the social situation.

To recognize the instinct of hostility and its effectiveness in social relations, even when it is a malevolent force, is not to eradicate it. Mead knew that the basic stuff of human nature, and the social attitudes generated therefrom, could not easily be dismissed. In fact, he acknowledged the social value of this basic human material. Hostility, we have already noted, is the cement of social cohesiveness in existing societies. It is the root of significant civic virtues—especially, the virtue of patriotism during war. Thus Mead could ponder the ques-

14 See below, p. 217.

tion whether it was possible to attain cohesiveness within a nation, except when readiness to wage wars against other nations was part of its outlook. In his still timely essay, "National-Mindedness and International-Mindedness" (1929), he examined the problem of finding "a moral equivalent for war," but he did not think, as William James had thought, that peace corps or elite humanitarian groups would suffice. The eradication of war as an instrument of national policy necessitated the removal of the instinct of hostility which expressed itself in armaments, without impairing the social cohesiveness that this instinct furnishes. Formal agreements, international laws, and world organizations cannot circumvent the presence and importance of the instinct of hostility, although at present, wars, the inevitable results of this instinct, are waged on so vast a scale that no nation can reasonably risk the costs. What is needed is an assurance of social cohesiveness without the cement of the belligerent instinct of hostility. Positive common interests among men have to be accentuated to weld them into real nations devoid of hostility toward outsiders. Nations which are cohesive by virtue of these common interests can live together at peace; no others can. Mead perceived prophetically how the Fascist nations would go down the path to war. Hopefully, although not unrealistically, he envisioned the possibility of world peace grounded upon a community of nations of men bound together by positive common interests.[15]

Evolution and Ideals

Cognizant of social realities and wary of utopian panaceas, resorting to the method of science in questions of morality rather than to authoritative religions or traditional customs, aware that men consist of impulses and instincts as well as of intelligence, Mead nevertheless discerned that there are ideal ends that operate as standards and goals for human conduct.

[15] Mead, "National-Mindedness and International-Mindedness," *International Journal of Ethics*, XXXIX (1929), 385–407. See below, p. 355.

In "The Philosophical Basis of Ethics," he explicitly ruled out an ideal order independent of the natural world, existing as the fixed, predetermined end toward which nature gropes.[16] He based his ethics on evolution, which he construed not as a mass of individual struggles for survival with victory exclusively won by the most physically fit, but rather as a social process in which the vying individuals in situations are reciprocals, adjusting to each other and obtaining an equilibrium of hostile and cooperative forces, whereby in some measure the interests of all or of most are satisfied. As the cosmological foundation of moral and social values, evolution dooms to falsity any ideology that attempts to forecast once and for all the values desiderated and the programs to be executed in the conduct of the practical life. Situations evolve toward ideal ends which themselves evolve concomitantly with the situations. When science studies society, it should be experimental, and the social policies it advocates should be tentative and hypothetical, because society changes and its goals change with it.

Although ideals do function in social evolution, they cannot be conceived as eternal fixities, subsisting apart from the flux, for they, too, evolve. However effective historically in assisting the rising bourgeoisie to obtain sound social objectives, the theory of natural rights, allegedly grounded on natural or divine laws, requires revision. As Mead pointed out in his penetrating article, "Natural Rights and the Theory of the Political Institution" (1915), the so-called natural rights derive their content from shifting social circumstances. Alterations in social relations reverberate upon the doctrine of rights and instigate changes in the material claims of the doctrine. Inherently rights are social; they consist in claims made by some individuals upon others in respect to certain objects or actions. No metaphysical eternity attaches to them. They are real, they exist and are effective within the course of human affairs only so far as the others upon whom the

16 See below, p. 86.

claims are made acknowledge the claims and either cooperate in fulfillment or refrain from obstruction. Political institutions, government, laws, and the courts are the instruments for establishing rights in social situations where the requisite recognition of the claims in existing social attitudes and habits is absent. Such rights are valid prior to widespread recognition when they represent the ideal ends, the maximal satisfactions possible, to which the situation evolves, and political institutions, by calling attention to these rights, hasten the day of their attainment. Once the claims are recognized widely and completely, once the rights are incarnate in the attitudes and interests of all members of the community, the resort to political institutions in their behalf abates.[17]

Rights are social ideals assisted by political institutions. All valid ideals are implicit in the situations to which they are relevant. They answer to the needs within the situation, but since the needs alter, the rights change. Valid ideals cannot be empty abstractions devoid of content, but must be rooted in social history and human nature. In his remarkable essay, "Philanthropy from the Point of View of Ethics," Mead has shown how even a benevolent impulse like charity, the desire to aid another human being in distress, is too fleeting and precarious to meet the needs in the situations which call it forth. These situations reveal, to the perceptive and sensitive person, objective obligations toward the individuals in distress, obligations which simply cannot be met by personal charity in place of institutionalized social welfare. The claims of those in distress are real; and given the structure of our industrial civilization, they are valid. As Mead wrote: "It is this feel for a social structure which is implicit in what is present that haunts the generous nature, and carries a sense of obligation which transcends any claim that his actual social order fastens upon him. It is an ideal world that lays the

[17] Mead, "Natural Rights and the Theory of the Political Institution," *The Journal of Philosophy, Psychology, and Scientific Methods*, XII (1915), 141–155. See below, p. 150.

claim upon him, but it is an ideal world which grows out of this world and its undeniable implications." [18]

V. COSMOLOGY

In a fragmentary note Mead singled out as major points of orientation for contemporary philosophy the concepts of emergence and of perspective (*PA*, p. 640). No doubt the concept of emergence owes its prestige to the spread of evolutionary cosmologies in the wake of Darwin's scientific revolution, while the centrality of the concept of perspective in much recent metaphysics stems, in large measure, from the influence of Einsteinian relativity on philosophy. Striving to understand and interpret these two crucial concepts that science has bequeathed to philosophy in the past century, Mead ventured, toward the end of his life, to expand his thought into a cosmology and a metaphysics. To find a speculative genius working from pragmatic principles who equals the daring of Mead, it is necessary to go back to Charles Peirce.[1] In a sensitive and balanced monograph on Mead's philosophy, David Victoroff has asserted that Mead's thought radiates out from his social psychology to a general philosophy, that, in effect, his cosmology is built in the image of his sociology.[2] The act as social is, in Stephen Pepper's term, "the root metaphor" of Mead's world hypothesis.[3] The act in its environment ex-

[18] Mead, "Philanthropy from the Point of View of Ethics." See below, p. 392.

[1] See Charles Morris, "Peirce, Mead and Pragmatism," *The Philosophical Review*, XLVII (1938), 109–127. Morris acknowledges the metaphysical bent in Peirce but minimizes it in Mead.

[2] David Victoroff, *G. H. Mead: Sociologue et Philosophe* (Paris: Presses Universitaires de France, 1953), p. 6.

[3] Stephen C. Pepper, *World Hypotheses; A Study in Evidence* (Berkeley and Los Angeles: University of California Press, 1942), p. 232. For a discussion of Mead's philosophy in terms of Pepper's account of contextual-

emplifies the categorical structure and qualitative character of the entire world.

After functionalism it was clear that the existence and nature of an environmental stimulus depend on the existence and nature of the organism just as much as the existence and nature of the response of the organism depend on the existence and nature of the environmental stimulus. No longer a static field in which an organism dwells, the environment has its texture and quality determined by the peculiar sensitivity of the organism. Continuous interaction prevails between organism and environment, each reciprocally determining the other. In his last years Dewey introduced the term "transaction" to designate this interaction.[4] A transaction is a situational process in which each element possesses a nature and performs a role, not intrinsically, but by virtue of its context, its relatedness to other elements with natures and roles similarly affected. For example, a commercial transaction between buyer and seller is a situational process in which there is a buyer only because there is a seller, and conversely.

Since, for Mead, acts constitute situations in which the characters of the environmental stimuli and the organic responses are codetermined, his philosophy is a form of what A. E. Murphy has termed "objective relativism."[5] Mead illustrated this type of theory with the existence and nature of food (*PA,* p. 71). Unless there are organisms capable of ingesting, digesting, and assimilating, there is no food, although such organisms may be present and nutriment still be absent. Food requires a biological situation, in which both organism and environment are adapted to each other. The

---

ism, see William C. Tremmel, "The Social Concepts of George Herbert Mead," *The Emporia State Research Studies,* V, No. 4 (1957), 6–11.

4 John Dewey and Arthur F. Bentley, *Knowing and the Known* (Boston: The Beacon Press, 1949), pp. 67–69.

5 A. E. Murphy, "Objective Relativism in Dewey and Whitehead," *The Philosophical Review,* XXXIV (1927), 121–144. See also A. E. Murphy's criticism of Mead's metaphysics: "Concerning Mead's *The Philosophy of the Act,*" *The Journal of Philosophy,* XXXVI (1939), 85–103.

dependence of qualities upon transactions between organism and environment, and their objectivity within the context of this relatedness, is generalized to bear upon all the categories of reality. Like food, space and time and causality are objectively relative.

Like Dewey, Mead abjured traditional metaphysics and cosmology. The term "metaphysics" bears pejorative connotations in his writings. Mead shared Dewey's disapproval of traditional philosophical systems because they allegedly and mistakenly focus on static values which transcend experience, because they bifurcate mind from nature and seek a finality alien to the scientist's method of "continued reconstruction in the face of events emerging in ceaseless novelty" (*PP*, p. 102). Nevertheless, he did not indict all general philosophical systems on these charges. On the contrary, he recognized the possibility of a metaphysics "that may be in some sense descriptive of the world so far as it comes within the range of our thought" (*PA*, p. 626). Writing before the publication of Dewey's *Quest for Certainty* (New York, 1929) and Alfred North Whitehead's *Process and Reality* (New York, 1929), Mead cited three treatises as outstanding illustrations of the office of philosophy: Bergson's *Creative Evolution* (Paris, 1907), Samuel Alexander's *Space, Time, and Deity* (London, 1920), and Dewey's *Experience and Nature* (Chicago, 1925). These works depict the world as unfractured and construe experience as "both the starting-point and goal of research science and the field of all our values and our meanings" (*PA*, p. 517).

In similar fashion Mead sought to construct a cosmological or metaphysical system. He has confessed his intention clearly: "I have merely wished to indicate that it is the technical function of philosophy so to state the universe that what we call our conscious life can be recognized as a phase of its creative advance" (*PA*, p. 515). Such a system as he intended, but never completed, is concerned "with the import of the appearance and presence in the universe of human reflective intelligence—that intelligence which transforms causes and effects into means and consequences, reactions into responses, and termini of natural processes into ends-in-view" (*PA*, p. 517).

Instead of dissipating himself in polemics against traditional doctrines, Mead sought to elucidate affirmatively, if tentatively, the processes of knowing and of reality. A. E. Murphy has consequently labeled his pragmatism "constructive" (*PP*, p. xiii). Because among the pragmatists Mead alone faced up to the revolutions triggered by physics, and because he strove to solve the theoretical problems generating therefrom, his constructive pragmatism belongs, as A. E. Murphy added, to that genre of the philosophy of nature which flourished in the 1920's and which culminated in Whitehead's philosophical development (*PP*, p. xv). Add to this, however, the pragmatist conception of thought as a problem-solving activity, and Mead's general philosophy is motivated always by definable problems which urge solution.

The Theory of Time

The problem Mead undertook to solve by means of his theory of time is so grave that in his Carus lectures he called it "the task of philosophy today"—namely, "to bring into congruence with each other this universality of determination which is the text of modern science, and the emergence of the novel which belongs not only to the experience of human social organisms, but is found also in a nature which science and the philosophy that has followed it have separated from human nature" (*PP*, p. 14). On the one hand, science posits emergence, the occurrence in the evolutionary process of novel elements. On the other hand, the rationalistic procedure of scientific method is deterministic, postulating that every event can be causally explained by its antecedent conditions. Hence a serious antinomy arises between the principle of emergence and the principle of causation, both espoused by science and scientific philosophy; and this antinomy illustrates the nature of a metaphysical problem, since the assertion of the reality of one side seems to entail the allegation of the unreality of the other. Its solution, Mead held, rests upon an adequate theory of time, which would reconcile emergent novelty with causal conditioning. In his essay, "The Nature of the Past" (1929), Mead stated the antinomy in terms of experience as well as scientific concepts.[6] On the one hand, there is the abrupt novelty emergent in experience; each present moment exhibits discontinuity. On the other hand, there is the continuity of experience implying some sort of temporal structure in which past and future extend in both directions from the present.

Mead's theory of time is a "philosophy of the present." As he declared: "Reality exists in a present" (*PP*, p. 1). As the locus of reality, a present is an occurrence of existence, an act, or an emergent event. The key to this theory of time is, therefore, the philosophy of the act. Within the context of the philosophy of the act, Mead incorporated those insights into the nature of time which he borrowed from the process philosophy of Bergson and Whitehead and upon which he leaned heavily. Mead said, "That which marks a present is its becoming and its disappearing," and he cited the flash of a meteor as an example of a present (*PP*, p. 1). Thus a present is an event—an act, however long it may take. When Mead rejected Bergsonian duration because of its psychological limitations, he praised that "correction of the Bergsonian philosophy which Mr. Whitehead has most effectively made, up to the present at least" (*MT*, p. 325). Unfortunately Mead never lived to know Whitehead's last works, such as *Process and Reality* (1929) and *Adventures of Ideas* (1933). Undoubtedly he would have found in them suggestions and principles in closer agreement with his own thinking than in those earlier Whiteheadian writings, *The Concept of Nature* (1919) and *The Principle of Relativity* (1922), from which he drew so

[6] Mead, "The Nature of the Past," in *Essays in Honor of John Dewey* (New York: Henry Holt and Co., 1929), pp. 235–242. See below, p. 345. For a lucid exposition and critique of Mead's theory, see H. N. Lee, "Mead's Doctrine of the Past," *Tulane Studies in Philosophy*, XII (1963), 52–75.

much, but not without pointed criticism. In making the present the locus of reality and in describing it as a becoming and a disappearing, Mead was in his own way formulating a concept akin to Whitehead's actual entity, or actual occasion. For what is seated in the present, the content essentially identical with the present, is the emergent event.

The emergent event as present is the basis of the structure of time. The future and the past both spread out from the present, but perhaps because of the paradox in asserting that the past expands from the present, Mead focused on the nature of the past. He boldly asserted, "The past is an overflow of the present. It is oriented from the present." Yet he was quick to deny that the past, like fancy, is a pure invention of the present. "The past is what must have been before it is present in experience as a past." [7]

While expounding his own conception of the past, Mead took care to repudiate another conception, although he conceded that it is "perhaps the common background of thinking" (*PP,* p. 9), cropping up in the metaphysics of the Minkowski space-time continuum and in certain uncritical methodological assumptions of research in history and science. According to this rejected conception, the past exists in itself as a scroll of elapsed presents independent of and unaffected by what is going on at present. Against this scroll concept of the past, Mead's fundamental objection is that it does not meet the methodological requirements of the past in historical or scientific research. No historian can find such a past; rather, he must reconstruct the past from evidences in the present.

Mead's theory of the past, clearly distinguished from a preexistent scroll, holds that there is some past somehow in the present, operating as a condition of the present. This does not mean that the present, as Bergson suggested, accumulates all the past, for Mead argued: "The present does not carry any

[7] Mead, "The Nature of the Past." See below, pp. 348–349.

such burden with it." [8] But it does mean a continuity of the past with the present. As the condition of the present, the past lies within the present and hence is not an external fixity. "The actual passage of reality is in the passage of one present into another, where alone is reality, and a present which has merged in another is not a past. Its reality is always that of a present." [9]

The appearance of the past in the present assumes the form of memory images and historical records. Here the past is conceived as the meaning of what has transpired for the present. In this connection Mead has alluded to two different senses of the past discernible upon consideration of the methods of historical research. First, there is the past ". . . when we are at grips with a problem and are seeking its solution. . . . It takes on now one sense and now another. We analyze it into one set of factors and then into another; we are seeking its meaning, endeavoring to find in it the course we should follow" (*PA*, p. 507). But once we have formed a solution to the problem, "the whole falls into a single story that we read in terms of a causal series. . . . We build up a hypothesis which we test and perhaps act successfully upon, and then the problem takes the interpretation which our hypothesis places upon it" (*PA*, p. 507). Here what we touch upon is not the mere occurrences that have been but the meaning of the past for what is now. Because with every present the meaning is revisable, it follows that the past, though real as the conditioning within the present, is fundamentally hypothetical. As Mead said: "Our reconstructions of the past vary in their extensiveness, but they never contemplate the finality of their findings. They are always subject to conceivable reformulations, on the discovery of later evidence" (*PP*, p. 29).

In the last analysis Mead's conception of the emergent event is the crux of his theory of time. An emergent event is

[8] See below, p. 349.
[9] See below, p. 345.

an event containing novel features not wholly derived from antecedent presents; at the same time it exists in a present and is conditioned by the past. As the source of novelty in life and in nature, the emergent event is not a deduction from what took place prior to its appearance; nevertheless, it is conditioned by the past, but only according to that sense of the past which it selects after its advent. Although every emergent event is produced by the past, since according to Mead production, or causation, is the "relation of any event to the conditions under which it occurs," and since this relation is established by the emergent event itself in the present, no emergent event can be reduced to what preceded it (*PP*, p. 33). Fundamentally, but not absolutely, the past of every emergent event is a past of its own making or choosing. Thus the novelty of the emergent event in the present is matched by the novelty of the past that it reconstructs.

The emergent event is, then, an act which both adds novelty to the world and socially establishes a relation to this world through adjustment and reconstruction. As unique and novel, the emergent event appears under the guise of discreteness, and seemingly disrupts the social process with discontinuity. As produced by the past, the emergent event appears as a part of the social process, further buttressing its continuity. Mead stressed that the present, the emergent event, the act, is social. "Sociality," he wrote, "is the capacity of being several things at once" (*PP*, p. 49). Since the "novel event is in both the old order and the new which its advent heralds," it exemplifies sociality par excellence.

Theory of Relativity

The discrepancy between objects as they are presented in experience—perceptual objects—and objects as they are conceived by science—scientific objects—led Mead to work on a theory of objects with metaphysical suggestions for a general theory of reality based upon the philosophy of the act. The classic form of this problem has to do with the distinction between objects composed merely of primary qualities as required by science and objects enriched with secondary qualities as they appear in ordinary experience. The most recent form of the problem, and perhaps the gravest, has to do with the nature of objects as conceived by relativity physics and quantum mechanics, the ultimate wavelike packets of energy in relative space-time, and the ordinary objects of common experience. Mead faced both forms of the problem and offered solutions based upon his theory of the act.

The Perceptual Object and the Act. The perceptual object [10] is for Mead the object of ordinary experience. It is an object that emerges within the social process, its qualities and contours determined by the act. In other words, objects are reified, that is, become real, within a process involving the interaction of organism and environment. In spite of multiple usages of the term "object," the primary meaning of this term in Mead's writings is an "expression of a peculiar relation between itself and the individual," the relation itself being "objective" (*PA,* p. 7). So awkward a formulation serves to underscore the reciprocity of object and organism. The situation that consists in the interaction of organism and environment exhibits elements denotable as "objects." These elements depend, of course, upon the biological constitution of the organism and its particular selectivity, while the organism within the situation is also an object when it is so regarded. Requisite to the existence and the nature of objects are the acts of organisms.

Now the act has three stages, with which the properties of the object of the act may be correlated. The object of the perceptual phase of the act is the object at a distance; it is made up of secondary qualities, such as color, sound, odor, etc. The object of the manipulatory phase is the contact object; it is comprised of the primary qualities of mass, solidity, figure, and motion. The object of the consummatory phase is the value; it is constituted by the satisfactions and dissatisfactions

[10] Mead, "The Mechanism of Social Consciousness." See below, p. 134.

registered in immediate experience. According to Mead, to
assign a subjective status to any properties of the object and
an objective status to other properties is an error which, in
fact, the traditional doctrine of primary and secondary qualities conspicuously exemplifies. No set of properties is exclusively subjective. All properties are functions of their contexts; they are "objectively relative."

Since the perceptual object, that is, the object of ordinary
experience, evolves along with the human organism, its properties, even its so-called primary qualities, exist within a context determined in part by the organism. The primary qualities,
including the physical causality of the thing, arise primarily when resistance is offered to the organism by the contact object in the manipulatory phase of the act. As it appears
in the manipulatory stage of the act, the perceptual object is identical with the physical thing. The genesis of the
physical thing in contact experience is explained in terms of
the transference of the pressures of bodily surfaces against
each other, pre-eminently of one hand against the other, to
the object. By virtue of this transference, which is facilitated
by the principle of sociality enabling the organism to adopt
the role of the other and to assume the attitude of the other,
the thing acquires an inside. Thus what the thing is, its essence or matter, the inside of the thing, the cluster of primary
qualities, is equated with the resistance which the organism
has transferred to the thing.

Hence the object of the act has its primary and its secondary qualities as objective but relative to the perceptual
and manipulatory phases of the act.

The Scientific Object and the Metaphysics of Relativity.
Whereas the philosophy of the act saves the properties of the
perceptual object from the erroneous ontological discrimination instigated by the doctrine of primary and secondary qualities, the metaphysics of relativity—the congeries of philosophical conceptions, such as the Minkowski space-time
continuum, inspired by the scientific theories of relativity—

proffers a yet more critical challenge to this object. The philosophies of classical Newtonian physics, with their distinction
between the primary and secondary qualities, provided an object which, so far as it was composed of primary qualities, re-
sembled the object of ordinary experience in the manipulatory stage of the act. The metaphysics of relativity, however,
posits objects wholly different from the objects of ordinary
experience. These scientific objects have apparently nothing
at all in common with perceptual objects. Expatiating on the
profound change relativity introduced into the scientific conceptions of objects, Mead noted the disappearance of motion
in Minkowski geometry, the abandonment of ether, the substitution of events for physical things, the fusion of space and
time, the curvature of space and time, and the concept of
perspectives and shifting frames of reference. In brief, the
metaphysics of relativity puts into question the reality of the
objects of ordinary experience.

Now this is a serious issue, for it cuts at the heart of physical thinghood. Lack of an answer puts in jeopardy the whole
physical world of objects, the study of which is the proper domain of the science of physics, of which one part is the theory
of relativity.

Mead met the challenge of relativity by maintaining the
methodological indispensability of the perceptual object, by
upholding relativity as a scientific theory—but repudiating its
metaphysics [11]—and by proposing a philosophical interpretation of relativity that would organize perspectives yet preserve the integrity of perceptual objects.

Scientific Method and the Perceptual Object. In the Introduction the editors of *The Philosophy of the Act* clearly delineated Mead's defense of the perceptual object in terms of
the requirements of scientific method. This defense, as they
rightly point out, is based upon wholly practical considera-

[11] For a fuller discussion of Mead's critique of the metaphysics of relativity, see my article, "The Philosophy of George Herbert Mead (1863–
1931)," *Tulane Studies in Philosophy*, XII (1963), esp. 44–47.

tions. As they state, " . . . when reason acts as a problem-solving procedure (as in scientific method), our total behavior, reflective and overt, unquestionably accepts as real the contact things of the laboratory" (*PA*, p. xxxvii). Helpfully, they have marshaled Mead's reasons for contending that the practice of scientific reasoning posits the reality of perceptual objects. First, at its outset science as reflective behavior accepts the reality of perceptual things (*PP*, p. 140). Secondly, the scientist returns to the perceptual world of perceptual things for verification of his hypotheses, a world he never questions (*PP*, p. 140). Thirdly, the scientific method of measurement, although its results are not statable in terms of physical things, nonetheless makes use of physical things, that is, the instruments of measurement, and so presupposes their reality (*PP*, p. 150). Fourthly, the "exception" that instigates the scientific investigation depends upon the acceptance of the reality of perceptual things in the manipulatory area of the act (*PP*, p. 149). Despite the discrepancy between perceptual and scientific objects, scientific methodology assumes that perceptual objects are functionally real. The research scientist, moreover, abstains from the dogmatic metaphysics of relativity. His goal in the pursuit of knowledge, Mead insisted, "is not a final world but the solution of his problem in the world that is there" (*PA*, p. 60). The conclusions of experimental science, the scientific objects, instead of enjoying final metaphysical reality, are socially developed symbols referring to characters in the world which the problematic situation has rendered prominent and science has abstracted (*PA*, p. 61). The analyzed elements of science cannot be more real than experience. "The ultimate touchstone of reality" in scientific investigation is, Mead said, " a piece of experience found in an unanalyzed world" (*PA*, p. 32).

Relativity and the Reality of Perspectives. Repudiating the metaphysics of relativity, Mead discarded those notions which prevent assigning a functional reality, defined by the act in its stages, to both perceptual and scientific objects. Though Mead dismissed the metaphysics of relativity, he vigorously upheld the scientific achievement of relativity. Mead concentrated on the "objective reality of perspectives" in his endeavor to provide a sound philosophical interpretation of relativity. "The conception of the perspective as there in nature is in a sense an unexpected donation by the most abstruse physical science to philosophy." [12] Etymologically linked to perception, the term "perspective" denotes that basic situation of which Mead declared, "The perceptual object is there over against the organism as a physical object" (*PA*, p. 151). Its "most unambiguous instance" is the relation between organism and environment. Perspectives, moreover, are objective, rooted in the constitution of the organism and its relation to its environment. "This perspective of the organism is then there in nature." [13]

Whereas classical Newtonian physics interpreted perspectives as loci in absolute space, relativity physics with its spatiotemporal continuum construes perspectives as spatiotemporal. Further, for relativity, since spatiotemporal characteristics vary with the events to which they pertain, the world of events divides into an indefinite multiplicity of perspectives. Unless the world is to be shattered into a plurality of perspectives without unity or community, the philosopher of relativity is confronted with the necessity of finding some principles for their organization. In quest of such principles, Mead emphatically rejected the solution of absolute idealism. "The grandiose undertaking of Absolute Idealism to bring the whole of reality within experience failed." [14]

The task, according to Mead, was not merely to assert the organization of perspectives within nature, but foremost to explain the mechanism of such an organization. He cited Whitehead for contributing the conception of nature as an organization of perspectives, and he commented upon Whitehead's affiliation with Leibnitzian monadology as a recent

[12] Mead, "The Objective Reality of Perspectives." See below, p. 308.
[13] See below, p. 307.
[14] See below, p. 306.

philosophical expression of the severity of the problem of
perspectives bequeathed to philosophy by relativity. While
Mead accepted Whitehead's formulation of the problem, he
rejected Whitehead's solution and sought his own in the field
of social psychology. Mead appealed to the principle of sociality. Human individuals are able to view objects with themselves as stationary points of reference or, for that matter, they
can project themselves into objects, that is, assume the attitudes of these objects, converting them into stationary points
of reference. So he asked, "Is this capacity for placing ourselves in the plane when we are on the earth, or on the earth
when we are in the plane . . . due to some power that belongs
to thought as such, or is this power of thought due to the
capacity to place ourselves in the attitude of the object which
presents itself in experience?" (*PA,* p. 545). Mead's answer
was, of course, the latter, namely, " . . . that meaning as such,
i.e., the object of thought, arises in experience through the
individual stimulating himself to take the attitude of the
other in his reaction toward the object" (*PA,* p. 545). The thinking individual is the key to the organization of perspectives
because the very structure of meaning enables him to occupy
the perspectives of others as well as his own. In assuming the
perspectives of others he approaches the "perspective of the
most universal community." The principle of sociality, expressed in social acts, undergirds nature and society.

VI. MEAD'S PHILOSOPHY IN ITS AMERICAN SETTING

Mead's life spanned the "golden age" of American philosophy. During this period that stretched from the Civil War
to the Great Depression and witnessed America's coming of
age as a world power, pragmatism was born. Conceived in
Cambridge, Massachusetts, and baptized in Berkeley, California, pragmatism was the first indigenous American philosophical movement to invade the capitals of Europe. Great

philosophers graced the American scene. Charles Peirce, William James, and Josiah Royce flourished during the first phase of the "golden age." In the second phase John Dewey, George Santayana, and Alfred North Whitehead came upon the stage. From the "canonical" list of six "classic" American philosophers Mead's name is omitted.[1] Yet, measured in all their scope and depth, Mead's contributions to the development of pragmatism, his social psychology and social philosophy, his work in intellectual history and in the philosophy of science, and his achievements in formulating a philosophy of act with its emergent temporalism and its concept of perspectives, assure him an eminent position in the history of American thought.

John Dewey has elegiacally described Mead as "the most original mind in philosophy in America of the last generation," and he has confessed: "I dislike to think what my own thinking might have been were it not for the seminal ideas which I derived from him." [2] Mead, in his turn, had complimented Dewey by the way he placed him, along with his predecessors, Royce and James, in their American setting. In a masterful essay, published near the end of his life, Mead held that the most striking character of American consciousness prior to the advent of pragmatism was the split between the directive currents of politics and business on the one hand, and the interpretive activities of history, literature, and speculation on the other.[3] Mead had admitted that the idealism of his teacher Josiah Royce, with its vision "of freedom of mind, and of dominance of thought in the universe, of a clear

[1] See *Classic American Philosophers,* edited by Max Fisch (New York: Appleton-Century-Crofts, 1951).

[2] Dewey, "George Herbert Mead," *The Journal of Philosophy,* XXVIII (1931), 310–311.

[3] Mead, "The Philosophies of Royce, James and Dewey in Their American Setting," *International Journal of Ethics,* XL (1929–1930), 211–231. Also in the cooperative volume, *John Dewey: The Man and His Philosophy* (Cambridge, Mass.: Harvard University Press, 1930), pp. 75–105. See below, p. 371.

unclouded landscape of spiritual reality where we sat like gods together," followed him for many years,[4] but, in the last analysis, he judged Royce's philosophy alien to American civilization as "part of the escape from the crudity of American life, not an interpretation of it." By comparison with Royce, Dewey fared exceedingly well. Pragmatism, as conceived by James and elaborated by Dewey, healed the breach between the interpretive cultural currents and the directive forces in American civilization. Where Royce had failed to articulate the implicit intelligence of the American community, Dewey had succeeded. "In the profoundest sense John Dewey is the philosopher of America." [5]

Having so ably placed the philosophies of his predecessors in their American setting, Mead invites a similar interpretation of his own thought. A student of James and Royce, Mead was connected with Peirce indirectly and tenuously, although like Peirce he examined language and meaning intently and he even arrived at a triadic theory of meaning. Like Peirce, moreover, he grappled with the problems of constructing a philosophical system only to leave it in an unfinished condition. Of Royce, Mead's later pronouncements were critical, since Mead deemed idealism inapplicable to the realities of America's urbanizing industrial civilization. Yet the idealist vision lingered, and Mead's own social goal of a universal community which fulfills human needs and aspirations is, in one sense, a naturalization of Royce's "Blessed Community." For Mead brought down to earth Royce's "Blessed Community"—which, as unveiled in *The Problem of Christianity* (1913), is nothing less than the ideal Christian Church—and converted it into a secular democracy in which intelligence and industry tackle social problems. Mead's debt to James is

---

[4] Mead, "Josiah Royce—A Personal Impression," *International Journal of Ethics*, XXVII (1917), 170.

[5] Mead, "The Philosophies of Royce, James and Dewey in Their American Setting"; see below, p. 391. See also Mead, "The Philosophy of John Dewey," *International Journal of Ethics*, XLVI (1935–1936), 64–81.

more obvious. His own work is founded on James's psychological and pragmatist theories. But while James sometimes veers toward a subjectivist empiricism, Mead is steadfast in his social objectivism. In emphasizing the social and behavioral elements in psychology and theory of knowledge, Mead's philosophy joins that of Dewey.

Without Mead's social psychology the history of social science in the United States would have been quite different. The "Chicago tradition" in social science, vitally influential today, stems in large measure from Mead's teachings. Role theory in sociology and symbolic interactionism in social psychology are traceable to Mead. Despite misgivings over the rationalistic tenor of symbolic interactionism as the key to both personality and society, at present Mead's social psychology, whatever the outcome of current discussions, occupies the center of the stage.[6] The unusual contemporaneity of Mead's psychology may be gauged by a brief comparison with the work of Santayana. After all, he and Santayana were born in the same year, 1863, and Santayana studied under Mead's teachers at Harvard—James and Royce. Further, Santayana survived Mead by over two decades, dying in 1952, the same year Dewey died. Yet Santayana's contributions to the philosophy of mind, at first in his renowned multivolume *Life of Reason* (1905–1906) and subsequently in his treatments of psyche in *The Realm of Matter* (1930) and of spirit in *The Realm of Spirit* (1940), belong to what he himself unmaliciously labeled "literary psychology." In contrast Mead's philosophy of mind is germane to existing scientific investigations of personality and society. Attending to the natural origin and social utility of mind and focusing on the social processes involved in the development of personality and of society, Mead has provided the most profound and comprehensive social psychology to emerge from pragmatism.

In social philosophy Mead's offerings, like those of Dewey,

[6] *Human Behavior and Social Processes; an Interactionist Approach,* edited by Arnold M. Rose (Boston: Houghton Mifflin Company, 1962).

were both theoretical and practical. The advocacy of scientific method for the solution of social problems, the analysis of the tentative mutability of social goals and the evolution of ends from natural processes in which they are interchangeable with means, the distrust of absolute panaceas and transcendent values, characterize Mead's thought as well as Dewey's. No doubt the influences of Dewey upon Mead were reciprocated. Like Dewey, too, Mead immersed himself in the practical affairs of his community, particularly in the fields of education, municipal government, and social welfare. In the hands of Dewey and Mead, pragmatism became a social philosophy, preoccupied with the reconstruction of problematic situations. To Mead goes the credit for furnishing the social psychology that accounts for reconstructionist programs in regard to personality and to society. Relevant here is Charles Morris' remark that while Dewey gave range and vision to pragmatic philosophy, Mead imparted analytical depth and scientific precision. "If Dewey is at once the rolling rim and many of the radiating spokes of the contemporary pragmatist wheel, Mead is the hub" (*MSS*, p. xi).

Not content to devote himself exclusively to the "problems of men," Mead faced up to the speculative issues generated by the science of his time. The first quarter of the twentieth century witnessed a revolution in physics comparable to the revolution in biology wrought in the nineteenth century. Mead discerned what no other pragmatist appreciated—the clash between the temporalist world view fostered by the theory of evolution in biology and the new metaphysics which was springing up in the wake of relativity physics. As a pragmatist Mead was loyal to temporalism, with its concepts of process, activity, and novelty. At the same time he perceived that relativity physics gravely challenged existing concepts of an unbroken creative advance in nature. Bergson and Whitehead also grasped the problem, but while Bergson resolved it by construing the time in relativity physics to be mathematical time distinct from real time, and Whitehead by rewriting the theory of relativity, Mead avoided such outright derogations from the attainments of the physical scientists. Instead, he questioned the explications of the philosophers. Mead's detailed criticisms of Whitehead have yet to be collated, systematically expounded, and critically interpreted; and with commentaries on Whitehead now in demand, a study of Mead's writings should be at a premium. Moreover, Mead's own positive theory, his philosophy of the act, or of the present, is a remarkable achievement in its own right. No metaphysics in recent American philosophy surpasses its striking originality. Its full import has still to be adequately probed and exploited. As long as Whitehead's cosmology captivates the attention of American philosophers, Mead's metaphysical temporalism will perhaps be eclipsed, but it continues to furnish a singular alternative for speculation.

Overshadowed by Dewey, whose ascendancy he acknowledged, Mead was nonetheless esteemed. Certainly his influence, though slow and limited, has been durable. Many of his students, attaining the stature of original thinkers in their own right, have carried on his work. To mention but a few, T. V. Smith, Charles Morris, and David Miller are outstanding examples of creative discipleship. Today a rising curve of interest in Mead's thought is in evidence. Far removed in spirit as well as in place and time from the seminars and lecture halls of the University of Chicago in the first quarter of this century, contemporary thinkers have revived Mead's ideas in psychoanalytic, phenomenological, and existential contexts. In the past decade Mead's philosophy has confronted Husserlian phenomenology through the writings of Maurice Natanson,[7] Martin Buber's social anthropology through the work of Paul Pfuetze,[8] and Sartre's existentialism and Zen

[7] Maurice Natanson, *The Social Dynamics of George H. Mead* (Washington, D. C.: Public Affairs Press, 1956).

[8] Paul E. Pfuetze, *The Social Self* (New York: Bookman Associates, 1954). Reprinted in 1961 as "Harper Torchbook" No. 1059, entitled *Self, Society, Existence*.

Buddhism through the studies of Van Meter Ames.[9] Mead's philosophy is winning a growing share of contemporary consideration, not only in America, but also abroad. Indeed, all the signs indicate that Mead's pragmatic, temporalist philosophy, so at home in its American setting and period, belongs to the world and to all time.

[9] Van Meter Ames, "Mead and Sartre on Man," *The Journal of Philosophy*, LIII (1956), 205–219, and "Zen to Mead," *Proceedings and Addresses of the American Philosophical Association*, XXXIII (1959–1960), 27–42.

BIBLIOGRAPHY

THE WRITINGS OF GEORGE HERBERT MEAD

Books

1. *The Philosophy of the Present.* Edited, with an Introduction, by ARTHUR E. MURPHY, and prefatory remarks by JOHN DEWEY. La Salle, Ill.: Open Court Publishing Company, 1932.

2. *Mind, Self and Society from the Standpoint of a Social Behaviorist.* Edited, with an Introduction, by CHARLES W. MORRIS. Chicago: University of Chicago Press, 1934.

3. *Movements of Thought in the Nineteenth Century.* Edited, with an Introduction, by MERRITT H. MOORE. Chicago: University of Chicago Press, 1936.

4. *The Philosophy of the Act.* Edited, with an Introduction, by CHARLES W. MORRIS, in collaboration with JOHN M. BREWSTER, ALBERT M. DUNHAM, and DAVID L. MILLER. Chicago: University of Chicago Press, 1938.

5. *The Social Psychology of George Herbert Mead.* Edited, with an Introduction, by ANSELM STRAUSS. "Phoenix Books." Chicago: University of Chicago Press, 1956.

Articles and Addresses

1. "Herr Lasswitz on Energy and Epistemology," *The Psychological Review*, I (1894), 172–175.

2. "The Relation of Play to Education," *The University Record* (Chicago), I (1896), 141–145.

3. "The Working Hypothesis in Social Reform," *The American Journal of Sociology*, V (1899), 369–371.

4. "Suggestions toward a Theory of the Philosophical Disciplines," *The Philosophical Review*, IX (1900), 1–17.

5. "The Definition of the Psychical," *The Decennial Publications of the University of Chicago.* "First Series." Volume III. Chicago: University of Chicago Press, 1903. Pp. 77–112.

6. "The Basis for a Parents' Association," *The Elementary School Teacher*, IV (1903–1904), 337–346.

7. "Image or Sensation," *The Journal of Philosophy, Psychology, and Scientific Methods*, I (1904), 604–607.

8. "The Relations of Psychology and Philology," *Psychological Bulletin*, I (1904), 375–391.

9. "The Teaching of Science in College," *Science*, XXIV (1906), 390–397.

10. "The Imagination in Wundt's Treatment of Myth and Religion," *Psychological Bulletin*, III (1906), 393–399.

11. "Science in the High School," *School Review*, XIV (1906), 237–249.

12. "Concerning Animal Perception," *The Psychological Review*, XIV (1907), 383–390.

13. "On the Educational Situation in the Chicago Public Schools," *City Club Bulletin* (Chicago), I (1907–1908), 131–138.

14. "The Philosophical Basis of Ethics," *International Journal of Ethics*, XVIII (1908), 311–323.

15. "The Social Settlement: Its Basis and Function," *The University Record* (Chicago), XII (1908), 108–110.

16. "Educational Aspects of Trade Schools," *Union Labor Advocate*, VIII, No. 7 (1908), 19–20.

17. "Industrial Education, the Working-Man, and the School," *The Elementary School Teacher*, IX (1908–1909), 369–383.

18. "Social Psychology as Counterpart to Physiological Psychology," *Psychological Bulletin*, VI (1909), 401–408.

19. "What Social Objects Must Psychology Presuppose?" *The Journal of Philosophy, Psychology, and Scientific Methods,* VII (1910), 174–180.

20. "The Psychology of Social Consciousness Implied in Instruction," *Science,* XXXI (1910), 688–693.

21. "Social Consciousness and the Consciousness of Meaning," *Psychological Bulletin,* VII (1910), 397–405.

22. "The Mechanism of Social Consciousness," *The Journal of Philosophy, Psychology, and Scientific Methods,* IX (1912), 401–406.

23. "The Social Self," *The Journal of Philosophy, Psychology, and Scientific Methods,* X (1913), 374–380.

24. "A Heckling School Board and an Educational Stateswoman," *Survey,* XXXI (1913–1914), 443–444.

25. "The Psychological Bases of Internationalism," *Survey,* XXXIII (1914–1915), 604–607.

26. "Natural Rights and the Theory of the Political Institution," *The Journal of Philosophy, Psychology, and Scientific Methods,* XII (1915), 141–155.

27. "Madison—The Passage of the University through the State Political Agitation of 1914; the Survey by Wm. H. Allen and His Staff and the Legislative Fight of 1915, with Indications these offer of the Place the State University Holds in the Community," *Survey,* XXXV (1915–1916), 349–351, 354–361.

28. "Smashing the Looking Glass, Rejoinder," *Survey,* XXXV (1915–1916), 607, 610.

29. "Professor Hoxie and the Community," *The University of Chicago Magazine,* IX (1916–1917), 114–117.

30. "Josiah Royce—A Personal Impression," *International Journal of Ethics,* XXVII (1917), 168–170.

31. "Scientific Method and Individual Thinker," *Creative Intelligence: Essays in the Pragmatic Attitude.* New York: Henry Holt and Co., 1917. Pp. 176–227.

32. "The Psychology of Punitive Justice," *The American Journal of Sociology,* XXIII (1917–1918), 577–602.

33. "Retiring President's Address," *City Club Bulletin* (Chicago), XIII (1920), 94–95, 97–99.

34. "A Behavioristic Account of the Significant Symbol," *The Journal of Philosophy*, XIX (1922), 157–163.

35. "Scientific Method and the Moral Sciences," *International Journal of Ethics*, XXXIII (1923), 229–247.

36. "The Genesis of the Self and Social Control," *International Journal of Ethics*, XXXV (1924–1925), 251–277.

37. "The Nature of Aesthetic Experience," *International Journal of Ethics*, XXXVI (1925–1926), 382–392.

38. "The Objective Reality of Perspectives," *Proceedings of the Sixth International Congress of Philosophy*. Edited by EDGAR SHEFFIELD BRIGHTMAN. New York: Longmans, Green and Co., 1927. Pp. 75–85. Reprinted in *The Philosophy of the Present*. LaSalle, Ill.: The Open Court Publishing Co., 1932.

39. "A Pragmatic Theory of Truth," *Studies in the Nature of Truth*. "University of California Publications in Philosophy," XI (1929), 65–88.

40. "The Nature of the Past," *Essays in Honor of John Dewey*. Edited by JOHN COSS. New York: Henry Holt and Co., 1929. Pp. 235–242.

41. "National-Mindedness and International-Mindedness," *International Journal of Ethics*, XXXIX (1929), 392–407.

42. "Bishop Berkeley and His Message," *The Journal of Philosophy*, XXVI (1929), 421–430.

43. "Cooley's Contribution to American Social Thought," *The American Journal of Sociology*, XXXV (1929–1930), 693–706.

44. "The Philosophies of Royce, James, and Dewey, in their American Setting," *International Journal of Ethics*, XL (1929–1930), 211–231. Also in the cooperative volume, *John Dewey: The Man and His Philosophy*. Cambridge, Mass.: Harvard University Press, 1930. Pp. 75–105.

45. "Philanthropy from the Point of View of Ethics," *Intelligent Philanthropy*. Edited by ELLSWORTH FARIS, FERRIS

LAUNE, and ARTHUR J. TODD. Chicago: University of Chicago Press, 1930. Pp. 133–148.

46. "Dr. A. W. Moore's Philosophy," *The University Record* (Chicago), New Series, XVII (1931), 47–49.

47. "The Philosophy of John Dewey," *International Journal of Ethics*, XLVI (1935–1936), 64–81.

48. "Two Unpublished Papers" ("Relative Space-Time and Simultaneity" and "Metaphysics"), edited, with an Introduction, by DAVID L. MILLER, *The Review of Metaphysics*, XVII (1963–1964), 511–556.

Book Reviews

1. K. LASSWITZ. *Die moderne Energetik in ihrer Bedeutung für Erkenntniskritik*. Reviewed in *The Psychological Review*, I (1894), 210–213.

2. C. L. MORGAN. *An Introduction to Comparative Psychology*. Reviewed in *The Psychological Review*, II (1895), 399–402.

3. G. LE BON. *The Psychology of Socialism*. Reviewed in *The American Journal of Sociology*, V (1899), 404–412.

4. D. DRAGHIESCO. *Du rôle de l'individu dans le déterminisme social,* and *Le problème du déterminisme, déterminisme biologique et déterminisme social*. Reviewed in *Psychological Bulletin*, II (1905), 399–405.

5. JANE ADDAMS. *The Newer Ideal of Peace*. Reviewed in *The American Journal of Sociology*, XIII (1907), 121–128.

6. B. M. ANDERSON, JR. *Social Value, A Study in Economic Theory*. Reviewed in *Psychological Bulletin*, VIII (1911), 432–436.

7. WARNER FITE. *Individualism: Four Lectures on the Significance of Consciousness for Social Relations*. Reviewed in *Psychological Bulletin*, VIII (1911), 323–328.

8. EDITH ABBOTT and SOPHONISBA P. BRECKINRIDGE. *Truancy*

and Non-Attendance in the Chicago Public Schools. Reviewed in *Survey,* XXXVIII (1917), 369–370.

Miscellany (Abstracts, Editorial Notes, and Other Materials)

1. "A Theory of Emotions from the Physiological Standpoint" (Abstract), *The Psychological Review,* II (1895), 162–164.

2. "Some Aspects of Greek Philosophy" (Abstract), *The University Record* (Chicago), I (1896–1897), 42.

3. "Editorial Notes," *School Review,* XV (1907), 160–165.

4. "The Relation of Imitation to the Theory of Animal Perception" (Abstract), *Psychological Bulletin,* IV (1907), 210–211.

5. "Editorial Notes" (Policy Statement), *The Elementary School Teacher,* VIII (1907–1908), 281–284.

6. "Editorial Notes: Industrial Education and Trade Schools," *The Elementary School Teacher,* VIII (1907–1908), 402–406.

7. "Editorial Notes" (N. E. A. Resolution on Industrial Education), *The Elementary School Teacher,* IX (1908–1909), 156–157.

8. "Editorial Notes" (Industrial Training), *The Elementary School Teacher,* IX (1908–1909), 212–214.

9. "Editorial Notes" (Moral Training in the Schools), *The Elementary School Teacher,* IX (1908–1909), 327–328.

10. "Editorial Notes" (The Problem of History in the Elementary School), *The Elementary School Teacher,* IX (1908–1909), 433–434.

11. Remarks on Exhibit of City Club Committee on Public Education, *City Club Bulletin* (Chicago), V (1912), 9.

12. Remarks on Labor Night Concerning Participation of Representatives of Labor in City Club, *City Club Bulletin* (Chicago), V (1912), 214–215.

13. *A Report on Vocational Training in Chicago and in Other Cities.* By a Committee of the City Club, GEORGE H. MEAD, Chairman. Chicago: City Club of Chicago, 1912.

14. *The Conscientious Objector.* "Patriotism through Education Series," Pamphlet No. 33. New York: National Security League, 1917.

NOTES ON THE TEXT

The present selection consists of twenty-five articles Mead published during his lifetime, twenty-two of which are reprinted in their entirety. The complete articles as numbered in the Bibliography and correlated with the roman numerals assigned to the essays in the Table of Contents are:

Article	Essay	Article	Essay	Article	Essay
4	II	22	XI	36	XVIII
9	IV	23	XII	37	XIX
12	V	26	XIII	38	XX
14	VI	31	XIV	39	XXI
18	VII	32	XV	40	XXII
19	VIII	34	XVI	44	XXIV
20	IX	35	XVII	45	XXV
21	X				

Three articles are presented in part, deletions having been prompted by the dependence of portions of the text upon extraneous material. In each case the deletions are clearly indicated by means of ellipses. The affected articles are:

Article	Essay
3	I
5	III
41	XXIII

The present volume presents Mead's thought as it developed and in all its scope and depth. As far as possible the material looks exactly as it appeared to Mead on first publication, even though this has meant repetition of ideas. The original source for each article appears as an unnumbered note, enclosed in square brackets and set off from the text, at the bottom of the first page of each essay. Typographical errors in spelling and punctuation have been corrected, and a uniform system of punctuation has been adopted—for example, the use of double quotation marks throughout the essays, although in some cases Mead used single quotation marks, in others double, to conform to the requirements of the original publications. For the scholar, references have been corrected or completed; for the student, translations of foreign phrases and annotations have been furnished, usually at the first appearance of unfamiliar or obscure phrases, concepts, and persons. In order to assure consecutive numbering, Mead's original footnote numbers have been changed. But in order to preserve as much as possible the original appearance of the essays, all material the editor has added to the text is enclosed in brackets.

From the standpoint of the intellectual historian, the philosopher, or the social psychologist, every selection in the present volume is of permanent value. Since the aim of this volume is to present only material Mead himself published during his lifetime, the editor did not draw upon Mead's book-length works and articles 47 and 48. Nor did he incorporate any material listed in the bibliography under the heading *Miscellany.* Except for the abstracts, which are too brief and which contain ideas more fully expressed in the articles, the miscellaneous material is too occasional in character to warrant inclusion in the present edition. Similarly, the book reviews, although furnishing valuable insights on the development of Mead's thought (Book Review 1 on the theory of the act, Book Reviews 3, 5, and 7 on social philosophy, Book Reviews 2 and 4 on social psychology), are excluded, since for the most part they are occupied with detailed critical discussion of minor works of no lasting worth and known only to a few scholars.

In a fundamental sense, of course, the scholar will always find of interest everything Mead wrote. And the specialist will wish, from time to time, to examine articles omitted from the present volume. For the social psychologist, Articles 1, 7, 8, and 10 may hold permanent value, although they are so wholly tied up with critical discussion of other theories that they do not stand on their own, and further, the ideas they express are to be found in other articles included in the present volume. Article 43, on Cooley, will perhaps interest the historian of social psychology, but he must first know Cooley's theories to make sense of Mead's judgment. Other articles of interest to the intellectual historian are Articles 30, 42, and 46, but again they are exceptionally specialized and contain ideas more adequately represented by the selections contained in the present volume—for example, Article 44 (Essay XXIV). Finally, the remaining articles that have been omitted may interest the social philosopher, but like the miscellaneous material, these articles, for the most part, are so occupied with the problems then current that they do not possess sufficient permanent worth to be included in the present volume. Perhaps Article 2, by its title, may invite the philosopher of education, but the theory of play this article advances is unoriginal and is superseded by the theory propounded in Article 36 (Essay XVIII).

A. J. R.

SELECTED WRITINGS

I

THE WORKING HYPOTHESIS
IN SOCIAL REFORM

. . . It is impossible to so forecast any future condition that depends upon the evolution of society as to be able to govern our conduct by such a forecast. It is always the unexpected that happens, for we have to recognize, not only the immediate change that is to take place, but also the reaction back upon this of the whole world within which the change takes place, and no human foresight is equal to this. In the social world we must recognize the working hypothesis as the form into which all theories must be cast as completely as in the natural sciences. The highest criterion that we can present is that the hypothesis shall *work* in the complex of forces into which we introduce it. We can never set up a detailed statement of the conditions that are to be ultimately attained. What we have is a method and a control in application, not an ideal to work toward. As has been stated, this is the attitude of the scientist in the laboratory, whether his work remains purely scientific or is applied immediately to conduct. His foresight does not go beyond the testing of his hypothesis. Given its success, he may restate his world from this standpoint and get the basis for further investigation that again always takes the form of a problem. The solution of this problem is found over again in the possibility of fitting his hypothetical proposition into the whole within which it arises. And he must recognize that this statement is only a working hypothesis at the best, i.e., he knows that further investigation will show that the former statement of his world is only provisionally true, and must be false from the standpoint of a larger knowledge, as every partial truth is necessarily false over against the fuller knowledge

[From *The American Journal of Sociology*, V (1899), 369–371.]

which he will gain later. Even the axioms of Euclid [1] are not true now in the sense of Euclid. In a word, our confidence in the results of science and the general application of intelligence to the control of the physical world is based, not upon a knowledge of the whole universe as it is, but upon a faith in its general rational character, that is perhaps best stated in the success of working hypotheses.

In social reform, or the application of intelligence to the control of social conditions, we must make a like assumption, and this assumption takes the form of belief in the essentially social character of human impulse and endeavor. We cannot make persons social by legislative enactment, but we can allow the essentially social nature of their actions to come to expression under conditions which favor this. What the form of this social organization will be depends upon conditions that lie necessarily beyond our ken. We assume that human society is governed by laws that involve its solidarity, and we seek to find these out that they may be used. In the same way the natural scientist assumes that the world is as a whole governed by laws that involve the interaction of all its forces, and that he may find these laws out, and use them for the further organization of his world, so far as he is a part of it.

There is here, however, a distinction that is of considerable importance. In the physical world we regard ourselves as standing in some degree outside the forces at work, and thus avoid the difficulty of harmonizing the feeling of human initiative with the recognition of series which are necessarily determined. In society we are the forces that are being investigated, and if we advance beyond the mere description of the phenomena of the social world to the attempt at reform, we seem to involve the possibility of changing what at the same time we

1 [Euclid (*ca.* 300 B.C.), Greek mathematician. Euclid's great work, the *Elements,* embraced and superseded the contributions of his predecessors. The famous 5th axiom concerning parallel lines could never be proved. In the 19th century several mathematicians, of whom the most notable were Lobachevsky in 1826 and Riemann in 1854, submitted other axioms for Euclid's 5th axiom and consequently developed non-Euclidean geometry.]

assume to be necessarily fixed. The question, stated more generally, is: What is the function of reflective consciousness in its attempt to direct conduct? The common answer is that we carry in thought the world as it should be, and fashion our conduct to bring this about. As we have already seen, if this implies a "vision given in the mount" which represents in detail what is to be, we are utterly incapable of conceiving it. And every attempt to direct conduct by a fixed idea of the world of the future must be, not only a failure, but also pernicious. A conception of a different world comes to us always as the result of some specific problem which involves readjustment of the world as it is, not to meet a detailed ideal of a perfect universe, but to obviate the present difficulty; and the test of the effort lies in the possibility of this readjustment fitting into the world as it is. Reflective consciousness does not then carry us on to the world that is to be, but puts our own thought and endeavor into the very process of evolution, and evolution within consciousness that has become reflective has the advantage over other evolution in that the form does not tend to perpetuate himself as he is, but identifies himself with the process of development. Our reflective consciousness as applied to conduct is, therefore, an identification of our effort with the problem that presents itself, and the developmental process by which it is overcome, and reaches its highest expression in the scientific statement of the problem, and the recognition and use of scientific method and control.

✍ II ◉✎

SUGGESTIONS TOWARD A THEORY OF THE · PHILOSOPHICAL DISCIPLINES

In *The Psychological Review* (Vol. III, pp. 357–70), Professor Dewey maintains in his discussion of the Reflex Arc that the sensation appears always in consciousness as a problem; that attention could not be centered upon a so-called element of consciousness unless the individual were abstracting from the former meaning of the object, and in his effort to reach a new meaning had fixed this feature of the former object as a problem to be solved. The illustration used is the well-worn one of the child and the candle. He has burned his fingers before in dealing with a moving bright object, and he has played with bright objects. There are then at least two tendencies to action, that of withdrawing the hand from the object that burns, and that of reaching out for a plaything. In the conflict between these two tendencies the bright yellow dancing something is shorn of its objective meaning in the child's former experience, and he is trying to learn what it is. While it is thus deprived of its objective value, while it is no longer a stimulus to action, it may become a sensation. But with knowledge of its real nature it ceases to appear in this form in consciousness. It can be sensation no longer until it again becomes the center of a problem episode in experience. I may have carried Mr. Dewey's doctrine beyond the statement given in the article on the Reflex Arc, but I think that the statement represents what Mr. Dewey would admit. At least such a statement is possible from the standpoint which Mr. Dewey takes, and admitting it

[From *The Philosophical Review*, IX (1900), 1–17. Reprinted by permission.]

6

for the sake of discussion, I wish to point out what its bearing upon the different philosophical disciplines may be.

The assumption made here is that all analytical thought commences with the presence of problems and the conflict between different lines of activity. The further assumption is that it continues always to be an expression of such conflict and the solution of the problems involved; that all reflective thought arises out of real problems present in immediate experience, and is occupied entirely with the solution of these problems or their attempted solution; that this solution finally is found in the possibility of continuing the activity, that has been stopped, along new or old lines, when such reflective thought ceases in the nature of the case. I shall not attempt to prove this to be true, but simply try to see where metaphysics, psychology, deductive and inductive logics (I refer here to the procedures of these sciences, not their general theories), ethics, aesthetics, and the general theory of logic would fall within a reflective process so stated.

The order of the disciplines stated above implies a dialectic within the act, which I wish to confess to at once. Metaphysics I wish to identify with the statement of the problem. It may take psychological form or not. If the result of the recognition of the problem is only to bring to consciousness the meaning of the object in terms of past experience, we get the universal—the ideal—and the use of the object thus defined can be systematized in a manner which is described in deductive logic. If, on the contrary, we abandon the old universals—the interpretations involved in the objects as we have constructed them—and frankly look forward to a new meaning, the immediate experience can claim only subjective validity, and we have the subject matter with which psychology deals. The use of this material to reach the new universal is evidently the procedure of inductive logic. The application of either of these methods to conduct as a whole, in their relation to the ideal or to the larger self to be attained, fulfils the function of ethics, while aesthetics deals with the artistic representations of the

object either as ideal or as a phase in the process of development. Finally, the general theory of the intelligent act as a
whole would fall within that of logic as treated in works such
as that of Hegel.[1]

Where our conscious activity finds itself unable to pass into
an objective world on account of the clash between different
tendencies to action, we are thrown back upon an analysis of
these spontaneous acts and therefore upon the objects which
get their content from them. I wish to emphasize this latter
assumption which is indeed in accord with some of the best
psychological analysis of the present time. It is otherwise stated
as the teleological nature of the concept, and affirms that the
meaning of the object is derived entirely from our reaction
upon it, or, in other words, our use of it.[2]

It would follow from this recognition of the nature of the
known object that the conflict of two uses or reactions in the
same instance would inevitably lead to an analysis of the activities themselves, if a complete abandonment of the action
did not take place. However, the analysis would not at first be
of the activity as a psychical state. The question would be
what the real nature of the object is. A case of doubt as to the
identity of a person just met, representing conflicting tendencies to greet him as an acquaintance and to treat him as a simple passer-by, does not at once suggest to us his form with its
color and other qualities as a series of sensations, though this
is implicitly involved. We are busy in the study of the object,
finally perhaps placing him as one whom we have not met before, but who bears a striking resemblance to some one of our
acquaintance. This involves the bringing to consciousness the
idea of the friend, his form and features, gestures and bearing,

1 [G. W. F. Hegel (1770–1831) wrote *Science of Logic* (2 vols., 1812–1816),
and *Shorter Logic,* Part One of his *Encyclopedia of Philosophical Sciences*
(1817). These works present a dialectical idealism which identifies the
real with the rational and embraces all reality within logic.]

2 [William] James, [*The Principles of*] *Psychology* [New York: Henry
Holt and Co., 1890], II, 332.

while the more or less unsuccessful attempt to make this image coalesce with the form before us, tends to emphasize the points of contrast, that is to form another image which is not able to represent the object before us satisfactorily. While we do not question the objective validity either of our mental pictures of the friend, or yet of the reality of the impression of the man whom we are in the presence of, there is little tendency to advance to the subjective character of the state of consciousness. Furthermore, if the image which is called up is one which represents fixed habits, especially those bearing pronounced moral sanction, we may affirm the reality of these ideas as over against the seeming contradiction before us. Such instances are found often enough in our lives. Every question of expediency is apt to lead to such a result. A moral line of conduct has become identified with certain objects. For example, the right to the use of what is termed property being once fixed, the expenditure of it in luxuries while others may be starving arouses, when the problem is felt, first of all the idea of property itself as it is represented in all the business transactions of life. This may be affirmed in spite of the contradiction between it and the tendencies to demand assistance for the suffering. The presence of such conflicts, between habitual interpretations of the meaning of the goods of life, and opposite lines of conduct with reference to them, tends to the conscious formulation by most of us of a moral code in more or less abstract terms. If we are able to live pretty consistently up to such a code, and to ignore the contradictions that persist, we have not yet reached the point of metaphysics.

A metaphysical situation implies that the problem persists and cannot be ignored. To affirm the reality of the idea, i.e., the meaning of the object in terms of past experience—our own or that of the community—we must deny to certain elements of experience, interpreted also in terms of the past activity, the like reality. A theological dogma may, for example, affirm the reality of our teleological interpretation of experience, and at the same time deny reality to the mechanical interpretation which the physical sciences suggest. Or, in the type of metaphysical thought found in Plato,[3] the reality of the idea may be affirmed at the expense of that of our entire sensuous experience. Metaphysics is then a statement of an essential problem in permanent form, in terms of the reality of an idea or system of ideas and the unreality of that which conflicts with it. The solution of the problem carries with it the disappearance of the problem and the metaphysical system at the same time. The conception of an immanent deity, making possible, for example, the harmonizing of the teleological and mechanical interpretations of nature, up to that point solves the problem and banishes the metaphysical *deus ex machina* from the system of thought. Of course this change will not necessarily affect other metaphysical features of theology. But in case it is accepted, special providences would be no longer necessary to explain what happens. Our modern teleological psychology which finds the unity of the object and of the world in our own activity, dissipates the conflict between the one and the many which lies at the bottom of the problem with which Plato was struggling. A psychological interpretation of experience makes it possible to affirm both the reality of the one, and the reality of the multitudinous elements that go to make up the object, and in so doing deprives the metaphysical system of its *raison d'être*.

The presence of such an idea, whose reality is maintained over against conflicting elements in experience, requires that we should rigidly distinguish in experience what is real and what is to be ignored or denied. We must be able to apply the idea, and the dominance of the idea cannot but bring to consciousness the method by which this must be done. Deductive reasoning is nothing but the organization of one's world upon the basis of certain ideas, implying that we either deny the

3 [Plato (427–347 B.C.), Greek philosopher who presented a philosophy of rational idealism in a series of dialogues. He maintained that universals (forms or ideas) are more real than individual things, and struggled with the problem of relating the universals to the things. His dialogue, *Parmenides*, dealt with this problem as the problem of the one and the many.]

existence of that which does not accord therewith, or else ignore it. When, however, the technique has in this manner
been made conscious, it may be used to aid us in the application of universals which are not necessarily metaphysical. Thus
while deductive logic had its rise as the organon of a metaphysical system, and served to separate the real from the unreal, it becomes a general organon that is applied universally,
serving to separate not the real from the unreal but the known
from that which is to be ignored for the time being only.

The next step in the dialectic of reflective consciousness is
found in the conscious solution of the problems which are
registered and systematized in metaphysics. A successful solution implies the recognition of the reality of all elements that
enter into the experience. Such reality implies further, in
logical terms, that all elements shall fall under universals
whose validity is recognized; for all our knowledge is through
universals and must be through universals. In psychological
terms, it implies that the concepts of the object, representing
the values of past reactions, though they are now in conflict,
shall be so harmonized that the values of each may appear
in a new concept, that each type of reaction shall be represented in the new activity. For example, if the problem, which
is implied in the essentially metaphysical substance of imponderable ether, is to be solved, both the elements which are
implied in the energy of mass (which should appear in any
medium as physics has defined media, but which is denied in
imponderable ether) and that of vibration must receive universal validity, or otherwise stated, and assuming that a theory of energy could solve the problem, a new method of
treating all physical phenomena, a new reaction which involves all that is true in all our processes of physical measurement and determination must take the place of those which
have come into conflict in this instance. If the conflict is not
a mere mistake, and if it is necessary within our known world,
it can be overcome only by the appearance of a new universal
or habit of reaction. In the second place, the solution of a
metaphysically stated problem can be achieved only by ad-

mitting, at least for the time being, the inadequacy of the old and so its lack of objective validity, and advancing toward a new universal whose objective validity cannot yet be recognized, with the hope that in this way a new known world shall arise in the place of the old. This, of course, holds only for the conscious solution of the problem. Countless necessary problems have arisen in the history of human society that have reached solution in the gradual appearance of new conceptions and the adaptation of old methods of action, which have thus become equal to situations in which irrepressible conflict first existed. The solution that we are referring to here is not this unconscious change by which one generation differs from the next with no historical sense of wherein this difference lies and with no anticipation of further fundamental change. It is the consciousness of the change that is the essential step in the dialectic of reflective consciousness. Furthermore, just as the metaphysical situation has given a technique in the statement of the problem, with the inestimable advantage that flows from it, so the consciousness of the process by which we change from the old universal to the new carries with it the acceleration which always accompanies the addition of reflection to any instinctive activity.

As indicated above, the necessary result of consciously advancing to the solution of an inevitable problem in human experience is the acceptance of a position midway between the old universals, whose validity is abandoned, and the new universal, which has not yet appeared. And this is a result that affects implicitly the whole world of knowledge; for that world is an organic whole in which no necessary part can be changed without involving all the rest. To assume the attitude, therefore, of solving a necessary problem, implies a willingness to completely invalidate one's known world. I am willing to admit that, even in an age of conscious progress, such an attitude is not explicitly taken by very many who are honestly attacking problems in a scientific spirit, that they not only make many reservations within which they do not expect scientific inquiry to reach, but also that they fail to recognize their known world as an organic whole which cannot be changed in essential parts without changing *in toto*. However, within the province where they do apply the scientific method they are ready to make the Cartesian clean sweep of all objective validity, and having adopted the method they cannot consistently hesitate to continue it as fast as they recognize that the province affects the whole.

In the third place, in the presence of the conflict we reach universals which are the result of abstraction from the immediate conflicting elements. The child has before him that which is neither the object which burned nor yet the plaything. It is something behind each and true of each—a bright moving object we will say. It carries with it a certain amount of the reality of each. It is insofar objectively valid. A primitive metaphysical attitude may maintain itself here as it did among the early Greek thinkers. It is that out of which they both or all spring, if the young child could only become metaphysical (and there is an early period within which the child is markedly so and is in search of pure being). But if he wishes to know, not that out of which they both spring, but which of the two it is, and if he insists on finding out how he can distinguish between the two, he makes the bright moving object merely the starting point of a scientific investigation. In doing this he must ascribe to it, hypothetically, different values for which he has as yet no sufficient objective validity. He knows that it is more than a bright moving object, but he is not sure that it is something that has burned him, nor yet that it is a possible plaything. If he could turn his attention upon it, he would have to say that it is for the time being simply an experience of his own that is confined to his consciousness, that represents experiences that have been objectively valid in the past and a possible future object. In a word, the result of consciously attempting to solve a necessary problem is to render one's world, insofar as it is affected by the problem, psychical, and the technique of the solution is psychology. I wish to insist that this consciousness does not become psychical with the mere abstraction resulting from the conflict of reactions. The bright moving object is objective. And it is conceivable that the analysis may stop here and go no further. It is only when the child refuses to accept the abstraction, and insists that his tendencies to action shall not be checked, but have the larger field for expression which will come with the new object, that the experience necessarily becomes psychical. And it becomes psychical, therefore, because the tendencies to action assert themselves, seeking to adjust themselves to each other. It is this process that falls peculiarly within the phase of attention. There is the hesitating movement of the finger toward the flame representing both tendencies, that to grasp and that to withdraw, but it is more than either. There is involved the assumption that the hand can be used to deal with hot objects, not simply to get out of their way. It is a hypothesis tested with fear and trembling. It includes both elements, both the readiness to withdraw from danger and to manipulate the distant object revealed by the eye, reacting upon each other so as to produce the action of dealing with an object in an entirely new way, and thus producing for the child a new object. Here we have the characteristics of attention, not simply the absorption in the bright moving object, but the control of different reactions upon it by each other [4] in the production of a new type of activity including both. One finds in attention not only concentration, but that which concentration implies, control, and control can exist only where there is something definite to be done which is consciously involved in the whole doing of it. This does not take place through a statement of what the ultimate meaning of the act is to be. The child cannot say to himself, "I must learn to handle a hot bright object." For to him there has been no element of handling in his experience of hot objects whether bright or not. The hot object was one to be withdrawn from. And in his manipulation

4 Contr[ibutions] of the Phil[osophy] Dep[artment] of the U[niversity] of C[hicago]. [James Rowland] Angell and [Addison W.] Moore, ["Reaction-Time: A Study in Attention and Habit"], I [1896], p. 8. [Also printed in The Psychological Review, III (1896).]

of playthings there had been nothing to be avoided. The two activities are here quite distinct, as therefore are the objects. The control lies in the fact that both reactions are excited at the same moment and must in some way both reach expression. The old world contained objects to be withdrawn from and those to be manipulated in play, the new world is to contain objects that are to be so manipulated that he does withdraw from the danger connected with them. Just what that object is to be, depends upon the result of the investigation. It cannot therefore serve as control. It is only the necessity of bringing both tendencies to expression in their interaction upon each other that does and can exercise such control. There is of course no place in this paper for an adequate analysis of attention. I wish only to point out that, in the attentive processes which arise at these problematic points in experience, the control which is an essential part of attention cannot be found in a world of objective validity—for, so to speak, the old is abandoned and the new is not yet in existence—but is found in the relation to each other of different tendencies to act which have been forcibly divorced from the old objects and can only find expression through the mediation of a new object. Both the subject matter of the experience and the process by which the new arises, are necessarily subjective.

We have identified the formation of the hypothesis with the psychical state. It is necessary to distinguish here between the psychical state, as it actually appears in the presence of problems, and the ghost of it which we deal with in psychological textbooks. In experimental psychology, for example, we generally deal with states of consciousness which do not appear as psychical to us in the slightest degree. What actually is taking place is the recognition of things whose objective reality we do not contest, and which we have no motive to state in terms of our own consciousness as distinct from that of anyone else, or in a state of consciousness which is distinguished from every one that has taken place before. The peculiarity of a psychical state is that it is absolutely *sui generis* in our life. It has elements of the immediate present that mark it off from any that has gone before or will come after. From all these peculiarities we necessarily abstract in objective knowledge. When, however, that objective knowledge is at fault and we are forced to correct and feel our way to something new, we bring out vividly the peculiar marks of the immediate experience and are in the presence of that which is psychical—as that of the individual and of a particular moment in his life to the complete distinction from every other moment present or past. It is evident that in the psychological experiment we are dealing with what is generally perfectly objective. It is only by an inference that we can go from this to the psychical, and that inference is too often one that rests upon an epistemological basis not distinguishable from Hume's or Berkeley's: [5] to wit, that we can reduce all experience to states of individual consciousness in which form we may recognize their ultimate validity. To do this, however, is to objectify the psychical state, and deprive it of the very elements that have rendered it psychical.

The marks of the psychical state are not such that they can be universalized to form a concept in the sense here implied. The peculiar content of them resists all such generalization. What can be generalized is their position in the act, the when and the how of their appearance. What we generally refer to, when we are speaking of psychical states, are elements of the objects which are simply abstracted from the objects themselves. I speak of the color "red," and in so doing have in mind something that I have abstracted from certain red objects. To get a concrete picture of this I call to mind the visual picture of the object, if I do not look at the object itself. In either case the object is itself known as objective; for even

---

[5] [George Berkeley (1685–1753), Irish philosopher and clergyman, presented his empirical epistemology in *A Treatise Concerning the Principles of Human Knowledge* (1710).—David Hume (1711–1776), Scottish philosopher, presented his empirical epistemology in *A Treatise of Human Nature* (1739–1740) and *An Inquiry Concerning Human Understanding* (1748).]

the picture of the imagination is objective so long as it is dealing with the elements of an objective world, which is not questioned, however fantastically it is put together. What fascinates is the presence of such a picture in the midst of such an unquestioned world. The red of a sunset never seen on sea or land is not one that is necessarily psychical, but one that is replete with the emotional value which is absolutely merged in the outer world. Our world is at best one of consciousness, and no amount of analysis of this world into elements will get to the psychical state unless the conditions out of which the psychical arises are present. Elements of consciousness are not as such elements of a psychical character. Nor yet are those which can be definitely connected with particular nervous phenomena of the individual psychical states. It is not the identification of the state with the individual that makes it psychical, but it is his recognition of it as his own, his attention to those peculiarities which mark it off not only from the consciousness of anyone else but also from any other state of his own life, that render it psychical. The parallelistic theory sets up the individual of experience and compares the world as he sees it with the world which our science assumes to exist free from all individual error, and tries to combine the two series. It is not denied that the individual's experience is entirely objective in its character. We are merely comparing the object of his perception with that which the scientist's methods of exact measurement reveal. I see a red house which is for me an object in a real world and in no sense psychical. The scientist measures the vibrations of light represented in that red, and shows that there is a complete gulf between the red of perception and the red of certain vibrations. He may call the one psychical and the other objective. But his observations are no more objective than is the original perception of the red house. He has taken a part of his experience which is more reliable than another and has shown that the two stand in a certain relation to each other, though it is not possible to carry this relation throughout. That one set can be related to his nervous

states, or at least that its errors are more completely stated
in certain nervous conditions than in the other, throws no
light upon the case. An engineer who estimates from a glance
the grade of a hill and then corrects his judgment from the
tracing of the leveler, is not entering into a distinction between a psychical and a physical world. He is comparing two
elements of his conscious world together and selecting that
which experience has shown to be more reliable. Parallelism
is pure epistemology, and does not get within the realm of
the psychical. The distinction between the immediate content of the world of perception, and the physical theory of
these perceptions, does not touch that distinction which lies
between the world of unquestioned validity, and the state
of consciousness which supervenes when it has lost that validity and there is nothing left but the subjectivity out of which
a new world may arise. This seems to indicate that there are
in reality two tasks which psychology has taken up, one that
of analysis of the objective world in terms of the consciousness of the objective individual—suggested in Hegel's *Phenomenology of the Spirit* [1807]—and the other, the analysis of
the situation within which the subjective consciousness arises
and the process by which it advances to the formation of the
new universal. To the former class most of the psychological
work that has been done belongs. It is indeed not different in
purpose from that undertaken by Kant,[6] being the study of
the structure of experience as necessarily found within the
consciousness of an objective individual. The other type is
represented in James's chapter on the Stream of Consciousness [7] and in some of the work that has gathered peculiarly
around the process of attention.

The typical situation is found in the attitude of the inductive scientist in the presence of a problem. The conflict of
given concepts has led to the abstraction, already described,

6 [Immanuel Kant (1724–1804), German philosopher whose *Critique of
Pure Reason* (1781) and *Critique of Practical Reason* (1788) founded the
critical philosophy and inspired transcendental idealism.]

7 [William James, *The Principles of Psychology*, Vol. I, chap. 9.]

in which what lies behind the conflict comes out as the fact of observation. I may refer again to the instance of ether, the fact of observation here being the actually given movements of heavenly bodies, with evidences of retardation or the opposite, and the transference of vibratory energy. The psychical phase appears when the scientist attempts to consciously solve the problem. This involves, first of all, the flexibility of movement by which he brings all his actual reactions into relation with each other. This freedom of movement, in which all the activities and tendencies to activity which have been confined by definite theory play without resistance into each other, seems to me the essence of subjectivity. A grouping takes place, now here and now there. To return to the illustration, the processes of exact determination of energy are stripped of the concepts of matter in terms of molecule and atom. There stands before the scientist only the multiple determinations. Energy of mass, vibration, etc., are represented only by the measurements that he undertakes to determine. Now the way in which these shall come together is not dependent upon any objective law. The only control lies in the necessity of bringing them all together. Only after they have been harmonized can the grouping take objective value. For the time being, the man is dependent upon the spontaneity of his own impulses—the genius for suggestion to which Whewell [8] refers. This may lead, in this case, to the positing of our own measuring processes as the substantial element about which all the facts of energy shall gather. As the result of physical science has been to state, not the movement in the terms of the body, but the body in terms of the

[8] [See William Whewell, *The Philosophy of Discovery* (London: John W. Parker and Son, 1860). Whewell (1794–1866), master of Trinity College, Cambridge, was a philosopher and historian of science. He maintained that each step in the advance of science "was a scientific *Discovery*, in which a new conception was applied in order to bind together observed facts." This conjunction of observed facts, he added, was not merely "an example of logical induction," since it included a crucial element of "novelty" which, though suggested by the situation, was supplied in part by the thinker (Preface, p. iv).]

movement, we may find the ultimate motions in which bodies are to be defined in our own reactions which we recognize as giving the content to the objective world. But the point which I wish to make clear is that we have here these various motions free from any bodies objectively determined, and are free to organize them at will if we only include them all. Another illustration may be found in the attitude of the inventor, who, facing a particular problem, is left to a constructive power proportional to the freedom with which the forces abstracted from their customary objects can be combined with each other into a new successful whole. It is the power of subjectivity that comes nearer answering to what we term genius than anything else.

The technique of the process, so far as it goes beyond this perfect freedom, lies in attention, in other words, in the control which arises through the interplay of the different activities. One must feel, in that which he does, not only the immediate action, but also all the others that are involved. In the case of the child he must grasp so as to avoid the burn. I am referring to so-called voluntary attention. In involuntary attention we have simply the process already become a habit and objectified. Perhaps the most primitive illustration can be found in the mutual control of the distance sense and the contact sense in the primal intelligent act. Here the fixing of the eye and its direction are continually determined by the process of locomotion and that of manipulation, while as obviously the manipulative and locomotive processes are controlled by the eye process. In this, as in the case of the child, we have not reached consciousness of what we are doing—not reflective consciousness. This statement also does justice to the modern psychological position that the stimulus, as psychology studies it, does not set off the activity, but is the sought occasion for activities that are demanding expression.

In this spontaneity and control we have the essential characteristics of the will, and when we pass beyond the limits of scientific investigation to conduct as a whole, we enter the field of ethics. Purely metaphysical ethics would carry us back to the promulgation of old universals with the ascetic demand that we ignore or suppress all tendencies to action, that do not fall under them, as interpreted by deductive logic. As in this situation we recognize the validity of only one set of impulses, and set them in hostile array against the other, there is no escape from a doctrine that action will be determined by the comparative strength of the two factions—determinism—unless we posit a will which is not represented in any of these impulses to action—an indeterminate will. Over against these positions, it becomes possible, from the standpoint taken above, to define freedom in terms of the identification of the self as a whole with the problem and its solution. The forces are not hostile if the aim is to represent all tendencies to action in the final act. The self is not identified with one tendency or any one set of tendencies more than with another, and the problem is recognized not as one that arises simply through the imperfect character of the self, but as one that springs from the essentially inadequate nature of the world of ends presented in knowledge. It is not a conflict between the good and bad elements of our nature, but between values and the impulses that these represent, meeting on a plane of absolute equality. Obligation lies in the demand that all these values and impulses shall be recognized. The binding nature of obligation is found in the necessity for action, and in the claim made by the whole self for representation within the action; while the consequences of failure to meet the obligation are found in the sacrifice of certain parts of the self which carries with it the friction and sense of loss that is characteristic of the immoral attitude. The ideal can be defined, not in the old universal nor in attempted delineation of what the future situation should be, for in advance of the solution such a delineation is quite impossible, but in the method of meeting the problem, in the statement of all that must be recognized in the solution to be attained; as the ideal of the scientist is found in the complete statement of the various conditions that must be recognized and met in any possible hypothesis. Finally the motive, as distinguished from the mere impulse, is found in the tendency to action when brought into conscious relation with the other conflicting tendencies, striving to estimate itself over against all. As the solution is one that arises from an unpredictable suggestion from within, the spontaneity of the individual is preserved beyond all question. The so-called moral struggle is found in the identification of the self with one set of tendencies to the exclusion of others. I do not mean by this statement that the self is something standing apart from the tendencies to conduct, but that it arises through the organization of these tendencies or impulses. Such an organization as is one-sided, leaving parts of the nature unrepresented, naturally leaves behind the continuous conflict which thus becomes chronic and destructive instead of being a moment in a process of natural development. The moral struggle always implies that an organization has been in some sense accomplished; or, better, that a working hypothesis or line of conduct has been adopted which is felt to be inadequate. The struggle does not lie in the process of forming the hypothesis, but in the friction in acting upon it. If the step has been in some sense irrevocable, the feeling of loss remains in the so-called emotional state of remorse. The natural trend is, however, forward, and looks to the reconsideration of the line of conduct adopted. It is only from the deterministic standpoint that retribution is called for. For in this case there is a hostile force that must, so to speak, be reduced.

Within such a conflict, even if it is not brought clearly to consciousness, and whether the result is simply the recognition of the old universal, or the conscious organization of the new world through the psychical phase, the sensuous objects—answering to the facts of scientific observation—take on a new form or meaning. They are the stimuli to, or occasions for, activities, for the time being abstracted therefrom by the conflict itself. But they stand for these activities, are the repositories of their meaning and value. In scientific observation, they are simply the conditions for the formation of the new universal, and we lose sight of the inherent value of these objects. But, where we are unable to reach the new universal, and are obliged to remain with the elements of the problem and to express our feeling for that which is not yet attained through the statement of these objects, they gain again this representative value. This representative value of the object resulting from conflict seems to me to be aesthetic. The term "conflict" may seem to be at variance with many features of aesthetic consciousness, but we must notice that within the attempted solution the hostility has ceased; for overt action has stopped and the state is preeminently one of calm, the absence of prejudice and rancorous feeling. We must remember also that it is by no means necessary that the conflict should take on the scientific form. The only element that comes above consciousness may be the new value of the object. This will depend upon the nature of the individual. The artist states the conditions for the solutions of his problems in terms of the sensuous objects of experience. The solution may be attained, supposing that it is attained, more or less unconsciously. Furthermore, there are certain problems that, like the poor, are always with us; for example, that between the mechanical and teleological statements of the world and its physical objects. Out of this springs decorative art and all the artistic representation of nature. In the utilitarian control of the world we lose sight of the end of this control. We fail to see the forest for the very trees. There are others connected with the primitive impulses of love and contest which are always with us; and, finally, the great moral problems never lose their eternal identity in whatever state of society they appear. The religious consciousness is preeminently one that recognizes in life a fundamental problem, while it clings to the reality of the great representative objects of conduct which the conflict has abstracted and set before us. In fact, it is allowable to define the religious object as one which, while transcending through its universality the particular situations of life, still is felt to be representative of its meaning and value. There is here indicated another characteristic of the object held in the abstraction of the unsolved problem. Insofar as it carries the meaning and value of the activity which it represents in actual conduct, it calls forth as emotions the feelings that accompany such activity. The subject is much too complex to be dealt with adequately here. I wish merely to indicate that the object that stands out in the midst of the problem, not only as a condition of its solution, but also, for the time being, as representative of the meaning and value of the act, would naturally gather about itself the emotional content that is so characteristic of aesthetic and religious experience.

Finally, the dialectic of this whole process of conscious analysis and reconstruction may be passed in review and be reduced to a technique, or at least be so treated that it tends to become such eventually. This science—the general theory of logic—does not deal with the statement of the problem as does metaphysics, nor with the immediate application of the abstracted universal—deductive logic—nor with the immediate formation of the hypothesis and its verification—inductive logic—but with the whole appearance of the objective world in thought terms and its passage into unanalyzed reality again. It deals therefore with the judgment and the different moments in the development of the judgment.

THE DEFINITION OF THE PSYCHICAL

There is greater uniformity in the use of the term "objectivity" than in that of the corresponding term "subjectivity." We know what we mean when we assert that we have an object before us, for the simple reason, if for no other, that we can act with reference to it. Objectivity is the characteristic of a cognitive process which has reached its goal. The success of the cognitive act furnishes the criterion of objectivity, and that without even defining what the nature of the category is. In contrast with the unequivocal character of objectivity stand the various significations attached to subjectivity. Historically it has completely boxed the compass. It meant some centuries ago what objectivity now connotes. The change is one that is parallel with the appearance of the modern individual, with the ascription of logical values to his peculiar consciousness which had belonged to the *mundus intelligibilis*.

Today subjectivity may connote that which is not-objective in the sense given above, that in whose regard one cannot or may not or should not act. Again, it may rather imply emotional coloring. It may be used with reference to psychical consciousness, and swallow up into itself all consciousness from the standpoint of a subjective idealism. To the dualist of one school it includes all that is conscious, and is contrasted with extended substance whose existence is largely an inference. Again, there is a subjectivity that is ascribed to the teleology of the acts of a person; thus the state of immediate purposeful consciousness would be subjective, while the abstract things of reflective scientific thought would be ob-

[From *The Decennial Publications of the University of Chicago,* "First Series," III (Chicago: University of Chicago Press, 1903), 77–78, 92–112.]

jects. Here subjectivity connotes immediacy, while objectivity means abstraction. Finally subjectivity may be found among the abstractions, belonging to the peculiar contents of a scientific psychology.

While many roads to objectivity may be taken by different types of thought the goal reached is identical. For practical purposes the object is recognizable, and the philosophical standpoint cannot affect its nature. But there is no such criterion of subjectivity, and its nature varies with the standpoint and system. There is, however, one constant characteristic which is a part of most definitions given it: the subjective is that which is identified with the consciousness of the individual qua individual. But the recognition of this does not locate subjectivity as the value of the object for action fixes objectivity. The process of reflection has ceased when action is reached, and no theory of reflection can change the object; but the peculiarities of individual consciousness lie well within the process of knowledge. Action takes place in a common world into which inference and interpretation have transmuted all that belonged solely to the individual subjectively considered. As subjectivity refers to the consciousness of the individual, and as the phase of consciousness which is peculiar to individual as such is generally placed within the process of reflection, the definition of subjectivity will depend upon the function which a theory of logic ascribes to the individual consciousness in the formation of the judgment. I can see no escape from this for our modern psychology, recognizing as it does that the subject-matter of its science is abstracted from concrete experience. Only an empiricism that assumes to start from sensations as concrete elements of reality can escape the necessity of accounting for the abstraction by which it obtains its material and of relating that process to the whole cognitive act of which reflection is a part. And yet modern psychology, that seeks to free its skirts from metaphysics, assumes that it may take its object as it finds it, and that it is given in the same sense and same general form as the object of the other sciences. While the relation of psychology to the other philosophical disciplines is undetermined, or, what is the same thing, while the peculiar abstraction which gives us the psychical content is not organically related to the other abstractions within the process of reflection, we shall have no certain criterion for recognizing the subject-matter of psychology.

. . . .

The problem may be now stated in the following form: Shall we assume, with Wundt, that the psychical elements arise from the analysis of reflection and that the result of that reflection is to substitute for the original object, first, a conceptual physical object which never may be actual—may never be presented—and, second, a still actual psychical content which has been withdrawn from the object [1] . . . ; or, shall we say with Külpe, that in a unitary experience reflection *reveals* a mechanical and an associative order, of which the mechanical or physical statement is methodologically the determining side, by relation to whose elements all the associative or psychical elements must be determined as correspondents, recognizing further that reflection reveals—does not create—this distinction, since "images," feelings, and volitions have always been necessarily subjective; [2] or with Bradley and Bosanquet, shall we consider the psychical merely the phenomenal appearance of the material which, to be cognized or rationally used in conduct, must cease to be psychical and become universal,[3] and maintain therefore that reflection does not create

[1] [For Wundt's theories on method in psychology, which Mead criticizes throughout the present essay, see Wilhelm Wundt, *Logik* (Stuttgart: Verlag von Ferdinand Enke, 1894–1895), Vol. II (*Methodenlehre*), Part II, chap. 2, pp. 151–303.]

[2] [Oswald Külpe,] *Einleitung in die Philosophie,* English translation [by W. B. Pillsbury and E. B. Titchener as *Introduction to Philosophy* (London and New York, 1897)], pp. 59, 205, note 6.

[3] It is agreed on both sides that, as psychical existences, ideas are particular like all other phenomena. The controversy is confined to the use we make of them. I should maintain that, so far as they remain particular, they are simple facts and not ideas at all, and that, where they are employed to extend or modify experience, they are never used in

or reveal the psychical, but ceaselessly transforms it, and that
the psychical is an abstraction which can never appear in its
own form in a cognitive consciousness, but must remain simply a presupposition of the theory of the attainment of knowledge by the individual; or with Ward,[4] shall we assert that
the subject of psychical experience and of objective experience are the same, that the transcendental *ego,* who has mas-
queraded in ethereal clothes in a world all his own, is nothing but the everyday *ego* of psychology; above all, that he is
to be unquestioningly accepted as one phase of the subject-
object form of experience, although he is neither the empirical self of psychology which can be an object, nor yet a mere
"function of unity," and although, further, this pious refusal
ever to put asunder subjectivity and objectivity is in crying
opposition to the fact that half the time subjectivity signifies
the denial of objectivity, and although it is not possible consistently to define the psychical by its reference to the subject
end of a polarized experience when the subject is hardly more
than an assertion which perpetually dodges definition; or,
with James,[5] shall we take up again with the soul and a dualistic theory of knowledge, in order that the psychical may
mirror the whole possibly known reality, and when we have
entered into this rich heritage, shall we promptly send the
soul to another and a metaphysical world and politely dismiss
the dualistic theory of knowledge as a great mystery, while we
dally with plural selves and spend our psychical substance in
phenomenalistic analyses and teleologically constructed objects; or shall we attempt some other definition of the psychical which will orient it with reference to immediate experience, to reflection, and the objects and conduct that arise
out of reflection, and which will vindicate the relation of the

their particular form.—Bradley, [*The Principles of*] *Logic* [London, 1893],
p. 37. [(2nd edn., rev.; London, 1922), I, p. 35. See also Bernard Bosanquet, *Logic* (2nd edn.; London: Oxford University Press, 1911), I, 44.]

4 [See James Ward, article on psychology, *Encyclopedia Britannica,* 9th
edn., XX, 38–39.]

5 [William James, *The Principles of Psychology,* I, 181.]

psychical to the individual and that of the individual to reflection? I think this would involve the recognition of a cognitive value in the individual qua individual over and above the "function of unity" and that function implied in the mere ascription of activities (identified in one way or another with attention) to the subject. Is it possible to regard the psychical, not as a permanent phase, nor even a permanent possible aspect of consciousness, but as a "moment" of consciousness or in a conscious process, and which has therefore cognitive value for that process? It is this suggestion that I wish to consider and discuss.

A variety of assumptions as to the existence of the psychical, some of which have been discussed, suggest themselves at once. We may assume that our consciousness is always psychical in content—that we can always reveal by analysis the psychical constituents, that the mind either adds meaning to these, and so makes knowledge out of them, or that this meaning arises simply through the fusing and assimilating of different states of consciousness by each other; or we may assume that the unitary character of consciousness involves the presence of both the subjective and objective as in some sense parallel, though our analysis reveals these as separate phases whose distinction appears only in the analysis. The difference between these points of view does not turn upon the question of the presence in psychical form of contents, but upon the question as to the way in which they appear—the question of elements, for example, and as to the fashion in which this psychical content becomes knowledge and the assumption of other processes of thought. Or a point of view may be taken which assumes that the psychical is a result of the analysis, not a discovery of it. And then the question may still further arise as to the destiny of this psychical content; does it disappear or does it persist as a necessary part of the more complex character of the analytical consciousness? Another aspect of this latter question would involve the theory of reflection itself. May this persist as an ultimate phase of consciousness, i.e., one that carries its own satisfaction within it; or does it necessarily lead up to a consciousness which is not reflective; or may it do either under different circumstances? The same question might be put in the form: Can reflection be conduct, or is it necessarily a phase in the preparatory stage of conduct? And having met the question as to the value of the psychical for knowledge, we could go on indefinitely asking questions. It is not my purpose to answer any of these questions dogmatically, but to take a point of view which seems to me to be involved in that of a number of thinkers, and which seems also to be peculiarly promising.

It is assumed, then, that the psychical does not appear until critical reflection in the process of knowledge analyzes our world. Up to this point the volition and emotions are not psychical, nor subjective in the sense of psychical. I do not mean that they are not recognized as such, but that their nature is not subjective in a psychical sense. With Wundt this position recognizes that the entire content of consciousness is subjective and objective at once in this unreflective stage. The world and the individual stand upon the same basis of reality. The distinction is one that is made within the universe of reality, not with a view to interpreting reflectively this reality. The analysis of this consciousness would not reveal a psychical, any more than it would reveal a conceptual atom or molecule. It does not seem to me that Wundt has consistently maintained this position, for he says that the presentation is withdrawn to the subjective phase of consciousness as a result of analysis, and that it—the presentation—continues to exist with the same immediacy that it had before, though without its objective reference, thus implying what he has explicitly denied, that the volitional and emotional phase is subjective in the sense that it is not also objective. . . . This Wundtian analysis leaves us with elements which have only symbolic value in the statement of the reality of experience. On the other hand, he has emphasized the constructive phases of psychology over against certain parallelists, insisting that psychology must recognize in perception and conception a result which is qualitatively different from the mere mass of elements which an analysis shows to have entered into the constructs of cognition. But though we seem to have our hands upon immediate psychical experience here, we find that it is only by a method of residues that he reaches this conclusion, comparing the elements of the analysis with the object which was dissected, and this is after all only an indirect analysis. His voluntaristic psychology suffers from the impossibility of getting anything more than the results of apperception into psychical consciousness. Before advancing to the consideration of Dewey's position, we must see whether his voluntaristic psychology introduces immediacy into the statement of the psychical.

There is a contradiction here between Wundt's theory . . . that the volitions and emotion have retained the original immediacy of unanalyzed experience, and the actual treatment in terms of presentation they have received at his hands. If these states of consciousness have been psychical from the start, if our logical criticism has simply withdrawn the presentation (*Vorstellung*) into a field of unquestioned subjectivity, it is strange that psychology has extended such a tardy recognition to this field. Why is it that the will has remained so long in the gall of metaphysics and the bonds of ontology, while the ideas have been psychologically studied for centuries? The fact of the case is that, historically considered, instead of the presentation becoming psychical by being withdrawn into the field of the unquestioned subjectivity of the will and the emotions, the will and the emotions have received psychological treatment insofar as they have been drawn or withdrawn into the field of the presentations. But even the treatment of attention in terms of results, and the description of the will in terms of the sensations of muscular contractions and joint movements, and of the emotions in terms of the feel of characteristic attitudes and visceral disturbances, are not immediate presentations of these phases of consciousness, but a reference to elements that answer to the conditions under which the feelings arise; and as the complete tale of these conditions includes a number of groups, some selection must be made. The most tempting group is that of the physiological organism and its physical environment. But the psychologist is as clearly justified in selecting another group, such as that which determines the appearance of the judgment. It is just as true that all our experience can be presented in the form of the judgment, as it is that it can be stated in the shiftings of the strains and stresses of the physical system made up of the animal and his surroundings. If the sociologist succeeds in analyzing the social objective content of experience into elements which he can show are conditions for social conduct, he will be at liberty to indicate the psychical correspondents of these elements and have his own parallelistic system of psychology for strictly private consumption.

In all these methods we start with the analysis of given experiences and obtain a statement of elements that must answer to the conditions of the experience. To obtain a psychology of the process the method is very simple. Find in each case the psychical element that corresponds to the objective condition, and there arises a complete psychological theory of the experience. It should be added, to show the perfection of the method, that the psychologist recognizes the psychical element by simply noting and picking up what he has stripped off from the original object in his scientific analysis, as unessential because purely individual. For instance, take emotion presented as an object in conduct. Secure a clever and accommodating actor, whose business it is to present this emotion. Analyze his conduct into its essential elements, which will then be the conditions for the appearance of the emotion as a part of social experience. These conditions will be a series and combination of characteristic attitudes and much less definitely determined vaso-motor upheavals. The states assumed to correspond to these are the psychical elements of the emotion. Finally, what is it that you have neglected in order to recognize that you have shaken your fist in the most terrifying manner of the profession? Obviously the feel of the emotion. In like manner attention as an object means the perception of certain things in some particular relation and the ignoring of other things. The objective analysis gives these certain things clear and distinct, and the rest vague, and certain connections or relations between these clear and distinct things in the events of experience. This may be translated into terms of the tensions of sense-organs and the postures of the body that make the sensing possible and of the functioning of the association fibers of the central nervous system. Even the recognition, that psychical elements corresponding to these elements are something less than the actual experience, and that there is an activity implied in the feelings of activity, does not bring this something more into the field of the psychical with which the science is occupied. The assertion that the subject to which these activities are referred along with other states is there because it must be there, or because the subject-object relation can't be got rid of, does not enable us to materialize anything more than corresponding elements. In a word, if the volitional and emotional phases of experience can be presented by the psychologist only in certain effects, we are forced to deal with these effects, after the fashion of the consistent parallelist, as elements corresponding to the conditions under which they arise. In general, the attempt to seize a psychical content which is only a by-product of an analysis undertaken in the search for an objective reality, results necessarily in a parallelistic statement— a statement in terms of the reality sought. This is as true of the older associationist and the modern logical school as of the physiological psychologists. One can see only that which he is looking for, and what else comes within the field of vision must be seen in terms of this. Sensations and other presentations rejected in the hunt for the reality of sensuous experience are no more positive psychical contents than the detected misstatements in a historical document are positive accounts of the process of consciousness by which they were introduced. If we have no direct knowledge of their appearance in the documents, we are helpless in our attempt to interpret them. It has been the acquaintance with the history,

with the growth and decay, of the religious and political institutions of the Greek and Hebrew peoples that has made positive data out of the products of destructive higher criticism.
Nor are the emotional and volitional rejects more direct and
immediate material, as long as we deal with them in terms of
that which does and does not make up the object of knowledge. This whole type of psychology can do no more than state
the objective conditions under which the criticized act of cognition with its content of feel, emotion, and effort took place.
That these psychologists have not confined themselves to this
is undoubtedly true, but their scientific method can only assume psychical elements that correspond to definite conditions
of objective experience.

The principal reason that one can be led astray in this matter is found in the fact that the statement of the logical
analysis is not made in terms of an immediate experience. We
transfer ourselves bag and baggage to the world of conceptual
objects, recognizing the sensuous object only as something abstracted from. And yet we know that controlled sensuous experience is the essential basis of all our science. Even the most
abstract speculation must have some point of sensuous contact with the world to render it real. We criticise various
sensuous experiences in their representative character, and
substitute for them the atoms and molecules of exact science.
This is done, however, upon the basis of experiences in the
laboratory, which are as sensuous as the experiences which we
criticise. To be sure, we generalize our criticism and so bring
the experiences in the experiment under the same statement,
and this subsumption as a later act is theoretically correct.
What is not legitimate is to assume that in the immediate experiment, the unquestioned data of the senses occupy logically
the same position as those which we have criticised. In all our
modern inductive science we deal with certain objects which
are not analyzed in our analysis of other objects. The ex post
facto legislation by which we transfer this analysis back to the
objects, whose immediacy was a precondition to it, is certainly
out of place in a science which is supposed to deal with im-

mediate experience. That is, it is not justifiable to demand of psychology that it regard all sensuous contents as psychical because analysis has shown certain of them not to be objective, while in the same experience other sensuous contents are necessarily regarded as objective. It would not be profitable here to enter into the logical question of the relation of the subject to the predicate, but it may be assumed that any theory of the judgment will imply the reality of some element of sensuous experience which is the contact point of the subject with the world. The reality of the sensuous "this" and "now" in any judgment, in any analysis, makes it impossible to present any immediate experience, however abstract, in which the sensuous content is entirely stripped off and relegated to the objectively unreal. Psychology cannot, then, pretend to be both a theory of perception by sensuous contents that can be only representative of the outer real object, themselves confined to the consciousness of the individual qua individual, and at the same time a theory of immediate experience. It is certainly curious that, while the long struggle of modern reflection has brought the world of knowledge into the experience of the self, the theory of the peculiar experience of that self should have no place in the doctrine of reflection. But how can one dodge this conclusion if his psychology deals only in rejects? For it cannot get its material till the reflection is complete, and an attempt to restate the process of reflection in the psychological terms which the reflection has furnished must presuppose the reflection itself. If we start our psychology with rejects, there is no stopping-point short of the dump heap. And an immediacy which is left over from an original immediate situation is a contradiction, since it has been confessedly obtained by a process of mediation.

For purposes of definition here "immediacy" implies the coincidence of presence and meaning, and "mediacy" means reference to something beyond. If the psychical is then to be immediate, it must be a part of the consciousness of the moment to which belongs the unitary act. It cannot be later discovered to have been a part of that moment, nor arise as a product in a reproduction of that unitary act or state. The individual must be conscious directly of all the predicates by which the psychical is defined before it can exist as such in his consciousness. Merely to demonstrate that there must be a psychical content is to take one's stand within the fallacy of the Cretan who affirmed the mendacity of all Cretans. Hence, if the psychical in this sense exist at all, there must be states of consciousness in which what is peculiar to the individual and a moment of his existence finds its meaning in these very peculiarities—not simply as contents which can be investigated because they happen to be there—but as contents whose very limitations make them organic phases in the cognitive act. They must be deprived of their reference to anything beyond, else they would not be peculiar to the individual and the moment; for if the momentary refer to that which transcends it, its presence is no longer coincident with its meaning. A reject has no meaning, even if we admit that it is present; or, if meaning is given to it—as that of the image providing content for the concept, or serving as representative of a neurological element which cannot yet be found—its meaning goes entirely beyond itself, and it ceases to be psychical at all. Unless we can show that the psychical as such is normally functional, we certainly can never produce it in the very peculiarities by which we must define it.

This is the position taken by Dewey in the article on "The Reflex Arc Concept." [6] He approaches the position from the discussion of the reflex-arc concept, but his quarrel with the psychologists he criticises is in the end the same as that which I have endeavored to present as inevitable—the quarrel with the doctrine that sensation is an isolated content analyzed out through its correspondence to an outside element.

> The result is that the reflex-arc idea leaves us with a disjointed psychology. . . . Failing to see the unity of activity, no matter how much it may prate of unity, it still leaves us with sensation or peripheral stimulus; idea or central process (the equivalent of attention); and motor response, or

act, as three disconnected existences, having somehow to be adjusted to each other, whether through the intervention of an extra-experimental soul, or by mechanical push and pull.[7]

And his proof of the futility of this psychology is that no such psychical elements answering to physical counterparts exist. Instead of a psychical state which is dependent upon a physical excitation, investigation shows in every case an activity which in advance must determine where attention is directed and give the psychical state the very content which is used in identifying it. In the simplest cases it is the direction of the sense-organs and their coordination in larger acts that is responsible for the actual contents of color, sound, odor, etc., which the psychologist treats as dependent only upon external physical conditions. To a reply that the psychologist assumes a complex coordinated nervous mechanism, with its inherited adaptations, over against which the outer physical stimulus is the only variable that needs to be taken into account, Dewey responds that either the physical mechanism must be taken as a bare system of motions, whose procedure is nothing but a shifting of stresses, in which case there is no such thing as stimulus and response at all, or else we must make our statement of the physiological system in terms of the same activity as those demanded for the psychological process. In the end what we see, hear, feel, taste, and smell depends upon what we are doing, and not the reverse. In our purposively organized life we inevitably come back upon previous conduct as the determining condition of what we sense at any one moment, and the so-called external stimulus is the occasion for this and not its cause. If we ask now for the results which such a disjointed psychology is actually able to present, the answer is that, just as the physical stimulus is reduced to nothing but a system of masses in motion in which the stimulus as such completely disappears, so the so-called psychical elements reduce to nothing but a series of sensations in which the character of response is as effectually de-

[7] *Ibid.,* p. 360.

stroyed as was that of the stimulus in the abstract physical world. We have sensations of motions as well as of colors, and nothing but sensations. Putting, then, the two parts of the argument together, in the first place, this disjointed psychology gives us nothing but sensations which cannot even be got into a sensory-motor arc, but are doomed to remain forever in their own abstract world of registration; and, in the second place, no such elements of sensations are found to exist, and what we have been pleased to call such have in them the whole content of the act of which we were supposed to make them a part.

The author concludes that the distinction between stimulus, whether psychologically or physiologically investigated, and response is not one between preexistent elements; that any phase of the act which could be obtained by analysis may be regarded as stimulus or response. The decision between the two predicates depends upon the direction in which the attention shifts. A type of analysis which follows in the wake of logical and physical sciences, gleaning that which they have dropped, harvests only unreal abstractions. Instead of attempting to identify elements, it is the duty of psychology to look upon these predicates as tools of interpretation. Which is another way of saying that sensation does not serve as a stimulus because of what it is as an independent content, but that it is a sensation because it serves as a stimulus. It is evident, then, that the definition must be made in terms of the act, not in terms of a content; and the following are the definitions given:

> Generalized, the sensation as stimulus is always that phase of activity requiring to be defined in order that a coordination may be completed. What the sensation will be in particular at a given time, therefore, will depend entirely upon the way in which an activity is being used. It has no fixed quality of its own. The search for the stimulus is the search for the exact conditions of action; that is, for the state of things which decides how a beginning coordination should be completed. Similarly, motion, as response, has only functional value. It is whatever will serve to complete

the disintegrating coordination. Just as the discovery of the sensation marks the establishing of the problem, so the constitution of the response marks the solution of this problem.[8]

And a little farther on:

The circle is a coordination, some of whose members have come into conflict with each other. It is the temporary disintegration and need of reconstitution which occasions, which affords the genesis of, the conscious distinction into sensory stimulus on the one side and motor response on the other. The stimulus is that phase of the forming coordination which represents the conditions which have to be met in bringing it to a successful issue; the response is that phase of one and the same forming coordination which gives the key to meeting these conditions, which serves as an instrument in effecting the successful coordination. They are therefore strictly correlative and contemporaneous. The stimulus is something to be discovered; to be made out; if the activity affords its own adequate stimulation, there is no stimulus save in the objective sense already referred to. As soon as it is adequately determined, then and then only is the response also complete. To attain either means that the coordination has completed itself.[9]

There are two situations suggested here—that in which the coordination is broken up by conflict between its members, and the other that in which the activity in its original form determines its own adequate stimulation. In the first case we have the presentation and solution of a problem, in terms of sensation and response. In the second instance, the author states that "there is no stimulus save in the objective sense." These so-called stimuli are further defined "as minor acts serving by their respective positions to the maintenance of some organized coordination."

Although the author has definitely postponed the application of this doctrine to the distinction between sensational and rational consciousness, and to the nature of the judgment, there seem to be some fairly evident conclusions that may be

8 *Ibid.*, p. 368.
9 *Ibid.*, p. 370.

drawn. In the first place, there are presented here certain situations in which the psychical is the nature of consciousness, not because any analysis, or even introspection, produces or, catching our thought as it disappears, reveals a phase of which we were not conscious before, but because the inevitable conflicts of conduct deprive us of the stimuli which further action requires; in other words, deprive us of the objective character of some part of our world. If we compare this position with Wundt's, the following distinction appears at once: Wundt assumes that the logical criticism arises when our anticipations are not satisfied and the interpretations of former experiences are contradicted. The result of this logical criticism, however, is simply to dislodge our objects from their objective position and relegate them to a subjective world, just as they are, deprived only of their validity. And their places are filled by the conceptual objects which a scientific imagination fashions out of figments light as air. That is, Wundt assumes that the criticised object may retain its organized content and yet lose its validity. He denies the mutual dependence of the validity and the form of the content. Dewey assumes that the object or stimulus loses its form in losing its validity. Furthermore, during this state the whole effort is toward a constitution of the object or stimulus again. The object loses its validity and organization as object at the same moment, and at the same moment it becomes psychical, but not as the shade of an object done to logical death, and doomed henceforth to haunt the shadows of a subjective Sheol. The illustration which is given in the article on the reflex arc is of the child of our modern psychology—not the child of the associational period, that meditative *Bambino* of the Milanese school with the orange in his hand; but that somewhat ponderously curious child with the candle, who seems to be taken out of a Dutch interior. Of this child and his candle the author says: "The question whether to reach or abstain from reaching is the question: What sort of a bright light have we here? Is it one which means playing with one's hands, eating milk, or burning one's fingers? The

stimulus must be constituted for the response to occur." [10]
Now, if these questions are the stuff that the psychical is made
of, we are dealing with states which do not have to be caught
from behind, as they whisk around the corner, and studied in
the faint aromas which they leave behind them. We are very
frankly conscious of our problems and the hypotheses which
they call forth, and the problems are not coy visitors that will
not remain to be interrogated. We are not dealing with images that have to be cautiously dissected out of our objects,
nor even with fancies that vanish as soon as we show an
interest in their pedigree and visible means of support. Other
theories of the psychical imply an analysis which preserves the
content of the criticised object as subjective experience. But
at once the difficulty arises of presenting this content. What
the psychologist has actual recourse to is the abstraction of
qualities from objects which have not been criticised. For
example, in dealing with color as psychical we assume at first
that, if we had not to distinguish the colored object as it appears to us from that object as our physical theory defines it,
it might never have been possible to separate the color from
the so-called real thing. But, in the second place, when we
ask for the color which has been stripped off from the object,
and which has in the process become psychical and subjective,
what is offered to us is the logical abstraction of color from
objects that remain objects for all the abstraction, under the
assumption that it must be the same as that which this critical
experience found on its hands when the object evanesced;
while the reject itself would be most difficult to reproduce,
and only the professional gymnastics of the trained introspectionist would be at all equal to the task, and he comes off
with aromas and suggestions, fearfully avoiding the Jabber-
wock of the psychological fallacy. We deal with substitutes
and correspondents in the place of the psychical material
which is too subtle for our grasp. And this holds not only for
the psychical derived from criticism of physical experience,
but also for that which comes to us from the criticism of

thought and imagination. Thought maintains its objectivity as proudly as does sense-perception and the analyst who tries to separate thought from the thing is apt to come off with all the object or nothing according to the school that he patronizes. But it is not difficult, of course, to abstract thought in logic, and it is easy to set up these abstractions as the psychical content, or, more correctly, the same thing as the psychical content which an epistemology has shown must be subjective purely.

The position taken by Dewey is that in this psychical situation the object is gone, and the psychical character of the situation consists in the disintegration and reconstruction. The question then arises: In what form do these contents appear when this disintegration and reconstitution takes place? It does not appear in the form of an object, for it is just this character that it has lost, and consciousness here certainly does not consist in the presentation of copies of objects that will not serve as stimuli, but in their analysis and reconstruction. An answer may be found in that classical description of psychical consciousness, James's chapter on "The Stream of Thought." [11] Are there any of the characteristics of the stream which are not unmistakably present when we face any problem and really construct any hypothesis? The kaleidoscopic flash of suggestion, and intrusion of the inapt, the unceasing flow of odds and ends of possible objects that will not fit, together with the continuous collision with the hard, unshakable objective conditions of the problem, the transitive feelings of effort and anticipation when we feel that we are on the right track and substantive points of rest, as the idea becomes definite, the welcoming and rejecting, especially the identification of the meaning of the whole idea with the different steps in its coming to consciousness—there are none of these that are not almost oppressively present on the surface of consciousness during just the periods which Dewey describes as those of distintegration and reconstitution of the

11 [William James, *The Principles of Psychology*, Vol. I, chap. 9.]

stimulus—the object. No person who bemoans insoluble diffi-culties in front of him that does not paint the same picture, though with no such brilliant brush. No scientist who de-scribes the steps of a dawning and solidifying hypothesis who does not follow in the same channel, with the same swirl and eddy of current, and the same dissolving views upon the shores. If there is ever a psychical feeling of relation, it is when the related object has not yet risen from the under-world. It is under these circumstances that identities and dif-ferences come with thrills and shocks. Most of the persons who bore us with themselves, and the novelists who bore us with others, are but dilating upon the evident traits of such phases of our life, and they need lay no claim to professional skill of the trained introspectionist to recognize these traits. Let me add also that James's account of the hunt for the middle term in the reasoning process,[12] and much that he writes of the concept, fit perfectly into this phase of experi-ence, and that here as well the psychologist's fallacy seems to have become perfectly innocuous. Consciousness here cannot help being psychical in its most evident form, and the recog-nition of it is unavoidable under whatever terminology, tech-nical, or nontechnical, we may cover it.

This real crux of the situation is to be found in the feelings of activity. Are they reduced to simple sensations of motion and effort, or may the activity appear directly, without repre-sentation? Can we psychically be consciously active, or is psy-chical consciousness confined to the results of activity? As long as the analysis is logical, i.e., as long as we simply abstract various characteristics of the objects and ascribe to the self assumed psychical elements corresponding to these, changes or motions will be inevitably translated into answering bodily changes or motions, and the only psychical elements that can be attained will be those presumed to accompany them. When psychology attempts to present these elements, it refers to cer-tain feels, as we indicated above. We are now in a position

12 [Ibid., chap. 22.]

to see where these contents come from. They cannot be the rejects, for reasons already adduced, but they may be the really psychical states forced into an integral act for purposes of interpretation. A successfully thrown ball means to us distance covered, weight of the ball, momentum attained, an entire objective situation. A mistake in the weight of the ball will give rise to a disorganized phase of consciousness, which will be subjective or psychical until it is readjusted. Here the efforts in their inhibition of each other provide us with states of feeling which we assume to be those which accompanied the coordinated process, though we could not detect them. This I take to be the real psychologist's fallacy, the attempt to introject a psychical state into a process which is not psychical. We assume that the individual who did move had an unanalyzed consciousness which contained the motion and this feeling of effort, whereas the feeling of effort belongs to a state in which the individual is not able to move, or in which at least the effort and the motion are in inverse proportion to each other. It is not the individual who could build up a world of masses and momentums, of carrying distances and varying velocities, that has feelings of effort. He has a universe of life and motion instead. Force these elements, however, into this universe by a reflective process, and the only statement you can make about them is that they are feelings *of* those motions. To generalize this statement: The psychical contents which belong to these phases of disintegration and reconstitution, if referred to physical or logical objects that belong to other phases of consciousness, can be only representative, can be only sensations *of* something. They inevitably lose their immediacy. To present a concrete instance: The man who hesitates before a ditch, which he is not sure that he can jump, is conscious of inhibited activity. If he were sure of his ability to jump it, in the place of that consciousness he would have an estimate of the width of the ditch and the spring as an objective motion. If now we say that the sense of effort which comes with the inhibition is the subjective side of that which is objectively expressed as motion, we introduce into the original process a complexity which was not there for our consciousness. We were consciously moving. But we are told that beside this conscious motion there was this feeling of effort which has been borrowed from the subjective phase. This is not the motion. At most it can be but a feeling of motion. We carry over as an element a content whose peculiar quality depends upon its functional value in one phase of consciousness into another, and insist that it exists there as the subjectivity of this second phase. Under these circumstances it is reduced to the position of standing for something, and this so-called subjective consciousness is made of nothing but sensations of registrations.

I should add that the experimental psychologist is apt to trouble himself comparatively little about this or any other content of subjectivity. He assumes its existence answering to the physical situation, and confines himself to determining these physical situations with reference to the conditions under which this subjectivity is supposed to appear.

If we do not confuse these two phases of consciousness, I see no more difficulty in the immediate consciousness of activity in the subjective situations than of the motion in the objective. It appears primarily in the shifting of attention in the adaptation of habitual tendencies to each other, when they have come into conflict within the coordination. They involve effort in the stresses and strains of these different activities over against each other. I cannot go into the discussion of the interpretation of attention in terms of the innervation of the muscles of the sense-organs and of the head and chest. I must confine myself to the demand that we leave different stages of conscious processes to themselves—to their immediacy—and to the assertion that, when we do this, no one phase can be made merely cognitive of another, whether we have reference to contents or activities.

The conclusion was reached above that psychical consciousness could be immediate only insofar as it was functional. We may go a step farther and add that, insofar as the psychical state is functional, it cannot be a sensation of something else that is not in that state. Its functional character confines its reference to this function, which is that of reconstruction of the disintegrated coordination.

The discussion so far has considered the immediate characteristic of the psychical. The other element in the definition is its identification with the experience of the individual qua individual. The implication of the functional conception of the psychical is very interesting. If the psychical is functional and the consciousness of the individual at the same time, it is hard to avoid the conclusion that this phase of our consciousness—or, in other words, the individual qua individual—is functional in the same sense. This individual cannot be the empirical "me" that exists in such profusion in the modern genetic and pathological psychologies; nor yet can it be the transcendental self that is nothing but the function of unity; nor the self whose realization is the goal of the ethics of Green and his ilk; [13] nor the individual whose whole content is the other way of stating the knowable universe. For this individual cannot be an object; and yet it must have a content, but that content cannot be an ideal either of conduct or of knowledge. It cannot be an object, because, for many reasons, some of which will be developed later, it belongs to the subject end of the polarized process of cognitive experience; it must have or be a content, because psychical consciousness does not belong to the normative phase of reflection, and deals therefore with relations and laws only in their

[13] [See T. H. Green, *Prolegomena to Ethics* (5th edn.; Oxford: Clarendon Press, 1906). Fellow of Balliol College and Whyte Professor of Moral Philosophy at Oxford, Green (1836–1882) was one of the most influential moral and political philosophers of the Victorian age. Unfinished at the time of Green's death, his *Prolegomena to Ethics* was edited by A. C. Bradley and published in 1883. A classic representation of the ethical theory of self-realization, this work, along with Green's *Lectures on the Principles of Political Obligation*, which was published posthumously in Volume II of *Works of T. H. Green*, edited by R. L. Nettleship (London: Longmans, 1885–1888), inspired the school of moral and political philosophers known as the Oxford Idealists. This school included Bernard Bosanquet, D. C. Ritchie, and Edward Caird in its membership.]

appearance within certain fields of experience; it cannot be an ideal, because it must be immediate, and therefore its reference, so far as it is psychical, must lie within its own phase of consciousness.

There is nothing that has suffered more through loss of dignity of content in modern positivistic psychology than the "I." The "me" has been most honorably dealt with. It has waxed in diameter and interest, not to speak of number, with continued analysis, while the "I" has been forced from its metaphysical throne, and robbed of all its ontological garments; and the rags of "feelings of effort about the head and chest," of the "focalization of sense-organs," the "furrowing of the eyebrows" seem but a sorry return for the antique dogmas. But the greatest loss is the constant drain from the "I" to the "me." No sooner is a content of subjectivity made out than it is at once projected into the object world. This is the peculiar theme of our social psychology.[14] The recognition of the social character of the self, that the *alii* of our experience are not secondary inferred objects with which our reason endows directly perceived physical things, but constructs whose content is derived from subjective consciousness—this recognition involves the objectifying of a content which used to belong to the subject. In Baldwin's address before the Yale Philosophical Club, upon "Mind and Body from the Genetic Point of View," [15] this exhaustion of the subjective content in socially organized, and therefore objective, minds is shown in a series of "progressions." Starting with a presumed "protoplasmic" condition of consciousness, out of which arise first the "projections," answering to persons and things, there appear next the "progression" of persons into selves, the *ego* and *alii;* and finally the recognition of the body, answering to the mind of the other and the corresponding relation of mind and body in the

14 See [James Mark] Baldwin, *Mental Development in the Child and the Race* [2nd edn.; New York, 1898], chap. 11, and *Social and Ethical Interpretations* [2nd edn.; New York, 1899], chap. 1.

15 Published in the May 1903 number of *The Psychological Review* [X, 225–247].

ego. In the final reflective attitude there is left nothing but mind and body. The subjectivity is entirely exhausted. The author is strictly logical in demanding that we recognize the completely correlative positions of mind and body in this position. Attempted reduction of the one to the other is a denial of their mutual dependence not only in their genesis, but in their functions in the reflective process. But this striking application of the results of genetic and social psychology to the epistemological problem leaves the same irreducible parallelism which we have discussed, and surrenders the problem of transcending this dualism to some other philosophic discipline.

The interesting situation suggested here is that, if we do accept this dualism for psychology, we do it at the sacrifice of a subject that is anything more than an assumption—possibly an assumption of some particular psychical processes such as attention, apperception, but still a subject that can never appear *in persona* within the domain of psychology. It is all very well to send a sergeant-at-arms into fields of the transcendental *ego* after him. If it actually appeared, its presence would, according to Baldwin, act like the nymph's magic kiss and reduce the whole experience to "protoplasmic" babyhood. That is, from this genetic standpoint the subject as a conscious stage must disappear before the reflective stage can arise. It must disappear in order that the contents of mind and body may arise. It is as much a presupposition here as it is over against the processes of attention or the activities in general; which is tantamount to saying that the relation of the psychical to the subject cannot be made a characteristic in the definition of the psychical. For the relation to an empirical "me" cannot be made particular. We inevitably generalize the experiences of these "me's" so that what belongs to one may belong to another. To say, with Wundt, that our concepts are used merely for the purposes of classification and arrangement, implies that we can present the material outside of the conceptual formulation. We have already seen that this is Wundt's assumption, but that it is an assumption which is hopelessly unproductive of any psychical content. These contents turn out to be nothing but the rejected elements of the object when it is subjected to logical analysis, and therefore stated in terms of the conceptual object in whose interest the abstraction is made. We have also seen that there is a phase that is not stated in terms of such an analysis, one that arises in the period of disintegration and reconstitution of the stimulus-object; that the content in this period is not what is abstracted from the former object when the conceptual object is erected in its place, but the content that appears when experience has lost its objectivity because of the conflicting tendencies to react, and that, instead of its being a reject, for the time being it includes all that is given at all. Not only this, but it is characterized by the consciousness of the reconstruction, of activities of attention and organization. We have seen that, as long as the activities of experience are present only in terms of their results, they can only appear in the form of sensations of the activities, but that in this stage the directing attention is immediately given. Thus, in the theories we have criticised, the subject is represented in two aspects, neither of which can presumably be present in the material with which the science deals; first as a content, the original subjectivity out of whose "projection" or "imitative introjection" arise not only the others' selves, but reactively our own, and second the "activities" that answer to attention or apperception; but in this phase of disintegration and reconstruction both these aspects *are* immediately given. The disintegration of the object means a return, with reference to a certain field, to the original phase of protoplasmic consciousness, and within these limits there is neither mind nor body, only subjectivity. The reconstruction is the immediate process of attention and apperception, of choice, of consciously directed conduct.

This stage of disintegration and reconstruction requires a more detailed description and analysis. The characteristics which identify it with the reflective consciousness are the sharp definition of the problem within one field of consciousness and the forms which the other contents of consciousness take in the statement and solution of the problem. The assumptions made in this description are: (1) that consciousness is so organized with reference to conduct that the objects in cognitive experience may all be regarded as means to the accomplishment of the end involved in that conduct; (2) that this end may be stated in psychological terms as the expression of an impulse; (3) that when the coordination is unbroken the stimulus is the object determined by the preceding processes of the act; and (4) that the rest of the field of consciousness is organized with reference to this object, and may be stated either in positive or negative terms of it; (5) that, insofar as the coordination is unbroken, the end is for the time being adequately expressed in terms of the means, i.e., the object and its background which provide an adequate stimulus for continuance of the activity, and thus the distinction between the act and the conditions of the act does not appear; (6) that when the coordination is broken up—or, in other words, when an adequate stimulus for the expression of the impulse is not given, but the conflicting tendencies to act deprive the object of its power as a stimulus—then consciousness is divided into two fields: that within which the new stimulus or object must be constructed, and the rest of experience which with reference to the new possible object can have no other content than that of conditions of its formation. An illustration of these characteristics can be found in social experiences in which we are forced to reconstruct our ideas of the character of our acquaintances. As long as we can act with reference to them successfully, that which we later consider our ideas of them constitute their characters as persons. That the organization of these characters springs from our mutual relations, and that the psychological statement of these relations would be found in our social impulses or activities, the analysis of social objects since Hegel, and the results of genetic and social psychology have, I think, abundantly demonstrated. It would also be admitted that the particular form which that character took on, in any instance, depends upon what particular social activity we are engaged in, and that the whole social environment would be more or less definitely organized as the background and sustaining whole of the individual or individuals who were the immediate stimuli of our conduct. If we assume now that some experience should run quite counter to the nature of an acquaintance as we have known him, the immediate result would be that we would be nonplussed and quite unable to act with reference to him for the time being. The immediate result would be a state of consciousness within which would appear mutually contradictory attitudes toward the acquaintance which would inevitably formulate themselves in a problem as to what the real nature of the man was, and over against this a mass of data drawn from our experience of him and of others that would constitute the conditions for the solution of the problem. The contradictory attitudes of approval and abhorrence include in their sweep not only the man in question, but also ourselves insofar as mutual interrelationship has helped to form our selves over against his. Or, in other words, we should be uncertain of our own capacity of judging him as the man himself. Insofar the subject and object relation, the *ego* and *alter,* would have disappeared temporarily within this field. The situation may be of such hopeless perplexity that consciousness in this regard could be well called protoplasmic; or at least would be of the same nature as the original subjectivity due to checks and inhibitions out of which is projected the other selves of a social consciousness.

There follows the definition of the problem, the delineation of which would be a task for logic. But there is a phase of the process with which logic does not deal or has not dealt; not because logic is a normative, while psychology is an explanatory and descriptive science simply, but because in that phase the content and the procedure cannot be distinguished. It is the hunt for a hypothesis, when the consciousness is more or less incoherent or, in other terms, the distinction between subject and predicate cannot be made. To return to the illustration, we are uncertain whether the conduct of our acquaintance is abhorrent, being logically a predicate and psychologically a stimulus to action, that of repulsion; or whether this possible predicate is not a prejudice of our own, being therefore subject. Given either alternative, and it takes its logical position, but for the time being it is actually neither, and cannot become such but by a further reconstruction in which there will emerge subjects and predicates which were never there before. Modern logic is ready enough to admit that the judgment is a process of reconstruction, by which, through ideal interpretation of our world, it becomes another world, but what it does not seem to me to recognize is that the idea has to arise, and that while it is arising it is not idea and cannot function as such; that the ideas we have are abstracted from our old world and cannot reconstruct it; and that we must allow for the situation in which what is essentially novel emerges before it even takes on the form of a hypothetical predicate. What I wish to insist upon is that, while we have not as yet a predicate, we also have no subject; that, while the negative statement of the problem clears the ground for its solution, it does not give that solution; and that the statement of the rest of experience in terms of the conditions of the solution of the problem, the gathering of data, does not give the positive touch of reconstruction which is involved in the presentation of a hypothesis, however slight and vague it may be; that this step takes place within the field of subjectivity, which insofar is neither me nor other, neither mind nor body. And it is in this phase of subjectivity, with its activities of attention in the solution of the problem, i.e., in the construction of the hypothesis of the new world, that the individual qua individual has his functional expression or rather is that function.

To appreciate this we need to consider this situation in consciousness from another point of view—that of the relation of the conditions for the solution, reflectively presented, to the problem itself. From the standpoint of science, these conditions are the data of investigation. They are abstractions which arise through the conflict. In the illustration used above the conduct is abstracted from the particular person and particular situation within which it appeared. This abstraction is due to our inability to treat the person as an acquaintance and continue our relations with him, or, on the other hand, to surrender him and pass judgment upon his conduct as we would but for our past knowledge of his character. This datum is therefore strictly correlative to the psychical consciousness of the conflicting tendencies and the disintegration of the object, but the ability to present this reflective content is due to the integral character of the rest of our world. This forms the basis upon which the reconstruction can take place. Not that this world will not eventually be brought within the reconstruction, at least by implication, but that for the time being the world and the individual have sufficient coherence to give the conditions under which the problem may be solved, representing, as they do, the organized system which remains the criterion of the reality of the result. The individual corresponding to the world of data or conditions is that given in the state of subjectivity. But it is evident that, as the function of the world is to provide the data for the solution, so it is the function of the individual to provide the hypothesis for that solution. It is equally evident that it is not the individual as a "me" that can perform this function. Such an empirical self belongs to the world which it is the function of this phase of consciousness to reconstruct. The selves of our scientific theory are part of the data which reflection presents to us. We have already seen that the content which is ascribed to them cannot be immediate. Furthermore, one of the results of the reconstruction will be a new individual as well as a new social environment. The reference which is made of this state of subjectivity to the presented self is therefore only in the sense of a statement of the conditions under which the new self is to be organized. In the meantime the experience in this psychical phase is not a presentation, but an immediate and direct experience. That is, this is the self in the disintegration and reconstruction of its universe, the self functioning, the point of immediacy that must exist within a mediate process. It is the act that makes use of all the data that reflection can present, but uses them merely as the conditions of a new world that cannot possibly be foretold from them. It is the self of un-necessitated choice, of undreamt hypotheses, of inventions that change the whole face of nature.

If we ask now what sort of scientific treatment this phase of consciousness may receive, we find the reply already given. It cannot be a presentation of contents. These presentations all take their place among the data or conditions of this activity. On the other hand, there is nothing mysterious about its flow. It may be as vividly and definitely described as any immediate experience, but it is not the content as content that constitutes the scientific character of the description, but its definition in terms of the laws of analysis and construction. It will not be a statement of the laws of these processes. This statement would belong to general logic, but the formulation of psychi-cal experience in terms of those laws. The theory of the con-flict within an organized universal whole is logical, but the statement of the conflict of an impulse with a coordination of impulses and the inhibition of these impulses will be a scientific treatment of the psychical. The theory of the recon-struction of a given world as subject through the interpreta-tion of a hypothetical idea or predicate lies in the sphere of logic, but the shifting of attention in the recoordination of the impulses, the control of the outgoing activities by the sense-processes during this coordination, and the like, will fall within the science of the psychical.

There appears to be, therefore, a field of immediate experi-ence within reflection that is open to direct observation, that does not have to be approached from the standpoint of paral-lelism, but which is a presuppostion of that parallelism, as it is of all presentation of data, which voluntaristic psychology pre-supposes, but does not directly deal with, and for which there is arising the modern discipline of functional psychology. Over against this would still stand the parallelistic psychology as presenting the conditions under which empirical bodies and minds must act in the reconstructions arising within the field of the psychical. For this functional psychology an explicit definition of its subject-matter seems highly important. That suggested in this paper is as follows: that phase of experience within which we are immediately conscious of conflicting impulses which rob the object of its character as object-stimulus, leaving us insofar in an attitude of subjectivity; but during which a new object-stimulus appears due to the reconstructive activity which is identified with the subject "I" as distinct from the object "me."

There are two illegitimate transfers in modern psychology. . . . In the first place, the psychologist who is interested in so-called psychical elements has abstracted the *qualia* [16] of sensation from the object of reflection by a process of simple analysis, and has assumed that he may transfer them in this form to the domain of the psychical (p. 41). In the second place, the voluntaristic psychologist has recognized the feelings of stress and strain that belong to the psychical phase of consciousness, and has transferred them to unanalyzed experience and its movements, where they are assumed to be the sensations of these movements (p. 43). It would be a mistake, however, to leave these treatments without some indication of their proper function, especially when an attempt is being made to relate psychical consciousness to other phases of the process of reflection.

The position of the "elements" is indicated at once by their origin. They are part of the data which define the conditions under which the immediate problem is to be solved. What distinguishes them from the data of the other sciences is their relation to the individual through physiological psychology. This science enables us to state all the data of the physical sciences in terms of the individual—the "corporeal individual." Their logical function must then be the same as that of the data of the other sciences, that of stating the conditions of the

[16] [In accord with *Webster's New International Dictionary* (2nd edn.), Mead's plural spelling *quales* is abandoned for the spelling *qualia* in this and in other instances of the term in the present essay.]

solution—the function of the subject of the judgment when the problem is as yet only stated. Now the hypothesis which is to arise must make its appearance in the individual qua individual. The general statement of conditions which are valid for all is not adequate for this situation. There must be a statement which will translate these into the conditions of this individual. The difficulty with the customary psychological statement is that they are not treated as conditions, but as contents which existed in advance of the appearance of the problem. It is, then, not remarkable that these so-called elements which have in reality been simply abstracted from scientifically determined objects do not appear in psychical consciousness at all, as introspection abundantly shows. What appear are the emerging objects, indistinct and still subject to the disintegration of conflicting impulses. But the conditions of the problem stand there as the form, so to speak, to which the hypothesis must conform itself. The attempt to give these conditions content apart from the immediate psychical experience inevitably drives the psychologist to borrow a filling from the abstractions of the outer scientific world—the "elements." Apart from the particular problem of constructing a sounding, colored, felt world, there is a certain legitimacy in referring to these conditions of individual reconstruction as sensations of color, sound, etc. But to assume that this content is determinable independently of the problem is utterly false. The only thing that is determinable in advance is the *function* of seeing, of hearing, and of feeling. What the content of this function is going to be is dependent upon the character of the process.

The legitimate result of this type of "elemental" psychology is found, not in the psychical correspondents of the physical originals, but in the physical statement itself. All the value of the study of so-called *qualia* of sensation is to be obtained eventually in the statement of the nervous mechanism. And this mechanism is only a series of paths. It is impossible to isolate anything in the nervous system except processes unless one arbitrarily assumes physical elements to answer to arbitrarily assumed psychical elements. To repeat the statement made above, the logical function of physiological psychology is to give a statement of the world of the physical sciences in terms of the individual so that the conditions of the hypotheses that can arise only in psychical consciousness may be so stated that they will hold for that consciousness. In my judgment, however, we must recognize not only a corporeal individual, but a social and even logical individual, each of whom would answer to the translation of the results of the social and logical sciences into terms of psychical consciousness. That is, if we find it convenient to set up a social environment or an epistemological environment in which we abstract from the physical statement, we must state the laws of these environments in terms of the individual, to put them at his disposal. In any case, such a statement is the subject-function of the judgment.

If we seek a psychological expression for the actual use of these conditions in experience we will find it in the term "image." However unfortunate the historical implications of the term may be, there is no other expression that answers to such an organization of a subjective state that it may become objective. The unfortunate implication of the term is still maintained in much of the psychological doctrine of the memory. The implication is that the memory image depends for its organization upon past experience, that the selection and ordering of its content looks back and not forward. There can be, however, no question that the activities with which psychology deals find their expression in the formation of the image, and that these activities are essentially forward-looking. The fallacy of referring these activities backward as the sensations of unanalyzed movements we have already commented upon at length (p. 44). As the statement in terms of elements stands only for the conditions of reconstruction, so these activities presented in the image stand only for the direction of the reconstruction. A psychology which assumes that these images are registrations of past experiences which exist ready to hand in some storehouse of the mind is as illegitimate as a psychology of "elements," even if it bring in attention or apperception as a force from the outside to order the material. For it has a material which is only made up out of logical abstractions. The ordering of this material by laws of the association of ideas or by attentive processes is unreal as long as these forces operate upon material which is quite separate from the immediate problem of consciousness. The image whose meaning alone makes association conceivable, and which can only arise through its successful reconstruction of the object, can no more be separated from the psychical state as a content than can the conditions discussed above. The image stands for the predicate as the *qualia* stand for the subject.

The image is the suggested object-stimulus, adapting itself to the conditions involved in the problem. It interprets the conditions as the predicate interprets the subject. But neither the subject nor the predicate is there in fixed form, but are present in process of formation. The value and content of the conditions is continually changing as the meaning of the problem develops, and this meaning grows as it recognizes and accepts the conditions that face it. It is evident that in this state of reflection it is impossible to present the elements out of which the new world is to be built up in advance, for disintegration and analysis of the old is as dependent upon the problem that arises as is the reconstruction. It is equally impossible to state the form which the world will take in advance. Neither elements nor image can be given in advance of the actual problem or, what is the same thing for psychology, in advance of the psychical state. For this psychical state they are reciprocal functions which have now this expression and now that. What this expression is depends upon the selective activity of attention or apperception—an activity that is practically coterminous with the psychical state as such.

The logical correspondent of this psychical state can be no other than the copula phase of the judgment; that in which subject and predicate determine each other in their mutual interaction. The subject and predicate—the conditions or elements and the images—may be reduced as contents to zero in the equation and be present only as felt functions. In this case we have the limit of subjectivity. Or we may have definite conditions and a working hypothesis, and then the state approaches objectivity. Here the elements of sensuous experience fit into the structure of the world perfectly under the interpretation of the image.

One word of recognition is due to the types of psychology which have been criticised. If we wish to make a symbolical statement of the conditions of organizing or coordinating experience, it may be legitimate to take colors, sounds, feels, and odors by logical abstraction from the objects around us, and if we wish to present the image symbolically it may be legitimate to use logical abstractions from our thought-objects—the ideas —as contents for this function. In actual psychical experience the material in which these functions express themselves are the disintegrating and reforming objects of the changing universe. The only justification, however, for these symbolical presentations must be found in their interpretation of actual psychical processes, and they can be properly used only as this function is kept in mind, and when the assumption is avoided that they offer a real account of what transpires in subjective consciousness.[17]

[17] It would be impossible for me to indicate in detail my obligations to Professor Dewey in the development of the thought of this paper, but the reference of the psychical phase of consciousness to the copula stage of the judgment, and its elaboration in the last three pages, should be credited directly to him.

✒❧ IV ❧✒

THE TEACHING OF SCIENCE IN COLLEGE

I wish to call attention to a situation which seems to me unnatural and unfortunate. It is unnecessary to present it in statistical form. No one will question that science in the colleges of this and other universities has not the importance and popularity that it should have, that this element of our modern education is by no means represented in the results of education in accordance with its importance.

It is not, however, to the failure to elect scientific courses as they are today or to enroll themselves for science degrees on the part of our students that I think especial attention should be directed. Nor do I think that we can explain this and other evidences of the deficiencies in this regard by the traditional prestige of the so-called humanities, or the prejudicing of the students' minds by preparatory courses inimical to scientific interest.

Scientific courses have not become popular as the old requirements in the languages have been decreased. It is rather the other courses such as the Ph.B. that have profited by the greater freedom of election. With considerable freedom of election in the preparatory schools the scientific courses are not sought out there by the children at a period when the concrete subject-matter of science properly presented should be immensely more attractive than the languages and many more abstract objects of study. The science courses in the high school are not at the present time popular, nor is the money spent upon them, either in equipment or in teaching force, comparable with their educational importance.

Address delivered before the Chicago Chapter, Sigma Chi, March 1906. [From *Science,* XXIV (1906), 390–397. Reprinted by permission.]

The result of this is that the majority of our students leave our colleges and universities, without being able to grasp the most important achievements in modern thought, without being able to take the point of view of those thinkers who are reconstructing our views of the physical universe and its constituent parts, and without being able to interpret what they see and hear and feel by means of the profoundest and most magnificent generalizations which the world has ever known.

I wish to present two reasons for this condition which seem to me more fundamental than those usually presented, and to discuss in connection with them the possibility of removing them or at least to invite discussion on the subject.

It is natural to compare the sciences so-called with the humanities. And yet in one respect the distinction between them has much decreased of late years and promises to continue to decrease. The method of study of the languages, history, literature and the so-called social sciences has become to a large degree that of the natural sciences. There is certainly no fundamental distinction between the researches of the historian, the philologist, the social statistician and those of the biologist, the geologist or even the physicist and chemist, in point of method. Each is approaching problems which must be solved, and to be solved must be presented in the form of carefully gathered data. For their solution hypotheses must be constructed and tested by means of experiment or observation. With the complexity of the phenomena, of course, the application of the scientific methods will vary. The processes of observation, for example, will vary enormously in the study of a historical problem in the ancient world, and in the study of the problem of variation where the material is immediately at hand. The methods of historical criticism—lower and higher—are nothing but methods of observations under conditions which are peculiarly difficult of access.

While it is true that in literature and other arts we do not go back of the aesthetic reaction in the judgment of beauty, or the study of this reaction in others as presented in literary criticism; outside this field of appreciation and criticism, the method of study in the field of the humanities is just as scientific as the subject-matter with which it deals allows.

This means for one thing that we no longer regard the acquirement of information as the legitimate object or method of education. The ideal of modern education is the solution of problems, the research method. And this research method is no less dominant in the humanities than it is in the natural sciences so far as the subject-matter permits.

The ground for the difference in attractive power of the natural sciences and the humanities cannot be laid up, therefore, to a difference in method. And if it could the prospect would be discouraging indeed and the judgment upon the students most unflattering, for the research method is, after all, nothing but the elaboration of the simple processes of perceiving and conceiving the world, elaborated in such a way that it can be applied to the complex and subtle problems of the physicist, the geologist, the biologist, etc. If the scientific method were the cause of unpopularity we should have to assume that the process of knowledge itself, the very function of cognition, was disagreeable to the average student.

If, however, we examine these two types of studies we do meet a distinction which holds for many if not for all. In the physical sciences the process of investigation involves the analysis of the objects, which are studied, into elements which are not present to immediate experience and which are with difficulty conceived and presented to the mind. The resolution of nature into atoms and molecules or corpuscles is an undertaking presenting itself at the beginning of scientific investigation, that is not forced upon the social sciences. Here the elements into which analysis reduces its objects are at bottom, but more or less reproducible states of our own consciousness, or still more direct objects of possible sense-perception. This was a difficulty that did not inhere in the old-time natural history. There the problem that aroused investigation was stated in terms of everyday experience, and for this very reason natural history was a more successful subject in the curriculum than our physics and chemistry. Its problems were real problems in the minds of the students. They were not located in a field as yet foreign to their acquaintance and, therefore, artificial and unmeaning.

The problems of biology and geology do not suffer as much from this remoteness, for to a large degree they can be stated in terms of a possible immediate experience of the student, and it is true that they make a more immediate appeal to the student than do the physical sciences. But it must not be forgotten that these biological and geological sciences are to no small degree applied physics and chemistry, and that this tendency is steadily increasing. That is, it is increasingly difficult to state the problems of these sciences in terms of immediate experience; their problems do not arise of themselves in the consciousness of the student, in other words, he is not immediately interested in the study.

We can generalize this in the following form: The result of the development of our sciences has been that their problems are no longer within the immediate experience of the student, nor are they always statable in terms of that experience. He has to be introduced to the science before he can reach the source of interest, i.e., problems which are his own and which he wants to solve by the process of his own thinking.

On the whole, the problems of the social sciences have a meaning to the student when he meets them, i.e., they can be his own problems from the start, and they do not have to be translated into terms which must be somewhat painfully acquired before they can be used.

In a certain sense mathematics has become the language of the physical sciences, and the student must have a command of this vernacular before he can read with interest that which is writ in the sciences, before he can attack their problems. But even where the vernacular of the science is not that of mathematics, it is still true, to a large extent, that the field of the real problems in the science lies outside of the direct experience of the student.

It hangs together with this, in the second place, that the

natural sciences are not interconnected in the minds of the students, that they exist in watertight compartments. There is no common field out of which they all spring. It seems to me that in this lies the great advantage which the humanities so-called have over the natural sciences in the curriculum. They all of them belong to one piece of human experience, and it remains true *nil humanum mihi alienum est*,[1] not simply because of the immediate human sympathy which unites men and women who are distant not only in space, but also in time, not only in speech, but also in state of civilization; there is a still more important hold which the social sciences and humanities have upon the interest of the student. It is that human history, human development, human institutions, its arts, its literature, its achievements, are so bound up together with each other, with the languages in which thought has been expressed, with the literature in which achievements have been recorded, with the movements of trade, commerce, colonization and discovery which have motived historic changes, that wherever one begins, problems of all sorts arise at once, interlacing with each other, so that the pursuit of one subject reinforces the interest in another, and vice versa. The whole group represents one social world which cannot be picked up piecemeal nor divided up into separate compartments, but is bound to exist in the mind as a whole.

This is not simply an advantage of an external sort. The logician tells us that, if we would expand it, the subject of every judgment would be found to be the universe itself, individualized in some immediate experience, but implying the whole world in its implicit relations. If we express this somewhat more modestly it would run, in educational terms, that it is only the implicit relation to other things that makes any subject teachable or learnable, and that the more evident and more pregnant these relations are the more readily is it assimilated. In a certain sense the more complex a thing is the more readily it is acquired, while its simplicity leaves it bare, without lines of connection, without retaining points. Of course

1 ["Nothing human is alien to me."]

this would not be the case if education were merely a process of storing away, a process of piling learning into the mind. But as the theory of science instruction, as well as scientific advance, is that of research, it is evident that the richer an object is in relation to other things the more suggestive it will be of solutions for problems, the more fertile it will be in arousing associations of kindred data. To bring out a problem then in a field which is already rich in interest is to insure not only its immediate attractiveness, but to provide the ideas and connections through which the problem may be studied and a solution reached.

It is this wealth of associations, this complex interrelation with a mass of other things, which the student fails to secure when he is introduced to modern science, through one door at a time, and that door leading into a specialized subject-matter whose relations with immediate experience are of the slightest character. A new subject should not be presented by itself, but in its relation to other things. It must grow in some fashion out of the student's present world.

The problem of college science is, therefore, very intimately connected with science in the secondary school. If the child were introduced to it in the proper way there the situation, which has just been described, would not exist in the college. He would come up into the college with the world of science already in existence, and that world as a field of his own experience. He would find problems arising there for whose solution he must look to the more specialized sciences. But the opposite of this is the case. Science in the high school, at the present time, is in a more parlous condition than it is in the college, because the child is farther away from the field of exact science than in the later college years. He finds fewer points of connection. His sciences remain for him located between impassable barriers. The college, therefore, at least until a reform can be wrought in the secondary school, is forced to face the problem within its own walls.

Its solution calls for introductory courses which will lead the student into the field of science, which will show the problems of his own experience in terms of this new field, and show them there capable of solution. There are two points of view from which such courses could be naturally presented; that of history, and that of a survey of the world analogous to what is given in introductory courses in sociology or social institutions.

The peculiar appropriateness of a course in the history of science for the junior college students, lies in the fact that the special character of modern science would grow out of the conditions that made it natural and necessary. There would be in it the inspiration of the personalities of the great scientific men, and the romance of their struggle with difficulties which beset their sciences from within and without. The conceptions of today would be found motived in the struggles of yesterday. But still more important the relations which have subsisted between scientific investigation and the whole field of human endeavor would appear—its relation to commerce, industry, the geographical distribution of men, their interconnection with each other, and the other sides of their intellectual life. Science would be interwoven with the whole human world of which it is actually a part. It is true that something of this is found in general history. It is there, however, presented not to lead up to further study of science, but to merely fill out the entire picture—a picture which is so crowded that many features are bound to be slighted, and among those which are slighted, science, just because it is a subject somewhat apart, is sure to be found.

We have of course the evidence of the import which such a course would have in the biographies of our scientific men— such as Darwin, Huxley, Pasteur, von Helmholtz.[2] But few of

2 [Charles Darwin (1809–1882), British naturalist, advanced the theory of evolution by natural selection in biology. His major works include *The Origin of the Species* (1859) and *The Descent of Man* (1871).— Thomas Henry Huxley (1825–1895), British scientist, became famous as an educator and a lecturer on evolution. His work, *Evolution and Ethics* (1893), was widely studied.—Louis Pasteur (1822–1895), French chemist, discovered the disease-causing micro-organisms that flourish in foodstuffs such as milk, and invented methods for eliminating them.—Hermann

our students in that period read them, and taken by themselves they do not have the educative power which the story of their efforts would have when presented in a course on the history of science. It is not, however, principally the personal note, which comes from the account of the men who have been the heroes of science, that would be found in such study. It is rather the form in which the scientific problem arose and the methods used for its solution which will carry the most valuable instruction. One scientific theory swallows up into itself what has preceded it, and the traces of the situation out of which the later doctrine arose are washed away. While our historical atlases present us in flaring colors the political situations out of which sprang present political conformations, the young student of science must pick up, as best he may, without assistance or interpretation, the explanation and historical interpretation of the conceptions he is forced to use. If an adequate comprehension of the powers of the American executive cannot be gained without a knowledge of the situation which preceded the formation of the constitution, no more can the uninstructed student comprehend the value of such terms as forces, energies, variations, atoms or molecules without understanding what the problems were which brought forth these hypotheses and scientific conceptions.

And there is no study like that of history to bring out the solidarity of human thought. The interdependence of scientific effort and achievement, and the interrelationship which exists between all science in presenting its world as a whole, can be brought out vividly only when its history is being presented, while in the midst of the arduous struggle with a single science these profound connections are quite overlooked. It is a fact that science is, from an important point of view, a single body of knowledge, whose different parts determine each other mutually, though this mutual influence is often overlooked. When the historian comes forward with the picture of a past

Ludwig Ferdinand von Helmholtz (1821–1894), a German scientist, made his most remarkable contributions in the fields of physiological optics and acoustics.]

age, such as Gomperz [3] has given us in his *Griechische Denker,* we recognize these interconnections and see that what has been done in one line has been now advanced because of the achievement of another, and now has been thwarted by the backwardness in still another. The Weltanschauung [4] of any age is at once the result of all its scientific achievements and a cause of each, by itself. We cannot finally understand any one without the comprehension of the whole, and it is the whole which is more comprehensible than any single science. It is a great deal easier to present the problem of evolution in the world as a whole than it is in the specific instance. It is easier to recognize the problem of matter, as it is presented in the book entitled *The New Knowledge,*[5] than it is to present the specific problem with which the physicist or chemist must wrestle. It may be a Hegelism, but it is good educational doctrine that the whole is more concrete than the part. A student who has first followed out the results of scientific evolution through the preceding centuries in their interconnection with each other, and meets then the problems of modern science as the growing points of the past, who understands somewhat what the controlling meanings are behind scientific concepts and terminology, who feels that he is entering into a battle that is going on, whose field he has surveyed before he has lost himself in the particular brigade, such a student is bound to enter into his study with both a comprehension and an interest which his brother will lack—his brother who must get the parts before he can have an inkling of the whole.

I am aware that, in the minds of a great many of you, there has arisen a spirit of contradiction to what has been presented, a spirit of contradiction which arises out of the very compe-

[3] [Theodore Gomperz (1832–1912), Austro-German historian of philosophy, was the author of *Griechische Denker,* 3 vols. (Leipzig: Veit & Co., 1896–1909), translated into English as *Greek Thinkers* by L. Magnus and G. G. Berry, 4 vols. (London and New York: J. Murray and Scribners, 1901–1912).]

[4] ["Conception of the world" or "philosophy of life."]

[5] [Probably a reference to *New Knowledge, Supplementing All Cyclopedias* (New York: Alden Brothers, 1905–1906).]

tency and exactness of the scientist. Such a type of instruction as that suggested above is felt to be superficial, inexact, and bound to be misleading to the person who is not scientifically trained. It would be information in a word, and the scientist does not hold it to be his position to impart information, nor can he promise any valuable educational result from a course whose content is one of information.

I wish to bring out the point because it seems to me fundamental to the question which has been broached. We need, in the first place, a definition of what information is and what knowledge is, as distinguished from it. I would suggest toward such a definition that nothing is information which helps anyone to understand better a question he is trying to answer, a problem he is trying to solve. Whatever bridges over a gap in a student's mind, enabling him to present concretely what otherwise would have been an abstract symbol, is knowledge and not mere information. Whatever is stored up, without immediate need, for some later occasion, for display or to pass examinations is mere information, and has no enduring place in the mind. From this standpoint nothing is superficial or inexact which gives concreteness and meaning to the problem before the student. Truth is a relative thing. We none of us have exact knowledge in the sense that our knowledge is exhaustive, and we none of us know the full import of what we do grasp. There can be no objection to the young student having a broad if seemingly superficial view of the scientific world, if it helps him to approach with more understanding the particular science he has before him. It is also certainly the pedagogic duty of the instructor in science to get far enough into the consciousness of the student to present the part to him by means of the whole.

The second point of view suggested for approach to the specialized study of science was that of the survey of the present field. If we can find the counterparts of the historical course in the biographies of great scientists, we can find that of the survey course in such treatises as the popular lectures of eminent scientists, such as those of Tyndall on *Sound,* or many of the popular lectures of men like von Helmholtz, du Bois-Reymond and a score of others.[6] We highly approve of such lectures when they appear on the lyceum or the university extension platform. We encourage the reading of such books, considering them distinctly educative, but we deny that they have a place in the university curriculum. The prevailing assumption is that when one cannot follow out the scientific process by which the results are reached, it is indeed better that he should have the result presented in a form which he can understand than not to have them at all, though it is not the place of the university to perform this function, except through its extension department. This statement, however, overlooks the fact that such acquaintance with the results of scientific research is also the source of interest in the research itself. What is merely keeping up with the progress of the world on the part of the businessman is preparation for the student who has to approach a new field. I presume that no one would question that those who had listened with intense interest and enthusiasm to an extension lecture upon the solar system would be better prepared for the study of astronomy. Indeed, we assume that university extension will serve in this fashion as a feeder of the university, but for some reason we feel that this same sort of preparatory work has no place inside of the university itself. From the point of view of education we are mistaken, for nothing is out of place which makes the approach of the students to the subject-matter a normal one. And until the student feels the problem of the science he undertakes to be a problem of his own, springing out of his own thought and experience, his approach is not a normal one.

6 [John Tyndall (1820–1893), British natural scientist, was noted for his books and lectures popularizing science. His work, *Sound*, appeared in 1867.—Von Helmholtz, *Popular Lectures on Scientific Subjects*, translated by E. Atkinson, with an Introduction by J. Tyndall (New York: Appleton, 1873).—Emil Heinrich du Bois-Reymond (1818–1896), a German physiologist, was singularly interested in the relation of science to general culture. A representative work of du Bois-Reymond is the essay, "On the Relation of Natural Science to Art," Smithsonian Institution, Annual Report, 1891 (Washington, D. C., 1893).]

One or two courses, then, from the standpoint of the history of science, and from that of the survey of the scientific field of today in the junior college, would organize the vague information of the student, would correlate it with the political and literary history with which he is familiar, would give him the sense of growth and vitality, would state the problems of science in his own terms, and awaken in him the passion to carry on the investigation himself which might otherwise remain dormant. They would be feeders to the specialized scientific courses that follow. They would break down the prejudice which most students bring against science from the high school. But not least, they would be as educative as any course in history could possibly be. They would serve as valuable a function as those courses which aim to acquaint the student with the social and political forces which dominate the world into which he is to enter.

What has been said so far has borne directly upon introductory courses in the junior college. It is only in the last remark that I have touched upon the demands which the university may make upon its scientists for the interpretation of the world for those who do not follow its special courses. If in the present day, under the sign of science in nature and society, anyone leaves an institution of higher learning without a comprehension of the results of science, which he can grasp in their relationship to the rest of human history and endeavor, he is certainly cheated out of one of the most valuable of the endowments which he has a right to demand from that institution. As I have already indicated, scientific method is dominant not only in the study of nature, but in the study of all the social subject-matters, in religion, politics, in all social institutions. Scientific discoveries have made over the answer even to the fundamental question of who is my neighbor. Science is responsible for the view of the universe as a whole which must be the background of our theology as well as our philosophy and much that is finest in our literature. Science has changed sentiment to intelligence in divine charity, and has substituted the virtue of reformation of evil for that of resignation thereto in religion. And yet a large percentage of our students leave the university without having any better opportunity of coming to close quarters with this science than those who are outside the university. They are compelled to get their science from the extension platform, or from the popular magazine. There should be unspecialized science for those who do not specialize in science, because they have the right to demand it of an educational institution.

There is still another demand that should be made upon the science faculties of the university, and that is that they should so organize the courses which their students take, that they will get the unity which every college course ought to give.

That unity of the social sciences which is given in subject-matter and human nature itself, is, as has been pointed out, absent from modern sciences which have become largely what Professor Wundt calls conceptual sciences. The interconnections are not apparent to the students who are in the special groups. Their attention is fixed within too narrow boundaries, the demands of their own subject is so great that they have no time to go beyond. They have a wealth which they cannot realize because they cannot put it into circulation.

Through the history of science, especially of the other sciences which they do not specialize in, through lecture courses which give them the results of these other sciences they should be able to get the unity of Weltanschauung, which is requisite for any college course.

It is requisite at the end as at the beginning that the student should see his world as a whole, should take up into it what he has acquired, and should get the mutual interpretation which the relation of his subject-matter has to what lies beyond it.

There is certainly no agent that can carry more profound culture than the sciences, but our science curriculum is poor in what may be called culture courses in the sciences, and the import of science for culture has been but slightly recognized and but parsimoniously fostered.

V

CONCERNING ANIMAL PERCEPTION

I wish to call attention to a phase of animal psychology which has received, it seems to me, but inadequate treatment. This inadequacy is evident not only in the general psychologies, but also in special experimental investigations of animal intelligence. The difficulty gathers about the doctrine of perception, and is due in part to the incomplete character of the theory of perception in human psychology, and in part to a failure to analyze sufficiently the conditions of possible perception in lower animal forms.

Can we draw a line between perception and higher cognitive processes, leaving below the line a cognition which is not rational though intelligent, such as characterizes the adaptations of a crab or a rat, and placing above the line all the consciousness of relation which makes human intelligence rational? Do our own predominately perceptive processes, such as those of rapidly climbing a steep, rocky cliff, or playing a game of tennis, where we are seemingly unconscious of anything except the physical environment and our reactions thereto, differ qualitatively from the more abstract processes in which we consciously deal in symbols and isolate the relations of things?

If these discursive processes are mere developments of contents which are implicitly present in perceptual consciousness, is there any definite line which can be drawn between the intelligence of man and that of the lower forms, unless we deny them the form of consciousness which we call perceptual in ourselves? Hobhouse,[1] for example, assumes that the cat, the

[From *The Psychological Review*, XIV (1907), 383–390. Reprinted by permission of the American Psychological Association.]

[1] *Mind in Evolution* [London and New York, 1901], p. 117.

dog and the monkey, which he observed, apprehend perceptual relations, which enabled them to learn by experience, without the ability to isolate the relations as elements in thought.

Stout [2] would grant to the chick that learns to reject a cinnabar caterpillar, an apprehension of meaning or significance, which would come to the same thing. On the other hand, Thorndyke [3] explains such learning by experience on the part of lower animals through the association of an "impulse" with a stimulus, which seems to imply a qualitatively different state of consciousness from that which would ordinarily be called perceptual in human experience. He undertakes to illustrate this by phases of human consciousness in which even perception would be reduced to a minimum. This latter illustration indicates a possibility of discrimination which seems to me to have been but inadequately recognized. In learning to play billiards or tennis, we are moving in a perceptual world, but the process of improvement takes place largely below even the perceptual level. We make certain movements which are more successful than others, and these persist. We are largely conscious only of the selection which has already begun. We emphasize this and control to some extent the conditions under which the selection takes place, but the actual assumption of the better attitude, the actual selection of the stroke, lies below even this level of consciousness. Thorndyke calls this selection a process of stamping in by the pleasure coming with success. This explanation, however, calls for its own explanation and ascribes active control to states of pleasure and pain, which is by no means proved and opens up another field of dubious animal psychology. Thorndyke calls the process of improvement an association of an impulse and a stimulus, which lies quite outside of associations of ideas. The phrase is perhaps a vague one, that calls for further specification, but it answers to a large number of instances which are commonly conceived of as percep-

2 *Manual of Psychology* [London and New York, 1899], pp. 84ff.

3 "Animal Intelligence," *Psy[chological] Rev[iew] Mon[ograph] Suppl[ement]*, II, No. 4 [1898], pp. 65ff.

tions by the animal psychologists, although it is to be presumed that Thorndyke himself assumes that these animals move in a perceptual world. The instances to which I refer may be well illustrated by the action of the chick in rejecting the cinnabar caterpillar or the orange-peel. Is there a revival of the past experiences which leads the chick to reject these disagreeable objects; or may we assume that the impulse to reject has become associated with this particular stimulus, without any intervening redintegrated psychoses?

This question is closely allied to that which arises with reference to the plasticity of the young form and the manner in which it acquires the specific habits which are not found performed in its nervous system. A chick learns to make use of the impulse to hide when a hawk sails overhead. A young fox learns to run away from the odor of man. The process of hiding and running away are indeed performed in these young animals. It is the association of the instinctive action with determinate stimuli which is acquired. What seems to take place is this: The animal tastes a disagreeable morsel when it instinctively strikes at a moving object before it. The action of the flavor of the morsel upon the organs of taste sets free an equally instinctive reaction of rejecting the morsel. At the same time, the chick eyes the caterpillar under the excitement of the disagreeable experience. Now the caterpillar hereafter to be avoided must be different from a mere moving object such as would have called forth the reaction of pecking. It is fair to assume that the condition for this discrimination made by the chick lies in the different reaction which it has called forth. The mere redintegration of the experience would not protect the chick. Either the chick would peck again, since presumably the same bad taste and same rejection would follow, simply reinforced by the revival of the past experience, and this would bring about no improvement in adaptation; or else the past experience would be revived with the appearance of the old stimulus. This stimulus was not a caterpillar with certain markings, but a moving object within reach. The revival of the experience with this generalized stimulus to which, as Lloyd Morgan's experiments show,[4] the chick reacts, would lead to the rejection, not of cinnabar caterpillars alone, but of all moving objects within reach. The ability to distinguish between stimuli which had been identical in their value before, arises together with the new reaction, that of rejection. The meaning of the plasticity of the young form seems to be that there exist in the form instinctive reactions which have not as yet determined external stimuli. Through the experience of the animal the appropriate stimuli are determined. One condition, at any rate, is found in the new visual or olfactory experience which arises when, for any reason, this new reaction takes place. A dog's shrinking from the sight of the whip involves not simply the revival of the painful experience of the flogging; it involves his reacting to characteristics in the sight of the whip which led to no reaction at first. It is not then so much the association of an old visual or olfactory experience with the impulse, as the arising of a new visual or olfactory experience which now becomes the stimulus for the particular impulse or reaction. If there be association of ideal contents, it is between this new visual or olfactory experience and the old experience which had not as yet been discriminated; of this association, Mr. Thorndyke remarks,[5] we have little or no evidence. What we must assume, in what is implied above, is that the animal gets the new visual or olfactory experience because it is carrying out a new reaction; that the ground for discrimination in sensation lies in the difference of reaction to that which is sensed, an assumption that is reinforced by the recognition that the process of sensing is controlled and directed by the reaction to the stimulus.

Now what is implied in perception is the association of the new sensory experience with the old. If the chick perceives a caterpillar as a "thing," he may associate the former experi-

4 [C. Lloyd Morgan, *Habit and Instinct* (London and New York: Edward Arnold, 1896), pp. 40–55.]

5 *Loc. cit.*

ence of pecking at a thing with the new experience of rejecting the peculiarly marked thing. But evidence for such
an association in the case of the chick certainly is lacking.
What has appeared in its conduct is a new stimulus of a visual character for a performed reaction, which up to this and
other like experiences had no determined visual stimulus.

The question then arises, what are the conditions for the
appearance of this permanent core to which varying sensory
elements may be associated? It is impossible to appeal directly
to the introspective analysis of human perception. We cannot
get inside the consciousness of the lower forms. It is, however,
possible to find in our own experience of physical objects
what constitutes this core which endows it with its Thinghood, and investigate the conduct and sensory equipment of
these forms, with a view to determining whether their experience can also contain this identical core to which varying
phases of the same object can be referred. Stout [6] finds this
core in what he terms "manipulation," understanding by this
any contact experiences which arise as the result of visual stimuli, such as the hearing, scratching, pulling, shoving, as well as
our actual handling of what we see. This he illustrates by the
visual experience of a hole to which an animal is fleeing and
which answers to an experience of contact, that enables the
animal to determine whether the opening is passable.

If this distinction be carried out somewhat further, we find
that the sensory experiences of animal life may be divided
into two categories: those that come through what may be
called the distance sense organs, the visual, olfactory and auditory senses, and those that come through the contact sensations. The distinction suggested by Stout's use of the term
"manipulation" is that intelligent conduct, when it reaches
the stage of perception, implies a reference of what comes
through the distance sensations to contact sensation. There is
perhaps nothing inherent in contact experiences which accounts for their being the substantial element in perception—

[6] *Loc. cit.*, pp. 326ff.

that to which, so far as physical, i.e., perceptual, experience goes, all other experience is referred. Visual discriminations are much finer and more accurate than those of manipulation. The auditory and olfactory experiences are richer in emotional valuations. But it remains true that our perception of physical objects always refers color, sound, odor, to a possibly handled substrate, a fact which was of course long ago recognized in the distinction between the so-called primary and secondary senses.

The ground of this is readily found in the nature of animal conduct, which, insofar as it is overt can be resolved into movements, stimulated by the distance senses, ending up in the attainment or avoidance of certain contacts. Overt food, protective, reproductive, fighting processes, all are made up of such movements toward or away from possible contacts, and the success of the conduct depends upon the accuracy with which the distance stimulation leads up to appropriate contacts. Consciously intelligent conduct within the perceptual field lies in the estimate of the sort of contact to which distance sensory [experience] stimulates the animal form, that is the conscious reference of experience resulting from the stimulation of the eye, the ear, the olfactory tracts, even the skin, by the movement of the air, etc., to the contacts which this stimulation tends to bring about.

The vast importance of the human hand for perception becomes evident when we recognize how it answers to the eye, especially among the distance senses. The development of space perception follows in normal individuals upon the interaction of the eye and the hand, and this interaction works a continual meeting of the discriminations of the eye by those of the skin, mediated through the manipulating hand. It is this contact experience which gives the identical core to which the contents coming from the distance senses are referred in the so-called process of complication. It is this core which answers to varying experiences while it remains the same. It is this core which is a *conditio sine qua non* of our perception of physical objects. Of course this content of contact experience is supplied by the process of association or complication out of past experience in most of our perceptions. The objects about us look hard or soft, large or small. But the reference is always there.

There are two respects in which the contact experiences of lower animal forms are inferior to those of man for the purposes of perception. The organs of manipulation are not as well adapted in form and function for manipulation itself, and, in the second place, the contact experiences of lower animals are, to a large extent, determined, not by the process of manipulation, but are so immediately a part of eating, fighting, repose, etc., that it is hard to believe that a consciousness of a "thing" can be segregated from these instinctive activities.

To develop this second point a little further, we need only to recall what has been brought out by Dewey [7] and Stout [8] that perception involves a continued control of such an organ as that of vision by such an organ as that of the hand, and vice versa. We look because we handle, and we are able to handle because we look. Attention consists in this mutual relationship of control between the processes of stimulation and response, each directing the other. But while this control is essential to perception, perception itself is neither eating, fighting, nor any other of the organic activities which commence overtly with stimulation and end with the response. On the contrary, perception lies within these activities, and represents a part of the mechanism by which these activities are carried out in highly organized forms. Perception is a process of mediation within the act; and that form of mediation by which the possible contact value of the distance stimulation appears with that stimulation, in other words, a mediation by which we are conscious of physical things. The actual eating, fighting or resting, etc., are not mediations

[7] ["The Reflex Arc Concept,"] *The Psychological Review*, III [1896], 359.

[8] *Loc. cit.*

within the act, but the culminations of the acts themselves. We could not perceive bread as a physical thing if that cognitive state grew out of the presentation of the mastication and taste which constitute eating. We perceive *what* we masticate, *what* we taste, etc., except insofar as we may perceive, through their movements, our various organs, as things.

The great importance of the human hand for perception lies in the fact that it is essentially mediatory within the organic acts out of which the physiological process of life is made up. The presentation of a physical thing which must be made up out of the contacts necessary to the actual processes of eating or those of locomotion cannot offer as fruitful a field for the growth of perception as those which are based upon the mediations of the hand within the act. And the contents of contact experience which a mouth or the paws can present must be very inadequate, for just that function of correspondence between the elements of the retinal and the tactual experience out of which the physical world of normal perception arises.

To assume that a chick can find in the contact of its bill together with those of its feet the materials that answer to the perception of a physical thing is almost inconceivable. Even the cat and the dog must find in their paws or mouths, fashioned seemingly for the purposes, not of "feeling things," but of locomotion or tearing and masticating, but a minimum of that material which goes into the structure of our perceptions. In the case of the monkey the question arises whether the function of locomotion is so dominant in use of the so-called hands that that of "feeling" can be isolated out of the monkey's contact experiences to build up perception.

Finally, to recur to the difficulties inherent in the doctrine of perception referred to at the opening of this paper, the assumption of a perception of things, that is, of what is mediatory in experience, carries with it the essence certainly of reasoning, i.e., the conscious use of something—a certain type of experience—for something else, another type of experience. Every perceived thing is insofar as perceived a recognized means to possible ends, and there can be no hard and fast line drawn between such perceptual consciousness and the more abstracted processes of so-called reasoning. Any form that perceives is insofar carrying on a process of conscious mediation within its act and conscious mediation is ratiocination.

VI

THE PHILOSOPHICAL BASIS OF ETHICS

The evolutionary point of view has had more than one important result for philosophical thought. Not the least important among these has been the conception of the evolution of evolution. Not only can we trace in the history of thought the evolution of the conception of evolution, but we find ourselves with a consciousness which we conceive of as evolved; the contents and the forms of these contents can be looked upon as the products of development. Among these contents and forms are found the temporal and spatial qualities of things, of the world. The very time process as well as the space of the universe lies in experience which is itself presented as the result of an evolution that arises in and through spatial conditions, which is first and foremost a temporal process.

The peculiarity of this situation lies in the fact that the evolution appears in the immediate findings of science. Our geological and biological sciences unhesitatingly present epochs antedating man in terms of man's consciousness, and biology and scientific psychology as unhesitatingly present that consciousness as an evolution within which all the distinctions must be explained by the same general laws as those which are appealed to to account for animal organs and functions. It is true that occasionally a scientist such as Poincaré [1] recognizes that even the number system, as well as Euclidean space, is but a construction which has arisen and maintained itself because of its practical advantages, though we can draw no conclusions from these practical advantages to their meta-

[From the *International Journal of Ethics*, XVIII (1908), 311–323.]

[1] [Henri Poincare (1854–1912), French mathematician and philosopher of science, author of *Science et méthode* (1905; English translation, 1914) and *La science et l'hypothèse* (1902; English translation, 1905).]

SELECTED WRITINGS 83

physical reality. If this position be generalized, there results the conception of an evolution within which the environment —that which our science has presented as a fixed datum in its physical nature—has been evolved as well as the form which has adapted itself to that environment; that the space within which evolution has taken place has arisen by the same laws; that the very time which makes an evolution presentable has arisen in like manner. Now, to a certain extent the conception of an evolution of environment as well as of the form has domesticated itself within our biological science. It has become evident that an environment can exist for a form only insofar as the environment answers to the susceptibilities of the organism; that the organism determines thus its own environment; that the effect of every adaptation is a new environment which must change with that which responds to it. The full recognition, however, that form and environment must be phases that answer to each other, character for character, appears in ethical theory.

In a certain sense this is found in the statement which genetic psychology makes of the development of the consciousness of the individual. Here there can be no evolution of the intelligence except insofar as the child's world answers to increased powers of conscious control. The world and the individual must keep pace with each other in the life history of the individual. But the child comes into a world which receives him as a child. The world of the adult, from the point of view of descriptive psychology, is an independent environment within which the child and his world evolve. Within the field of ethics, on the other hand, the moral individual and his world cannot consistently be presented as themselves lying inside another moral field. The growth of moral consciousness must be coterminous with that of the moral situation. The moral life lies in the interaction of these two; the situation rises up in accusation of the moral personality which is unequal to it, and the personality rises to the situation only by a process which reconstructs the situation as profoundly as it reconstructs the self. No man has found moral power within himself except insofar as he has found a meaning in his world that answered to the new-found power, or discovered a deeper ethical meaning in his environment that did not reveal new capacities for activities within himself. Moral evolution takes place then as does that of the child; the moral personality and its world must arise *pari passu,* but, unlike the psychologist's statement of the development of the child, it does not lie inside a larger determining environment.

I am not ignorant of evolutionary ethics, nor that every type of ethical theory in these days has felt itself bound to interpret the development of moral consciousness in terms of custom and institutions. Thus we seem to postulate not only a community moral consciousness, a moral world which determines the growth of the moral consciousness of the individual, but also we imply that this determining moral environment goes back into a past that antedates moral consciousness itself. From this point of view, morality, i.e., control by community habit, has determined the development of individual moral consciousness as tyrannically as the intellectual world has controlled the growth of intelligence in the members of society. But this paradox disappears when we recognize that this control by the community over its members provides indeed the material out of which reflective moral consciousness builds up its own situation, but cannot exist as a situation until the moral consciousness of the individual constructs it.

It is another statement of the same thing that moral consciousness is the most concrete consciousness—the most inclusive statement which can be given of immediate experience. There is no phase of activity, intellectual or physical, no type of inner experience, no presentation of outer reality, which does not find its place within the moral judgment. There is nothing which may not be a condition or an element of conduct, and moral consciousness reaches its climax in the estimation of every possible content of the individual and his situation. There is no other type of consciousness which must not abstract from other phases to assure its own existence. One cannot carry out an acute analysis and respond to the beauty of the object of analysis, one cannot swell with emotion and dispassionately observe. But we place every phase of our experience within the sweep of conscience; there is no one of these phases of consciousness which has not its legitimate function within the activity when viewed as moral. It is but a step further to claim that the abstractions of science and the expressions of the emotion and the direction of attention in perception and inference must find their functions, and hence their reason for existence, in the act; and that morality inheres in the act alone, but in none of these functions of the act (if I may be allowed two meanings of function in the same sentence).

It is, of course, possible to make this a metaphysical doctrine. If one finds reality in immediate experience and admits that the various intellectual, aesthetic, and perceptual processes exist only as parts and functions of an act which is the ultimate form of immediate experience, then the recognition of the ethical statement of this act as its fullest statement would found metaphysics upon ethics. The presentation of such a doctrine, however, would demand first of all a discussion of the meaning of the terms "immediate experience," of "reality," and the "cognitive state" that answers to it. I have no wish to enter this debatable field, that is loosely defined by the term "pragmatism."

There are, however, certain implications of modern ethical doctrine which fall within the lines which I have indicated above; that are of interest quite apart from their relation to metaphysical and logical speculations. The implications to which I refer are those that flow from evolutionary doctrine on the one side and from the identification of purposive activity with moral activity, and the recognition that our intelligence is through and through purposive. The first implication that flows from this position is that the fundamental necessity of moral action is simply the necessity of action at all; or stated in other terms, that the motive does not arise from the relations of antecedently given ends of activities, but rather that the motive is the recognition of the end as it arises in consciousness. The other implication is that the moral interpretation of our experience must be found within the experience itself.[2]

We are familiar with three ethical standpoints, that which finds in conscious control over action only the further development of conduct which has already unconsciously been determined by ends, that which finds conduct only where reflective thought is able to present a transcendental end, and that which recognizes conduct only where the individual and the environment—the situation—mutually determine each other. In the first case, moral necessity in conduct, for the conscious individual, is quite relative. It depends upon the degree of recognition which he reaches of the forces operating through him. Furthermore, the motive to act with reference to the end of the fullest life of the species is one which is primarily quite narrowly individualistic, and depends for a social interpretation upon the community of which the individual is a member. Moral necessity in conduct from this point of view is quite independent of the activity itself. So far from being the most fundamental reality it is a derivative by which, through what it is hard not to call a hocus-pocus, the individual acts, for what is only indirectly his own—a distant end, through a social *Dressur*.[3] It is, of course, natural that this point of view should mediate the process of training by which men are to be led unwittingly to socially worthy action, rather than the immediate conduct of the individual who finds himself face to face with a moral problem. It is the standpoint of the publicist and the reformer of social institutions.

But if we admit that the evolutionary process consists in a mutual determination of the individual and his environment —not the determination of the individual by his environment, moral necessity in conduct is found in the very evolutionary

[2] The full analysis of the position assumed here has been given by Prof. John Dewey in his article, "The Logical Conditions of a Scientific Treatment of Morality," in Vol. III of *The Decennial Publications of the University of Chicago*.

[3] ["Training" or "breaking in."]

situation. The possibility of intelligent action waits upon the determination of the conditions under which that action is to take place. The statement of these conditions becomes the end, when it is recognized that the statement is in terms of the activities that make up the personality of the individual. The content of the end is the mutuality of statement of personality, i.e., the tendencies to activity, in terms of the personalities who make up the environment, i.e., the conditions of the expression of the activities. It is because the man must recognize the public good in the exercise of his powers, and state the public good in terms of his own outgoing activities that his ends are moral. But it is not the public good which comes in from outside himself and lays a moral necessity upon him, nor is it a selfish propensity that drives him on to conduct.

It is inconceivable that such an outside end should have any but an extraneous position. It could never come into a personality except by the door of its own interest. The end could not be a social end. Nor could a purely individual propensity through the agency of community training become social. The moral necessity lies not in the end acting from without, nor in the push of inclination from within, but in the relation of the conditions of action to the impulses to action. The motive is neither a purely rational, external end, nor a private inclination, but the impulse presented in terms of its consequences over against the consequences of the other impulses. The impulse so conditioned, so interpreted, becomes a motive to conduct. The moral necessity is that all activity which appears as impulse and environment should enter into the situation, and there is nothing which ensures this completeness of expression except the full interrelationship of the self and the situation. That one fully recognized the conflict which the impulse involves in its consequences with the consequences of all the other social processes that go to make him up, is the moral dictum. From the reconstructions that this recognition involves the immediate statement of the end appears. To enforce this dictum is simply to live as fully and consciously and as determinedly as possible.

The moral necessity for education is not an ideal of intelligence that lies before us of the clear refulgence of the intellect. It is the necessity of knowledge to do what is trying to be done, the dependence of the uninformed impulse upon means, method, and interpretation. The necessity of uprightness in public affairs does not rest upon a transcendental ideal of perfection of the self, nor upon the attainment of the possible sum of human happiness, but upon the economy and effectiveness, and consistency demanded in the industrial, commercial, social, and aesthetic activities of those that make up the community. To push reform is to give expression to all these impulses and present them in their consequences over against those of all the other social impulses out of which an organism of personalities arises.

There is abroad a feeling of lack of moral force; we look before and after—to our ancestors, our posterity—for incentive to right conduct, when in fact there is no moral necessity which is not involved in the impulses to conduct themselves. To correct one abuse we must emphasize the interests it jeopardizes. There is no reservoir of moral power, except that which lies in the impulses behind these interests. To correct the sin of the individual is to awaken through the consequences of the sin the normal activities which are inhibited by the excess. It is this healthful, aggressive, moral attitude, which it seems to me is encouraged by the recognition that moral consciousness is the most concrete, the most inclusive of all. Here we must abstract from nothing, and here we cannot appeal from ourselves to a power without ourselves that makes for righteousness. In the fullness of immediate experience, with the consciousness that out of the struggle to act must arise all power to mediate action, lies salvation. In like manner evolution in moral conduct can appeal to no environment without to stamp itself upon the individual; nor to him to adapt himself to a fixed order of the universe, but environment as well as individual appears in immediate experience; the one coterminous with the other, and moral endeavor appears in the mutual determination of one by the other.

Nowhere is this point of view more needed than in the struggles which fill our industrial and commercial life. The individual is treated as if he were quite separable from his environment; and still more is the environment conceived as if it were quite independent of the individual. Both laborer and the society which employs him are exhorted to recognize their obligations to each other, while each continues to operate within its own narrow radius; and because the employer regards the labor union as a fixed external environment of his activity, and would have all the relations between laborer and employer determined by the method in which he bargains and does business, he becomes a narrow individualist; and because the laborer would determine these same relations by the methods which he has used in building up this union, he becomes a socialist. What will take that and other allied problems out of the vicious circles in which they are at present found, is the recognition that it is the incompleteness with which the different social interests are present that is responsible for the inadequacy of the moral judgments. If the community educated and housed its members properly, and protected machinery, food, market, and thoroughfares adequately, the problems at present vexing the industrial world would largely disappear. We resent the introduction of the standard of life into the question of the wages; and yet if the social activities involved in the conception of the standard of life were given full expression, the wage question would be nearly answered. Every such problem is the inevitable indication of what has been left undone, of impulses checked, or interest overlooked. We turn back to history and talk about the evolution of man as if his environment were not the projection of himself in the conditions of conduct, as if the fulfillment of the Law and the Prophets were not the realization of all that is in us. The sources of power lie in that which has been overlooked. Again and again we are surprised to find that the moral advance has not been along the straight line of the moral struggles in which a sin seemed to be faced by righteous effort, but by the appearance of a novel interest which has changed the whole nature of the problem. If we were willing to recognize that the environment which surrounds the moral self is but the statement of the conditions under which his different conflicting impulses may get their expression, we would perceive that the reorganization must come from a new point of view which comes to consciousness through the conflict. The environment must change *pari passu* with the consciousness. Moral advance consists not in adapting individual natures to the fixed realities of a moral universe, but in constantly reconstructing and recreating the world as the individuals evolve.

The second implication to which reference has been made, is that we must find the interpretation of moral consciousness within the act. The appeal to a moral order which transcends either metaphysically or temporally the moral situation; the besetting assumption of the moralist that a moral reconstruction can be made intelligible only by a perfect moral order from which we have departed, or toward which we are moving, have very grave practical consequences which it becomes us to consider. In the first place these assumptions rob our moral consciousness of the intellectual interest which belongs to them of right. If morality connotes merely conformity to a given order, our intellectual reaction is confined to the recognition of agreement and disagreement, beyond that the moral reaction can be only emotional and instinctive. There may be, indeed, intellectual processes involved in stating this moral order, but such statement is confined, in the nature of the case, to apologetic and speculative thought, to thought which cannot be a part of the immediate moral consciousness.

A moral order to which we must conform can never be built up in thought in the presence of an exigency. There are only two types of reaction in a practical situation. One may respond to well-recognized cues by well-formed habits, or one may adapt and reconstruct his habits by new interpretation of the situation. In the first instance we have habitual conduct, in the second that type of reaction which has been most explicitly worked out by the natural sciences. Most of our action, of course, falls within the first category, and involves no moral struggle. The second type, on the other hand, is that in which practically all our moral issues arise. If a practical scientific problem arises, such as the engineering problems in constructing railroads or driving tunnels, we recognize that the intellectual process by which the problem is solved cannot be a mere reference to a perfect model of conduct already in existence. On the contrary, just because the engineer is face to face with a real problem he must find in the physical situation facts of which he is at present ignorant, and at the same time readjust his habits; in fact, it is the possible readjustment of the habit that directs his attention in investigating the situation, and, on the other hand, what is discovered serves to mediate the formation of the new habit. In a word, there is the typical play of attention back and forth between perception and response. In any such process the criterion which governs the whole and its two phases—three phases if we distinguish between perception of the new data and the formation of the hypothesis by which they are interpreted and mediated in the response—can never be external to the process. There exists as yet no plan of procedure which the engineer discovers or receives as a vision in the mount. The control is found in the relation of the different phases of the act which have been sketched above. It is the possibility of reaction to a stimulus that holds the reaction in the field of investigation and it is the continued investigation of the field of stimulus which keeps the reaction continuous and pertinent. The control is then that which was earlier referred to as the process of evolution in which individual and environment mutually determine each other. It is the criterion of action, which uses working hypotheses, but which cannot possibly be identified with an external ideal. This process, whether met in the field of mechanical invention, or the range of engineering, or that of scientific research, is recognized as the most absorbing, most interesting, most fascinating intellectually with which the mind of man can occupy itself, and this interest belongs legitimately to the solution of every moral problem, for the procedure is identical intellectually.

Yet we succeed in robbing our reflective moral consciousness of a great part of this interest. For there is and can be no interest in merely identifying certain types of conduct with those found in a given theory. For example, there is no intellectual interest involved in merely identifying the control exercised by a financier over an industry with the concept of property, and justifying him in doing what he will, within the limits of the law, with his own. There may be a very vigorous emotional reaction against the suggestion that he be interfered with in these vested rights; or, on the other hand, against an institution of property which permits such individualistic exploitation of social values, but there is no intellectual interest except that which is either apologetic or purely speculative. It does not come into the moral reaction to the situation. And yet the enormous content of interest which does attach to these moral questions is attested by the social sciences which have sprung up and expanded in every college and university.

It is interesting to compare the intellectual treatment which such problems receive at the hands of the scientific investigator and the pulpit. In the latter there is at present no apparatus for investigation. The pulpit is committed to a right and wrong which are unquestioned, and from its point of view unquestionable. Its function then is not the intellectual one of finding out what in the new situation is right, but in inspiring to a right conduct which is supposed to be so plain that he who runs may read. The result has been that in the great moral issues of recent industrial history, such as the child labor, woman's labor, protection of machinery, and a multitude more, the pulpit has been necessarily silent. It had not the means nor the technique for finding out what was the right thing to do. The science of hygiene threatens the universal issue of temperance, while we can look forward to the time when investigation may enable us to approach understandingly the prostitute and her trade, and change the social conditions which have made her possible instead of merely scourging an abstract sin.

The loss to the community from the elimination of the

intellectual phase of moral conduct it would be difficult to overestimate and this loss is unavoidable as long as the interpretation of conduct lies outside the immediate experience, as long as we must refer to a moral order without, to intellectually present the morality of conduct.

In conclusion may I refer to another loss which moral conduct dependent upon an external ideal involves. The interpretation of sin and wrong with reference to a moral order external to the conduct fails to identify the moral defect with the situation out of which it springs and by whose reconstruction it may be eliminated. An illustration will at once indicate, I think, what I have in mind. The responsibility for death and accident upon our railroads cannot be laid at the doors of the system and those that work it, if an abstract doctrine of property and contract is used to judge the conduct of railroad managers and directors. The imperative necessity of the situation is that responsibility should be tested by the consequences of an act; that the moral judgment should find its criterion in the mutual determination of the individual and the situation. As it is, men who would risk their own lives to save a drowning man, regard themselves as justified in slaughtering others by the thousand to save money. Abstract valuations take the place of concrete valuations, and as the abstract external valuations are always the precipitations of earlier conduct, they are pretty uniformly inadequate.

But not only does an external moral ideal rob immediate moral conduct of its most important values, but it robs human nature of the most profound solace which can come to those who suffer—the knowledge that the loss and the suffering, with its subjective poignancy, has served to evaluate conduct, to determine what is and what is not worthwhile.

✦ VII ✦

SOCIAL PSYCHOLOGY AS COUNTERPART
TO PHYSIOLOGICAL PSYCHOLOGY

There is the widest divergence among psychologists as to the nature of Social Psychology. The most recent textbook under this title—the *Social Psychology* of Professor Ross—opens with this sentence: "Social Psychology, as the writer conceives it, studies the psychic planes and currents that come into existence among men in consequence of their association." [1] That is, it must confine itself to the "uniformities in feeling, belief, or volition—and hence in action—which are due to the interaction of human beings." Here we find a certain field of human experience cut off from the rest, because men and women influence each other within that field. There result certain uniformities from this interaction and this makes the subject-matter of the science of social psychology. In the same manner one might investigate the psychology of mountain tribes because they are subject to the influence of high altitudes and rugged landscape. Sociality is for Professor Ross no fundamental feature of human consciousness, no determining form of its structure.

In the *Social Psychology* [2] of McDougall, which appeared but a few months before the treatise we have just mentioned, human consciousness is conceived of as determined by social

[From the *Psychological Bulletin*, VI (1909), 401–408. Reprinted by permission of the American Psychological Association.]

1 [Edward Alsworth Ross, *Social Psychology; an Outline and a Source Book* (New York: The Macmillan Company, 1908), p. 1.]
2 [William McDougall, *An Introduction to Social Psychology* (London: Methuen & Co., 1908).]

94

instincts, whose study reveals sociality not as the result of interaction but as the medium within which intelligence and human emotion must arise.

If we turn to standard treatises on psychology, we find the social aspect of human consciousness dealt with in very varying fashion. Royce, both in his psychology and in the volume, *Studies of Good and Evil*,[3] makes out of the consciousness of one self over against other selves the source of all reflection. Thought, according to Professor Royce, in its dependence upon symbolic means of expression, has arisen out of intercourse, and presupposes, not only in the forms of language, but in the meanings of language, social consciousness. Only through imitation and opposition to others could one's own conduct and expression gain any meaning for one's self, not to speak of the interpretation of the conduct of others through one's own imitative responses to their acts. Here we stand upon the familiar ground of Professor Baldwin's studies of social consciousness.[4] The *ego* and the *socius* are inseparable, and the medium of alternative differentiation and identification is imitation. But from the point of view of their psychological treatises we feel that these writers have said too much or too little of the form of sociality. If we turn to the structural psychologists we find the social aspect of consciousness appearing only as one of the results of certain features of our affective nature and its bodily organism. The self arises in the individual consciousness through apperceptive organization and enters into relation with other selves to whom it

3 [Josiah Royce, *Studies of Good and Evil; a Series of Essays upon Problems of Philosophy and of Life* (New York: D. Appleton and Company, 1898). See especially Essay VIII, "Self-Consciousness, Social Consciousness and Nature," pp. 198–248.]

4 [James Mark Baldwin (1861–1934), American psychologist and philosopher, compiler of the *Dictionary of Philosophy and Psychology* (1901–1906) and editor of *The Psychological Review* (1894–1909). Baldwin is remembered for his genetic theories of consciousness and of reality. On the point made by Mead, see J. M. Baldwin, *Mental Development in the Child and the Race, Methods and Processes* (3rd edn. rev.; New York and London: The Macmillan Company, 1906), pp. 321–322.]

is adapted by organic structure. In Professor James's treatise the self is brilliantly dealt with in a chapter by itself.[5] Within that chapter we see that, as a self, it is completely knit into a social consciousness, that the diameter of the self waxes and wanes with the field of social activity, but what the value of this nature of the self is for the cognitive and emotional phases of consciousness we do not discover. In the genetic treatment given by Professor Angell, the last chapter deals with the self.[6] Here indeed we feel the form of sociality is the culmination, and the treatment of attention, of the impulses, and the emotions, and finally of volition involves so definitely a social organization of consciousness, that in the light of the last chapter the reader feels that a rereading would give a new meaning to what has gone before. If we except Professor Cooley, in his *Human Nature and the Social Order*,[7] and his *Social Organization*,[8] the sociologists have no adequate social psychology with which to interpret their own science. The modern sociologists neither abjure psychology with Comte,[9] nor determine what the value of the social character of human consciousness is for the psychology which they attempt to use.

To repeat the points of view we have noted, some see in social consciousness nothing but uniformities in conduct and feeling that result from the interaction of men and women, others recognize a consciousness that is organized through social instincts, others still find in the medium of communica-

5 [William James, *The Principles of Psychology*, Vol. I, chap. 10.]

6 [James Rowland Angell, *Psychology; an Introductory Study of the Structure and Function of Human Consciousness* (4th edn. rev.; New York: Henry Holt and Co., 1908), chap. 23, pp. 440–457.]

7 [Charles Horton Cooley, *Human Nature and the Social Order* (New York: C. Scribner's Sons, 1902; rev. edn., 1922).]

8 [*Social Organization; a Study of the Larger Mind* (New York: C. Scribner's Sons, 1909).]

9 [Auguste Comte (1798–1857), French philosopher and sociologist who founded positivism. Comte's classification of the sciences in his *Cours de philosophie positive* (1830–1842; English translation, 1853) excludes psychology, moving directly from biology to sociology.]

tion and the thought that depends upon it, a social origin for reflective consciousness itself, still others find the social aspect of human nature to be only the product of an already organized intelligence responding to certain social impulses, while others find that an organized intelligence in the form of a self could arise only over against other selves that must exist in consciousness as immediately as the subject self, still others are content to recognize necessary social conditions in the genesis of volition and the self that expresses itself in volition.

Now it is evident that we cannot take both positions. We cannot assume that the self is both a product and a presupposition of human consciousness, that reflection has arisen through social consciousness and that social intercourse has arisen because human individuals had ideas and meanings to express.

I desire to call attention to the implications for psychology of the positions defended by McDougall, by Royce and Baldwin respectively, if they are consistently maintained. The positions I have in mind are the following: that human nature is endowed with and organized by social instincts and impulses; that the consciousness of meaning has arisen through social intercommunication; and finally that the *ego,* the self, that is implied in every act, in every volition, with reference to which our primary judgments of valuation are made, must exist in a social consciousness within which the *socii,* the other selves, are as immediately given as is the subject self.

McDougall lists eleven human instincts: flight, repulsion, curiosity, pugnacity, subjection, self-display, the parental instinct, the instinct of reproduction, the gregarious instinct, the instinct of acquisition, and the instinct of construction. Six of these are social, without question: pugnacity, subjection, self-display, the parental instinct, the instinct of reproduction, and the gregarious instinct. These would probably be the instincts most widely accepted by those who are willing to accept human instincts at all. Four of the others, repulsion, curiosity, acquisition, and construction, would be questionable, or conceivably to be resolved into other instincts. The fact is that McDougall has his doctrine of instincts so essentially bound up with a doctrine of emotions and sentiments that he is evidently forced to somewhat strain his table of instincts to get in the proper number of corresponding emotions. But the fact that is of moment is that the psychologist who recognizes instincts and impulses will find among them a preponderating number that are social. By a social instinct is meant a well-defined tendency to act under the stimulation of another individual of the same species. If self-conscious conduct arises out of controlled and organized impulse, and impulses arise out of social instincts, and the responses to these social stimulations become stimuli to corresponding social acts on the part of others, it is evident that human conduct was from the beginning of its development in a social medium. The implication is highly important for its bearing upon the theory of imitation, which, as is indicated above, plays a great part in current social psychology.

There are two implications of the theory that important social instincts lie behind developed human consciousness—two to which I wish to call attention. The first is that any such group of instincts inevitably provides the content and the form of a group of social objects. An instinct implies first of all a certain type of stimulus to which the organism is attuned. This sensuous content will attract the attention of the individual to the exclusion of other stimuli. And the organism will respond to it by a certain attitude that represents the group of responses for which such an instinct is responsible. These two are the characteristics of an object in our consciousness—a content toward which the individual is susceptible as a stimulus, and an attitude of response toward this peculiar type of content. In our consciousness of this sensuous content and of our attitude toward it we have both the content of the object as a thing and the meaning of it, both the perception and the concept of it, at least implicit in the experience. The implication of an organized group of social instincts is the implicit presence in undeveloped human consciousness of both the matter and the form of a social object.

The second implication has to do with the theory of imitation. Social instincts imply that certain attitudes and movements of one form are stimuli in other forms to certain types of response. In the instinct of fighting these responses will be of one sort, in that of parental care another. The responses will be adapted to the stimulus and may vary from it or may approach it in its own form or outward appearance. It may be that, as in the case of the gregarious instinct, the action of one form may be a stimulus to the other to do the same thing—to the member of the herd, for example, to run away in the direction in which another member of the herd is running. We have no evidence that such a reaction is any more an imitation than if the instinctive response were that of running away from an enemy which threatened the animal. Furthermore, a group of well organized social instincts will frequently lead one form to place another under the influence of the same stimuli which are affecting it. Thus a parent form, taking a young form with it in its own hunting, subjects the instincts which the child form has inherited to the same stimuli as those which arouse the hunting reaction in the parent form. In various ways it is possible that the action of one form should serve directly or indirectly to mobilize a similar instinct in another form where there is no more question of imitation than there is in the case in which the action of one form calls out, for the protection of life, a diametrically opposite reaction. Another phase of the matter is also of importance for the interpretation of the so-called imitative processes, in lower animal forms and in the conduct of young children. I refer to what Professor Baldwin has been pleased to call the circular reaction, the instance in which, in his terminology, the individual imitates himself. One illustration of this, that of mastication, which sets free the stimuli which again arouse the masticating reflexes, is a purely mechanical circle, similar to that which is responsible for the rhythmical processes of walking, but which has no important likeness to such processes as that of learning to talk. In the latter experiences the child repeats continually a sound which

he has mastered, perhaps without being perceptibly influenced by the sounds about him—the da-da-da, the ma-ma-ma,
of the earliest articulation. Here we have the child producing
the stimulus which in a socially organized human animal
calls for a response of another articulation. We see the same
thing probably in a bird's insistent repetition of its own notes.
The child is making the first uncertain efforts to speak—in this
case to himself, that is, in response to an articulate sound
which operates as a stimulus upon his auditory apparatus as
inevitably as if the sound were made by another. The bird is
responding to the note he sings himself as definitely as if he
responded to a note uttered by another bird. In neither case
is there any evidence that the sound which is the stimulus
operates by its quality to induce the child or the bird to produce a sound which shall be like that which is heard. Under
the influence of social instincts, animals and young children
or primitive peoples may be stimulated to many reactions
which are like those which directly or indirectly are responsible for them without there being any justification for the
assumption that the process is one of imitation—in any sense
which is connoted by that term in our own consciousness.
When another self is present in consciousness doing something, then such a self may be imitated by the self that is conscious of him in his conduct, but by what possible mechanism,
short of a miracle, the conduct of one form should act as a
stimulus to another to do, not what the situation calls for,
but something like that which the first form is doing, is beyond ordinary comprehension. Imitation becomes comprehensible when there is a consciousness of other selves, and not
before. However, an organization of social instincts gives rise
to many situations which have the outward appearance of
imitation, but these situations—those in which, under the influence of social stimulation, one form does what others are
doing—are no more responsible for the appearance in consciousness of other selves that answer to our own than are the
situations which call out different and even opposed reactions. Social consciousness is the presupposition of imitation,

and when Professor Royce, both in the eighth chapter of *Studies of Good and Evil,* and in the twelfth chapter of his *Outlines of Psychology* [10] makes imitation the means of getting the meaning of what others and we ourselves are doing, he seems to be either putting the cart before the horse, or else to be saying that the ideas which we have of the actions of others are ideomotor in their character, but this does not make out of imitation the means of their becoming ideomotor. The sight of a man pushing a stone registers itself as a meaning through a tendency in ourselves to push the stone, but it is a far call from this to the statement that it is first through imitation of him or some one else pushing stones that we have gained the motor-idea of stone-pushing.

The important character of social organization of conduct or behavior through instincts is not that one form in a social group does what the others do, but that the conduct of one form is a stimulus to another to a certain act, and that this act again becomes a stimulus at first to a certain reaction, and so on in ceaseless interaction. The likeness of the actions is of minimal importance compared with the fact that the actions of one form have the implicit meaning of a certain response to another form. The probable beginning of human communication was in cooperation, not in imitation, where conduct differed and yet where the act of the one answered to and called out the act of the other. The conception of imitation as it has functioned in social psychology needs to be developed into a theory of social stimulation and response and of the social situations which these stimulations and responses create. Here we have the matter and the form of the social object, and here we have also the medium of communication and reflection.

The second position to which I wish to call attention, and whose implications I wish to discuss, is that the consciousness of meaning is social in its origin. The dominant theory at

[10] [Josiah Royce, *Outlines of Psychology; an Elementary Treatise with Some Practical Applications* (New York: The Macmillan Company, 1903), chap. 12, pp. 274–298.]

present, that which is most elaborately stated by Wundt in the first volume of his *Völkerpsychologie*,[11] regards language as the outgrowth of gesture, the vocal gesture. As a gesture, it is primarily an expression of emotion. But the gesture itself is a syncopated act, one that has been cut short, a torso which conveys the emotional import of the act. Out of the emotional signification has grown the intellectual signification. It is evident that but for the original situation of social interaction the bodily and vocal gestures could never have attained their signification. It is their reference to other individuals that has turned expression, as a mere outflow of nervous excitement, into meaning, and this meaning was the value of the act for the other individual, and his response to the expression of the emotion, in terms of another syncopated act, with its social signification, gave the first basis for communication, for common understanding, for the recognition of the attitudes which men mutually held toward each other within a field of social interaction. Attitudes had meanings when they reflected possible acts. And the acts could have meanings when they called out definite reactions which call out still other appropriate responses; that is, when the common content of the act is reflected by the different parts played by individuals, through gestures—truncated acts. Here is the birth of the symbol, and the possibility of thought. Still, thought remains in its abstractest form sublimated conversation. Thus reflective consciousness implies a social situation which has been its precondition. Antecedent to the reflective consciousness within which we exist, in the beginnings of the society of men and in the life of every child that arises to reflective consciousness, there must have been this condition of interrelation by acts springing from social instincts.

Finally, Professor Baldwin has abundantly exemplified the interdependence of the *ego* and the *socius*, of the self and the other. It is still truer to say the self and the *others*, the *ego*

11 [Wilhelm Max Wundt, *Völkerpsychologie; Eine Untersuchung der Entwicklungsgesetze von Sprache, Mythus und Sitte*, 2 vols. (Leipzig: W. Engelmann, 1900–1909).]

and the *socii*. If the self-form is an essential form of all our consciousness it necessarily carries with it the other-form. Whatever may be the metaphysical impossibilities or possibilities of solipsism, psychologically it is nonexistent. There must be other selves if one's own is to exist. Psychological analysis, retrospection, and the study of children and primitive people give no inkling of situations in which a self could have existed in consciousness except as the counterpart of other selves. We even can recognize that in the definition of these selves in consciousness, the child and primitive man have defined the outlines and the character of the others earlier than they have defined their own selves. We may fairly say a social group is an implication of the structure of the only consciousness that we know.

If these positions are correct it is evident that we must be as much beholden to social science to present and analyze the social group with its objects, its interrelations, its selves, as a precondition of our reflective and self-consciousness, as we are beholden to physiological science to present and analyze the physical complex which is the precondition of our physical consciousness. In other words, a social psychology should be the counterpart of physiological psychology. In each case the conditions under which certain phases of consciousness arise must be studied by other sciences, because the consciousness which the psychologist analyzes presupposes objects and processes which are preconditions of itself and its processes. It is true that our reflection can sweep the very physical and social objects which the physical and social sciences have presented within itself, and regard them as psychical presentations. But in doing this it is presupposing another brain that conditions its action, and whose defection would bring collapse to the very thought that reduced the brain to states of consciousness. In the same manner we may wipe the *alteri* [12] out of existence and reduce our social world to our individual selves, regarding the others as constructions of our own, but we can only do it to some other audience with whom our

[12] ["Others."]

thought holds converse, even if this self is only the I and the Me of actual thought, but behind these protagonists stand the chorus of others to whom we rehearse our reasonings by word of mouth or through the printed page.

The evolutionary social science which shall describe and explain the origins of human society, and the social sciences which shall finally determine what are the laws of social growth and organization, will be as essential for determining the objective conditions of social consciousness, as the biological sciences are to determine the conditions of consciousness in the biological world. By no possibility can psychology deal with the material with which physiology and the social sciences deal, because the consciousness of psychological science arises within a physical and a social world that are presuppositions of itself. From a logical point of view a social psychology is strictly parallel to a physiological psychology.

⚶⚶ VIII ⚶⚶

WHAT SOCIAL OBJECTS MUST PSYCHOLOGY PRESUPPOSE?

There is a persistent tendency among present-day psychologists to use consciousness as the older rationalistic psychology used the soul. It is spoken of as something that appears at a certain point, it is a something into which the object of knowledge in some sense enters from without. It is conceived to have certain functions—in the place of faculties. It is as completely separated from the physical body by the doctrine of parallelism as the metaphysical body was separated from the metaphysical soul by their opposite qualities.

Functional psychology has set itself the program of assimilating the purposive character of conscious processes—or of consciousness as it is termed—to the evolutionary conception of adaptation, but instead of making consciousness in human individuals a particular expression of a great process, as is demanded of a philosophy of nature, it comes in generally as a new and peculiar factor which even demands a new formula of evolution for its explanation; it involves a new evolution superinduced upon the old.

In spite of much philosophizing, consciousness is identified in current psychological practice with the field which is open to introspection, and the object of knowledge is placed within this field, and related to the physical world—spoken of as an external field of reality—by a parallelistic series. This psychological practice tends to accept the conceptual objects of science, the atoms, molecules, ether vortex rings, ions, and elec-

Given at the meeting of the Psychological Association in Boston, December 31, 1909. [From *The Journal of Philosophy, Psychology, and Scientific Methods*, VII (1910), 174–180. Reprinted by permission of *The Journal of Philosophy*.]

trons, as the substantial realities of the physical world, and, by implication at least, to relegate the sensuous content of objects of direct physical experience to this separate field of consciousness. The old-fashioned idealist has then only to point out the thought structure of these hypothetical objects of science to sweep triumphantly, with one stroke of his wand, the whole world of nature within this limited field of the consciousness open to introspection. Whereupon the solipsistic spook arises again to reduce one's world to a nutshell.

The way out of these crude psychological conceptions, in my mind, lies in the recognition that psychical consciousness is a particular phase in development of reality, not an islanded phase of reality connected with the rest of it by a one to one relationship of parallel series. This point of view I have elsewhere developed somewhat obscurely and inffectually, I am afraid.[1]

What I wish to call to your attention in the few moments at my disposal, is another phase of this situation which is itself psychological in its character;[2] the presupposition of selves as already in existence before the peculiar phase of consciousness can arise, which psychology studies.

Most of us admit the reality of the objects of direct physical experience until we are too deeply entangled in our psychological analyses of cognition. Unless we subject ourselves to the third degree of criticism, the parallelism of which we speak lies between the processes of brain tissues which can be seen and smelt and handled and the states of consciousness which are conditioned by them. While this admission guarantees the physical bodies of our fellows as equally real, the self is relegated to the restricted field of introspected consciousness and enjoys not the reality of a so-called external object, but only

[1] "The Definition of the Psychical," *The University of Chicago Decennial Publications*. [Essay III in the present volume.]

[2] I have discussed the implications of this position from a somewhat different point of view in the *Psychological Bulletin*, Vol. VI, No. 12, December 15, 1909. [Essay VII in the present volume: "Social Psychology as Counterpart to Physiological Psychology."]

that of a combination of states of consciousness. Into the existence of those states of consciousness in another, we are solemnly told we can only inferentially enter by a process of analogy from the relations of our own introspected states and the movements of our bodies to the movements of other bodies and the hypothetical conscious states that should accompany them. If we approach the self from within, our analysis recognizes, to be sure, its close relationship to, if not its identity with, the organization of consciousness, especially as seen in conation, in apperception, in voluntary attention, in conduct, but what can be isolated as self-consciousness as such reduces to a peculiar feeling of intimacy in certain conscious states, and the self gathers, for some unexplained reason, about a core of certain vague and seemingly unimportant organic sensations—a feeling of contraction in the brow, or in the throat, or goes out to the muscular innervations all over the body which are not involved directly in what we are doing or perceiving. And yet when we proceed introspectively the whole field of consciousness is ascribed to this self, for it is only insofar as we are self-conscious that we can introspect at all.

But what I wish to emphasize is that the other selves disappear as given realities even when we are willing to admit the real objects of physical experience. The self arises within the introspected field. It has no existence outside that introspected field, and other selves are only projects and ejects of that field. Each self is an island, and each self is sure only of its own island, for who knows what mirages may arise above this analogical sea.

It is fair to assume that if we had exact social sciences which could define persons precisely and determine the laws of social change with mathematical exactness, we should accept selves, as there, in the same sense in which we accept physical objects. They would be guaranteed by their sciences. For in the practice of thought, we are as convinced as the Greeks that exact knowledge assures the existence of the object of knowledge.

It is evident that the assumption of the self as given by social science in advance of introspection would materially and fundamentally affect our psychological practice. Consciousness as present in selves would be given as there, outside the field of introspection. Psychological science would have to presuppose selves as the precondition of consciousness in individuals just as it presupposes nervous systems and vascular changes. In actual psychological analysis we should condition the existence and process of states and streams of consciousness upon the normal presence and functioning of these selves, as we condition the appearance and functioning of consciousness upon the normal structure and operation of the physical mechanism, that our psychology presupposes.

In a manner we do this in treatises on mob psychology, in such a treatise on social psychology as that of Cooley's *Human Nature and the Social Order*. McDougall's [*Introduction to*] *Social Psychology* prepares the way for it in carrying back the processes of consciousness to social impulses and instincts—to those terms in which, somewhat vaguely, selves are stated in an evolutionary theory of society.

The economic man of the dismal science was an attempt to state the self in terms of an objective and exact social science. But fortunately the economic man has proved spurious. He does not exist. The economic man is as little guaranteed by the orthodox political economy, as *realia* were by the metaphysics of scholasticism.

Social science in anthropology, in sociology pure and impure, dynamic and static, has not as yet found its scientific method. It is not able to satisfactorily define its objects, nor to formulate their laws of change and development. Until the social sciences are able to state the social individual in terms of social processes, as the physical sciences define their objects in terms of physical change, they will not have risen to the point at which they can force their object upon an introspective psychology. We can today foresee the possibility of this. Eugenics, education, even political and economic sciences, pass beyond the phase of description and look toward the formation of the social object. We recognize that we control the conditions which determine the individual. His errors and shortcomings can be conceivably corrected. His misery may be eliminated. His mental and moral defects corrected. His heredity, social and physical, may be perfected. His very moral self-consciousness through normal and healthful social conduct, through adequate consciousness of his relations to others, may be constituted and established. But without awaiting the development of the social sciences it is possible to indicate in the nature of the consciousness which psychology itself analyzes, the presuppostion of social objects, whose objective reality is a condition of the consciousness of self.

The contribution that I wish to suggest toward the recognition of the given character of other selves is from psychology itself, and arises out of the psychological theory of the origin of language and its relation to meaning.

This theory, as you know, has been considerably advanced by Wundt's formulation of the relation of language to gesture. From this point of view language in its earliest form comes under that group of movements which, since Darwin, have been called expressions of the emotions. They fall into classes which have been regarded as without essential connection. Either they are elements—mainly preparatory—beginnings of acts—social acts, i.e., actions and reactions which arise under the stimulation of other individuals, such as clenching the fists, grinding the teeth, assuming an attitude of defense—or else they are regarded as outflows of nervous energy which sluice off the nervous excitement or reinforce and prepare indirectly for action. Such gestures, if we may use the term in this generalized sense, act as stimuli to other forms which are already under social stimulation.

The phase of the subject which has not been sufficiently emphasized is the value which these truncated acts, these beginnings of inhibited movements, these gestures, have as appropriate stimulations for the conduct of other individuals. Inevitably, forms that act and react to and upon each other come to prepare for each other's reaction by the early movements in the act. The preliminaries of a dog or cock fight amply illustrate the sensitiveness of such individuals to the earliest perceptible indications of coming acts. To a large degree forms, which live in groups or in the relation of the animals of prey and those they prey upon, act upon these first signs of oncoming acts. All gestures, to whatever class they belong, whether they are the beginnings of the outgoing act itself or are only indications of the attitude and nervous tension which these acts involve, have this value of stimulating forms, socially organized, to reactions appropriate to the attack, or flight, or wooing, or suckling, of another form. Illustrations are to be found in human conduct, in such situations as fencing, where one combatant without reflection makes his parry from the direction of the eye and the infinitesimal change of attitude which are the prelude to the thrust.

Gestures then are already significant in the sense that they are stimuli to performed reactions, before they come to have significance of conscious meaning. Allow me to emphasize further the value of attitudes and the indications of organized preparation for conduct, especially in the change of the muscles of the countenance, the altered breathing, the quivering of tense muscles, the evidence of circulatory changes, in such minutely adapted social groups, because among these socially significant innervations will be found all these queer organic sensations about which the consciousness of the self is supposed to gather as a core.

Human conduct is distinguished primarily from animal conduct by that increase in inhibition which is an essential phase of voluntary attention, and increased inhibition means an increase in gesture in the signs of activities which are not carried out; in the assumptions of attitudes whose values in conduct fail to get complete expression. If we recognize language as a differentiation of gesture, the conduct of no other form can compare with that of man in the abundance of gesture.

The fundamental importance of gesture lies in the development of the consciousness of meaning—in reflective consciousness. As long as one individual responds simply to the gesture of another by the appropriate response, there is no necessary consciousness of meaning. The situation is still on a level of that of two growling dogs walking around each other, with tense limbs, bristly hair, and uncovered teeth. It is not until an image arises of the response, which the gesture of one form will bring out in another, that a consciousness of meaning can attach to his own gesture. The meaning can appear only in imaging the consequence of the gesture. To cry out in fear is an immediate instinctive act, but to scream with an image of another individual turning an attentive ear, taking on a sympathetic expression and an attitude of coming to help, is at least a favorable condition for the development of a consciousness of meaning.

Of course the mere influence of the image, stimulating to reaction, has no more meaning value than the effect of an external stimulus, but in this converse of gestures there is also a consciousness of attitude, of readiness to act in the manner which the gesture implies. In the instance given the cry is part of the attitude of flight. The cry calls out the image of a friendly individual. This image is not merely a stimulus to run toward the friend, but is merged in the consciousness of inhibited flight. If meaning is consciousness of attitude, as Dewey, Royce, and Angell among others maintain, then consciousness of meaning arose only when some gesture that was part of an inhibited act itself called up the image of the gesture of another individual. Then the image of the gesture means the inhibited act to which the first gesture belonged. In a word, the response to the cry has the meaning of inhibited flight.

One's own gestures could not take on meaning directly. The gestures aroused by them in others would be that upon which attention is centered. And these gestures become identified with the content of one's own emotion and attitude. It is only through the response that consciousness of meaning appears, a response which involves the consciousness of another self as the presupposition of the meaning in one's own attitude. Other selves in a social environment logically antedate the consciousness of self which introspection analyzes. They must be admitted as there, as given, in the same sense in which psychology accepts the given reality of physical organisms as a condition of individual consciousness.

The importance for psychology of this recognition of others, if thus bound up with the psychology of meaning, may need another word of emphasis. Consciousness could no longer be regarded as an island to be studied through parallel relations with neuroses. It would be approached as experience which is socially as well as physically determined. Introspective self-consciousness would be recognized as a subjective phase, and this subjective phase could no longer be regarded as the source out of which the experience arose. Objective consciousness of selves must precede subjective consciousness, and must continually condition it, if consciousness of meaning itself presupposes the selves as there. Subjective self-consciousness must appear *within* experience, must have a function in the development of that experience, and must be studied from the point of view of that function, not as that in which self-consciousness arises and by which through analogical bridges and self-projections we slowly construct a hypothetically objective social world in which to live. Furthermore, meaning in the light of this recognition has its reference not to agglomerations of states of subjective consciousness, but to objects in a socially conditioned experience. When in the process revealed by introspection we reach the concept of self, we have attained an attitude which we assume not toward our inner feelings, but toward other individuals whose reality was implied even in the inhibitions and reorganizations which characterize this inner consciousness.

If we may assume, then, that meaning is consciousness of attitude, I would challenge any one to show an adequate motive for directing attention toward one's attitudes, in a consciousness of things that were merely physical; neither control over sense-perception nor over response would be directly forwarded by attention directed toward a consciousness of readiness to act in a given situation. It is only in the social situation of converse that these gestures, and the attitudes they express could become the object of attention and interest. Whatever our theory may be as to the history of things, social consciousness must antedate physical consciousness. A more correct statement would be that experience in its original form became reflective in the recognition of selves, and only gradually was there differentiated a reflective experience of things which were purely physical.

IX

THE PSYCHOLOGY OF SOCIAL CONSCIOUSNESS IMPLIED IN INSTRUCTION

I have been asked to present the social situation in the school as the subject of a possible scientific study and control.

The same situation among primitive people is scientifically studied by the sociologist (folk-psychologist). He notes two methods in the process of primitive education. The first is generally described as that of play and imitation. The impulses of the children find their expression in play, and play describes the attitude of the child's consciousness. Imitation defines the form of unconscious social control exercised by the community over the expression of childish impulse.

In the long ceremonies of initiation education assumed a more conscious and almost deliberate form. The boy was inducted into the clan mysteries, into the mythology and social procedure of the community, under an emotional tension which was skillfully aroused and maintained. He was subjected to tests of endurance which were calculated not only to fullfil this purpose, but also to identify the ends and interests of the individual with those of the social group. These more general purposes of the initiatory ceremonies were also at times cunningly adapted to enhance the authority of the medicine man or the control over food and women by the older men in the community.

Whatever opinion one may hold of the interpretation which folk-psychology and anthropology have given of this early phase of education, no one would deny, I imagine, the possi-

Read before Section L—Education. American Association for the Advancement of Science, Boston, December 1909. [From *Science*, XXXI (1910), 688–693. Reprinted by permission.]

bility of studying the education of the savage child scientifically, nor that this would be a psychological study. Imitation,
play, emotional tensions favoring the acquirement of clan
myths and cults, and the formation of clan judgments of evaluation, these must be all interpreted and formulated by some
form of psychology. The particular form which has dealt with
these phenomena and processes is social psychology. The important features of the situation would be found not in the
structure of the idea to be assimilated considered as material
of instruction for any child, nor in the lines of association
which would guarantee their abiding in consciousness. They
would be found in the impulse of the children expressed in
play, in the tendency of the children to put themselves in the
place of the men and women of the group, i.e., to imitate
them in the emotions which consciousness of themselves in
their relationship to others evoke, and in the import for the
boy which the ideas and cults would have when surcharged
with such emotions.

If we turn to our system of education we find that the materials of the curriculum have been presented as percepts
capable of being assimilated by the nature of their content to
other contents in consciousness, and the manner has been indicated in which this material can be most favorably prepared
for such assimilation. This type of psychological treatment of
material and the lesson is recognized at once as Herbartian.[1]
It is an associational type of psychology. Its critics add that it
is intellectualistic. In any case it is not a social psychology,
for the child is not primarily considered as a self among other
selves, but as an *Apperceptionsmasse*.[2] The child's relations to

[1] [Johann Friedrich Herbart (1776–1841) was a German philosopher
and educator, the author of several works which, translated into English,
exerted considerable influence upon educational theories in the United
States during the late nineteenth and early twentieth centuries. See J. F.
Herbart, *The Science of Education*, translated with a biographical introduction by Henry M. and Emmie Felkin (Boston: Heath and Co., 1891).]

[2] [*Apperceptionsmasse* is a German technical philosophical term meaning "a mass of presentations." In the article on "apperception" in the
Dictionary of Philosophy and Psychology (New York: The Macmillan

the other members of the group, to which he belongs, have no immediate bearing on the material nor on the learning of it. The banishment from the traditional school work of play and of any adult activities in which the child could have a part as a child, i.e., the banishment of processes in which the child can be conscious of himself in relation to others, means that the process of learning has as little social content as possible.

An explanation of the different attitudes in the training of the child in the primitive and in the modern civilized communities is found, in part, in the division of labor between the school on the one side, and the home and the shop or the farm on the other. The business of storing the mind with ideas, both materials and methods, has been assigned to the school. The task of organizing and socializing the self to which these materials and methods belong is left to the home and the industry or profession, to the playground, the street and society in general. A great deal of modern educational literature turns upon the fallacy of this division of labor. The earlier vogue of manual training and the domestic arts before the frank recognition of their relation to industrial training took place, was due in no small part to the attempt to introduce those interests of the child's into the field of his instruction which gathers about a socially constituted self, to admit the child's personality as a whole into the school.

I think we should be prepared to admit the implication of this educational movement—that however abstract the material is which is presented and however abstracted its ultimate use is from the immediate activities of the child, the situation implied in instruction and in the psychology of that instruction is a social situation; that it is impossible to fully interpret or control the process of instruction without recognizing the child as a self and viewing his conscious processes from

---

Company, 1911), II, 61, J. M. Baldwin and G. F. Stout wrote: "The treatment of apperception by Herbart forms a turning-point in the history of the subject. Apperception, for him, is the process by which a mass of presentations (*Apperceptionsmasse*) assimilates relatively new elements, the whole forming a system (*Apperceptionssystem*)."]

the point of view of their relation in his consciousness to his self, among other selves.

In the first place, back of all instruction lies the relation of the child to the teacher and about it lie the relations of the child to the other children in the schoolroom and on the playground. It is, however, of interest to note that so far as the material of instruction is concerned an ideal situation has been conceived to be one in which the personality of the teacher disappears as completely as possible behind the process of learning. In the actual process of instruction the emphasis upon the relation of pupil and teacher in the consciousness of the child has been felt to be unfortunate. In like manner the instinctive social relations between the children in school hours is repressed. In the process of memorizing and reciting a lesson, or working out a problem in arithmetic a vivid consciousness of the personality of the teacher in his relationship to that of the child would imply either that the teacher was obliged to exercise discipline to carry on the process of instruction, and this must in the nature of the case constitute friction and division of attention, or else that the child's interest is distracted from the subject-matter of the lesson, to something in which the personality of the teacher and pupil might find some other content; for even a teacher's approval and a child's delight therein has no essential relation to the mere subject-matter of arithmetic or English. It certainly has no such relationship as that implied in apprenticeship, in the boy's helping on the farm or the girl's helping in the housekeeping, has no such relationship as that of members of an athletic team to each other. In these latter instances the vivid consciousness of the self of the child and of his master, of the parents whom he helps and of the associates with whom he plays is part of the child's consciousness of what he is doing, and his consciousness of these personal relationships involves no division of attention. Now it had been a part of the fallacy of an intellectualistic pedagogy that a divided attention was necessary to insure application of attention—that the rewards, and especially the punishments, of the school hung before the child's mind to catch the attention that was wandering from the task, and through their associations with the schoolwork to bring it back to the task. This involves a continual vibration of attention on the part of the average child between the task and the sanctions of school discipline. It is only the psychology of school discipline that is social. The pains and penalties, the pleasures of success in competition, of favorable mention of all sorts implies vivid self-consciousness. It is evident that advantage would follow from making the consciousness of self or selves which is the life of the child's play—on its competition or cooperation—have as essential a place in instruction. To use Professor Dewey's phrase, instruction should be an interchange of experience in which the child brings his experience to be interpreted by the experience of the parent or teacher. This recognizes that education is interchange of ideas, is conversation—belongs to a universe of discourse. If the lesson is simply set for the child—is not his own problem— the recognition of himself as facing a task and a taskmaster is no part of the solution of the problem. But a difficulty which the child feels and brings to his parent or teacher for solution is helped on toward interpretation by the consciousness of the child's relation to his pastors and masters. Just insofar as the subject-matter of instruction can be brought into the form of problems arising in the experience of the child—just so far will the relation of the child to the instructor become a part of the natural solution of the problem—actual success of a teacher depends in large measure upon this capacity to state the subject-matter of instruction in terms of the experience of the children. The recognition of the value of industrial and vocational training comes back at once to this, that what the child has to learn is what he wants to acquire, to become the man. Under these conditions instruction takes on frankly the form of conversation, as much sought by the pupil as the instructor.

I take it therefore to be a scientific task to which education should set itself that of making the subject-matter of its instruction the material of personal intercourse between pupils and instructors, and between the children themselves. The substitution of the converse of concrete individuals for the pale abstractions of thought.

To a large extent our school organization reserves the use of the personal relation between teacher and taught for the negative side, for the prohibitions. The lack of interest in the personal content of the lesson is in fact startling when one considers that it is the personal form in which the instruction should be given. The best illustration of this lack of interest we find in the problems which disgrace our arithmetics. They are supposed matters of converse, but their content is so bare, their abstractions so raggedly covered with the form of questions about such marketing and shopping and building as never were on sea or land, that one sees that the social form of instruction is a form only for the writer of the arithmetic. When further we consider how utterly inadequate the teaching force of our public schools is to transform this matter into concrete experience of the children or even into their own experience, the hopelessness of the situation is overwhelming. Ostwald has written a textbook of chemistry for the secondary school which has done what every textbook should do.[3] It is not only that the material shows real respect for the intelligence of the student, but it is so organized that the development of the subject-matter is in reality the action and reaction of one mind upon another mind. The dictum of the Platonic Socrates,[4] that one must follow the argument where it leads in the dialogue, should be the motto of the writer of textbooks.

It has been indicated already that language being essentially in its nature thinking with the child is rendered con-

[3] [Wilhelm Ostwald, *The Fundamental Principles of Chemistry; an Introduction to All Text-books of Chemistry*, translated by Harry W. Morse (New York: Longmans, Green and Co., 1909).]

[4] [Socrates (*ca.* 470–399 B.C.), Athenian philosopher who was martyred for philosophy. Socrates' most famous pupil, Plato, built his dialogues around the Socratic dialectic, with Socrates usually playing the role of the central character.]

crete by taking on the form of conversation. It has been also indicated that this can take place only when the thought has reference to a real problem in the experience of the child. The further demand for control over attention carries us back to the conditions of attention. Here again we find that traditional school practice depends upon social consciousness for bringing the wandering attention back to the task, when it finds that the subjective conditions of attention to the material of instruction are lacking, and even attempts to carry over a formal self-consciousness into attention, when through the sense of duty the pupil is called upon to identify the solution of the problem with himself. On the other hand, we have in vocational instruction the situation in which the student has identified his impulses with the subject-matter of the task. In the former case, as in the case of instruction, our traditional practice makes use of the self-consciousness of the child in its least effective form. The material of the lesson is not identified with the impulses of the child. The attention is not due to the organization of impulses to outgoing activity. The organization of typical school attention is that of a school self, expressing subordination to school authority and identity of conduct with that of all the other children in the room. It is largely inhibitive—a consciousness of what one must not do, but the inhibitions do not arise out of the consciousness of what one is doing. It is the nature of school attention to abstract from the content of any specific task. The child must give attention *first* and *then* undertake any task which is assigned to him, while normal attention is essentially selective and depends for its inhibitions upon the specific act.

Now consciousness of self should follow upon that of attention, and consists in a reference of the act, which attention has mediated, to the social self. It brings about a conscious organization of this particular act with the individual as a whole—makes it his act, and can only be effectively accomplished when the attention is an actual organization of impulses seeking expression. The separation between the self, implied in typical school attention, and the content of the school tasks, makes such an organization difficult if not impossible.

In a word attention is a process of organization of consciousness. It results in the reenforcement and inhibitions of perceptions and ideas. It is always a part of an act and involves the relation of that act to the whole field of consciousness. This relation to the whole field of consciousness finds its expression in consciousness of self. But the consciousness of self depends primarily upon social relations. The self arises in consciousness *pari passu* with the recognition and definition of other selves. It is therefore unfruitful if not impossible to attempt to scientifically control the attention of children in their formal education, unless they are regarded as social beings in dealing with the very material of instruction. It is this essentially social character of attention which gives its peculiar grip to vocational training. From the psychological point of view, not only the method and material but also the means of holding the pupils' attention must be socialized.

Finally a word may be added with reference to the evaluations—the emotional reactions—which our education should call forth. There is no phase of our public school training that is so defective as this. The school undertakes to acquaint the child with the ideas and methods which he is to use as a man. Shut up in the history, the geography, the language and the number of our curricula should be the values that the country, and its human institutions, have; that beauty has in nature and art; and the values involved in the control over nature and social conditions.

The child in entering into his heritage of ideas and methods should have the emotional response which the boy has in a primitive community when he has been initiated into the mysteries and the social code of the group of which he has become a citizen. We have a few remainders of this emotional response, in the confirmation or conversion and entrance into the church, in the initiation into the fraternity, and in the passage from apprenticeship into the union. But the complexities of our social life, and the abstract intellectual character of the ideas which society uses have made it increasingly difficult to identify the attainment of the equipment of a man with the meaning of manhood and citizenship.

Conventional ceremonies at the end of the period of education will never accomplish this. And we have to further recognize that our education extends for many far beyond the adolescent period to which this emotional response naturally belongs. What our schools can give must be given through the social consciousness of the child as that consciousness develops. It is only as the child recognizes a social import in what he is learning and doing that moral education can be given.

I have sought to indicate that the process of schooling in its barest form cannot be successfully studied by a scientific psychology unless that psychology is social, i.e., unless it recognizes that the processes of acquiring knowledge, of giving attention, of evaluating in emotional terms must be studied in their relation to selves in a social consciousness. So far as education is concerned, the child does not become social by learning. He must be social in order to learn.

X

SOCIAL CONSCIOUSNESS AND
THE CONSCIOUSNESS OF MEANING

In an earlier publication [1] I have supported the position that gestures in their original forms are the first overt phases in social acts, a social act being one in which one individual serves in his action as a stimulus to a response from another individual. The adaptation of these individuals to each other implies that their conduct calls out appropriate and valuable responses from each other. Such adjustment on the part of each form to the action of the other naturally leads to the direction of the action of the one form by the earliest phases of the conduct of the other. The more perfect the adaptation of the conduct of a social form the more readily it would be able to determine its actions by the first indications of an act in another form. From such a situation there follows a peculiar importance attaching to these earlier stages of social acts, serving as they do to mediate the appropriate responses of other forms in the same group. The earlier stages in social acts involve all the beginnings of hostility, wooing and parental care, all the control of the sense-organs which precede the overt conduct directed by the sense-organ, the attitudes of the body expressing readiness to act and the direction which the act will take, and finally the vasomotor preparations for action, such as the flushing of the blood vessels, the change in the rhythm of breathing and the explosive sounds which accompany the change in the breathing rhythm and circulation.

[From the *Psychological Bulletin,* VII (1910), 397–405. Reprinted by permission of the American Psychological Association.]

[1] The *Psychological Bulletin,* VI [1909], 401. [Essay VII in the present volume: "Social Psychology as Counterpart to Physiological Psychology."]

All of these early stages in animal reaction are of supreme importance as stimuli to social forms—i.e., forms whose lives are conditioned by the conduct of other forms—and must become in the process of evolution peculiarly effective as stimuli, or, put the other way around, social forms must become peculiarly sensitive to these earliest overt phases in social acts. The import which these early stages in social acts have is a sufficient explanation for their preservation even though some of them may have lost their original function in the social act. The gesture as the beginning of a social activity has become provocative of a certain response on the part of another form. It serves in wooing and quarreling to produce a summation of stimuli for reproductive and hostile reactions. This interplay of preliminary and preparatory processes even in the conduct of animal forms lower than man places the animals *en rapport* with each other, and leads in wooing, quarreling, and animal play to relatively independent activities that answer to human intercourse.

There exists thus a field of conduct even among animals below man, which in its nature may be classed as gesture. It consists of the beginnings of those actions which call out instinctive responses from other forms. And these beginnings of acts call out responses which lead to readjustments of acts which have been commenced, and these readjustments lead to still other beginnings of response which again call out still other readjustments. Thus there is a conversation of gesture, a field of palaver within the social conduct of animals. Again the movements which constitute this field of conduct are themselves not the complete acts which they start out to become. They are the glance of the eye that is the beginning of the spring or the flight, the attitude of body with which the spring or flight commences, the growl, or cry, or snarl with which the respiration adjusts itself to oncoming struggle, and they all change with the answering attitudes, glances of the eye, growls and snarls which are the beginnings of the actions which they themselves arouse.

Back of these manifestations lie the emotions which the

checking of the acts inevitably arouse. Fear, anger, lust of hunger and sex, all the gamut of emotions arise back of the activities of fighting, and feeding, and reproduction, because these activities are for the moment stopped in the process of readjustment. While these gestures thus reveal emotion to the observer their function is not that of revealing or expressing emotion. While the very checking of activity and readiness, straining to adjust oneself to indications of action on the part of the other individual, imply excess of energy seeking outlet, the setting free of surplus energy is not the function of the gesture. Nor yet is it an adequate explanation to find in the gesture the psychophysical counterpart of the emotional consciousness. The first function of the gesture is the mutual adjustment of changing social response to changing social stimulation, when stimulation and response are to be found in the first overt phases of the social acts.

I desire in this paper to emphasize and elaborate the position taken earlier that only in the relation of this mutual adjustment of social stimulation and response to the activities which they ultimately mediate, can the consciousness of meaning arise.

It is the assumption of the author that the consciousness of meaning consists mainly in a consciousness of attitude, on the part of the individual, over against the object to which he is about to react. The feeling of attitude represents the coordination between the process of stimulation and that of response when this is properly mediated. The feelings of readiness to take up or read a book, to spring over a ditch, to hurl a stone, are the stuff out of which arises a sense of the meaning of the book, the ditch, the stone. Professor Royce has perhaps given the most simple and convincing statement of the doctrine, in his *Psychology*.[2]

It is important to thus identitfy the sense of meaning with the consciousness of response or readiness to respond, because such an identification throws some light on the conditions un-

[2] [Josiah Royce, *Outlines of Psychology*, pp. 285–290.]

der which the sense of meaning can arise. The power of distinguishing clearly the different elements in contents of consciousness belongs peculiarly to the field of stimulation and its imagery. Such sharp distinction of contents is not characteristic of the consciousness of response.

Vision with its assimilated imagery of contact sensation readily distinguishes the form, shadings, and colors of a rock, and can mark the different areas of color and brightness, the changing curve of line and plane, but the tendencies to react to each of these different stimulations lie back in a field into which we can only indirectly introduce clear distinctions of content. We may detect a tendency of the eye to follow the curving line and to arrest its movement with its breaks in the contour. We may catch the finger in a readiness to follow a like path, or we may be unable to analyze out these contents, and these are but a minimal fraction of the responses which are indicated in our sense of familiarity with the boulder.

The motor imagery which lies in the background of the sensuous discriminations is notably difficult to detect, and even when consciously aroused, to differentiate into clearly distinguishable parts. This difficulty in presenting the contents of response—either in terms of the attitude of body, the position of the limbs, feel of contracting muscles, or in terms of the memory of past responses—indicates that these contents, at least in their analyzed elements, are of negligible importance in the economy of immediate conduct. On the contrary, conduct is controlled by recognized differences in the field of stimulation. It is the difference in the visual or auditory or tactual experience which results in changed response. It is the failure to secure a difference in these fields that leads to renewed effort. We are conscious of muscular strain to some degree, but attention follows the changing objects about us that register the success or failure of the activity. It is further true that the more perfect the adjustment between the stimulation and response within the act the less conscious are we of the response itself. Of incomplete adjustment we are aware as awkwardness of movement and uncontrolled reactions. Perfection of adjustment leaves us with only the recognition of the sensuous characteristics of the objects about, and we have only the attitude of familiarity to record the readiness to make a thousand responses to distinctions of vision, sound and feel that lie in our field of stimulation. Yet the meaning of these distinctions in sense experience must lie in the relation of the stimulation to the response.

The recurrence in memory of the past experience is the content that is commonly supposed to mediate this consciousness of meaning. The burnt child avoids the fire. Something to be shunned has become to him the most important element of the fascinating flame, and it is the *consequence* of the response that is supposed to give the child the all-important content. The recurrence of the imagery of the past disaster insures the avoidance of the flame. Does it give the child a consciousness that this is the meaning of the fire? There is wide difference between merging the memory of the past experience with the present sensuous stimulation leading to the withdrawal of the child's hand, and a consciousness that hot fire *means* withdrawal. In the first case an immediate content of sensation assimilates a content of imagery that ensures a certain response. This assimilation in no sense guarantees a consciousness of a distinguishable meaning. As indicated above the more complete the assimilation the less conscious are we of the actual content of response. That with which we are most familiar is least likely to be distinguished in direct conduct in terms of meaning. That this familiarity is still a guarantee that upon demand we can give a meaning illustrates the point I desire to make, that the bringing into consciousness of a meaning content is an act which must in every instance be distinguished from the mere consciousness of stimulation resulting in response. To see one's hat may at once lead to picking it up and putting it on. This sureness and immediacy of action is not the same as the consciousness that it is his hat. In fact it is essential to the economy of our conduct that the connection between stimulation and response should become habitual and should sink below the threshold of consciousness. Furthermore if the relation between stimulation and response is to appear as the meaning of the object,—if the characters of the stimulation are to be referred to the appropriate characters in response, we find ourselves before the difficulty presented above. There is in our response so little content which can be distinguished and related to the characters in the content of stimulation. There is the leaping flame which means to the child a plaything, there is heat which means a burn. In this case the results of the past responses are related to characters in the content of stimulation—movement means plaything, heat means burn. Still the meaning of plaything is playing and the meaning of burn is drawing back the hand. The association of these contents with the dancing flame does not enable the child to present to himself the playing or hurried withdrawal. It simply gives other contents, other stimulation values to his immediate experience. The association of one content with another content is not the symbolism of meaning. In the consciousness of meaning the symbol and that which is symbolized—the thing and what it means—must be presented separately. Association of contents of stimulation tends to become a complete merging and loss of distinction. And these contents of imagery which are merged are not the attitudes, the feels of readiness to act which lie back of our consciousness of meaning. The general habit of reacting to objects of a certain class, such as a book, must be got before the mind's eye before a recognition of the meaning of a book can appear. No amount of enrichment of the sensuous content of the book through the eye, hand or memory image will bring this habitual generalized attitude into consciousness. Unquestionably these enrichments furnish us with more cues for setting off this habitual reaction. But this is their entire function, to act as cues to habitual reactions, not to appear as symbols of these reactions, as separate contents. The facility of habitual conduct forbids such separation between the stimulation-cue and the response. The more perfect the habit the less possibility would there be that the content which serves to stimulate could serve directly as the symbol of the response, could bring out separately and relate to itself the reaction for which it is responsible. If the fact be simple, consisting only in well-organized stimulation and response, there cannot be found in its mechanism the occasion for the appearance of the consciousness of meaning. The perfection of adjustment between these two parts of the act leaves no opening for the distinction between characteristic and its meaning, and without such a distinction, involved in the process of relation, there can be no recognition of meaning. Furthermore the contents in consciousness which answer to the meaning of objects are our generalized habitual responses to them. These contents are the consciousness of attitudes, of muscular tensions and the feels of readiness to act in presence of certain stimulations. There is nothing in the economy of the act itself which tends to bring these contents above the threshold, nor distinguish them as separable elements in a process of relation, such as is implied in the consciousness of meaning.

The foregoing analysis has considered only the act made perfect in habit. This act is of course the basis of the consciousness of meaning. Meaning is a statement of the relation between the characteristics in the sensuous stimulation and the responses which they call out. While therefore there is nothing in the mechanism of the act which brings this relation itself to consciousness the consciousness of the relation rests upon the perfection of the act.

If the occasion for the consciousness of meaning is not found in the habitual act may it not be found in the conflict of acts? The same psychology that states meaning in terms of the attitudes which are the registrations in consciousness of habits of reaction is wont to find in conflicting activities occasion for reflective consciousness. Thinking for this psychology is always the solution of a problem. It would then be consonant with this point of view to find in conflicting activities just that conscious distinction between the characteristic in the stimulation and the attitude of response which is the prerequisite of the consciousness of meaning. For example, a man is in doubt whether the clouds and wind mean rain or fair weather. His inclination to walk abroad, and his inclination to seek shelter are in conflict. This conflict is precisely the situation which brings sharply into consciousness the characteristics of sky and atmosphere which are signs of fair and of foul weather. A certain direction of the wind and dampness in the air are so merged in experience with the imagery of rainy weather that one instinctively draws back from expeditions far from shelter, while a still unclouded sky arouses the inclinations to wander abroad. Does this conflict which must emphasize the opposing characteristics of the morning heavens also lead to that relation of the characteristics to response which is implied in the consciousness of meaning? A legitimate guide in seeking an answer to this question will be found in the direction of attention; and attention under such conditions is directed toward the differences in the characteristics of weather, and not toward the feels of attitude which reveal our habits of response. The man so situated studies the heavens, sniffs the air, detects a thickening of the sky which would otherwise have passed unnoticed, but does not immediately become conscious that rain means his habit of withdrawing from its inclemency, nor is he impelled to define to himself fair weather in terms of far-ranging expeditions. The connections are of course there, but the conflict of tendencies directs the attention not to these connections but toward the sharper definition of the objects which constitute the stimulation.

In the field of gesture, on the other hand, the interplay of social conduct turns upon changes of attitude, upon signs of response. In themselves these signs of response become simply other stimulations to which the individual replies by means of other responses and do not at first seem to present a situation essentially different from that of the man hesitating before the uncertainties of the morning sky. The difference is found, however, in the fact that we are conscious of interpreting the gestures of others by our own responses or tendencies to respond. We awaken to the hostility of our neighbors' attitudes by the arising tendency to attack or assume the attitude of defense. We become aware of the direction of another's line of march by our tendencies to step one side or the other.

During the whole process of interaction with others we are analyzing their oncoming acts by our instinctive responses to their changes of posture and other indications of developing social acts. We have seen that the ground for this lies in the fact that social conduct must be continually readjusted after it has already commenced, because the individuals to whose conduct our own answers, are themselves constantly varying their conduct as our responses become evident. Thus our adjustments to their changing reactions take place, by a process of analysis of our own responses to their stimulations. In these social situations appear not only conflicting acts with the increased definition of elements in the stimulation, but also a consciousness of one's own attitude as an interpretation of the meaning of the social stimulus. We are conscious of our attitudes because they are responsible for the changes in the conduct of other individuals. A man's reaction toward weather conditions has no influence upon the weather itself. It is of importance for the success of his conduct that he should be conscious not of his own attitudes, of his own habits of response, but of the signs of rain or fair weather. Successful social conduct brings one into a field within which a consciousness of one's own attitudes helps toward the control of the conduct of others.

In the field of social conduct, attention is indeed directed toward the stimulation existing in the overt actions and preparations for action on the part of others, but the response to these indications of conduct leads to change in this conduct. The very attention given to stimulation may throw one's attention back upon the attitude he will assume toward the challenging attitude in another, since this attitude will change the stimulation. To make the two situations somewhat more specific we may compare the state of consciousness of a man running through a forest or over broken ground, with that of a man face to face with a number of enemies. The first is constantly faced by problems requiring rapid solution, problems of the pace he can keep up, and the direction he should take in the midst of the crowded obstacles to his progress. He responds instantaneously to indications of distance, of contour, and of resistance by rapid movements toward which as attitudes he has not the slightest temptation to turn his attention.

The second is subject to the same type of stimulation. He must act instantaneously and judge as quickly the characters of the stimulations to which he must respond. His situation however differs in this, that the attitude he assumes to meet an anticipated blow may lead his opponent to change the attack, and he must if he is to survive be aware of this value. His own gesture thus interprets his opponent's attitude and must be held in consciousness as changing the situation to which he must respond. In a word, within social conduct the feels of one's own responses become the natural objects of attention, since they interpret first of all attitudes of others which have called them out, in the second place, because they give the material in which one can state his own value as a stimulus to the conduct of others. Thus we find here the opportunity and the means for analyzing and bringing to consciousness our responses, our habits of conduct, as distinguished from the stimulations that call them out. The opportunity is found in the import of the response in determining the conduct of others. The means are our gestures as they appear in the feel of our own attitudes and movements, which are the beginnings of social reactions.

I may refer in closing to the accepted doctrine that language, in which our meanings almost exclusively arise in consciousness, is but a form—a highly specialized form—of gesture, and to the other important fact that in these presentations of others' attitudes and our own we have the material out of which selves are constructed, and to the fact that consciousness of meaning is so intimately bound up with self-consciousness.

Thus the consciousness of meaning at least at this stage is a consciousness of one's own attitudes of response as they answer to, control, and interpret the gestures of others. The elements in this consciousness are first of all a social situation, i.e., stimulation by another's act with tendencies to respond revealing themselves in our own reactions, these tendencies and the stimulations which call them out mutually influencing each other; secondly, the consciousness of this value of one's own gesture in terms of the change in the gesture of the other form, i.e., one is conscious of the relation between the stimulation and the response; thirdly, the terms in which this relation appears in consciousness, i.e., the feel of one's own attitude arising spontaneously to meet the gesture of the other, then the imagery of the change in the gesture of the other which would answer this expression, which again would arouse the tendency to respond in still different fashion. It must remain for a later paper to analyze the process of language in these terms, and to indicate the fundamental character of this consciousness of meaning in the consciousness of self, and finally to present the process of thought itself as such a play of gesture between selves, even when those selves are a part of our inner self-consciousness.

ꟾ XI ꟾ

THE MECHANISM OF SOCIAL CONSCIOUSNESS

The organization of consciousness may be regarded from the standpoint of its objects and the relation of these objects to conduct. I have in mind to present somewhat schematically the relation of social objects or selves to the form of social conduct, and to introduce this by a statement of the relation of the physical object to the conduct within which it appears.

A physical object or percept is a construct in which the sensuous stimulation is merged with imagery which comes from past experience. This imagery on the cognitive side is that which the immediate sensuous quality stands for, and insofar satisfies the mind. The reason for this satisfaction is found in the fact that this imagery arises from past experience of the result of an act which this stimulus has set going. Thus the wall as a visual stimulus tends to set free the impulse to move toward it and push against it. The perception of the wall as distant and hard and rough is related to the visual experience as response to stimulation. A peculiar stimulus value stands for a certain response value. A percept is a collapsed act in which the result of the act to which the stimulus incites is represented by imagery of the experience of past acts of a like nature.

Insofar as our physical conduct involves movements toward or away from distant objects and their being handled when we come into contact with them, we perceive all things in terms of distance sensation—color, sound, odor—which stand for hard or soft, big or little, objects of varying forms, which actual contact will reveal.

Read at the meeting of the Western Philosophical Association held in Chicago, April 5 and 6, [1912. From *The Journal of Philosophy, Psychology, and Scientific Methods,* IX (1912), 401–406. Reprinted by permission of *The Journal of Philosophy.*]

Our conduct in movement and manipulation, with its stimulations and responses, gives the framework within which objects of perception arise—and this conduct is in so far responsible for the organization of our physical world. Percepts —physical objects—are compounds of the experience of immediate stimulation and the imagery of the response to which this stimulation will lead. The object can be properly stated in terms of conduct.

I have referred to percepts as objects which arise in physical experience because it is a certain phase of conduct which, with its appropriate stimuli and responses, gives rise to such products, i.e., movement under the influence of distant stimuli leading to contact experiences of manipulation.

Given a different type of conduct with distinguishable stimulations and responses, and different objects would arise— such a different field is that of social conduct. By social conduct I refer simply to that which is mediated by the stimulations of other animals belonging to the same group of living forms, which lead to responses which again affect these other forms—thus fighting, reproduction, parental care, much of animal play, hunting, etc., are the results of primitive instincts or impulses which are set going by the stimulation of one form by another, and these stimulations again lead to responses which affect other forms.

It is of course true that a man is a physical object to the perception of another man, and as real as is a tree or a stone. But a man is more than a physical object, and it is this more which constitutes him a social object or self, and it is this self which is related to that peculiar conduct which may be termed social conduct.

Most social stimulation is found in the beginnings or early stages of social acts which serve as stimuli to other forms whom these acts would affect. This is the field of gestures, which reveal the motor attitude of a form in its relation to others; an attitude which psychologists have conceived of as predominantly emotional, though it is emotional only insofar as an ongoing act is inhibited. That certain of these early indications of an incipient act have persisted, while the rest of the act has been largely suppressed or has lost its original value, e.g., the baring of the teeth or the lifting of the nostrils, is true, and the explanation can most readily be found in the social value which such indications have acquired. It is an error, however, to overlook the relation which these truncated acts have assumed toward other forms of reactions which complete them as really as the original acts, or to forget that they occupy but a small part of the whole field of gesture by means of which we are apprised of the reactions of others toward ourselves. The expressions of the face and attitudes of body have the same functional value for us that the beginnings of hostility have for two dogs, who are maneuvering for an opening to attack.

This field of gesture does not simply relate the individual to other individuals as physical objects, but puts him *en rapport* with their actions, which are as yet only indicated, and arouses instinctive reactions appropriate to these social activities. The social response of one individual, furthermore, introduces a further complication. The attitude assumed in response to the attitude of another becomes a stimulus to him to change his attitude, thus leading to that conversation of attitudes which is so vividly illustrated in the early stages of a dog fight. We see the same process in courting and mating, and in the fondling of young forms by the mother, and finally in much of the play of young animals.

It has been recognized for some time that speech belongs in its beginnings, at least, to this same field of gesture, so-called vocal gesture. Originally indicating the preparation for violent action, which arises from a sudden change of breathing and circulation rhythms, the articulate sounds have come to elaborate and immensely complicate this conversation of attitudes by which social forms so adjust themselves to each other's anticipated action that they may act appropriately with reference to each other.

Articulate sounds have still another most important result. While one feels but imperfectly the value of his own facial expression or bodily attitude for another, his ear reveals to him his own vocal gesture in the same form that it assumes to his neighbor. One shakes his fist primarily only at another, while he talks to himself as really as he talks to his vis-à-vis. The genetic import of this has long been recognized. The young child talks to himself, i.e., uses the elements of articulate speech in response to the sounds he hears himself make, more continuously and persistently than he does in response to the sounds he hears from those about him, and displays greater interest in the sounds he himself makes than in those of others. We know also that this fascination of one's own vocal gestures continues even after the child has learned to talk with others, and that the child will converse for hours with himself, even constructing imaginary companions, who function in the child's growing self-consciousness as the processes of inner speech—of thought and imagination—function in the consciousness of the adult.

To return to the formula given above for the formation of an object in consciousness, we may define the social object in terms of social conduct as we defined the physical object in terms of our reactions to physical objects. The object was found to consist of the sensuous experience of the stimulation to an act plus the imagery from past experience of the final result of the act. The social object will then be the gestures, i.e., the early indications of an ongoing social act in another plus the imagery of our own response to that stimulation. To the young child the frowns and smiles of those about him, the attitude of body, the outstretched arms, are at first simply stimulations that call out instinctive responses of his own appropriate to these gestures. He cries or laughs, he moves toward his mother, or stretches out his arms. When these gestures in others bring back the images of his own responses and their results, the child has the material out of which he builds up the social objects that form the most important part of his environment. We are familiar with this phase of a baby's development, being confident that he recognizes the different members of the group about him. He acts then with confidence toward them since their gestures have come to have meaning for him. His own response to their stimulations and its consequences are there to interpret the facial expressions and attitudes of body and tones of voice. The awakening social intelligence of the child is evidenced not so much through his ready responses to the gestures of others, for these have been in evidence much earlier. It is the inner assurance of his own readiness to adjust himself to the attitudes of others that looks out of his eyes and appears in his own bodily attitudes.

If we assume that an object arises in consciousness through the merging of the imagery of experience of the response with that of the sensuous experience of the stimulation, it is evident that the child must merge the imagery of his past responses into the sensuous stimulation of what comes to him through distance senses. His contact and kinesthetic experiences must be lodged in the sensuous experiences that call them out if they are to achieve objective character in his consciousness.

It will be some time before he can successfully unite the different parts of his own body, such as his hands and feet, which he sees and feels, into a single object. Such a step must be later than the formation of the physical objects of his environment. The form of the object is given in the experience of things, which are not his physical self. When he has synthesized his various bodily parts with the organic sensations and affective experiences, it will be upon the model of objects about him. The mere presence of experiences of pleasure and pain, together with organic sensations, will not form an object unless this material can fall into the scheme of an object—that of sensuous stimulation plus the imagery of the response.

In the organization of the baby's physical experience the appearance of his body as a unitary thing, as an object, will be relatively late, and must follow upon the structure of the objects of his environment. This is as true of the object that appears in social conduct, the self. The form of the social object must be found first of all in the experience of other selves. The earliest achievement of social consciousness will be the merging of the imagery of the baby's first responses and their results with the stimulations of the gestures of others. The child will not succeed in forming an object of himself—of putting the so-called subjective material of consciousness within such a self—until he has recognized about him social objects who have arisen in his experience through this process of filling out stimulations with past experiences of response. And this is indeed our uniform experience with children. The child's early social percepts are of others. After these arise incomplete and partial selves—or "me's"—which are quite analogous to the child's percepts of his hands and feet, which precede his perception of himself as a whole. The mere presence of affective experience, of imagery, of organic sensations, does not carry with it consciousness of a self to which these experiences belong. Nor does the unitary character of the response which tends to synthesize our objects of perception convey that same unitary character to the inner experience until the child is able to experience himself as he experiences other selves.

It is highly probable that lower animals never reach any such objective reference of what we term subjective experiences to selves, and the question presents itself—what is there in human social conduct that gives rise to a "me," a self which is an object? Why does the human animal transfer the form of a social object from his environment to an inner experience?

The answer to the question is already indicated in the statement of vocal gesture. Certainly the fact that the human animal can stimulate himself as he stimulates others and can respond to his stimulations as he responds to the stimulations of others, places in his conduct the form of a social object out of which may arise a "me" to which can be referred so-called subjective experiences.

Of course the mere capacity to talk to oneself is not the whole of self-consciousness, otherwise the talking birds would have souls or at least selves. What is lacking to the parrot are the social objects which can exist for the human baby. Part of the mechanism for transferring the social objects into an inner experience the parrot possesses, but he has nothing to import into such an inner world. Furthermore, the vocal gesture is not the only form which can serve for the building-up of a "me," as is abundantly evident from the building-up gestures of the deaf mutes. Any gesture by which the individual can himself be affected as others are affected, and which therefore tends to call out in him a response as it would call it out in another, will serve as a mechanism for the construction of a self. That, however, a consciousness of a self as an object would ever have arisen in man if he had not had the mechanism of talking to himself, I think there is every reason to doubt.

If this statement is correct the objective self of human consciousness is the merging of one's responses with the social stimulation by which he affects himself. The "me" is a man's reply to his own talk. Such a "me" is not then an early formation, which is then projected and ejected into the bodies of other people to give them the breadth of human life. It is rather an importation from the field of social objects into an amorphous, unorganized field of what we call inner experience. Through the organization of this object, the self, this material is itself organized and brought under the control of the individual in the form of so-called self-consciousness.

It is a commonplace of psychology that it is only the "me" —the empirical self—that can be brought into the focus of attention—that can be perceived. The "I" lies beyond the range of immediate experience. In terms of social conduct this is tantamount to saying that we can perceive our responses only as they appear as images from past experience, merging with the sensuous stimulation. We cannot present the response while we are responding. We cannot use our responses to others as the materials for construction of the self— this imagery goes to make up other selves. We must socially stimulate ourselves to place at our own disposal the material out of which our own selves as well as those of others must be made.

The "I" therefore never can exist as an object in consciousness, but the very conversational character of our inner experience, the very process of replying to one's own talk, implies an "I" behind the scenes who answers to the gestures, the symbols, that arise in consciousness. The "I" is the transcendental self of Kant, the soul that James conceived behind the scene holding on to the skirts of an idea to give it an added increment of emphasis.

The self-conscious, actual self in social intercourse is the objective "me" or "me's" with the process of response continually going on and implying a fictitious "I" always out of sight of himself.

Inner consciousness is socially organized by the importation of the social organization of the outer world.

THE SOCIAL SELF

Recognizing that the self cannot appear in consciousness as an "I," that it is always an object, i.e., a "me," I wish to suggest an answer to the question, What is involved in the self being an object? The first answer may be that an object involves a subject. Stated in other words, that a "me" is inconceivable without an "I." And to this reply must be made that such an "I" is a presupposition, but never a presentation of conscious experience, for the moment it is presented it has passed into the objective case, presuming, if you like, an "I" that observes—but an "I" that can disclose himself only by ceasing to be the subject for whom the object "me" exists. It is, of course, not the Hegelism of a self that becomes another to himself in which I am interested, but the nature of the self as revealed by introspection and subject to our factual analysis. This analysis does reveal, then, in a memory process an attitude of observing oneself in which both the observer and the observed appear. To be concrete, one remembers asking himself how he could undertake to do this, that, or the other, chiding himself for his shortcomings or pluming himself upon his achievements. Thus, in the redintegrated self of the moment passed, one finds both a subject and an object, but it is a subject that is now an object of observation, and has the same nature as the object self whom we present as in intercourse with those about us. In quite the same fashion we remember the questions, admonitions, and approvals addressed to our fellows. But the subject attitude which we instinctively

Read at the Annual Meeting of the Western Philosophical Association, March 1913. [From *The Journal of Philosophy, Psychology, and Scientific Methods,* X (1913), 374–380. Reprinted by permission of *The Journal of Philosophy.*]

take can be presented only as something experienced—as we can be conscious of our acts only through the sensory processes set up after the act has begun.

The contents of this presented subject, who thus has become an object in being presented, but which still distinguish him as the subject of the passed experience from the "me" whom he addressed, are those images which initiated the conversation and the motor sensations which accompany the expression, plus the organic sensations and the response of the whole system to the activity initiated. In a word, just those contents which go to make up the self which is distinguished from the others whom he addresses. The self appearing as "I" is the memory image of the self who acted toward himself and is the same self who acts toward other selves.

On the other hand, the stuff that goes to make up the "me" whom the "I" addresses and whom he observes, is the experience which is induced by this action of the "I." If the "I" speaks, the "me" hears. If the "I" strikes, the "me" feels the blow. Here again the "me" consciousness is of the same character as that which arises from the action of the other upon him. That is, it is only as the individual finds himself acting with reference to himself as he acts towards others, that he becomes a subject to himself rather than an object, and only as he is affected by his own social conduct in the manner in which he is affected by that of others, that he becomes an object to his own social conduct.

The differences in our memory presentations of the "I" and the "me" are those of the memory images of the initiated social conduct and those of the sensory responses thereto.

It is needless, in view of the analysis of Baldwin, of Royce and of Cooley and many others, to do more than indicate that these reactions arise earlier in our social conduct with others than in introspective self-consciousness, i.e., that the infant consciously calls the attention of others before he calls his own attention by affecting himself and that he is consciously affected by others before he is conscious of being affected by himself.

The "I" of introspection is the self which enters into social relations with other selves. It is not the "I" that is implied in the fact that one presents himself as a "me." And the "me" of introspection is the same "me" that is the object of the social conduct of others. One presents himself as acting toward others—in this presentation he is presented in indirect discourse as the subject of the action and is still an object,—and the subject of this presentation can never appear immediately in conscious experience. It is the same self who is presented as observing himself, and he affects himself just insofar and only insofar as he can address himself by the means of social stimulation which affect others. The "me" whom he addresses is the "me," therefore, that is similarly affected by the social conduct of those about him.

This statement of the introspective situation, however, seems to overlook a more or less constant feature of our consciousness, and that is that running current of awareness of what we do which is distinguishable from the consciousness of the field of stimulation, whether that field be without or within. It is this "awareness" which has led many to assume that it is the nature of the self to be conscious both of subject and of object—to be subject of action toward an object world and at the same time to be directly conscious of this subject as subject,—"Thinking its nonexistence [1] along with whatever else it thinks." Now, as Professor James pointed out, this consciousness is more logically conceived of as sciousness—the thinker being an implication rather than a content, while the "me" is but a bit of object content within the stream of sciousness.[2] However, this logical statement does not do justice to the findings of consciousness. Besides the actual stimulations and responses and the memory images of these, within which lie perforce the organic sensations and responses which

[1] [Mead probably meant "own existence." William James ascribed the quotation as amended to the Scottish metaphysician, James F. Ferrier (1808–1864), author of *Institutes of Metaphysic* (Edinburgh, 1854). See William James, *The Principles of Psychology*, I, 304.]

[2] [For the term "sciousness," see William James, *ibid.*, I, 304–305.]

make up the "me," there accompanies a large part of our conscious experience, indeed all that we call self-conscious, an inner response to what we may be doing, saying, or thinking. At the back of our heads we are a large part of the time more or less clearly conscious of our own replies to the remarks made to others, of innervations which would lead to attitudes and gestures answering our gestures and attitudes towards others.

The observer who accompanies all our self-conscious conduct is then not the actual "I" who is responsible for the conduct in *propria persona* [3]—he is rather the response which one makes to his own conduct. The confusion of this response of ours, following upon our social stimulations of others with the implied subject of our action, is the psychological ground for the assumption that the self can be directly conscious of itself as acting and acted upon. The actual situation is this: The self acts with reference to others and is immediately conscious of the objects about it. In memory it also redintegrates the self acting as well as the others acted upon. But besides these contents, the action with reference to the others calls out responses in the individual himself—there is then another "me" criticising, approving, and suggesting, and consciously planning, i.e., the reflective self.

It is not to all our conduct toward the objective world that we thus respond. Where we are intensely preoccupied with the objective world, this accompanying awareness disappears. We have to recall the experience to become aware that we have been involved as selves, to produce the self-consciousness which is a constituent part of a large part of our experience. As I have indicated elsewhere, the mechanism for this reply to our own social stimulation of others follows as a natural result from the fact that the very sounds, gestures, especially vocal gestures, which man makes in addressing others, call out or tend to call out responses from himself. He can not hear himself speak without assuming in a measure the attitude

[3] ["One's own character."]

which he would have assumed if he had been addressed in the same words by others.

The self which consciously stands over against other selves thus becomes an object, an other to himself, through the very fact that he hears himself talk, and replies. The mechanism of introspection is therefore given in the social attitude which man necessarily assumes toward himself, and the mechanism of thought, insofar as thought uses symbols which are used in social intercourse, is but an inner conversation.

Now it is just this combination of the remembered self which acts and exists over against other selves with the inner response to his action which is essential to the self-conscious ego—the self in the full meaning of the term—although neither phase of self-consciousness, insofar as it appears as an object of our experience, is a subject.

It is also to be noted that this response to the social conduct of the self may be in the role of another—we present his arguments in imagination and do it with his intonations and gestures and even perhaps with his facial expression. In this way we play the roles of all our group; indeed, it is only insofar as we do this that they become part of our social environment—to be aware of another self as a self implies that we have played his role or that of another with whose type we identify him for purposes of intercourse. The inner response to our reaction to others is therefore as varied as is our social environment. Not that we assume the roles of others toward ourselves because we are subject to a mere imitative instinct, but because in responding to ourselves we are in the nature of the case taking the attitude of another than the self that is directly acting, and into this reaction there naturally flows the memory images of the responses of those about us, the memory images of those responses of others which were in answer to like actions. Thus the child can think about his conduct as good or bad only as he reacts to his own acts in the remembered words of his parents. Until this process has been developed into the abstract process of thought, self-consciousness remains dramatic, and the self which is a fusion of the remembered actor and this accompanying chorus is somewhat loosely organized and very clearly social. Later the inner stage changes into the forum and workshop of thought. The features and intonations of the dramatis personae fade out and the emphasis falls upon the meaning of the inner speech, the imagery becomes merely the barely necessary cues. But the mechanism remains social, and at any moment the process may become personal.

It is fair to say that the modern western world has lately done much of its thinking in the form of the novel, while earlier the drama was a more effective but equally social mechanism of self-consciousness. And, in passing, I may refer to that need of filling out the bare spokesman of abstract thought, which even the most abstruse thinker feels, in seeking his audience. The import of this for religious self-consciousness is obvious.

There is one further implication of this nature of the self to which I wish to call attention. It is the manner of its reconstruction. I wish especially to refer to it, because the point is of importance in the psychology of ethics.

As a mere organization of habit the self is not self-conscious. It is this self which we refer to as character. When, however, an essential problem appears, there is some disintegration in this organization, and different tendencies appear in reflective thought as different voices in conflict with each other. In a sense the old self has disintegrated, and out of the moral process a new self arises. The specific question I wish to ask is whether the new self appears together with the new object or end. There is of course a reciprocal relation between the self and its object, the one implies the other and the interests and evaluations of the self answer exactly to the content and values of the object. On the other hand, the consciousness of the new object, its values and meaning, seems to come earlier to consciousness than the new self that answers to the new object.

The man who has come to realize a new human value is more immediately aware of the new object in his conduct than of himself and his manner of reaction to it. This is due to the fact to which reference has already been made, that direct attention goes first to the object. When the self becomes an object, it appears in memory, and the attitude which it implies has already been taken. In fact, to distract attention from the object to the self implies just that lack of objectivity which we criticise not only in the moral agent, but in the scientist.

Assuming as I do the essentially social character of the ethical end, we find in moral reflection a conflict in which certain values find a spokesman in the old self or a dominant part of the old self, while other values answering to other tendencies and impulses arise in opposition and find other spokesmen to present their cases. To leave the field to the values represented by the old self is exactly what we term selfishness. The justification for the term is found in the habitual character of conduct with reference to these values. Attention is not claimed by the object and shifts to the subjective field where the affective responses are identified with the old self. The result is that we state the other conflicting ends in subjective terms of other selves and the moral problem seems to take on the form of the sacrifice either of the self or of the others.

Where, however, the problem is objectively considered, although the conflict is a social one, it should not resolve itself into a struggle between selves, but into such a reconstruction of the situation that different and enlarged and more adequate personalities may emerge. Attention should be centered on the objective social field.

In the reflective analysis, the old self should enter upon the same terms with the selves whose roles are assumed, and the test of the reconstruction is found in the fact that all the personal interests are adequately recognized in a new social situation. The new self that answers to this new situation can appear in consciousness only after this new situation has been realized and accepted. The new self can not enter into the field as the determining factor because he is consciously present only after the new end has been formulated and accepted.

The old self may enter only as an element over against the other personal interests involved. If he is the dominant factor it must be in defiance of the other selves whose interests are at stake. As the old self he is defined by his conflict with the others that assert themselves in his reflective analysis.

Solution is reached by the construction of a new world harmonizing the conflicting interests into which enters the new self.

The process is in its logic identical with the abandonment of the old theory with which the scientist has identified himself, his refusal to grant this old attitude any further weight than may be given to the other conflicting observations and hypotheses. Only when a successful hypothesis, which overcomes the conflicts, has been formulated and accepted, may the scientist again identify himself with this hypothesis as his own, and maintain it *contra mundum*.[4] He may not state the scientific problem and solution in terms of his old personality. He may name his new hypothesis after himself and realize his enlarged scientific personality in its triumph.

The fundamental difference between the scientific and moral solution of a problem lies in the fact that the moral problem deals with concrete personal interests, in which the whole self is reconstructed in its relation to the other selves whose relations are essential to its personality.

The growth of the self arises out of a partial disintegration, —the appearance of the different interests in the forum of reflection, the reconstruction of the social world, and the consequent appearance of the new self that answers to the new object.

4 ["Against the world."]

❧ XIII ❧

NATURAL RIGHTS AND THE THEORY OF
THE POLITICAL INSTITUTION

The term "natural rights" suggests the political speculations of the seventeenth and eighteenth centuries in Europe, and the various revolutions that took them in some sense as their slogans. These revolutionary movements were one after the other increasingly forward-looking, constructive undertakings, until we may fairly say that as their results we find in representative government and growing democracy, revolution incorporated in the institution of government itself. That is, the form of government has become such that in its own operation the people can by legislation and amendment change it into any form they desire and still will have acted in a strictly legal and constitutional fashion. Furthermore, in the interplay of legislation and the execution and judicial interpretation of the legislation there arise not only the opportunities, but also the legally recognized occasions for the continual reconstruction of governmental institutions, so that a constant growth may take place in the form of institutions, and government may become in its own operation something entirely different from what it was, without any break or overthrow of constituted authority. Revolution has been incorporated into the constituted form of government itself.

And this has involved a revolution itself, for such an institutionalizing of revolution has been no less revolutionary with

Read at the joint session of the American and Western Philosophical Associations with the American Political Science Association and Conference on Legal and Social Philosophy, at Chicago, December 29, 1914. [From *The Journal of Philosophy, Psychology, and Scientific Methods*, XII (1915), 141–155. Reprinted by permission of *The Journal of Philosophy*.]

reference to revolution itself than it has been with reference to fixed forms of government. The tendency of each revolutionary movement had been to fix itself in relatively unchangeable governmental structure, that the successes it has spent and fought for might be preserved and entrenched, and thus had prepared the appropriate situation for the next revolution that sought in its turn to build its achievements into a new structure that should hold out

Against the wreckful siege of battering days.[1]

In fact, the form of government in democratic countries has responded more completely to the demand for the opportunity for continual change than have the customs and attitudes of the community itself. The embedded structure of society has become more conservative than its more external forms and machinery. The possible revolutions, in the old sense, which we can envisage today are supposed to be directed against this inner structure such as the very producing and holding of wealth, or the procreating and nurture of children, and it is quite on the cards that these revolutions might be carried out by methods which would be strictly constitutional and legal.

It is not remarkable, then, that rights which looked very definite to the gentlemen who drew up the American Declaration of Independence, or those who formulated the bills of rights that were to justify the French revolutions, should have an entirely different aspect and meaning today. Life, liberty, security, property, and even the pursuit of happiness took on a definite connotation from the dangers and hindrances men sought to eliminate, the dangers and hindrances which an autocratic government could put in the way of the enjoyment of these imprescriptible rights. And when these dangers and hindrances had been removed the definitions of the rights which had been given in terms of what threatened them lost their bearings and at the same time their content. How simple and self-evident are the following definitions, taken from the

[1] [Shakespeare, Sonnet No. LXV.]

declaration of rights and duties prefixed to the French constitution of September 23, 1795:

The rights of man in society are liberty, equality, security, property.

Liberty consists in the power to do that which does not injure the rights of others.

Equality consists in this, that the law is the same for all, whether it protects, or whether it punishes.

Equality does not admit any distinction of birth, or any inheritance of power.

Security results from the coöperation of all to assure the rights of each.

Property is the right to enjoy and dispose of one's goods, one's revenues, of the fruit of one's labor, and of one's industry.

The law is the general will expressed by the majority of all the citizens or of their representatives.

That which is not forbidden by law may not be prohibited. No one may be constrained to do that which the law does not ordain.

No one may be summoned before court, accused, arrested, or detained, except in cases determined by law, according to the forms prescribed by law.

Those who incite, give legal form to, sign, execute, or have executed arbitrary acts are culpable and are to be punished.

All unnecessary severity in securing the person of the accused is to be severely repressed by law.

No man may be judged until he has been heard or legally summoned.

The law may only judge such penalties as are strictly necessary and proportioned to the offense.

All treatment which aggravates the penalty set by the law is a crime.

No law either criminal or civil may be applied retroactively.

Every individual may dispose of his time and his services,

but he may not offer himself for sale or be sold. His person is not alienable property.

All taxes are established for the common good. It should be divided among those contributing to it, according to their abilities.

The sovereignty resides essentially in the entirety of the citizens.

No individual and no group of citizens may take to himself or itself sovereignty.

No one without legal commission may exercise any authority or fill any public office.

Everyone has the right to take equal part in the formation of the law, in the nomination of the representatives of the people, and of public officers.

Public offices may not become the property of those who hold them.

Social security cannot exist if the division of powers has not been established, if their limits have not been fixed, and if the responsibility of public officers has not been assured.

Here we find liberty defined in terms of taking away liberty and other rights to be defined, equality in terms of the absence of legal distinctions, security in terms of its source, property in terms of the absence of interference with its use, whatever it may be. But to the minds of men of the year four,[2] these definitions had definite contents, because they were undertaking to determine the conditions under which certain powers which it did not even occur to them to define might be exercised.

Now that these conditions are in large measure assured, that the danger of inherited dynastic autocratic power has largely disappeared, these same powers lack the definition which the

[2] [The year four in the French Revolutionary calendar is September 22, 1795, through September 21, 1796. The National Convention promulgated the Revolutionary calendar in order to count time from the establishment of the Republic and to strike a blow against the Church and the clergy by abandoning the standard Gregorian calendar.]

outlining of certain conditions of their exercise gave to them, and with Taine [3] we may criticise the working conceptions of the French Revolution as abstract.

It is to be remembered, however, that a *working* conception can be abstract only insofar as that to which it refers for its functioning, needs only to be designated, not to be analytically defined. The abstract political individual of the seventeenth and eighteenth centuries and the abstract economic individual of the nineteenth century were quite concrete, everyday persons. They were pointed out by the negative definitions of those who speculated about them, and the negative definitions had reference to the hindrances to their activities which most interested the individuals. Thus Spinoza [4] was interested in a community in which the inherent reason of the individual should find its natural expression, and the passions should be relegated to their proper place. Such a state would be founded by and through a *libera multitudo*,[5] free in the Spinozistic sense that it would be conscious of its essentially rational nature. It is from the standpoint of Spinoza's theory of the passions as passive and privations that he is led to regard man as the embodiment of an abstract *potentia*, which by his definition comes to consciousness and so to freedom by the very disappearance of those privations which are our passions. It is the irony of Spinoza's speculation that for his conduct it was the passions, the negations, which were after all defined as to their content, while the *potentia* which was to exist in positive consciousness is defined only in terms of the cessation of the passions, and the conditions under which this may take

[3] [Hippolyte Adolphe Taine (1828–1893), French historian and critic. His criticism of the French Revolution, on the grounds that instead of destroying absolute power it merely placed this power in other hands, and that instead of increasing liberty it reduced liberty by increasing centralization, is presented in his *Les origines de la France contemporaine* (1876–1894).]

[4] [Benedictus de Spinoza (1632–1677), Dutch philosopher and maker of lenses, was author of the *Tractatus Theologico-Politicus* (1670) and *Ethics* (1677).]

[5] ["Free masses" or "free multitude (of people)."]

SELECTED WRITINGS

in the denouement of his *Ethics* is a mystical emotion. But in
his own struggle and in that which he predicated of all human
conduct it was through the definition of what he had to overcome that he designated the individual which was to rise
triumphant. This *potentia* has the right to express itself, but
the right is defined in terms of the obstacles to its expression.

The timorous Hobbes [6] facing the disturbances of the Puritan revolution and the worse conditions which were likely to
ensue defined the individual in terms of those hostile impulses
which must lead to a *bellum omnium contra omnes*.[7] It was
this human being, lifted through Hobbes's fear out of all human relationship, whose rights, recognized only in a state of
nature, must be entirely surrendered to an autocratic sovereign, who is defined entirely in terms of what he must surrender to be safely admitted within a human society. There
could and can be no doubt to whom Hobbes referred in his
abstract definition of the individual, nor can there be any
question that the definition indicates the hindrances which
keep the individual out of the social state to which he belongs.
In the case of Hobbes the rights—so-called—of man are positive. They are the concrete satisfactions of every desire, just
insofar as the man is able to attain that satisfaction. The individual who surrenders these rights, on the contrary, is entirely
empty as a social being. He is the mere creature of the absolute sovereign.

The revolution of 1688 found its philosopher in John
Locke,[8] and its theory in his *Treatise of Civil Government*.

[6] [Thomas Hobbes (1588–1679), English philosopher, author of the
Leviathan (1651). This treatise on political philosophy advocates absolute
government founded on social compact in order to secure men against
civil disorder.]

[7] ["War of all against all."]

[8] [John Locke (1632–1704), English empiricist philosopher, author of
An Essay Concerning Human Understanding (1690) and two *Treatises of
Civil Government* (1690). The second *Treatise of Civil Government* presents the political theory that government is founded on contract to
secure the liberty and property of the citizens.]

Building on the very foundations which had seemed so abhorrent to Hobbes, the party that dethroned James and brought in by act of Parliament William and Mary appealed to a certain common interest which they felt to be the interest of the individual. Thus we find in Locke's account of the state of nature the whole content of social existence which, according to Hobbes, was possible only under the absolute autocrat. There is lacking only a settled statement of law, received by common consent, an indifferent judge to administer it, and an executive to enforce the decisions. But this legislation, justice, and execution is only the carrying out of actions with reference to common ends which are already in the natures and conduct of men, before the government is constituted. The government comes in only to give adequate expression and effect to natural social attitudes and conduct of men in a state of nature. There is to be found property, the family, and neighborly interest in one another. Was ever human nature so quickly regenerated as between the publications of the *Leviathan* and the *Treatise of Civil Government?* With such a human nature, so admirable in its native state, the emphasis must now be laid upon the restrictions to be placed upon government, not those to be placed upon the individual. The laws must be free from the influence of private interest, they must have in view alone the public good. The taxes raised must be by common consent, and the original power of the people to fashion its own government for its own ends must not be placed in any other hands or power.

Here we have a statement of rights of the people against any usurping, misgoverning government. And they again are negative, and yet they are the issues of the revolution of 1688, the elimination of court and dynastic interests in legislation, the vigor of Parliament, and, in especial, its unquestioned hold upon the purse strings. But none of these human rights which Locke affirms over against a dethroned monarch is stated in positive form. There is no definition of the common good, nor of the purposes for which taxes should be raised and expended, nor what is the essential function of Parliament.

And for the purposes of presenting the case of the revolutionary party the statement was far more effective than one which had undertaken to state what the common good of the community was or in what lay the authority of the supreme legislative body.

With Rousseau [9] the affirmation of the social character of human nature is still more emphatic. There is not only a common good that exists, and can be recognized by all, there is also a common will by which it can be affirmed and enforced. The government which Locke calls out to carry out the social nature of men is but the expression of Rousseau's *volonté générale* [10] which, it is true, constructs a government as an instrument to carry out its purposes. This government, however, is but a means to accomplish a definite common purpose, commonly conceived, and the execution of which is commonly determined. Over against such a mere instrument, such a servant of the common interest and will, the rights of the men who make up the state are the more sharply defined, but for that very purpose negatively stated. A statement of them was given in the form of the preamble to the constitution of the year four.

The rights of man, especially those which have been called natural rights, have been the expression of certain negative conditions under which men in society and under government could express themselves. And they have been formulated with reference to definite hindrances which have brought to consciousness the powers which were seeking expression, but only in terms of the obstacles themselves. In the *Areopagitica*, in the whole eloquent plea for freedom of publication, Milton undertakes no definition of what is good to print, and we are in the same case today.[11] After all we are legally free to say and to print what a jury of twelve talesmen think it proper

[9] [Jean Jacques Rousseau (1712–1778), French philosopher and man of letters. His *Social Contract* (1762) influenced the makers of the French Revolution.]

[10] [Rousseau's phrase, in the *Social Contract*, for the "general will."]

[11] [John Milton (1608–1674), English poet. His pamphlet, *Areopagitica* (1644), is a classic defense of freedom of the press.]

for us to say and print. If this legal situation were the actual situation and the determination of what we might say or publish did lie with any twelve theoretically good men and true, picked by the sheriff, and not with what we call public sentiment, the situation would be ludicrously absurd. However, public sentiment does not undertake to define what it is proper to print except over against the dictum of a legislature or a judge, and then it does not speak positively as to what is the nature of what may be said or printed. It approves or disapproves of the particular law or decision that is applied in the particular case, and if you undertake to formulate a right out of this, you find that you have only an abstraction.

The natural right to liberty may be rendered by the pregnant phrase that there is no freedom except under the law, which is another way of saying that nothing may be forbidden to you which must not, by the same act, be forbidden to everyone else under the same conditions, although this is not all that this phrase implies; but it will tell you nothing of what you are at liberty to do. It has always been for the crushing-out of exceptional privileges that our wars of freedom have been fought. Not even the statement that a man must be an end and never a means can be made a positive content, i.e., can be made into a positive statement of what responsible personality consists in. In general no man is free who has not the means of expressing himself, but just what is necessary to that self-expression cannot be made clear. It is probable that Epictetus [12] was far freer than was his master, and at the present time millions of men are expressing their freedom in exposing their bodies to torture and death. I do not say that we cannot formulate a fairly comprehensive statement of what has come to be the stature and measure of what the citizen should be in our minds at the present moment. We would give him undoubtedly economic freedom, an education, an association with his fellow citizens and fellow workmen that would ensure him the means of control over situations affect-

12 [Epictetus (ca. A.D. 60), Greek Stoic philosopher who was also a slave.]

ing his physical, social, and intellectual well-being. But of one thing we may be sure—that the next struggle for liberty, or our liberties, will arise out of some infraction that will not have reference to the definition which we have formulated of what the man should be and, consequently, of what constitute his liberties. On the contrary, we will find in all probability that the struggle will lead to a quite different definition from the one with which we started. No more illuminating instance of such a struggle can be found than in the fight of laborers for liberty to combine. The contests have always been over concrete restrictions, and every victory and defeat has left the question of what is the right to liberty of combination still undecided, though it has settled possibly for long periods to come a certain class of cases. The contents of our so-called natural rights have always been formulated negatively, with reference to restrictions to be overcome. When these restrictions have been overcome they represent a positive content of what we call for the time being our liberties. Thus we claim freedom of conscience in religious conduct. Slavery has gone by the board. Popular education, freedom of laborers to combine, etc., are milestones in our progress, and at each struggle we have added something to the fundamental rights of the man who is a part of the modern community. But we have also discovered that we never fight our battles over again. It is never the same question that arises again, and over against the new situation we find ourselves as unable satisfactorily to define the content of what our liberties are as our forefathers have been before us. We feel the narrow walls and brace ourselves to burst open the doors of opportunity that we find shut, but we can never apply the keys by which former doors were locked.

Historians of the theory of natural rights take pains to point out that the question of the inherent character of these rights has been confused with that of their priority to the society within which they find their expression. The most glaring instance of this error is to be found in the common assumption of the contract theorists of society, that we can conceive of the individual citizen existing before the community, in the possession of the rights which afterward the society undertakes to protect. On the contrary, it is pointed out that a right implies a recognition, and that this is a recognition which cannot be found outside of an organized social group. Thus they deny the possibility of rights inhering in the men in the state of nature as presented by Spinoza and Hobbes, for these men have only powers, such as have the beasts of the field, but no rights. On the other hand, the state of nature which upon Locke's hypothesis precedes the compact forming the state is already a society, however deficient it may have been in governmental institutions. Had Locke had the acquaintance of our anthropologists with primitive groups he would have recognized that his precontract men would have possessed an organized group of social habits out of which indeed governmental institutions were to arise, but which already performed the functions of government as definitely as the later institutions were destined to do. Rousseau of course is subject to the same error of supposing that his socially endowed men with their recognition of each other's personalities could have existed without some form of social organization that must have fulfilled the function in some way of social control. If we are to correct their history we would substitute, for the coming together of these Lockean and Rousseauian precontract men, the situations in which tribes that include a number of clans find the blood feuds so costly in life and tribe strength, that they get together to formulate a graduated set of fines and primitive courts to enforce these penalties. Here governmental institutions arise out of communities that have been controlled largely by customs that needed no institutional instruments for the exercise of their function. Here the rights that are formulated and enforced have already existed and hence have been already recognized in another form, and indeed in a true sense have been already enforced.

If we rob the term "natural right" of this implication of nature—that the right existed in a previous state of nature—can the term still be retained? We find that the term "natural right" is bound up with another very important conception in the history of political theory, that of natural law. Here the reference to nature does not imply a prior existence, but points rather to the fundamental character of the law, or in the other case to the fundamental character of the right. Here the emphasis upon *natural* sets it off against what is left to be unnatural. Thus there is supposed to be a natural law of propinquity in marriage which throws into sharp contrast instances of unnatural marriages. And there are in the same sense the natural rights which may be contrasted with the unnatural rights which have been conferred upon privileged classes or individuals. Thus equality has been asserted as natural to man, and freedom of movement in the satisfaction of his wants. And the term may have either a backward or a forward look.

> When Adam dug and Eve span
> Who was then the gentleman? [13]

looked backward for the typical expression of human nature. Nature as Aristotle conceived it,[14] on the other hand, reached its typical expression at the end of a period of growth or realization. And a modern evolutionist, Herbert Spencer,[15] has presented the hypothesis of a human society that is to be the result of a process of evolution, within which there is to be complete adaptation, so that finally there will arise a human nature that is as yet only in embryo.

This conception of a right that belongs to the nature of society and that of the men who constitute that society brings us finally to the question, what beyond its recognition is in-

---

[13] [John Ray, *English Proverbs* (1678).]

[14] [Aristotle (384–322 B.C.), Greek philosopher whose theories of logic, knowledge, and reality have shaped Western thought. His concepts of nature and man are presented in his treatises *Physics* and *On the Soul*, and his treatments of morality and politics are to be found in his *Nicomachean Ethics* and *Politics*.]

[15] [Herbert Spencer (1820–1903), English philosopher, author of *Synthetic Philosophy*, 10 vols. (1860–1896). In social philosophy he advanced the theory of social evolution through natural selection and individual competition.]

volved in a right. We have seen that it comes to consciousness
through some infraction, but this does not reveal its essential
character. It can only exist in a society. Is it, then, conferred
upon the individual by the group or society? From the standpoint of Bentham [16] and Austin [17] there are no natural rights,
all rights being conferred, unless we accept Spencer's criticism
on Benthamism that there must be assumed an original right
to the enjoyment of pleasure. In any case it is the *common
interest* on the part of society or those who constitute society
in that which is the right of the individual which gives that
right its recognition, and gives the ground for the enforcement of the right.

The attitude of the individual and of society may, however,
be quite different, depending upon the point of view we adopt
as to the character of the object which the individual sets before himself as his end. Is he pursuing a private end which
chances to have the approval of the rest of the community?
Or is his object one that is to him also a common good? Even
Mill [18] has sought to show that through indissoluble association the private end may become the common end in the view
of the individual himself. Kant [19] sought, approaching the
problem from the opposite pole to reach a like goal through
substituting the good will itself for the universal form of the
act, advancing then from the good will as an end to a society
of good wills as a kingdom of ends. It remained for post-
Kantian philosophy to find in the doctrine of the universality

16 [Jeremy Bentham (1748–1832), English philosopher and jurist. His
Introduction to the Principles of Morals and Legislation (1789) applied
the principle of utility to ethics and law.]

17 [John Austin (1790–1859), English jurist. His *Province of Jurisprudence* (1832) and *Lectures on Jurisprudence* (1862) proposed a legal
positivism that distinguished law from morals.]

18 [John Stuart Mill (1806–1873), English philosopher and economist.
His essays, *On Liberty* (1859) and *Considerations on Representative Government* (1860), are classic documents of liberalism.]

19 [Kant's conceptions of the universality of law proceeding from the rational will and of humanity as a kingdom of ends are expressed in his
Fundamental Principles of the Metaphysic of Ethics (1785).]

of the end of the individual's act, and the fact that that end must be social, being an objectification of the self, the starting point for a theory of the state. I have no intention of discussing this theory. I wish simply to point out that Kant, Hegel, and Mill all assume that the individual in society does in large measure pursue ends which are not private, but are in his own mind public goods and his own good because they are public goods. Here we have a basis for a doctrine of rights which can be natural rights without the assumption of the existence of the individual and his right prior to society. The right is arbitrary from the standpoint of neither the individual nor the community. Insofar as the end is a common good, the community recognizes the individual's end as a right because it is also the good of all, and will enforce that right in the interest of all. An evident illustration is found in property. The individual seeks property in a form which at the same time recognizes the property of others. In the same fashion the community in recognizing property as a common social object, which is yet the end of the individual, enforces the right of the individual to his own possession. This character certainly inheres in all so-called natural rights. In all of them we recognize that the individual in asserting his own right is also asserting that of all other members of the community, and that the community can only exist insofar as it recognizes and enforces these common ends, in which both the individual and the community are expressed.

It follows from this conception that the number of natural rights will be limited and in some sense defined at any time, depending upon the meaning we give to the term "enforce." If by that we imply the exercise of *force majeure* through the judicial and executive institutions of the community, the number of kinds or rights which can be enforced at any one time in a community will be necessarily limited. If by enforcement we imply as well the action of custom, public opinion, and sympathetic response, and indeed these are the chief forces that enforce the will of the community, then the number of natural rights which men may possess will be practically unlimited, for their common objects may not be counted. Even the most selfish end must have the form of a public good, to have any value to the private individual, otherwise it cannot be his to have and to hold. It is evident that in one sense we have boxed the compass. We started with life, liberty, security, equality, pursuit of happiness, as natural rights. They were recognized as present in happiness, as natural rights. They were recognized as present in consciousness only when they were in some manner trenched upon. They were found to be incapable of definition as to their content. From the point of view just suggested, every object that is pursued in a common or social form, implies a common good, that may demand recognition and the enforcement of the right of the individual. Here there is no limit to the number of such goods, and hence no limit to such rights. They seem to be definable in terms of contents, for they are all the common interests of men and mankind, and we have them as contents ever in mind, as they are prizes of our effort, and the solace of our hours of relaxation.

This anomalous situation repeats itself when we look to the nature of human rights and to their guaranties in our political and judicial institutions. What is evident at once is the difficulty of formulating fundamental rights which are to be distinguished from the multitudinous objects, the ends of actions, that are sought through our government and courts. The problem is that of determining the distinction that is to be made between the private right which must take its chances against other demands of a like sort and the specific common good which is endangered and calls for the especial protection of our institutions. I think I shall not be subject to contradiction if I assert that in this country at least, where we have gone further than men have gone in other countries in the attempt to formulate fundamental rights in our written constitutions, and in the use of the courts in their protection, we have not succeeded in rendering definite what the rights are which should receive these guaranties, and that behind the effort to state and defend these rights have always loomed other issues, which theoretically should be kept out of the question, but which come to be the deciding influences in the action of the courts.

It is evident that we do not assume that in other cases than those especially protected human rights are to be sacrificed. On the contrary, we assume that they are protected in the ordinary process of social conduct, both within and without the courts. Nor do we or should we assume that the rights which are so protected are less precious than those which call for the unusual action provided by our state and federal constitutions. On the contrary, must we not assume that issues which arise under the application of these guaranties are those leading to the formulation of new objects and the rights which attach to them? It is largely under the doctrine of the police power, that such new objects and rights are emerging in our kingdom of ends, and here what is demanded is not an exact definition of abstract human liberties, of the right to the due process of law, but that these new interests which have been what we have been pleased to call private interests in the past, should have the opportunity to appear as common goods. It is evident that categories which are to serve all these purposes must be abstract and empty of content and that they should get their content through the struggle which arises on the bare floor and between their distant walls.

It is not for me to discuss the architecture, curious and at times fascinating in its archeological interest, of the staircases and corridors and doorways by which these modern throbbing issues reach these halls, nor the strange garbs that they have to assume to be presented at court. It is important to recognize what is going on, and to distinguish between that part of the process which merely holds the issue back from making its plea, and that which allows it to become gradually formulated. And it is important that we should realize the relation between these two phases of the process. This can be recognized in the instances which are most in evidence in the courts, those having to do with the protection of rights involved in property. In the social legislation which is appearing in such volume in all our states, rights which have in the past inhered in property are seriously affected. Now it is not of importance that these earlier rights should be protected if some common good which they have failed to recognize is at stake, nor should there be obstacles placed in the way of the appearance of this common good involved, in the interest of the ancient right. What is of importance is that all the interests which are involved should come to expression. For this purpose it is of importance that no hasty action should take place. And from this standpoint it is clear that political guaranties which delay action in the legislatures and constitutional provisions which are enforced in the courts have the same function.

On the face of it the former method, that of political guaranties, is the more logical, for it is in the legislature that it is possible to present more fully the human interests that are involved. Especially in a legislature such as the English, in which the responsibility for the execution of the laws is and must be felt. And in England the political guaranties are practically the only ones in existence. But I cannot discuss the relative value of these two types of guaranties, I can only insist that we should recognize that the drag which we put by means of both of them upon the changes in the structure in our society serves only the purpose of enabling all the interests that are involved in the issue at stake to come to the surface and be adequately estimated. Let us labor under no delusion; while we do not want hasty or ill-considered action, there is after all no right that must not eventually get its formulation in terms of a common good so universal that even those most opposed in the struggle will accept and acclaim it. And such a formulation must eventually take place in terms of concrete living interests.

In other words, we must recognize that the most concrete and most fully realized society is not that which is presented in institutions as such, but that which is found in the interplay of social habits and customs, in the readjustments of personal interests that have come into conflict and which take place outside of court, in the change of social attitude that is not dependent upon an act of legislature. In the society which is closest to that of the primitive man we find the reality of all that is prefigured and set out in the institutions, and while problems that are not and cannot be solved through the readjustments of the individual's habit and the immediate change in social attitudes have to be dealt with in the halls of legislature and the rooms of our high courts, they are only brought there to enable men to envisage them more clearly and especially to become conscious of interests which could not appear immediately in their reactions to each other. When, however, this has taken place and the essential meaning of the problem has been grasped, its solution lies in the action of common citizens with reference to the common goods, which our institutions have brought to their view and so analyzed that they can react to these new interests as they have to those to which they are already adjusted.

In these days of discussion over the meaning of *Kultur*, we may entertain a false view of institutions. They are the tools and implements of the community; they are not civilization itself. Society has progressed by a process of integration which has gradually brought men and women who have been separated by physical and social distances so close together that they have come to react to those who have been afar off as to those with whom they have been in immediate sympathetic relation, and political institutions have held people together in these as yet not fully integrated groups and in part have helped them to get still closer together and in part have kept them still farther apart. The political institution has especially held men together because it has represented and in some sense undertaken to make good, what was lacking through the absence of immediate social interrelationship. Thus through military activity men of different groups and different localities have been brought into a relationship which could be but the shadow of a real human community. And yet the relation of those thus socially and geographically at a distance could be mediated by the direct connection to the monarch. Here was a common bond, though it did not run from man to man directly, but from each to the sovereign. It became, of course, a basis for direct relationship in war through the attitude toward the common leader. But it also served other purposes. It gave in the first place a sense of the larger social whole to which men belonged. In the second place, the subjection to the monarch carried with it the theory at least of his protection. Thus the relation to the king could serve to replace in some degree the complete socialization of the whole realm. The king was the guarantee for all the rights that were not respected because men belonged to so many different groups and classes and districts instead of to one self-conscious community. Not only military activity has thus brought men of different groups together and held them together by means of a political institution till social integration could take place. Religion has served the same purpose. In Europe Pope and Emperor were together the institutional figures which in the Holy Roman Empire drew the shadowy outlines of Christendom and made it possible for men to realize that theoretically they belonged to a single society. But even more compelling than the influence of arms and religious faiths has been the influence of barter and trade and the wealth which they have procreated. Exchange of goods does not wait upon the decision of the clanging fight nor the acceptance of the prophet's message. It has undistanced the Alexanders and the Gregorys,[20] and has set up a tenuous society of economic men from which no accessible member of the human race is excluded. Thus has money, that root of all evil, set the most grandiose problem to human kind of achieving the completed society which wealth-in-exchange has sketched. But if men that are otherwise hostile to each other will trade together there must be some guarantee that

[20] [Alexander the Great (356–323 B.C.), king of Macedonia, united the Greeks and conquered the known world of the Near East. His conquests spread Greek culture and ushered in the Hellenistic Age.

Gregory was the name of sixteen popes. The first was Gregory the Great, later St. Gregory (*ca.* 540–604), who increased the authority of the Roman See over other Christian churches. Others of the same name, most notably Gregory VII, who was pope from 1073 to 1085, carried on the organization of the Church with final authority located at Rome.]

the human rights which neither is bound to respect in the other shall be regarded at least insofar as they continue to trade and barter. Let these same economic processes within a community force men from different classes together into relations which do not carry with them their own social organization and hence their own guarantee of mutual rights, and again some outside institution must arise to act as a surrogate for the control which a completely organized group would exercise directly. In a word, the political institution presupposes first, relations set up between those at an effective distance from each other, distance which may be measured in miles and days, or in unsurmounted barriers of social classes and castes; and secondly, that the social control over the conduct of men in this relationship, which would arise through the other social relations if these distances were overcome, must in the interest of the whole be exercised by some compelling social force within the radius of whose action the distant individuals fall; and thirdly, that with the completion of the socialization of those who lie within this relationship the function of the institution, its guarantee of rights, ceases. Most of our quarrels are settled out of court, and except at the street corners within the loop district few of our actions are governed by the police, nor are human rights the less carefully guarded; they are infinitely better protected than the most vigilant police administration or system of courts could guard them. Human rights are never in such danger as when their only defenders are political institutions and their officers.

If this is in any sense a true account of the situation, every right that comes up for protection by our courts or other constitutional institution is confessedly in a form which is incomplete and inadequate, because it represents a social situation which is incomplete and inadequate. Until that situation can change the right may demand such defense as an institution can give it. But to stereotype the incomplete social situation even in the interest of action which should be neither hasty nor inconsiderate is not the proper function of the institution. It is true that until the human interests involved can be brought to public consciousness action should halt. But is it wise to have one organ to halt action and quite others or perhaps none at all for bringing these issues to the surface when the actual right is being safeguarded?

Furthermore, whatever confidence we may have in the brakes and drags which we put upon the wheels of popular action, we should not forget that the ultimate guarantee must be found in the reaction of men and women to a human situation so fully presented that their whole natures respond. However lacking in rigidity and solidity this may seem, it is at bottom the only guarantee of a human right to which we can finally appeal. Our other appeals are to institutions which delay the action in this highest court, and are legitimate when they make possible the complete presentation of the case. But is it wise to put our faith entirely in the valiant delayer of action, rather than in the agencies which will lead to the final social readjustments through their adquate presentation of the issues involved? Is it not true that our confidence in our courts has worked in no small degree with other causes to weaken the responsibility of our legislatures on the one hand, and on the other, to lead many of us to face social problems by turning our backs upon them, and approach them only when we have exhausted every delay the constitution provides?

✒ XIV ✒

SCIENTIFIC METHOD AND
INDIVIDUAL THINKER

The scientist in the ancient world found this test of reality in the evidence of the presence of the essence of the object. This evidence came by way of observation, even to the Platonist. Plato could treat this evidence as the awaking of memories of the ideal essence of the object seen in a world beyond the heavens during a former stage of the existence of the soul.[1] In the language of *Theaetetus*[2] it was the agreement of fluctuating sensual content with the thought-content imprinted in or viewed by the soul. In Aristotle[3] it is again the agreement of the organized sensuous experience with the vision which the mind gets of the essence of the object through the perceptual experience of a number of instances. That which gives the stamp of reality is the coincidence of the percept with a rational content which must in some sense be in the mind to ensure knowledge, as it must be in the cosmos to ensure existence, of the object. The relation of this test of reality to an analytical method is evident. Our perceptual world is always more crowded and confused than the ideal contents by which the reality of its meaning is to be tested.

[From *Creative Intelligence: Essays in the Pragmatic Attitude* (New York: Henry Holt and Co., 1917), pp. 176–227. Reprinted by permission of Holt, Rinehart and Winston, Inc.]

[1] [Plato presented this theory in his dialogue, *Meno.*]

[2] [A dialogue by Plato devoted to the definition of knowledge and its relation to sense perception and opinion.]

[3] [Aristotle's major works in logic, natural science, epistemology, and metaphysics include: *Organum* (six treatises on logic), *Metaphysics, Physics, On the Heavens, History of Animals, Parts of Animals,* and *On the Soul.*]

The aim of the analysis varies with the character of the science. In the case of Aristotle's theoretical sciences, such as mathematics and metaphysics, where one proceeds by demonstration from the given existences, analysis isolates such elements as numbers, points, lines, surfaces, and solids, essences and essential accidents. Aristotle approaches nature, however, as he approaches the works of human art. Indeed, he speaks of nature as the artificer par excellence. In the study of nature, then, as in the study of the practical and productive arts, it is of the first importance that the observer should have the idea—the final cause—as the means of deciphering the nature of living forms. Here analysis proceeds to isolate characters which are already present in forms whose functions are assumed to be known. By analogy such identities as that of fish fins with limbs of other vertebrates are assumed, and some very striking anticipations of modern biological conceptions and discoveries are reached. Aristotle recognizes that the theory of the nature of the form or essence must be supported by observation of the actual individual. What is lacking is any body of observation which has value apart from some theory. He tests his theory by the observed individual which is already an embodied theory, rather than by what we are wont to call the facts. He refers to other observers to disagree with them. He does not present their observations apart from their theories as material which has existential value, independent for the time being of any hypothesis. And it is consistent with this attitude that he never presents the observations of others in support of his own doctrine. His analysis within this field of biological observation does not bring him back to what, in modern science, are the data, but to general characters which make up the definition of the form. His induction involves a gathering of individuals rather than of data. Thus analysis in the theoretical, the natural, the practical, and the productive sciences, leads back to universals. This is quite consistent with Aristotle's metaphysical position that since the matter of natural objects has reality through its realization in the form, whatever appears without such meaning can be accounted for only as the expression of the resistance which matter offers to this realization. This is the field of a blind necessity, not that of a constructive science.

Continuous advance in science has been possible only when analysis of the object of knowledge has supplied not elements of meanings as the objects have been conceived but elements abstracted from those meanings. That is, scientific advance implies a willingness to remain on terms of tolerant acceptance of the reality of what cannot be stated in the accepted doctrine of the time, but what must be stated in the form of contradiction with these accepted doctrines. The domain of what is usually connoted by the term facts or data belongs to the field lying between the old doctrine and the new. This field is not inhabited by the Aristotelian individual, for the individual is but the realization of the form or universal essence. When the new theory has displaced the old, the new individual appears in the place of its predecessor, but during the period within which the old theory is being dislodged and the new is arising, a consciously growing science finds itself occupied with what is on the one hand the debris of the old and on the other the building material of the new. Obviously, this must find its immediate *raison d'être* in something other than the meaning that is gone or the meaning that is not yet here. It is true that the barest facts do not lack meaning, though a meaning which has been theirs in the past is lost. The meaning, however, that is still theirs is confessedly inadequate, otherwise there would be no scientific problem to be solved. Thus, when older theories of the spread of infectious diseases lost their validity because of instances where these explanations could not be applied, the diagnoses and accounts which could still be given of the cases of the sickness themselves were no explanation of the spread of the infection. The facts of the spread of the infection could be brought neither under a doctrine of contagion which was shattered by actual events nor under a doctrine of the germ theory of disease, which was as yet unborn. The logical import of the dependence of these facts upon observation, and hence upon the individual experience of the scientist, I shall have occasion to discuss later; what I am referring to here is that the conscious growth of science is accompanied by the appearance of this sort of material.

There were two fields of ancient science, those of mathematics and of astronomy, within which very considerable advance was achieved, a fact which would seem therefore to offer exception to the statement just made. The theory of the growth of mathematics is a disputed territory, but whether mathematical discovery and invention take place by steps which can be identified with those which mark the advance in the experimental sciences or not, the individual processes in which the discoveries and inventions have arisen are almost uniformly lost to view in the demonstration which presents the results. It would be improper to state that no new data have arisen in the development of mathematics, in the face of such innovations as the minus quantity, the irrational, the imaginary, the infinitesimal, or the transfinite number, and yet the innovations appear as the recasting of the mathematical theories rather than as new facts. It is of course true that these advances have depended upon problems such as those which in the researches of Kepler [4] and Galileo [5] led to the early concepts of the infinitesimal procedure, and upon such undertakings as bringing the combined theories of geometry and algebra to bear upon the experiences of continuous change. For a century after the formulation of the infinitesimal method men were occupied in carrying the new tool of analysis into every field where its use promised advance. The conceptions of the method were uncritical. Its applications were the center of attention. The next century undertook to bring order into the concepts, consistency into the doctrine, and rigor into the reasoning. The dominating trend of this move-

[4] [Johannes Kepler (1571–1630), German astronomer who discovered that planetary orbits are elliptical and formulated mathematically the laws of the motions of the planets in their orbits around the sun.]

[5] [Galileo Galilei (1564–1642), Italian astronomer, mathematician, and physicist. He constructed astronomical telescopes, theorized that the planets move, and applied mathematics to physical phenomena.]

ment was logical rather than methodological. The development was in the interest of the foundations of mathematics rather than in the use of mathematics as a method for solving scientific problems. Of course this has in no way interfered with the freedom of application of mathematical technique to the problems of physical science. On the contrary, it was on account of the richness and variety of the contents which the use of mathematical methods in the physical sciences imported into the doctrine that this logical housecleaning became necessary in mathematics. The movement has been not only logical as distinguished from methodological but logical as distinguished from metaphysical as well. It has abandoned a Euclidean space with its axioms as a metaphysical presupposition, and it has abandoned an Aristotelian subsumptive logic for which definition is a necessary presupposition. It recognizes that everything cannot be proved, but it does not undertake to state what the axiomata shall be; and it also recognizes that not everything can be defined, and does not undertake to determine what shall be defined implicitly and what explicitly. Its constants are logical constants, as the proposition, the class and the relation. With these and their like and with relatively few primitive ideas, which are represented by symbols, and used according to certain given postulates, it becomes possible to bring the whole body of mathematics within a single treatment. The development of this pure mathematics, which comes to be a logic of the mathematical sciences, has been made possible by such a generalization of number theory and theories of the elements of space and time that the rigor of mathematical reasoning is secured, while the physical scientist is left the widest freedom in the choice and construction of concepts and imagery for his hypotheses. The only compulsion is a logical compulsion. The metaphysical compulsion has disappeared from mathematics and the sciences whose techniques it provides.

It was just this compulsion which confined ancient science. Euclidian geometry defined the limits of mathematics. Even mechanics was cultivated largely as a geometrical field. The metaphysical doctrine according to which physical objects had their own places and their own motions determined the limits within which astronomical speculations could be carried on. Within these limits Greek mathematical genius achieved marvelous results. The achievements of any period will be limited by two variables: the type of problem against which science formulates its methods, and the materials which analysis puts at the scientist's disposal in attacking the problems. The technical problems of the trisection of an angle and the duplication of a cube are illustrations of the problems which characterize a geometrical doctrine that was finding its technique. There appears also the method of analysis of the problem into simpler problems, the assumption of the truth of the conclusion to be proved and the process of arguing from this to a known truth. The more fundamental problem which appears first as the squaring of the circle, which becomes that of the determination of the relation of the circle to its diameter and development of the method of exhaustion, leads up to the sphere, the regular polyhedra, to conic sections and the beginnings of trigonometry. Number was not freed from the relations of geometrical magnitudes, though Archimedes [6] could conceive of a number greater or smaller than any assignable magnitude. With the method of exhaustion, with the conceptions of number found in writings of Archimedes and others, with the beginnings of spherical geometry and trigonometry, and with the slow growth of algebra finding its highest expression in that last flaring up of Greek mathematical creation, the work of Diophantus; [7] there were present all the conceptions which were necessary for attack upon the problems of velocities and changing velocities, and the development of the method of analysis which has been

[6] [Archimedes (287–212 B.C.), Greek mathematician, physicist, and inventor. His treatise, *Arenarius,* presented a system for counting into very high numbers.]

[7] [Diophantus (*ca.* 3rd century B.C.), Greek algebraist who specialized in solving a special kind of indeterminate algebraic equations.]

the revolutionary tool of Europe since the Renaissance. But the problems of a relation between the time and space of a motion that should change just as a motion, without reference to the essence of the object in motion, were problems which did not, perhaps could not, arise to confront the Greek mind. In any case its mathematics was firmly embedded in a Euclidian space. Though there are indications of some distrust, even in Greek times, of the parallel axiom, the suggestion that mathematical reasoning could be made rigorous and comprehensive independently of the specific content of axiom and definition was an impossible one for the Greek, because such a suggestion could be made only on the presupposition of a number theory and an algebra capable of stating a continuum in terms which are independent of the sensuous intuition of space and time and of the motion that takes place within space and time. In the same fashion mechanics came back to fundamental generalizations of experience with reference to motions which served as axioms of mechanics, both celestial and terrestrial: the assumptions of the natural motion of earthly substances to their own places in straight lines, and of celestial bodies in circles and uniform velocities, of an equilibrium where equal weights operate at equal distances from the fulcrum.

The incommensurable of Pythagoras [8] and the paradoxes of Zeno [9] present the "no thoroughfares" of ancient mathematical thought. Neither the continuum of space nor of motion could be broken up into ultimate units, when incommensurable ratios existed which could not be expressed, and when motion refused to be divided into positions of space or time since these are functions of motion. It was not until an

[8] [Pythagoras (*ca.* 582–507 B.C.), Greek philosopher who taught that number is the essence of all things, and who is credited with having discovered the theorem that bears his name in geometry.]

[9] [Zeno of Elea (*ca.* 490–430 B.C.), Greek philosopher who sought to demonstrate the unreality of motion and of multiplicity by a series of paradoxes.]

algebraic theory of number led mathematicians to the use of expressions for the irrational, the minus, and the imaginary numbers through the logical development of generalized expressions, that problems could be formulated in which these irrational ratios and quantities were involved, though it is also true that the effort to deal with problems of this character was in no small degree responsible for the development of the algebra. Fixed metaphysical assumptions in regard to number, space, time, motion, and the nature of physical objects determined the limits within which scientific investigation could take place. Thus though the hypotheses of Copernicus [10] and in all probability of Tycho Brahe [11] were formulated by Greek astronomers, their physical doctrine was unable to use them because they were in flagrant contradiction with the definitions the ancient world gave to earthly and celestial bodies and their natural motions. The atomic doctrine with Democritus' [12] thoroughgoing undertaking to substitute a quantitative for a qualitative conception of matter with the location of the qualitative aspects of the world in the experience of the soul appealed only to the Epicurean who used the theory as an exorcism to drive out of the universe the spirits which disturbed the calm of the philosopher.

There was only one field in which ancient science seemed to break away from the fixed assumptions of its metaphysics and from the definitions of natural objects which were the bases for their scientific inferences, this was the field of astron-

10 [Nicholas Copernicus (1473–1543), Polish astronomer whose work, *De revolutionibus orbium coelestium* (1543), advanced the heliocentric hypothesis according to which the sun is in the center of the system and all the planets, including the earth, revolve around the sun.]

11 [Tycho Brahe (1546–1601), Danish astronomer whose system offered a compromise between the Ptolemaic (geocentric) and Copernican (heliocentric) astronomies. Brahe's observations of planetary motions were the most exact of his time, and upon these observations Kepler, his successor, built his astronomical laws.]

12 [Democritus (*ca.* 460–370 B.C.), Greek philosopher who advanced the atomic theory of matter and who held that sense perceptions of quality are merely the result of quantitative distributions of atoms.]

omy in the period after Eudoxus.[13] Up to and including the
theories of Eudoxus, physical and mathematical astronomy
went hand in hand. Eudoxus' nests of spheres within spheres
hung on different axes revolving in different uniform periods
was the last attempt of the mathematician philosopher to state
the anomalies of the heavens, and to account for the stations,
the retrogressions, and varying velocities of planetary bodies
by a theory resolving all phenomena of these bodies into motions of uniform velocities in perfect circles, and also placing
these phenomena within a physical theory consistent with the
prevailing conceptions of the science and philosophy of the
time. As a physicist Aristotle felt the necessity of introducing
further spheres between the nests of spheres assigned by Eudoxus to the planetary bodies, spheres whose peculiar motions
should correct the tendency of the different groups of spheres
to pass their motions on to each other. Since the form of the
orbits of heavenly bodies and their velocities could not be
considered to be the results of their masses and of their relative positions with reference to one another; since it was not
possible to calculate the velocities and orbits from the physical characters of the bodies, since in a word these physical
characters did not enter into the problem of calculating the
positions of the bodies nor offer explanations for the anomalies which the mathematical astronomer had to explain, it
was not strange that he disinterested himself from the metaphysical celestial mechanics of his time and concentrated his
attention upon the geometrical hypotheses by means of which
he could hope to resolve into uniform revolutions in circular
orbits the anomalous motions of the planetary bodies. The
introduction of the epicycle with the deferent and the eccentric as working hypotheses to solve the anomalies of the heavens is to be comprehended largely in view of the isolation of
the mathematical as distinguished from the physical problem

[13] [Eudoxus of Cnidus (*ca.* 408–355 B.C.), Greek astronomer, mathematician, and physicist. The first Greek astronomer to offer a scientific explanation of planetary motions, he postulated a number of concentric
spheres to support the planets in their paths.]

of astronomy. In no sense were these conceptions working hypotheses of a celestial mechanics. They were the only means of an age whose mathematics was almost entirely geometrical for accomplishing what a later generation could accomplish by an algebraic theory of functions. As has been pointed out, the undertaking of the ancient mathematical astronomer to resolve the motions of planetary bodies into circular, uniform, continuous, symmetrical movements is comparable to the theorem of Fourier [14] which allows the mathematician to replace any one periodic function by a sum of circular functions. In other words, the astronomy of the Alexandrian period is a somewhat cumbrous development of the mathematical technique of the time to enable the astronomer to bring the anomalies of the planetary bodies, as they increased under observation, within the axioms of a metaphysical physics. The genius exhibited in the development of the mathematical technique places the names of Apollonius of Perga,[15] Hipparchus of Nicaea,[16] and Ptolemy [17] among the great mathematicians of the world, but they never felt themselves free to attack by their hypotheses the fundamental assumptions of the ancient metaphysical doctrine of the universe. Thus it was said of Hipparchus by Adrastus, a philosopher of the first century A.D., in explaining his preference for the epicycle to the eccentric as a means of analyzing the motions of the planetary bodies:

> He preferred and adopted the principle of the epicycle as more probable to his mind, because it ordered the sys-

14 [Jean Baptiste Joseph Fourier (1768–1830), French mathematician and physicist, noted for his researches on numerical functions.]

15 [Apollonius of Perga (247–205 B.C.), Greek mathematician of the Alexandrian school. His treatise on conic sections, which contained the work of his predecessors, including Euclid, has survived.]

16 [Hipparchus of Nicaea (190–125 B.C.), the first systematic astronomer of antiquity, discoverer of the order of the equinoxes.]

17 [Ptolemy of Alexandria (*fl*. A.D. 127–151), famous mathematician, astronomer, and geographer. His geocentric conception of the cosmos, with its theory of epicycles to account for planetary movements, dominated astronomy until the time of Copernicus.]

tem of the heavens with more symmetry and with a more intimate dependence with reference to the center of the universe. Although he guarded himself from assuming the role of the physicist in devoting himself to the investigations of the real movements of the stars, and in undertaking to distinguish between the motions which nature has adopted and those which the appearances present to our eyes, he assumed that every planet revolved along an epicycle, the center of which describes a circumference concentric with the earth.[18]

Even mathematical astronomy does not offer an exception to the scientific method of the ancient world, that of bringing to consciousness the concepts involved in their world of experience, organizing these concepts with reference to each, analyzing and restating them within the limits of their essential accidents, and assimilating the concrete objects of experience to these typical forms as more or less complete realizations.

At the beginning of the process of Greek self-conscious reflection and analysis, the mind ran riot among the concepts and their characters until the contradictions which arose from these unsystematized speculations brought the Greek mind up to the problems of criticism and scientific method. Criticism led to the separation of the many from the one, the imperfect copy from the perfect type, the sensuous and passionate from the rational and the intrinsically good, the impermanent particular from the incorruptible universal. The line of demarcation ran between the lasting reality that answered to critical objective thought and the realm of perishing imperfect instances, of partially realized forms full of unmeaning differences due to distortion and imperfection, the realm answering to a sensuous passionate unreflective experience. It would be a quite inexcusable mistake to put all that falls on the wrong side of the line into a subjective experience, for these char-

18 [The remarks by Adrastus of Aphrodisias on Hipparchus, as preserved by Adrastus' disciple, Theonis of Smyrna, in *Liber de Astronomia*, chap. 34. See Pierre Duhem, *Le système du monde* (Paris: Librairie scientifique, Hermann et cie, 1954), I, 454.]

acters belonged not alone to the experience, but also to the
passing show, to the world of imperfectly developed matter
which belonged to the perceptual passionate experience.
While it may not then be classed as subjective, the Greeks of
the Sophistic period felt that this phase of existence was an
experience which belongs to the man in his individual life,
that life in which he revolts from the conventions of society,
in which he questions accepted doctrine, in which he differentiates himself from his fellows. Protagoras [19] seems even
to have undertaken to make this experience of the individual,
the stuff of the known world. It is difficult adequately to assess
Protagoras' undertaking. He seems to be insisting both that
the man's experience as his own must be the measure of reality as known and on the other hand that these experiences present norms which offer a choice in conduct. If this is true Protagoras conceived of the individual's experience in its atypical
and revolutionary form as not only real but the possible
source of fuller realities than the world of convention. The
undertaking failed both in philosophic doctrine and in practical politics. It failed in both fields because the subjectivist,
both in theory and practice, did not succeed in finding a place
for the universal character of the object, its meaning, in the
mind of the individual and thus in finding in this experience the hypothesis for the reconstruction of the real world.
In the ancient world the atypical individual, the revolutionist,
the nonconformist was a self-seeking adventurer or an anarchist, not an innovator or reformer, and subjectivism in ancient
philosophy remained a skeptical attitude which could destroy
but could not build up.

Hippocrates [20] and his school came nearer consciously using
the experience of the individual as the actual material of the
object of knowledge. In the skeptical period in which they

[19] [Protagoras of Abdera (*ca*. 480–410 B.C.), Greek sophist who taught
that man is the measure of all things.]
[20] [Hippocrates (*ca*. 460–370 B.C.), Greek physician recognized as the
father of medicine.]

flourished they rejected on the one hand the magic of traditional medicine and on the other the empty theorizing that had been called out among the physicians by the philosophers. Their practical tasks held them to immediate experience. Their functions in the gymnasia gave their medicine an interest in health as well as in disease, and directed their attention largely toward diet, exercise, and climate in the treatment even of disease. In its study they have left the most admirable sets of observations, including even accounts of acknowledged errors and the results of different treatments of cases, which ancient science can present. It was the misfortune of their science that it dealt with a complicated subject-matter dependent for its successful treatment upon the whole body of physical, chemical, and biological disciplines as well as the discovery and invention of complicated techniques. They were forced after all to adopt a hopelessly inadequate physiological theory—that of the four humors—with the corresponding doctrine of health and disease as the proper and improper mixture of these fluids. Their marvelously fine observation of symptoms led only to the definition of types and a medical practice which was capable of no consistent progress outside of certain fields of surgery. Thus even Greek medicine was unable to develop a different type of scientific method except insofar as it kept alive an empiricism which played a not unimportant part in post-Aristotelian philosophy. Within the field of astronomy in explaining the anomalies of the heavens involved in their metaphysical assumptions, they built up a marvelously perfect Euclidian geometry, for here refined and exhaustive definition of all the elements was possible. The problems involved in propositions to be proved appeared in the individual experience of the geometrician, but this experience in space was uniform with that of everyone else and took on a universal not an individual form. The test of the solution was given in a demonstration which holds for everyone living in the same Euclidian space. When the mathematician found himself carried by his mathematical technique beyond the assumptions of a metaphysical physics he abandoned the field of physical astronomy and confined himself to the development of his mathematical expressions.

In other fields Greek science analyzed with varying success and critical skill only the conceptions found in the experience of their time and world. Nor did Greek thought succeed in formulating any adequate method by which the ultimate concepts in any field of science were to be determined. It is in Aristotle's statement of induction and the process of definition that we appreciate most clearly the inadequacy of their method. This inadequacy lies fundamentally in Aristotle's conception of observation which, as I have already noted, implies the recognition of an individual, that is, an object which is an embodied form or idea. The function of knowledge is to bring out this essence. The mind sees through the individuals the universal nature. The value of the observation lies, then, not in the controlled perception of certain data as observed facts, but in the insight with which he recognizes the nature of the object. When this nature has been seen it is to be analyzed into essential characters and thus formulated into the definition. In Aristotle's methodology there is no procedure by which the mind can deliberately question the experience of the community and by a controlled method reconstruct its received world. Thus the natural sciences were as really fixed by the conceptions of the community as were the exact sciences by the conceptions of a Euclidian geometry and the mathematics which the Greeks formulated within it. The individual within whose peculiar experience arises a contradiction to the prevailing conceptions of the community and in whose creative intelligence appears the new hypothesis which makes possible a new heaven and a new earth could utilize his individual experience only in destructive skepticism. Subjectivism served in ancient thought to invalidate knowledge not to enlarge it.

Zeller [21] has sketched a parallelism between the ideal state

21 [Edward Zeller (1814–1908), German philosopher whose *Greek Philosophy* (1844–1852; English translation, 1881) established his fame. On

of Plato and the social structure of the medieval world. The philosopher-king is represented by the Pope, below him answering to the warrior class in the Platonic state stands the warrior class of the Holy Roman Empire, who in theory enforce the dictates of the Roman curia, while at the bottom in both communities stand the mass of the people bound to obedience to the powers above. There is, however, one profound difference between the two, and that is to be found in the relative positions of the ideal worlds that dominate each. Plato's ideal world beyond the heavens gives what reality it has to this through the participation by the world of becoming in the ideas. Opinion dimly sensed the ideas in the evanescent objects about it, and though Plato's memory theory of knowledge assumed that the ideas had been seen in former existence and men could thus recognize the copies here, the ideal world was not within the mind but without. In a real sense the Kingdom of Heaven was within men in the medieval world, as was the Holy Roman Empire. They were ideal communities that ought to exist on earth, and it was due to the depravity of men that they did not exist. From time to time men undertook in various upheavals to realize in some part these spiritual and political ideals which they carried within them. And men not only carried within them the ideas of a New Jerusalem in which the interest of one was the interest of all and of an earthly state ordered by a divine decree to fulfill this Christian ideal, but the determining causes of the present condition and the future realization depended also upon the inner attitudes and experiences of the individuals themselves.

Without carrying the analogy here too far, this relation between the experience of the individual and the world which may arise through the realization of his ideas is the basis of the most profound distinction between the ancient world and the modern. Before the logic of this attitude could appear in

the point mentioned by Mead, see Vol. II of Zeller's *Plato and the Older Academy*, translated by S. F. Alleyne and A. Goodwin (London and New York: Longmans, Green and Co., 1888), pp. 490–491.]

science a long period of intellectual and social growth was necessary. The most essential part of this growth was the slow but steady development of psychological doctrine which placed the objective world in the experience of the individual. It is not of interest here to bring out the modern epistemological problem that grew out of this, or to present this in the world of Leibnitzian monads [22] that had no windows or in the Berkeleyan subjective idealism.[23] What is of interest is to point out that this attitude established a functional relationship between even the subjective experience of the individual and the object of knowledge. A skepticism based upon subjectivism might thereafter question the justification of the reference of experience beyond itself; it could not question knowledge and its immediate object.

Kant formalizes the relation of what was subjective and what was objective by identifying the former with the sensuous content of experience and the latter with the application of the forms of sensibility and understanding to this content. The relationship was formal and dead. Kant recognized no functional relationship between the nature of the *Mannigfaltigkeit* [24] of sensuous experience and the forms into which it was poured. The forms remained external to the content, but the relationship was one which existed within experience, not without it, and within this experience could be found the necessity and universality which had been located in the world independent of experience. The melting of these fixed Kantian categories came with the spring floods of the romantic idealism that followed Kant.

The starting point of this idealism was Kantian. Within experience lay the object of knowledge. The Idealist's principal undertaking was to overcome the skepticism that attached to

22 [A startling metaphysical theory advanced by G. W. Leibnitz (1646–1716), German philosopher and mathematician, in his *Monadology* (1714).]

23 [The doctrine that *esse* is *percipi* (to be is to be perceived) advanced by George Berkeley (1685–1753), Irish philosopher and clergyman, in his *Treatise Concerning the Principles of Human Knowledge* (1710).]

24 ["Manifold."]

the object of knowledge because of its reference to what lies outside itself. If, as Kant had undertaken to prove, the reality which knowledge implies must reach beyond experience, then, on the Kantian doctrine that knowledge lies within experience, knowledge itself is infected with skepticism. Kant's practical bridge from the world of experience to the world of things-in-themselves, which he walked by faith and not by sight, was found in the postulates of the conduct of the self as a moral being, as a personality. The romantic idealists advance by the same road, though as romanticists not critical philosophers, they fashioned the world of reality, that transcends experience, out of experience itself, by centering the self in the absolute self and conceiving the whole infinite universe as the experience of the absolute self. The interesting phase of this development is that the form which experience takes in becoming objective is found in the nature and thought of the individual, and that this process of epistemological experience becomes thus a process of nature, if the objective is the natural. In Kant's terms our minds give laws to nature. But this nature constantly exhibits its dependence upon underlying noumena that must therefore transcend the laws given by the understanding. The Romanticist insists that this other reality must be the same stuff as that of experience, that in experience arise forms which transcend those which bound the experience in its earlier phase. If in experience the forms of the objective world are themselves involved, the process of knowledge sets no limits to itself, which it may not, does not, by implication transcend. As further indication of the shift by which thought had passed into possession of the world of things-in-themselves stands the antimony which in Kantian experience marks the limit of our knowledge while in post-Kantian idealism it becomes the antithesis that leads to the synthesis upon the higher plane. Contradiction marks the phase at which the spirit becomes creative, not simply giving an empty formal law to nature, but creating the concrete universe in which content and form merge in true actuality. The relation of the sensuous content to the conceptual form is not dead, as in Kant's doctrine. It is fused as perception into concept and carries its immediacy and concreteness of detail into the concrete universal as the complete organization of stimulation and response pass into the flexible habit. And yet in the Hegelian logic, the movement is always away from the perceptual experience toward the higher realm of the *Idee*. Thought is creative in the movement, but in its ultimate reality it transcends spatial and temporal experience, the experience with which the natural and mathematical sciences deal. Thought is not a means of solving the problems of this world as they arise, but a great process of realization in which this world is forever transcended. Its abstract particularities of sensuous detail belong only to the finite experience of the partial self. This world is, therefore, always incomplete in its reality and, insofar, always untrue. Truth and full reality belong not to the field of scientific investigation.

In its metaphysics Romantic Idealism, though it finds a place for scientific discovery and reconstruction, leaves these disdainfully behind, as incomplete phases of the ultimate process of reality, as infected with untruth and deceptive unwarranted claims. The world is still too much with us. We recognize here three striking results of the development of reflective consciousness in the modern world:—first, it is assumed that the objective world of knowledge can be placed within the experience of the individual without losing thereby its nature as an object, that all characters of that object can be presented as belonging to that experience, whether adequately or not is another question; and secondly, it is assumed that the contradictions in its nature which are associated with its inclusion in individual experience, its references beyond itself when so included, may themselves be the starting point of a reconstruction which at least carries that object beyond the experience within which these contradictions arose; and thirdly, it is assumed that this growth takes place in a world of reality within which the incomplete experience of the individual is an essential part of the process, in which it is not a mere fiction, destroying reality by its representation, but is a growing point in that reality itself.

These characters of philosophic interpretation, the inclusion of the object of knowledge in the individual experience and the turning of the conflicts in that experience into the occasion for the creation of new objects transcending these contradictions, are the characters in the conscious method, of modern science, which most profoundly distinguish it from the method of ancient science. This, of course, is tantamount to saying that they are those which mark the experimental method in science.

That phase of the method upon which I have touched already has been its occupation with the so-called data or facts as distinguished from Aristotelian individuals.

Whenever we reduce the objects of scientific investigation to facts and undertake to record them as such, they become events, happenings, whose hard factual character lies in the circumstance that they have taken place, and this quite independently of any explanation of their taking place. When they are explained they have ceased to be facts and have become instances of a law, that is, Aristotelian individuals, embodied theories, and their actuality as events is lost in the necessity of their occurrence as expressions of the law; with this change their particularity as events or happenings disappears. They are but the specific values of the equation when constants are substituted for variables. Before the equation is known or the law discovered they have no such ground of existence. Up to this point they find their ground for existence in their mere occurrence, to which the law which is to explain them must accommodate itself.

There are here suggested two points of view from which these facts may be regarded. Considered with reference to a uniformity or law by which they will be ordered and explained they are the phenomena with which the positivist deals; as existences to be identified and localized before they are placed within such a uniformity they fall within the domain of the psychological philosopher who can at least place them in their relation to the other events in the experience of the individual who observes them. Considered as having a residual meaning apart from the law to which they have become exceptions, they can become the subject-matter of the rationalist. It is important that we recognize that neither the positivist nor the rationalist is able to identify the nature of the fact or datum to which they refer. I refer to such stubborn facts as those of the sporadic appearance of infectious diseases before the germ theory of the disease was discovered. Here was a fact which contradicted the doctrine of the spread of the infection by contact. It appeared not as an instance of a law, but as an exception to a law. As such, its nature is found in its having happened at a given place and time. If the case had appeared in the midst of an epidemic, its nature as a case of the infectious disease would have been cared for in the accepted doctrine, and for its acceptance as an object of knowledge its location in space and time as an event would not have been required. Its geographical and historical traits would have followed from the theory of the infection, as we identify by our calculations the happy fulfilment of Thales' prophecy.[25] The happening of an instance of a law is accounted for by the law. Its happening may and in most instances does escape observation, while as an exception to an accepted law it captures attention. Its nature as an event is, then, found in its appearance in the experience of some individual, whose observation is controlled and recorded as his experience. Without its reference to this individual's experience it could not appear as a fact for further scientific consideration.

Now the attitude of the positivist toward this fact is that induced by its relation to the law which is *subsequently* discovered. It has then fallen into place in a series, and his doctrine is that all laws are but uniformities of such events. He treats the fact when it is an exception to law as an instance of

25 [Thales of Miletus (*ca.* 636–546 B.C.), one of the Seven Wise Men of Greece and the father of Western philosophy. He predicted the eclipse of May 28, 585 B.C.]

the new law and assumes that the exception to the old law and the instance of the new are identical. And this is a great mistake,—the mistake made also by the neo-realist when he assumes that the object of knowledge is the same within and without the mind, that nothing happens to what is to be known when it by chance strays into the realm of conscious cognition. Any as yet unexplained exception to an old theory can happen only in the experience of an individual, and that which has its existence as an event in someone's biography is a different thing from the future instance which is not beholden to anyone for its existence. Yet there are, as I indicated earlier, meanings in this exceptional event which, at least for the time, are unaffected by the exceptional character of the occurrence. For example, certain clinical symptoms by which an infectious disease is identified have remained unchanged in diagnosis since the days of Hippocrates. These characters remain as characters of the instance of the law of germ-origin when this law has been discovered. This may lead us to say that the exception which appears for the time being as a unique incident in a biography is identical with the instance of a germ-induced disease. Indeed, we are likely to go further and, in the assurance of the new doctrine, state that former exceptions can (or with adequate acquaintance with the facts could) be proved to be necessarily an instance of a disease carried by a germ. The positivist is therefore confident that the field of scientific knowledge is made up of events which are instances of uniform series, although under conditions of inadequate information some of them appear as exceptions to the statements of uniformities, in truth the latter being no uniformities at all.

That this is not a true statement of the nature of the exception and of the instance, it is not difficult to show if we are willing to accept the accounts which the scientists themselves give of their own observation, the changing forms which the hypothesis assumes during the effort to reach a solution and the ultimate reconstruction which attends the final tested solution. Wherever we are fortunate enough, as in the biographies of men such as Darwin and Pasteur, to follow a number of the steps by which they recognized problems and worked out tenable hypotheses for their solution, we find that the direction which is given to attention in the early stage of scientific investigation is toward conflicts between current theories and observed phenomena, and that since the form which these observations take is determined by the opposition, it is determined by a statement which itself is later abandoned. We find that the scope and character of the observations change at once when the investigator sets about gathering as much of the material as he can secure, and changes constantly as he formulates tentative hypotheses for the solution of the problem, which, moreover, generally changes its form during the investigation. I am aware that this change in the form of the data will be brushed aside by many as belonging only to the attitude of mind of the investigator, while it is assumed that the "facts" themselves, however selected and organized in his observation and thought, remain identical in their nature throughout. Indeed, the scientist himself carries with him in the whole procedure the confidence that the fact-structure of reality is unchanged, however varied are the forms of the observations which refer to the same entities.[26]

[26] An analysis which has been many times carried out has made it clear that scientific data never do more than approximate the laws and entities upon which our science rests. It is equally evident that the forms of these laws and entities themselves shift in the reconstructions of incessant research, or where they seem most secure could consistently be changed, or at least could be fundamentally different were our psychological structure or even our conventions of thought different. I need only refer to the *Science et Hypothèse* of Poincaré and the *Problems of Science* of Enriques. The positivist who undertakes to carry the structure of the world back to the data of observation, and the uniformities appearing in the accepted hypotheses of growing sciences cannot maintain that we ever succeed in isolating data which must remain the same in the kaleidoscope of our research science; nor are we better served if we retreat to the ultimate elements of points and instants which our pure mathematics assumes and implicitly defines, and in connection with which it has worked out the modern theory of the number and continuous series, its statements of continuity and infinity.

The analysis of the fact-structure of reality shows in the first place that the scientist undertakes to form such a hypothesis that all the data of observation will find their place in the objective world, and in the second place to bring them into such a structure that future experience will lead to anticipated results. He does not undertake to preserve facts in the form in which they existed in experience before the problem arose nor to construct a world independent of experience or that will not be subject itself to future reconstructions in experience. He merely insists that future reconstructions will take into account the old in readjusting it to the new. In such a process it is evident that the change of the form in the data is not due to a subjective attitude of the investigator which can be abstracted from the facts. When Darwin, for instance, found that the marl dressings which farmers spread over their soil did not sink through the soil by the force of gravity as was supposed, but that the earthworm castings were thrown up above these dressings at nearly the same rate at which they disappeared, he did not correct a subjective attitude of mind. He created in experience a humus which took the place of a former soil, and justified itself by fitting it into the whole process of disintegration of the earth's surface. It would be impossible to separate in the earlier experiences certain facts and certain attitudes of mind entertained by men with reference to these facts. Certain objects have replaced other objects. It is only after the process of analysis, which arose out of the conflicting observations, has broken up the old object that what was a part of the object, heavier-things-pushing-their-way-through-soil-of-lighter-texture, can become a mere idea. Earlier it was an object. Until it could be tested the earthworm as the cause of the disappearance [of] the dressings was also Darwin's idea. It became fact. For science at least it is quite impossible to distinguish between what in an object must be fact and what may be idea. The distinction when it is made is dependent upon the form of the problem and is functional to its solution, not metaphysical. So little can a consistent line of cleavage between facts and ideas be indicated, that we can never tell where in our world of observation the problem of science will arise, or what will be regarded as structure of reality or what erroneous idea.

There is a strong temptation to lodge these supposititious fact-structures in a world of conceptual objects, molecules, atoms, electrons, and the like. For these at least lie beyond the range of perception by their very definition. They seem to be in a realm of things-in-themselves. Yet they also are found now in the field of fact and now in that of ideas. Furthermore, a study of their structure as they exist in the world of constructive science shows that their infra-sensible character is due simply to the nature of our sense-processes, not to a different metaphysical nature. They occupy space, have measurable dimensions, mass, and are subject to the same laws of motion as are sensible objects. We even bring them indirectly into the field of vision and photograph their paths of motion.

The ultimate elements referred to above provide a consistent symbolism for the finding and formulating of applied mathematical sciences, within which lies the whole field of physics, including Euclidian geometry as well. However, they have succeeded in providing nothing more than a language and logic pruned of the obstinate contradictions, inaccuracies, and unanalyzed sensuous stuff of earlier mathematical science. Such a rationalistic doctrine can never present in an unchanged form the objects with which natural science deals in any of the stages of its investigation. It can deal only with ultimate elements and forms of propositions. It is compelled to fall back on a theory of analysis which reaches ultimate elements and an assumption of inference as an indefinable. Such an analysis is actually impossible either in the field of the conceptual objects into which physical science reduces physical objects, or in the field of sensuous experience. Atoms can be reduced into positive and negative electrical elements and these may, perhaps do, imply a structure of ether that again invites further analysis and so on ad infinitum. None of the hypothetical constructs carry with themselves the character of being ultimate elements unless they are purely metaphysical. If they are fashioned to meet the actual problems of scientific research they will admit of possible further analysis, because they must be located and defined in the continuity of space and time. They cannot *be* the points and instants of modern mathematical theory. Nor can we reach ultimate elements in sensuous experience, for this lies also within a continuum. Furthermore, our scientific analyses are dependent upon the form that our objects assume. There is no general analysis which research in science has ever used. The assumption that psychology provides us with an analysis of experience which can be carried to ultimate elements or facts, and which thereby provides the elements out of which the objects of our physical world must be constructed, denies to psychology its rights as a natural science of which it is so jealous, turning it into a Berkeleyan metaphysics.

This most modern form of rationalism being unable to find ultimate elements in the field of actual science is compelled to take what it can find there. Now the results of the analysis of the classical English psychological school give the impression of being what Mr. Russell calls "hard facts," i.e., facts which cannot be broken up into others.[27] They seem to be the data of experience. Moreover, the term "hard" is not so uncompromising as is the term "element." A fact can be more or less hard, while an ultimate element cannot be more or less ultimate. Furthermore, the entirely formal character of the logic enables it to deal with equal facility with any content. One can operate with the more or less hard sense-data, putting them in to satisfy the seeming variables of the propositions, and reach conclusions which are formally correct. There is no necessity for scrutinizing the data under these circumstances, if one can only assume that the data are those which science is actually using. The difficulty is that no scientist ever analyzed his objects into such sense-data. They exist only in

[27] [Mead must have had in mind Bertrand Russell's conception of "hard data." See Bertrand Russell, *Our Knowledge of the External World* (Chicago and London: Open Court Publishing Company, 1914), pp. 70–71.]

philosophical textbooks. Even the psychologists recognize that these sensations are abstractions which are not the elements out of which objects of sense are constructed. They are abstractions made from those objects whose ground for isolation is found in the peculiar problems of experimental psychology, such as those of color or tone perception. It would be impossible to make anything in terms of Berkeleyan sense-data and of symbolic logic out of any scientific discovery. Research defines its problem by isolating certain facts which appear for the time being not as the sense-data of a solipsistic mind, but as experiences of an individual in a highly organized society, facts which, because they are in conflict with accepted doctrines, must be described so that they can be experienced by others under like conditions. The ground for the analysis which leads to such facts is found in the conflict between the accepted theory and the experience of the individual scientist. The analysis is strictly *ad hoc*. As far as possible the exception is stated in terms of accepted meanings. Only where the meaning is in contradiction with the experience does the fact appear as the happening to an individual and become a paragraph out of his biography. But as such an event, whose existence for science depends upon the acceptance of the description of him to whom it has happened, it must have all the setting of circumstantial evidence. Part of this circumstantial evidence is found in so-called scientific control, that is, the evidence that conditions were such that similar experiences could happen to others and could be described as they are described in the account given. Other parts of this evidence which we call corroborative are found in the statements of others which bear out details of this peculiar event, though it is important to note that these details have to be wrenched from their settings to give this corroborative value. To be most conclusive they must have no intentional connection with the experience of the scientist. In other words, those individuals who corroborate the facts are made, in spite of themselves, experiencers of the same facts. The perfection of this evidence is attained when the fact can happen to others and the observer simply details the conditions under which he made the observation, which can be then so perfectly reproduced that others may repeat the exceptional experience.

This process is not an analysis of a known world into ultimate elements and their relations. Such an analysis never isolates this particular exception which constitutes the scientific problems as an individual experience. The extent to which the analysis is carried depends upon the exigencies of the problem. It is the indefinite variety of the problems which accounts for the indefinite variety of the facts. What constitutes them facts in the sense in which we are using the term is their *exceptional* nature; formally they appear as particular judgments, being denials of universal judgments, whether positive or negative. This exceptional nature robs the events of a reality which would have belonged to them as instances of a universal law. It leaves them, however, with the rest of their meaning. But the value which they have lost is just that which was essential to give them their place in the world as it has existed for thought. Banished from that universally valid structure, their ground for existence is found in the experience of the puzzled observer. Such an observation was that of the moons of Jupiter made possible by the primitive telescope of Galileo. For those who lived in a Ptolemaic cosmos, these could have existence only as observations of individuals. As moons they had distinct meaning, circling Jupiter as our moon circles the earth, but being in contradiction with the Ptolemaic order they could depend for their existence only on the evidence of the senses, until a Copernican order could give them a local habitation and a name. Then they were observed not as the experiences of individuals but as instances of planetary order in a heliocentric system. It would be palpably absurd to refer to them as mere sense-data, mere sensations. They are for the time being inexplicable experiences of certain individuals. They are inexplicable because they have a meaning which is at variance with the structure of the whole world to which they belong. They are the phenomena termed accidental by Aristotle and rejected as full realities by him, but which have become, in the habitat of individual experience, the headstone of the structure of modern research of science.

A rationalism which relegates implication to the indefinables cannot present the process of modern science. Implication is exactly that process by which these events pass from their individual existence into that of universal reality, and the scientist is at pains to define it as the experimental method. It is true that a proposition implies implication. But the proposition is the statement of the result of the process by which an object has arisen for knowledge and merely indicates the structure of the object. In discovery, invention, and research the escape from the exceptional, from the data of early stages of observation, is by way of an hypothesis; and every hypothesis so far as it is tenable and workable in its form is universal. No one would waste his time with a hypothesis which confessedly was not applicable to all instances of the problem. A hypothesis may be again and again abandoned, it may prove to be faulty and contradictory, but insofar as it is an instrument of research it is assumed to be universal and to perfect a system which has broken down at the point indicated by the problem. Implication and more elaborated instances flow from the structure of this hypothesis. The classical illustration which stands at the door of modern experimental science is the hypothesis which Galileo formed of the rate of the velocity of a falling body. He conceived that this was in proportion to the time elapsed during the fall and then elaborated the consequences of this hypothesis by working it into the accepted mathematical doctrines of the physical world, until it led to an anticipated result which would be actually secured and which would be so characteristic an instance of a falling body that it would answer to every other instance as he had defined them. In this fashion he defined his inference as the anticipation of a result because this result was a part of the world as he presented it amended by his hypothesis. It is true that back of the specific implication of this result lay a mass of other implications, many not even presented specifically in thought and many others presented by symbols which generalized innumerable instances. These implications are for the scientist more or less implicit meanings, but they are meanings each of which may be brought into question and tested in the same fashion if it should become an actual problem. Many of them which would not have occurred to Galileo as possible problems have been questioned since his day. What has remained after this period of determined questioning of the foundations of mathematics and the structure of the world of physical science is a method of agreement with oneself and others, in (a) the identification of the object of thought, in (b) the accepted values of assent and denial called truth and falsehood, and in (c) referring to meaning, in its relation to what is meant. In any case the achievement of symbolic logic, with its indefinables and axioms, has been to reduce this logic to a statement of the most generalized form of possible consistent thought intercourse, with entire abstraction from the content of the object to which it refers. If, however, we abstract from its value in giving a consistent theory of number, continuity, and infinity, this complete abstraction from the content has carried the conditions of thinking in agreement with self and others so far away from the actual problem of science that symbolic logic has never been used as a research method. It has indeed emphasized the fact that thinking deals with problems which have reference to uses to which it can be put, not to a metaphysical world lying beyond experience. Symbolic logic has to do with the world of discourse, not with the world of things.

What Russell pushes to one side as a happy guess is the actual process of implication by which, for example, the minute form in the diseased human system is identified with unicellular life and the history of the disease with the life history of this form. This identification implies reclassification of these forms and a treatment of the disease that answers to their life history. Having made this identification we anticipate the result of this treatment, calling it an inference.

Implication belongs to the reconstruction of the object. As long as no question has arisen, the object is what it means or means what it is. It does not imply any feature of itself. When through conflict with the experience of the individual some feature of the object is divorced from some meaning the relationship between these becomes a false implication. When a hypothetically reconstructed object finds us anticipating a result which accords with the nature of such objects we assert an implication of this meaning. To carry this relation of implication back into objects which are subject to no criticism or question would of course resolve the world into elements connected by external relations, with the added consequence that these elements can have no content, since every content in the face of such an analysis must be subject to further analysis. We reach inevitably symbols such as X, Y, and Z, which can symbolize nothing. Theoretically we can assume an implication between any elements of an object, but in this abstract assumption the symbolic logician overlooks the fact that he is also assuming some content which is not analyzed and which is the ground of the implication. In other words this logician confuses the scientific attitude of being ready to question anything with an attitude of being willing to question everything at once. It is only in an unquestioned objective world that the exceptional instance appears and it is only in such a world that an experimental science tests the implications of the hypothetically reconstructed object.

The guess is happy because it carries with it the consequences which follow from its fitting into the world, and the guess, in other words the hypothesis, takes on this happy form solely because of the material reconstruction which by its nature removes the unhappy contradiction and promises the successful carrying out of the conflicting attitudes in the new objective world. There is no such thing as formal implication.

Where no reconstruction of the world is involved in our identification of objects that belong to it and where, therefore, no readjustment of conduct is demanded, such a logic symbolizes what takes place in our direct recognition of objects and our response to them. Then "X is a man implies X is mortal for all values of X" exactly symbolizes the attitude toward a man subject to a disease supposedly mortal. But it fails to symbolize the biological research which starting with inexplicable sporadic cases of an infectious disease carries over from the study of the life history of infusoria a hypothetical reconstruction of the history of disease and then acts upon the result of this assumption. Research science presents a world whose form is always universal, but this universal form is neither a metaphysical assumption nor a fixed form of the understanding. While the scientist may as a metaphysician assume the existence of realities which lie beyond a possible experience, or be a Kantian or neo-Kantian, neither of these attitudes is necessary for his research. He may be a positivist—a disciple of Hume [28] or of John Stuart Mill.[29] He may be a pluralist who conceives, with William James, that the order which we detect in parts of the universe is possibly one that is rising out of the chaos and which may never be as universal as our hypothesis demands. None of these attitudes has any bearing upon his scientific method. This simplifies his thinking, enables him to identify the object in which he is interested wherever he finds it, and to abstract in the world as he conceives it those features which carry with them the occurrence he is endeavoring to place. Especially it enables him to make his thought a part of the socially accepted and socially organized science to which his thought belongs. He is far too modest to demand that the world be as his inference demands.

He asks that his view of the world be cogent and convincing to all those whose thinking has made his own possible, and be an acceptable premise for the conduct of that society to which he belongs. The hypothesis has no universal and necessary characters except those that belong to the thought which preserves the same meanings to the same objects, the same relations between the same relata, the same attributes of assent and dissent under the same conditions, the same results of the same

[28] [David Hume (1711–1776), Scottish philosopher and historian. His *Treatise of Human Nature* (1739–1740) and *Inquiry Concerning Human Understanding* (1748) are classics of empirical philosophy.]

[29] [John Stuart Mill's *System of Logic* (1843) formulates the basic principles of inductive logic, since known as "Mill's Methods."]

combinations of the same things. For scientific research the meanings, the relations with the relata, the assent and dissent, the combinations and the things combined are all in the world of experience. Thinking in its abstractions and identifications and reconstructions undertakes to preserve the values that it finds, and the necessity of its thinking lies in its ability to so identify, preserve, and combine what it has isolated that the thought structure will have an identical import under like conditions for the thinker with all other thinkers to whom these instruments of research conduct are addressed. Whatever conclusions the scientist draws as necessary and universal results from his hypothesis for a world independent of his thought are due, not to the cogency of his logic, but to other considerations. For he knows if he reflects that another problem may arise which will in its solution change the face of the world built upon the present hypothesis. He will defend the inexorableness of his reasoning, but the premises may change. Even the contents of tridimensional space and sensuous time are not essential to the cogency of that reasoning nor can the unbroken web of the argument assure the content of the world as invariable. His universals, when applied to nature, are all hypothetical universals; hence the import of experiment as the test of an hypothesis. Experience does not rule out the possible cropping up of a new problem which may shift the values attained. Experience simply reveals that the new hypothesis fits into the meanings of the world which are not shaken; it shows that, with the reconstruction which the hypothesis offers, it is possible for scientific conduct to proceed.

But if the universal character of the hypothesis and the tested theory belong to the instrumental character of thought in so reconstructing a world that has proved to be imperfect, and inadequate to conduct, the stuff of the world and of the new hypothesis are the same. At least this is true for the scientist who has no interest in an epistemological problem that does not affect his scientific undertakings in one way nor another. I have already pointed out that from the standpoint of logical and psychological analysis the things with which science deals can be neither ultimate elements nor sense-data; but that they must be phases and characters and parts of things in some whole, parts which can only be isolated because of the conflict between an accepted meaning and some experience. I have pointed out that an analysis is guided by the practical demands of a solution of this conflict; that even that which is individual in its most unique sense in the conflict and in attempts at its solution does not enter into the field of psychology—which has its own problems peculiar to its science. Certain psychological problems belong to the problems of other sciences, as, for example, that of the personal equation belongs to astronomy or that of color vision to the theory of light. But they bulk small in these sciences. It cannot be successfully maintained that a scientific observation of the most unique sort, one which is accepted for the time being simply as a happening in this or that scientist's experience, is as such a psychological datum, for the data in psychological textbooks have reference to *psychological* problems. Psychology deals with the consciousness of the individual in its dependence upon the physiological organism and upon those contents which detach themselves from the objects outside the individual and which are identified with his inner experience. It deals with the laws and processes and structures of this consciousness in all its experiences, not with *exceptional* experiences. It is necessary to emphasize again that for science these particular experiences arise within a world which is in its logical structure organized and universal. They arise only through the conflict of the individual's experience with such an accepted structure. For science individual experience *presupposes* the organized structure; hence it cannot provide the material out of which the structure is built up. This is the error of both the positivist and of the psychological philosopher, if scientific procedure gives us in any sense a picture of the situation.

A sharp contrast appears between the accepted hypothesis with its universal form and the experiences which invalidate the earlier theory. The reality of these experiences lies in their happening. They were unpredictable. They are not instances of a law. The later theory, the one which explains these occurrences, changes their character and status, making them necessary results of the world as that is conceived under this new doctrine. This new standpoint carries with it a backward view, which explains the erroneous doctrine, and accounts for the observations which invalidated it. Every new theory must take up into itself earlier doctrines and rationalize the earlier exceptions. A generalization of this attitude places the scientist in the position of anticipating later reconstructions. He then must conceive of his world as subject to continuous reconstructions. A familiar interpretation of his attitude is that the hypothesis is thus approaching nearer and nearer toward a reality which would never change if it could be attained, or, from the standpoint of the Hegelian toward a goal at infinity. The Hegelian also undertakes to make this continuous process of reconstruction an organic phase in reality and to identify with nature the process of finding exceptions and of correcting them. The fundamental difference between this position and that of the scientist who looks before and after is that the Hegelian undertakes to make the exception in its exceptional character a part of the reality which transcends it, while the scientist usually relegates the exception to the experience of individuals who were simply caught in an error which later investigation removes.

The error remains as a historical incident explicable perhaps as a result of the conditions under which it occurred, but insofar as it was an error, not a part of reality. It is customary to speak of it as subjective, though this implies that we are putting the man who was unwittingly in error into the position of the one who has corrected it. To entertain that error in the face of its correction would be subjective. A result of this interpretation is that the theories are abstracted from the world and regarded as something outside it. It is assumed that the theories are mental or subjective and change while the facts remain unchanged. Even when it is assumed that theories and facts agree, men speak of a correspondence or parallelism between idea and the reality to which it refers. While this attitude seems to be that of science toward the disproved theories which lie behind it, it is not its attitude to the theories which it accepts. These are not regarded as merely parallel to realities, as abstracted from the structure of things. These meanings go into the makeup of the world. It is true that the scientist who looks before and after realizes that any specific meaning which is now accepted may be questioned and discarded. If he carries his reflection far enough he sees that a complete elimination of all the meanings which might conceivably be so discredited would leave nothing but logical constants, a world with no facts in any sense. In this position he may of course take an agnostic attitude and be satisfied with the attitude of Hume or Mill or Russell. But if he does so, he will pass into the camp of the psychological philosophers and will have left the position of the scientist. The scientist always deals with an *actual* problem, and even when he looks before and after he does so insofar as he is facing in inquiry some actual problem. No actual problem could conceivably take on the form of a conflict involving the whole world of meaning. The conflict always arises between an individual experience and certain laws, certain meanings while others are unaffected. These others form the necessary field without which no conflict can arise. They give the man of research his ποῦ στῶ [30] upon which he can formulate his problem and undertake its solution. The possible calling in question of any content, whatever it may be, means always that there is left a field of unquestioned reality. The attitude of the scientist never contemplates or could contemplate the possibility of a world in which there would be no reality by which to test his hypothetical solution of the problem that arises. Nor does this attitude when applied to past discarded theories necessarily carry with it the implication that these older theories were subjective ideas in men's minds, while the reality lay beside and beyond them unmingled with ideas. It always finds a

[30] ["Standpoint" or "starting-point"; literally, "Where do I stand?"]

standpoint from which these ideas in the earlier situation are still recognized as reliable, for there are no scientific data without meanings. There could be no history of science on any other basis. No history of science goes back to ultimate elements or sense-data, or to any combination of bare data on one hand and logical elements on the other. The world of the scientist is always there as one in which reconstruction is taking place with continual shifting of problems, but as a real world within which the problems arise. The errors of the past and present appear as untenable hypotheses which could not bear the test of experiment if the experience were sufficiently enlarged and interpreted. But they are not mere errors to be thrown into the scrap heap. They become a part of a different phase of reality which a fuller history of the past records or a fuller account of the present interprets, giving them thereby their proper place in a real world.[31]

The completion of this program, however, awaits the solution of the scientific problem of the relation of the psychical and the physical with the attendant problem of the meaning of the so-called origin of consciousness in the history of the world. My own feeling is that these problems must be attacked from the standpoint of the social nature of so-called consciousness. The clear indications of this I find in the reference of our logical constants to the structure of thought as a means of communication, in the explanation of errors in the history of science by their social determination, and in the interpretation of the inner field of experience as the importation of social intercourse into the conscious conduct of the individual. But whatever may be the solution of these problems, it must carry with it such a treatment of the experience of the individual that the latter will never be regarded merely as a subjective state, however inadequate it may have proved itself as a scientific hypothesis. This seems to me to be involved in the con-

[31] In other words, science assumes that every error is *ex post facto* explicable as a function of the real conditions under which it really arose. Hence, "consciousness," set over against Reality, was not its condition.

ception of psychology as a natural science and in any legitimate carrying out of the Hegelian program of giving reality and creative import to individual experience. The experience of the individual in its exceptional character is the growing point of science, first of all in the recognition of data upon which the older theories break, and second in the hypothesis which arises in the individual and is tested by the experiment which reconstructs the world. A scientific history and a scientific psychology from which epistemology has been banished must place these observations and hypotheses together with erroneous conceptions and mistaken observations *within* the real world in such a fashion that their reference to the experience of the individual and to the world to which he belongs will be comprehensible. As I have indicated, the scientific theory of the physical and conscious individual in the world implied in this problem has still to be adequately developed. But there is implied in the conception of such a theory such a location of the process of thought in the process of reality as will give it an import both in the meanings of things and in the individual's thinking. We have the beginning of such a doctrine in the conception of a functional value of consciousness in the conduct of living forms, and the development of reflective thought out of such a consciousness which puts it within the act and gives it the function of preparation where adjustment is necessary. Such a process creates the situation with reference to which the form acts. In all adjustment or adaptation the result is that the form which is adjusted finds that by its adjustment it has created an environment. The ancients by their formulation of the Ptolemaic theory committed themselves to the world in which the fixed values of the heavenly over against the earthly obtained. Such a world was the interpretation of the experience involved in their physical and social attitudes. They could not accept the hypothesis of Aristarchus [32] because it conflicted with the world which they

[32] [Aristarchus of Samos (*ca.* 3rd century B.C.), Greek astronomer of the Alexandrian school who anticipated the Copernican theory that the sun is at rest and that the earth revolves around the sun.]

had created, with the values which were determining values for them. The same was true of the hypothesis of Democritus. They could not, as they conceived the physical world, accept its purely quantitative character. The conception of a disinterested truth which we have cherished since the Middle Ages is itself a value that has a social basis as really as had the dogma of the church. The earliest statement of it was perhaps that of Francis Bacon.[33] Freeing investigation from the church dogma and its attendant logic meant to him the freedom to find in nature what men needed and could use for the amelioration of their social and physical condition. The full implication of the doctrine has been recognized as that of freedom, freedom to effect not only values already recognized, but freedom to attain as well such complete acquaintance with nature that new and unrecognized uses would be at our disposal; that is, that progress should be one toward any possible use to which increased knowledge might lead. The cult of increasing knowledge, of continually reconstructing the world, took the place both of the ancient conception of adequately organizing the world as presented in thought, and of the medieval conception of a systematic formulation on the basis of the statement in church dogma of social values. This modern conception proceeds from the standpoint not of formulating values, but giving society at the moment the largest possible number of alternatives of conduct, i.e., undertaking to fix from moment to moment the widest possible field of conduct. The purposes of conduct are to be determined in the presence of a field of alternative possibilities of action. The ends of conduct are not to be determined in advance, but in view of the interests that fuller knowledge of conditions awakens. So there appears a conception of determining the field that shall be quite independent of given values. A real world which consists not of an unchanged universe, but of a universe which may be con-

---

[33] [Sir Francis Bacon (1561–1626), English philosopher, essayist, and statesman, author of *The Advancement of Learning* (1605) and the *Novum Organum* (1620), which aimed at grounding the sciences in induction.]

tinually readjusted according to the problems arising in the consciousness of the individuals within society. The seemingly fixed character of such a world is found in the generally fixed conditions which underlie the type of problems which we find. We determine the important conditions incident to the working out of the great problems which face us. Our conception of a given universe is formed in the effort to mobilize all the material about us in relation to these problems—the structure of the self, the structure of matter, the physical process of life, the laws of change and the interrelation of changes. With reference to these problems certain conditions appear fixed and become the statement of the world by which we must determine by experimental test the viability of our hypotheses. There arises then the conception of a world which is unquestioned over against any particular problem. While our science continually changes that world, at least it must be always realized as there. On the other hand, these conceptions are after all relative to the ends of social conduct which may be formulated in the presence of any freedom of action.

We postulate freedom of action as the condition of formulating the ends toward which our conduct shall be directed. Ancient thought assured itself of its ends of conduct and allowed these to determine the world which tested its hypothesis. We insist such ends may not be formulated until we know the field of possible action. The formulation of the ends is essentially a social undertaking and seems to follow the statement of the field of possible conduct, while in fact the statement of the possible field of conduct is actually dependent on the push toward action. A moving end which is continually reconstructing itself follows upon the continually enlarging field of opportunities of conduct.

The conception of a world of existence, then, is the result of the determination at the moment of the conditions of the solution of the given problems. These problems constitute the conditions of conduct, and the ends of conduct can only be determined as we realize the possibilities which changing conditions carry with them. Our world of reality thus becomes independent of any special ends or purposes and we reach an entirely disinterested knowledge. And yet the value and import of this knowledge is found in our conduct and in our continually changing conditions. Knowledge for its own sake is the slogan of freedom, for it alone makes possible the continual reconstruction and enlargement of the ends of conduct.

The individual in his experiences is continually creating a world which becomes real through his discovery. Insofar as new conduct arises under the conditions made possible by his experience and his hypothesis the world, which may be made the test of reality, has been modified and enlarged.

I have endeavored to present the world which is an implication of the scientific method of discovery with entire abstraction from any epistemological or metaphysical presuppositions or complications. Scientific method is indifferent to a world of things-in-themselves, or to the previous condition of philosophic servitude of those to whom its teachings are addressed. It is a method not of knowing the unchangeable but of determining the form of the world within which we live as it changes from moment to moment. It undertakes to tell us what we may expect to happen when we act in such or such a fashion. It has become a matter of serious consideration for a philosophy which is interested in a world of things-in-themselves, and the epistemological problem. For the cherished structures of the metaphysical world, having ceased to house the values of mankind, provide good working materials in the hypothetical structures of science, on condition of surrendering their metaphysical reality; and the epistemological problem, having seemingly died of inanition, has been found to be at bottom a problem of method or logic. My attempt has been to present what seems to me to be two capital instances of these transformations. Science always has a world of reality by which to test its hypotheses, but this world is not a world independent of scientific experience, but the immediate world surrounding us within which we must act. Our next action may find these conditions seriously changed, and then science will formulate this world so that in view of this problem we may logically construct our next plan of action. The plan of action should be made self-consistent and universal in its form, not that we may thus approach nearer to a self-consistent and universal reality which is independent of our conduct, but because our plan of action needs to be intelligent and generally applicable. Again science advances by the experiences of individuals, experiences which are different from the world in which they have arisen and which refer to a world which is not yet in existence, so far as scientific experience is concerned. But this relation to the old and new is not that of a subjective world to an objective universe, but is a process of logical reconstruction by which out of exceptions the new law arises to replace a structure that has become inadequate.

In both of these processes, that of determining the structure of experience which will test by experiment the legitimacy of the new hypothesis, and that of formulating the problem and the hypothesis for its solution, the individual functions in his full particularity, and yet in organic relationship with the society that is responsible for him. It is the import for scientific method of this relationship that promises most for the interpretation of the philosophic problems involved.

XV

THE PSYCHOLOGY OF PUNITIVE JUSTICE

The study of instincts on the one side and of the motor character of human conduct upon the other has given us a different picture of human nature from that which a dogmatic doctrine of the soul and an intellectualistic psychology presented to an earlier generation.

The instincts even in the lower animal forms have lost their rigidity. They are found to be subject to modification by experience, and the nature of the animal is found to be not a bundle of instincts but an organization within which these congenital habits function to bring about complex acts—acts which are in many cases the result of instincts which have modified each other. Thus new activities arise which are not the simple expression of bare instincts. A striking illustration of this is found in play, especially among young animal forms, in which the hostile instinct is modified and held in check by the others that dominate the social life of the animals. Again the care which the parent form gives to the infant animal admits of hostile features which, however, do not attain the full expression of attack and destruction usually involved in the instinct from which they arise. Nor is this merging and interaction of such divergent instinctive acts a process of alternate dominance of now one and now another instinct. Play and parental care may be and generally are of a piece, in which the inhibition of one tendency by the others has entered into the structure of the animal's nature and seemingly even of its congenital nervous organization. Another illustration of such a merging of divergent instincts is found in the elaborate wooing of the female among the birds.

[From *The American Journal of Sociology*, XXIII (1917–1918), 577–602.]

Back of all this type of organization of instinctive conduct lies the social life within which there must be cooperation of the different individuals, and therefore a continual adjustment of the responses to the changing attitudes of the animals that participate in the corporate acts. It is this body of organized instinctive reactions to one another which makes up the social nature of these forms, and it is from a social nature of this kind exhibited in the conduct of lower forms that our human nature is evolved. An elaborate analysis of this is still in the making, but certain great features in it stand out with sufficient clearness to warrant comment. We find two opposing groups of instincts, those which we have named hostile and those which may be termed friendly, the latter being largely combinations of the parental and sexual instincts. The import of a herding instinct lying back of them all is still very uncertain if not dubious. What we do find is that individuals adjust themselves to each other in common social processes, but come into conflict with each other frequently in the process, that the expression of this individual hostility within the whole social act is primarily that of the destructive hostile type, modified and molded by the organized social reaction, that where this modification and control breaks down, as, e.g., in the rivalry of males in the herd or pack, the hostile instinct may assert itself in its native ruthlessness.

If we turn to the human nature that has developed out of the social nature of lower animals, we find in addition to the organization of social conduct that I have indicated a vast elaboration of the process of adjustment of individuals to each other. This elaboration of gesture, to use Wundt's generalized term, reaches its most developed expression in language. Now language was first the attitude, glance of the eye, movement of the body and its parts indicating the oncoming social act to which the other individuals must adjust their conduct. It becomes language in the narrower sense when it is a common speech of whatever form; that is when through his gesture the individual addresses *himself* as well as the others who are involved in the act. His speech is their speech.

He can address himself in their gestures and thus present to himself the whole social situation within which he is involved, so that not only is conduct social but consciousness becomes social as well.

It is out of this conduct and this consciousness that human society grows. What gives it its human character is that the individual through language addresses himself in the role of the others in the group and thus becomes aware of them in his own conduct. But while this phase of evolution is perhaps the most critical in the development of man, it is after all only an elaboration of the social conduct of lower forms. Self-conscious conduct is only an exponent which raises the possible complications of group activity to a higher degree. It does not change the character of the social nature that is elaborated and complicated, nor does it change the principles of its organization. Human nature still remains an organization of instincts which have mutually affected each other. Out of such fundamental instincts as those of sex, parenthood, and hostility has arisen an organized type of social conduct, the conduct of the individual within the group. The attack upon the other individuals of the group has been modified and softened so that the individual asserts himself as over against the others in play, in courting, in care of the young, in certain common attitudes of attack and defense, without the attempted destruction of the individuals attacked. If we use the common terminology we shall account for these modifications by the process of trial and error within the evolution out of which has arisen the social form. Out of the hostile instinct has arisen conduct modified by the social instincts that has served to delimit the conduct springing from sex, parenthood, and mutual defense and attack. It has been the function of the hostile instinct to provide the reaction by which the individual asserts himself within a social process, thus modifying that process while the hostile conduct is itself modified *pro tanto*.[1] The result is the appearance of new individuals, certain types of sex mates, playmates, parent and child forms, mates in fight and mates in

1 ["To that extent."]

defense. While this assertion of the individual within the social process delimits and checks the social act at various points, it leads to a modified social response with a new field of operation which did not exist for the unmodified instincts. The source of these higher complexes of social conduct appears suddenly when through a breakdown of the organization of the social act there is enacted a crime of passion, the direct outcome of self-assertion within sex, family, or other group responses. Unmodified self-assertion under these conditions means the destruction of the individual attacked.

When now, through the exponent of self-consciousness, the complexities of social conduct are raised to the nth power, when the individual addresses himself as well as the others, by his gestures, when in the role of another he can respond to his own stimulus, all the range of possible activities is brought within the field of social conduct. He finds himself within groups of varied sorts. The size of the group to which he can belong is limited only by his ability to cooperate with its members. Now the common control over the food process lifts these instincts out of the level of the mechanical response to biologically determined stimuli and brings them within the sweep of self-conscious direction inside of the larger group activity. And these varied groupings multiply the occasions of individual oppositions. Here again the instinct of hostility becomes the method of self-assertion, but while the oppositions are self-conscious the process of readjustment and the molding of the hostile attitudes by the larger social process remains in principle the same, though the long road of trial and error may be at times abandoned for the short cuts which the symbolism of language provides.

On the other hand the consciousness of self through consciousness of others is responsible for a more profound sense of hostility—that of the members of the groups to those opposed to it, or even to those merely outside it. And this hostility has the backing of the whole inner organization of the group. It provides the most favorable condition for the sense of group solidarity because in the common attack upon the common enemy the individual differences are obliterated. But in the development of these group hostilities we find the same self-assertion with the attempted elimination of the enemy giving way before the larger social whole within which the conflicting groups find themselves. The hostile self-assertion passes over into functional activities in the new type of conduct as it has taken place in play even among lower animal forms. The individual becomes aware of himself, not through the conquest of the other, but through the distinction of function. It is not so much that the actual hostile reactions are themselves transformed as that the individual who is conscious of himself as over against the enemy finds other opportunities for conduct which remove the immediate stimuli for destroying the enemy. Thus the conqueror who realized himself in his power of life or death over the captive found in the industrial value of the slave a new attitude which removed the sense of hostility and opened the door to that economic development which finally placed the two upon the same ground of common citizenship.

It is insofar as the opposition reveals a larger underlying relationship within which the hostile individuals arouse non-hostile reactions that the hostile reactions themselves become modified into a type of self-assertion which is balanced against the self-assertion of those who had been enemies, until finally these oppositions become the compensating activities of different individuals in a new social conduct. In other words the hostile instinct has the function of the *assertion* of the social self when this self comes into existence in the evolution of human behavior. The man who has achieved an economic, a legal, or any type of social triumph does not feel the impulse to physically annihilate his opponent, and ultimately the mere sense of the security of his social position may rob the stimulus to attack of all of its power.

The moral of this is, and one is certainly justified in emphasizing it at this time of a profound democratic movement in the midst of a world war, that advance takes place in bringing to consciousness the larger social whole within which hostile attitudes pass over into self-assertions that are functional instead of destructive.

The following pages discuss the hostile attitude as it appears especially in punitive justice.

In the criminal court it is the purpose of the proceeding to prove that the defendant did or did not commit a certain act, that in case the defendant did commit the act this act falls under such and such a category of crime or misdemeanor as defined by the statute, and that, as a consequence, he is subject to such and such punishment. It is the assumption of this procedure that conviction and punishment are the accomplishment of justice and also that it is for the good of society, that is, that it is both just and expedient, though it is not assumed that in any particular case the meting out to a criminal of the legal recompense of his crime will accomplish an immediate social good which will outweigh the immediate social evil that may result to him, his family, and society itself from his conviction and imprisonment. Galsworthy's play *Justice* [2] turns upon the wide discrepancy between legal justice and social good in a particular case. On the other side lies the belief that without this legal justice with all its miscarriages and disintegrating results society itself would be impossible. In the back of the public mind lie both these standards of criminal justice, that of retribution and that of prevention. It is just that a criminal should suffer in proportion to the evil that he has done. On the other hand it is just that the criminal should suffer so much and in such a manner that his penalty will serve to deter him and others from committing the like offense in the future. There has been a manifest shift in the emphasis upon these two standards. During the Middle Ages, when courts of justice were the antechambers to chambers of torture, the emphasis lay upon the nice proportioning of the suffering to the offense. In the grand epic manner Dante

[2] [John Galsworthy (1867–1933), English novelist and dramatist. *Justice* was produced in 1910.]

projected this torture chamber, as the accomplishment of justice, against the sphere of the heavens, and produced those magnificent distortions and magnifications of human primitive vengeance that the medieval heart and imagination accepted as divine.[3]

There existed, however, even then no commensurability between retributory sufferings and the evil for which the criminal was held responsible. In the last analysis he suffered until satisfaction had been given to the outraged sentiments of the injured person, or of his kith and kin, or of the community, or of an angry God. To satisfy the latter an eternity might be too short, while a merciful death ultimately carried away from the most exacting community the victim who was paying for his sin in the coin of his own agony. Commensurability does not exist between sin and suffering but does exist roughly between the sin and the amount and kind of suffering that will satisfy those who feel themselves aggrieved and yet it has become the judgment of our common moral consciousness that satisfaction in the suffering of the criminal has no legitimate place in assessing his punishment. Even in its sublimated form, as a part of righteous indignation, we recognize its legitimacy only in resenting and condemning injury, not in rendering justice for the evil done. It was therefore natural that in measuring the punishment the emphasis should shift from retribution to prevention, for there is a rough quantitative relation between the severity of the penalty and the fear which it inspires. This shift to the standard of expediency in determining the severity of the penalty does not mean that retribution is no longer the justification for punishment either in the popular mind or in legal theory, for however expedient it may be to visit crimes with condign punishments in the interest of the welfare of society, the justification for inflicting the suffering at all is found in the assumption that the crimi-

[3] [Dante Alighieri (1265–1321), Italian poet born in Florence. His greatest work, the *Commedia*, embodies the notion of symbolic justice. In the first part, the *Inferno*, Dante describes hell in detail as a place in which punishment fits the sin.]

nal owes retributive suffering to the community; a debt which the community may collect in the form and amount which is most expedient to itself.

This curious combination of the concepts of retributive suffering which is the justification for punishment but may not be the standard for the amount and degree of the punishment, and of a social expediency which may not be the justification for the punishment itself but is the standard of the amount and kind of punishment inflicted, is evidently not the whole story. If retribution were the only justification for punishment it is hard to believe that punishment would not itself have disappeared when society came to recognize that a possible theory of punishment could not be worked out or maintained on the basis of retribution; especially when we recognize that a system of punishments assessed with reference to their deterrent powers not only works very inadequately in repressing crime but also preserves a criminal class. This other part of the story, which neither retribution nor social expediency tells, reveals itself in the assumed solemnity of criminal court procedure, in the majesty of the law, in the supposedly impartial and impersonal character of justice. These characters are not involved in the concept of retribution nor in that of deterrence. Lynch law is the very essence of retribution and is inspired with the grim assurance that such summary justice must strike terror into the heart of the prospective criminal, and lynch law lacks solemnity, and majesty, and is anything but impersonal or impartial. These characters inhere, not in the primitive impulses out of which punitive justice has arisen nor in the cautious prudence with which society devises protection for its goods, but in the judicial institution which theoretically acts on rule and not upon impulse and whose justice is to be done though the heavens fall. What, then, are these values evidenced in and maintained by the laws of punitive justice? The most patent value is the theoretically impartial enforcement of the common will. It is a procedure which undertakes to recognize and protect the individual in the interest of the common good and by the common will. In

his acceptance of the law and dependence upon it the individual is at one with the community, while this very attitude carries with it the recognition of his responsibility to obey and support the law in its enforcement. So conceived the common law is an affirmation of citizenship. It is, however, a grave mistake to assume that the law itself and men's attitudes toward it can exist *in abstracto*.[4] It is a grave mistake, for too often the respect for law as law is what we demand of members of the community, while we are able to regard with comparative indifference defects both in the concrete laws and in their administration. It is not only a mistake, it is also a fundamental error, for all emotional attitudes—and even respect for law and a sense of responsibility are emotional attitudes—arise in response to concrete impulses. We do not respect law in the abstract but the values which the laws of the community conserve. We have no sense of responsibility as such but an emotional recognition of duties which our position in the community entails. Nor are these impulses and emotional reactions less concrete because they are so organized into complex habits that some slight but appropriate stimulus sets a whole complex of impulses into operation. A man who defends an apparently unimportant right on principle is defending the whole body of analogous rights which a vast complex of social habits tends to preserve. His emotional attitude, which is seemingly out of proportion to the immediate issue, answers to all of those social goods toward which the different impulses in the organized body of habits are directed. Nor may we assume that because our emotions answer to concrete impulses they are therefore necessarily egoistic or self-regarding. No small portion of the impulses which make up the human individual are immediately concerned with the good of others. The escape from selfishness is not by the Kantian road of an emotional response to the abstract universal, but by the recognition of the genuinely social character of human nature. An important instance of this illusory respect for abstract law appears in our attitude of dependence upon the law and its en-

4 ["In abstraction."]

forcement for the defense of our goods and those of others with whom we identify our interests.

A threatened attack upon these values places us in an attitude of defense, and as this defense is largely entrusted to the operation of the laws of the land we gain a respect for the laws which is in proportion to the goods which they defend. There is, however, another attitude more easily aroused under these conditions which is, I think, largely responsible for our respect for law as law. I refer to the attitude of hostility to the lawbreaker as an enemy to the society to which we belong. In this attitude we are defending the social structure against an enemy with all the animus which the threat to our own interests calls out. It is not the detailed operation of the law in defining the invasion of rights and their proper preservation that is the center of our interest but the capture and punishment of the personal enemy, who is also the public enemy. The law is the bulwark of our interests, and the hostile procedure against the enemy arouses a feeling of attachment due to the means put at our disposal for satisfying the hostile impulse. The law has become the weapon for overwhelming the thief of our purses, our good names, or even of our lives. We feel toward it as we feel toward the police officer who rescues us from a murderous assault. The respect for the law is the obverse side of our hatred for the criminal aggressor. Furthermore the court procedure, after the man accused of the crime is put under arrest and has been brought to trial, emphasizes this emotional attitude. The state's attorney seeks a conviction. The accused must defend himself against this attack. The aggrieved person and the community find in this officer of the government their champion. A legal battle takes the place of the former physical struggle which led up to the arrest. The emotions called out are the emotions of battle. The impartiality of the court who sits as the adjudicator is the impartiality of the umpire between the contending parties. The assumption that contending parties will each do his utmost to win, places upon each, even upon the state's attorney, the obligation to get a verdict for his own side rather than to bring about a result which will be for the best interests of all concerned. The doctrine that the strict enforcement of the law in this fashion is for the best interest of all concerned has no bearing upon the point which I am trying to emphasize. This point is that the emotional attitude of the injured individual and of the other party to the proceedings—the community— toward the law is that engendered by a hostile enterprise in which the law has become the ponderous weapon of defense and attack.[5]

There is another emotional content involved in this attitude of respect for law as law, which is perhaps of like importance with the other. I refer to that accompanying stigma placed upon the criminal. The revulsions against criminality reveal themselves in a sense of solidarity with the group, a sense of being a citizen which on the one hand excludes those who have transgressed the laws of the group and on the other inhibits tendencies to criminal acts in the citizen himself. It is this emotional reaction against conduct which excludes from society that gives to the moral taboos of the group such impressiveness. The majesty of the law is that of the angel with the fiery sword at the gate who can cut one off from the world to which he belongs. The majesty of the law is the dominance of the group over the individual, and the paraphernalia of

[5] I am referring here to criminal law and its enforcement, not only because respect for the law and the majesty of the law have reference almost entirely to criminal justice, but also because a very large part, perhaps the largest part, of civil law proceedings are undertaken and carried out with the intent of defining and readjusting social situations without the hostile attitudes which characterize the criminal procedure. The parties to the civil proceedings belong to the same group and continue to belong to this group, whatever decision is rendered. No stigma attaches to the one who loses. Our emotional attitude toward this body of law is that of interest, of condemnation and approval as it fails or succeeds in its social function. It is not an institution that must be respected even in its disastrous failures. On the contrary it must be changed. It is hedged about in our feelings by no majesty. It is efficient or inefficient and as such awakens satisfaction or dissatisfaction and an interest in its reform which is in proportion to the social values concerned.

criminal law serves not only to exile the rebellious individual from the group, but also to awaken in law-abiding members of society the inhibitions which make rebellion impossible to them. The formulation of these inhibitions is the basis of criminal law. The emotional content that accompanies them is a large part of the respect for law as law. In both these elements of our respect for law as law, in the respect for the common instrument of defense from and attack upon the enemy of ourselves and of society, and in the respect for that body of formulated custom which at once identifies us with the whole community and excludes those who break its commandments, we recognize concrete impulses—those of attack upon the enemy of ourselves and at the same time of the community, and those of inhibition and restraint through which we feel the common will, in the identity of prohibition and of exclusion. They are concrete impulses which at once identify us with the predominant whole and at the same time place us on the level of every other member of the group, and thus set up that theoretical impartiality and evenhandedness of punitive justice which calls out in no small degree our sense of loyalty and respect. And it is out of the universality that belongs to the sense of common action springing out of these impulses that the institutions of law and of regulative and repressive justice arise. While these impulses are concrete in respect of their immediate object, i.e., the criminal, the values which this hostile attitude toward the criminal protects either in society or in ourselves are negatively and abstractly conceived. Instinctively we estimate the worth of the goods protected by the procedure against the criminal and in terms of this hostile procedure. These goods are not simply the physical articles but include the more precious values of self-respect, in not allowing one's self to be overridden, in downing the enemy of the group, in affirming the maxims of the group and its institutions against invasions. Now in all of this we have our backs toward that which we protect and our faces toward the actual or potential enemy. These goods are regarded as valuable because we are willing to fight and even die for them in certain exigencies, but their intrinsic value is neither affirmed nor considered in the legal proceeding. The values thus obtained are not their values in use but sacrifice values. To many a man his country has become infinitely valuable because he finds himself willing to fight and die for it when the common impulse of attack upon the common enemy has been aroused, and yet he may have been, in his daily life, a traitor to the social values he is dying to protect because there was no emotional situation within which these values appeared in his consciousness. It is difficult to bring into commensurable relationship to each other a man's willingness to cheat his country out of its legitimate taxes and his willingness to fight and die for the same country. The reactions spring from different sets of impulses and lead to evaluations which seem to have nothing in common with each other. The type of valuation of social goods that arises out of the hostile attitude toward the criminal is negative, because it does not present the positive social function of the goods that the hostile procedure protects. From the standpoint of protection one thing behind the wall has the same import as anything else that lies behind the same defense. The respect for law as law thus is found to be a respect for a social organization of defense against the enemy of the group and a legal and judicial procedure that are oriented with reference to the criminal. The attempt to utilize these social attitudes and procedures to remove the causes of crime, to assess the kind and amount of punishment which the criminal should suffer in the interest of society, or to reinstate the criminal as a law-abiding citizen has failed utterly. For while the institutions which inspire our respect are concrete institutions with a definite function, they are responsible for a quite abstract and inadequate evaluation of society and its goods. These legal and political institutions organized with reference to the enemy or at least the outsider give a statement of social goods which is based upon defense and not upon function. The aim of the criminal proceeding is to determine whether the accused is innocent, i.e., still belongs to the group or whether he is guilty, i.e., is put under the ban which criminal punishment carries with it. The technical statement of this is found in the loss of the privileges of a citizen, in sentences of any severity, but the more serious ban is found in the fixed attitude of hostility on the part of the community toward a jailbird. One effect of this is to define the goods and privileges of the members of the community as theirs in virtue of their being law-abiding, and their responsibilities as exhausted by the statutes which determine the nature of criminal conduct. This effect is not due alone to the logical tendency to maintain the same definition of the institution of property over against the conduct of the thief and that of the law-abiding citizen. It is due in far greater degree to the feeling that we all stand together in the protection of property. In the positive definition of property, that is in terms of its social uses and functions, we are met by wide diversity of opinion, especially where the theoretically wide freedom of control over private property, asserted over against the thief, is restrained in the interest of problematic public goods. Out of this attitude toward the goods which the criminal law protects arises that fundamental difficulty in social reform which is due, not to mere difference in opinion nor to conscious selfishness, but to the fact that what we term opinions are profound social attitudes which, once assumed, fuse all conflicting tendencies over against the enemy of the people. The respect for law as law in its positive use in defense of social goods becomes unwittingly a respect for the conceptions of these goods which the attitude of defense has fashioned. Property becomes sacred not because of its social uses but because all the community is as one in its defense, and this conception of property, taken over into the social struggle to make property serve its functions in the community, becomes the bulwark of those in possession, *beati possidentes*.[6]

Beside property other institutions have arisen, that of the person with its rights, that of the family with its rights, and that of the government with its rights. Wherever rights exist, invasion of those rights may be punished, and a definition of

[6] ["Blessed (are) the possessors."]

these institutions is formulated in protecting the right against trespass. The definition is again the voice of the community as a whole proclaiming and penalizing the one whose conduct has placed him under the ban. There is the same unfortunate circumstance that the law speaking against the criminal gives the sanction of the sovereign authority of the community to the negative definition of the right. It is defined in terms of its contemplated invasion. The individual who is defending his own rights against the trespasser is led to state even his family and more general social interests in abstract individualistic terms. Abstract individualism and a negative conception of liberty in terms of the freedom from restraints become the working ideas in the community. They have the prestige of battle cries in the fight for freedom against privilege. They are still the countersigns of the descendants of those who cast off the bonds of political and social restraint in their defense and assertion of the rights their forefathers won. Wherever criminal justice, the modern elaborate development of the taboo, the ban, and their consequences in a primitive society, organizes and formulates public sentiment in defense of social goods and institutions against actual or prospective enemies, there we find that the definition of the enemies, in other words the criminals, carries with it the definition of the goods and institutions. It is the revenge of the criminal upon the society which crushes him. The concentration of public sentiment upon the criminal which mobilizes the institution of justice, paralyzes the undertaking to conceive our common goods in terms of their uses. The majesty of the law is that of the sword drawn against a common enemy. The evenhandedness of justice is that of universal conscription against a common enemy, and that of the abstract definition of rights which places the ban upon anyone who falls outside of its rigid terms.

Thus we see society almost helpless in the grip of the hostile attitude it has taken toward those who break its laws and contravene its institutions. Hostility toward the lawbreaker inevitably brings with it the attitudes of retribution, repression, and exclusion. These provide no principles for the eradication of crime, for returning the delinquent to normal social relations, nor for stating the transgressed rights and institutions in terms of their positive social functions.

On the other side of the ledger stands the fact that the attitude of hostility toward the lawbreaker has the unique advantage of uniting all members of the community in the emotional solidarity of aggression. While the most admirable of humanitarian efforts are sure to run counter to the individual interests of very many in the community, or fail to touch the interest and imagination of the multitude and to leave the community divided or indifferent, the cry of thief or murder is attuned to profound complexes, lying below the surface of competing individual effort, and citizens who have separated by divergent interests stand together against the common enemy. Furthermore, the attitude reveals common, universal values which underlie like a bedrock the divergent structures of individual ends that are mutually closed and hostile to each other. Seemingly without the criminal the cohesiveness of society would disappear and the universal goods of the community would crumble into mutually repellent individual particles. The criminal does not seriously endanger the structure of society by his destructive activities, and on the other hand he is responsible for a sense of solidarity, aroused among those whose attention would be otherwise centered upon interests quite divergent from those of each other. Thus courts of criminal justice may be essential to the preservation of society even when we take account of the impotence of the criminal over against society, and the clumsy failure of criminal law in the repression and suppression of crime. I am willing to admit that this statement is distorted, not however in its analysis of the efficacy of the procedure against the criminal, but in its failure to recognize the growing consciousness of the many common interests which is slowly changing our institutional conception of society, and its consequent exaggerated estimate upon the import of the criminal. But it is important that we should realize what the implications of this attitude of hostility are within our society. We should especially recognize the inevitable limitations which the attitude carries with it. Social organization which arises out of hostility at once emphasizes the character which is the basis of the opposition and tends to suppress all other characters in the members of the group. The cry of "stop thief" unites us all as property owners against the robber. We all stand shoulder to shoulder as Americans against a possible invader. Just in proportion as we organize by hostility do we suppress individuality. In a political campaign that is fought on party lines the members of the party surrender themselves to the party. They become simply members of the party whose conscious aim is to defeat the rival organization. For this purpose the party member becomes merely a Republican or a Democrat. The party symbol expresses everything. Where simple social aggression or defense with the purpose of eliminating or encysting an enemy is the purpose of the community, organization through the common attitude of hostility is normal and effective. But as long as the social organization is dominated by the attitude of hostility the individuals or groups who are the objectives of this organization will remain enemies. It is quite impossible psychologically to hate the sin and love the sinner. We are very much given to cheating ourselves in this regard. We assume that we can detect, pursue, indict, prosecute, and punish the criminal and still retain toward him the attitude of reinstating him in the community as soon as he indicates a change in social attitude himself, that we can at the same time watch for the definite transgression of the statute to catch and overwhelm the offender, and comprehend the situation out of which the offense grows. But the two attitudes, that of control of crime by the hostile procedure of the law and that of control through comprehension of social and psychological conditions, cannot be combined. To understand is to forgive and the social procedure seems to deny the very responsibility which the law affirms, and on the other hand the pursuit by criminal justice inevitably awakens the hostile attitude in the offender and renders the attitude of mutual comprehension practically impossible. The social worker in the court is the sentimentalist, and the legalist in the social settlement in spite of his learned doctrine is the ignoramus.

While then the attitude of hostility, either against the transgressor of the laws or against the external enemy, gives to the group a sense of solidarity which most readily arouses like a burning flame and which consumes the differences of individual interests, the price paid for this solidarity of feeling is great and at times disastrous. Though human attitudes are far older than any human institutions and seem to retain identities of structure that make us at home in the heart of every man whose story has come down to us from the written and unwritten past, yet these attitudes take on new forms as they gather new social contents. The hostilities which flamed up between man and man, between family and family, and fixed the forms of old societies have changed as men came to realize the common whole within which these deadly struggles were fought out. Through rivalries, competitions, and cooperations men achieved the conception of a social state in which they asserted themselves while they at the same time affirmed the status of the others, on the basis not only of common rights and privileges but also on the basis of differences of interest and function, in an organization of more varied individuals. In the modern economic world a man is able to assert himself much more effectively against others through his acknowledgment of common property rights underlying their whole economic activity; while he demands acknowledgment for his individual competitive effort by recognizing and utilizing the varied activities and economic functions of others in the whole business complex.

This evolution reaches a still richer content when the self-assertion appears in the consciousness of social contribution that obtains the esteem of the others whose activities it complements and renders possible. In the world of scientific research rivalries do not preclude the warm recognition of the service which the work of one scientist renders to the whole cooperative undertaking of the *monde savant*.[7] It is evident that such a social organization is not obtainable at will, but is dependent upon the slow growth of very varied and intricate social mechanisms. While no clearly definable set of conditions can be presented as responsible for this growth, it will I think be admitted that a very necessary condition, perhaps the most important one, is that of overcoming the temporal and spatial separations of men so that they are brought into closer interrelation with each other. Means of intercommunications have been the great civilizing agents. The multiple social stimulation of an indefinite number of varied contacts of a vast number of individuals with each other is the fertile field out of which spring social organizations, for these make possible the larger social life that can absorb the hostilities of different groups. When this condition has been supplied there seems to be an inherent tendency in social groups to advance from the hostile attitudes of individuals and groups toward each other through rivalries, competitions, and cooperations toward a functional self-assertion which recognizes and utilizes other selves and groups of selves in the activities in which social human nature expresses itself. And yet the attitude of hostility of a community toward those who have transgressed its laws or customs, i.e., its criminals, and toward the outer enemies has remained as a great solidifying power. The passionate appreciation of our religious, political, property, and family institutions has arisen in the attack upon those who individually or collectively have assailed or violated them, and hostility toward the actual or prospective enemies of our country has been the never-failing source of patriotism.

If then we undertake to deal with the causes of crime in a fundamental way, and as dispassionately as we are dealing with the causes of disease, and if we wish to substitute negotiation and international adjudication for war in settling disputes between nations, it is of some importance to consider

[7] ["Learned world."]

what sort of emotional solidarity we can secure to replace that which the traditional procedures have supplied. It is in the juvenile court that we meet the undertaking to reach and understand the causes of social and individual breakdown, to mend if possible the defective situation and reinstate the individual at fault. This is not attended with any weakening of the sense of the values that are at stake, but a great part of the paraphernalia of hostile procedure is absent. The judge sits down with the child who has been committed to the court, with members of the family, parole officers, and others who may help to make the situation comprehensible and indicates what steps can be taken to bring matters to a normal condition. We find the beginnings of scientific technique in this study in the presence of the psychologist and medical officer who can report upon the mental and physical condition of the child, of the social workers who can report upon the situation of the families and neighborhood involved. Then there are other institutions beside the jails to which the children can be sent for prolonged observation and change of immediate environment. In centering interest upon reinstatement the sense of forward-looking moral responsibility is not only not weakened but is strengthened, for the court undertakes to determine what the child must do and be to take up normal social relations again. Where the responsibility rests upon others this can be brought out in much greater detail and with greater effect since it is not defined under abstract legal categories and the aim in determining responsibility is not to place punishment but to obtain future results. Out of this arises a much fuller presentation of the facts that are essential for dealing with the problem than can possibly appear in a criminal court procedure that aims to establish simply responsibility for a legally defined offense with the purpose of inflicting punishment. Of far greater importance is the appearance of the values of family relations, of schools, of training of all sorts, of opportunities to work, and of all the other factors that go to make up that which is worthwhile in the life of a child or an adult. Before the juvenile court it is possible to present all of these and all of them can enter the consideration of what action is to be taken. These are the things that are worthwhile. They are the ends that should determine conduct. It is impossible to discover their real import unless they can all be brought into relationship with each other.

It is impossible to deal with the problem of what the attitude and conduct of the community should be toward the individual who has broken its laws, or what his responsibility is in terms of future action, unless all the facts and all the values with reference to which the facts must be interpreted are there and can be impartially considered, just as it is impossible to deal scientifically with any problem without recognizing all the facts and all the values involved. The attitude of hostility which places the criminal under the ban, and thus takes him out of society, and prescribes a hostile procedure by which he is secured, tried, and punished can take into account only those features of his conduct which constitute infraction of the law, and can state the relation of the criminal and society only in the terms of trial for fixing guilt and of punishment. All else is irrelevant. The adult criminal court is not undertaking to readjust a broken-down social situation, but to determine by the application of fixed rules whether the man is a member of society in good and regular standing or is an outcast. In accordance with these fixed rules what does not come under the legal definition not only does not naturally appear but it is actually excluded. Thus there exists a field of facts bearing upon the social problems that come into our courts and governmental administrative bureaus, facts which cannot be brought into direct use in solving these problems. It is with this material that the social scientist and the voluntary social worker and his organizations are occupied. In the juvenile court we have a striking instance of this material forcing its way into the institution of the court itself and compelling such a change in method that the material can be actually used. Recent changes of attitude toward the family permit facts bearing upon the care of children which earlier lay outside the purview of the court to enter into its consideration.

Other illustrations could be cited of this change in the structure and function of institutions by the pressure of data which the earlier form of the institution had excluded. One may cite the earlier theory of charity that it was a virtue of those in fortunate circumstances which is exercised toward the poor whom we have always with us, in its contrast with the conception of organized charity whose aim is not the exercise of an individual virtue but such a change in the condition of the individual case and of the community within which the cases arise that a poverty which requires charity may disappear. The author of a medieval treatise on charity considering the lepers as a field for good works contemplated the possibility of their disappearance with the ejaculation "which may God forbid!" The juvenile court is but one instance of an institution in which the consideration of facts which had been regarded as irrelevant or exceptional has carried with it a radical change in the institution. But it is of particular interest because the court is the objective form of the attitude of hostility on the part of the community toward the one who transgresses its laws and customs, and it is of further interest because it throws into relief the two types of emotional attitudes which answer to two types of social organization. Over against the emotional solidarity of the group opposing the enemy we find the interests which spring up around the effort to meet and solve a social problem. These interests are at first in opposition to each other. The interest in the individual delinquent opposes the interest in property and the social order dependent upon it. The interest in the change of the conditions which foster the delinquent is opposed to that identified with our positions in society as now ordered, and the resentment at added responsibilities which had not been formerly recognized or accepted.

But the genuine effort to deal with the actual problem brings with it tentative reconstructions which awaken new interests and emotional values. Such are the interests in better housing conditions, in different and more adequate schooling, in playgrounds and small parks, in controlling child labor and in vocational guidance, in improved sanitation and hygiene, and in community and social centers. In the place of the emotional solidarity which makes us all one against the criminal there appears the cumulation of varied interests unconnected in the past which not only bring new meaning to the delinquent but which also bring the sense of growth, development, and achievement. This reconstructive attitude offers the cumulative interest which comes with interlocking diversified values. The discovery that tuberculosis, alcoholism, unemployment, school retardation, adolescent delinquency, among other social evils, reach their highest percentages in the same areas not only awakens the interest we have in combating each of these evils, but creates a definite object, that of human misery, which focuses endeavor and builds up a concrete object of human welfare which is a complex of values. Such an organization of effort gives rise to an individual or self with a new content of character, a self that is effective since the impulses which lead to conduct are organized with reference to a clearly defined object.

It is of interest to compare this self with that which responds to the community call for defense of itself or its institutions. The dominant emotional coloring of the latter is found in the standing together of all the group against the common enemy. The consciousness which one has of others is stripped of the instinctive oppositions which in varying forms are aroused in us by the mere presence of others. These may be merely the slight rivalries and differences of opinion and of social attitude and position, or just the reserves which we all preserve over against those about us. In the common cause these can disappear. Their disappearance means a removal of resistance and friction and adds exhilaration and enthusiasm to the expression of one of the most powerful of human impulses. The result is a certain enlargement of the self in which one seems to be at one with everyone else in the group. It is not a self-consciousness in the way of contrasting one's self with others. One loses himself in the whole group in some sense, and may attain the attitude in which he undergoes suffering and death for the common cause. In fact just as war removes the inhibitions from the attitude of hostility so it quickens and commends the attitude of self-assertion of a self which is fused with all the others in the community. The ban upon self-assertion which the consciousness of others in the group to which one belongs carries with it disappears when the assertion is directed against an object of common hostility or dislike. Even in times of peace we feel as a rule little if any disapproval of arrogance toward those of another nationality, and national self-conceit and the denigration of the achievements of other peoples may become virtues. The same tendency exists in varying degree among those who unite against the criminal or against the party foe. Attitudes of difference and opposition between members of the community or group are in abeyance and there is given the greater freedom for self-assertion against the enemy. Through these experiences come the powerful emotions which serve to evaluate for the time being what the whole community stands for in comparison with the interests of the individual who is opposed to the group. These experiences, however, serve only to set off against each other what the group stands for and the meager birthright of the individual who cuts himself off from the group.

What we all fight for, what we all protect, what we all affirm against the detractor, confers upon each in some measure the heritage of all, while to be outside the community is to be an Esau [8] without heritage and with every man's hand against him. Self-assertion against the common enemy, suppressing as it does the oppositions of individuals within the group and thus identifying them all in a common effort, is after all the self-assertion of the fight in which the opposing selves strive each to eliminate the other, and in so doing are setting up their own survival and the destruction of the others as the

[8] [Esau, the son of Isaac and twin brother of Jacob, was deprived of his birthright and forced into exile by Jacob's trickery.]

end. I know that many ideals have been the ends of war, at least in the minds of many of the fighters; that insofar the fighting was not to destroy the fighters but some pernicious institution, such as slavery, that many have fought bloody wars for liberty and freedom. No champions, however, of such causes have ever failed to identify the causes in the struggle with themselves. The battle is for the survival of the right party and the death of the wrong. Over against the enemy we reach the ultimate form of self-assertion, whether it is the patriotic national self, or the party, or the schismatic self, or the institutional self, or simply the self of the hand-to-hand melee. It is the self whose existence calls for the destruction, or defeat, or subjection, or reduction of the enemy. It is a self that finds expression in vivid, concentrated activity and under appropriate conditions of the most violent type. The instinct of hostility which provides the structure for this self when fully aroused and put in competition with the other powerful human complexes of conduct, those of sex, of hunger, and of parenthood and of possession has proved itself as more dominant than they. It also carries with it the stimulus for readier and, for the time being, more complete socialization than any other instinctive organization. There is no ground upon which men get together so readily as that of a common enemy, while a common object of the instinct of sex, of possession, or of hunger leads to instant opposition, and even the common object of the parental instinct may be the spring of jealousy. The socializing agency of common hostility is marked, as I have above indicated, by its own defects. Insofar as it is the dominant instinct it does not organize the other instincts for its object. It suppresses or holds the others in abeyance. While hostility itself may be a constituent part of the execution of any instinct, for they all involve oppositions, there is no other instinctive act of the human self which is a constituent part of the immediate instinctive process of fighting, while struggle with a possible opponent plays its part in the carrying out of every other instinctive activity. As a result those who fight together against common enemies instinctively tend to ignore the other social activities within which oppositions between the individuals engaged normally arise.

It is this temporary relief from the social frictions which attend upon all other cooperative activities which is largely responsible for the emotional upheavals of patriotism, of mob consciousness, and the extremes of party warfare, as well as for the gusto of malicious gossiping and scandalmongering. Furthermore, in the exercise of this instinct success implies the triumph of the self over the enemy. The achievement of the process is the defeat of certain persons and the victory of others. The end takes the form of that sense of self-enlargement and assurance which comes with superiority of the self over others. The attention is directed toward the relative position of the self toward others. The values involved are those that only can be expressed in terms of interests and relations of the self in its differences from others. From the standpoint of one set of antagonists their victory is that of efficient civilization while the other regards their victory as that of liberal ideas. All the way from the Tamerlanes [9] who create a desert and call it peace to the idealistic warriors who fight and die for ideas, victory means the survival of one set of personalities and the elimination of others, and the ideas and ideals that become issues in the contest must perforce be personified if they are to appear in the struggles that arise out of the hostile instinct. War, whether it is physical, economic, or political, contemplates the elimination of the physical, economic, or political opponent. It is possible to confine the operation of this instinct within certain specific limitations and fields. In the prize fights as in the olden tourneys the annihilation of the enemy is ceremonially halted at a fixed stage in the struggle. In a football game the defeated team leaves the field to the champion. Successful competition in its sharpest form eliminates its competitor. The victor at the polls drives the op-

[9] [Tamerlane (*ca.* 1336–1405), Mongol conqueror whose military expeditions ravaged Asia.]

ponent from the field of political administration. If the struggle can be *à outrance* [10] within any field and contemplates the removal of the enemy from that field, the instinct of hostility has this power of uniting and fusing the contesting groups, but since victory is the aim of the fight and it is the victory of one party over the other, the issues of battle must be conceived in terms of the victor and the vanquished.

Other types of social organization growing out of the other instincts, such as possession, hunger, or parenthood, imply ends which are not as such identified with selves in their oppositions to other selves, though the objects toward which these instinctive activities are directed may be occasion for the exercise of the hostile instinct. The social organizations which arise about these objects are in good part due to the inhibitions placed upon the hostile impulse, inhibitions which are exercised by the other groups of impulses which the same situations call out. The possession by one individual in a family or clan group of a desirable object is an occasion for an attack on the part of other members of the group, but his characters as a member of the group are stimuli to family and clan responses which check the attack. It may be mere repression with smoldering antagonisms, or there may be such a social reorganization that the hostility can be given a function under social control, as in the party, political, and economic contests, in which certain party, political, and economic selves are driven from the field leaving others that carry out the social activity. Here the contest being restricted the most serious evils of the warfare are removed, while the contest has at least the value of the rough selection. The contest is regarded in some degree from the standpoint of the social function, not simply from that of the elimination of an enemy. As the field of constructive social activity widens the operation of the hostile impulse in its instinctive form decreases. This does not, however, mean that the reactions that go to make up the impulse or instinct have ceased to function. It does mean that the im-

[10] ["To the bitter end" or "to the last extremity."]

pulse ceases to be an undertaking to get rid of the offending object by injury and destruction, that is, an undertaking directed against another social being with capacities for suffering and death—physical, economical or political—like his own. It becomes in its organization with other impulses an undertaking to deal with a situation by removing obstacles. We still speak of him as fighting against his difficulties. The force of the original impulse is not lost but its objective is no longer the elimination of a person, but such a reconstruction that the profounder social activities may find their continued and fuller expression. The energy that expressed itself in burning witches as the causes of plagues expends itself at present in medical research and sanitary regulations and may still be called a fight with disease.

In all these changes the interest shifts from the enemy to the reconstruction of social conditions. The self-assertion of the soldier and conqueror becomes that of the competitor in industry or business or politics, of the reformer, the administrator, of the physician or other social functionary. The test of success of this self lies in the change and construction of the social conditions which make the self possible, not in the conquest and elimination of other selves. His emotions are not those of mass consciousness dependent upon suppressed individualities, but arise out of the cumulative interests of varied undertakings converging upon a common problem of social reconstruction. This individual and his social organization are more difficult of accomplishment and subject to vastly greater friction than those which spring out of war. Their emotional content may not be so vivid, but they are the only remedy for war, and they meet the challenge which the continued existence of war in human society has thrown down to human intelligence.

XVI

A BEHAVIORISTIC ACCOUNT OF
THE SIGNIFICANT SYMBOL

The statement I wish to present rests upon the following assumptions, which I can do no more than state: I assume, provisionally, the hypothesis of the physical sciences, that physical objects and the physical universe may be analyzed into a complex of physical corpuscles. I assume that the objects of immediate experience exist in relationship to the biologic and social individuals whose environments they make up. This relationship involves on the one hand the selection through the sensitivities and reactions of the living forms of those elements that go to make up the object. On the other hand these objects affect the plants and animals whose natures are responsible for them as objects, e.g., food exists as an immediate experience in its relation to the individuals that eat it. There is no such thing as food apart from such individuals. The selection of the characters which go to make up food is a function of living individuals. The effect of this food upon the living individuals is what we call adaptation of the form to the environment or its opposite. Whatever may be said of a mechanical universe of ultimate physical particles, the lines that are drawn about objects in experience are drawn by the attitudes and conduct of individual living forms. Apart from such an experience involving both the form and its environment, such objects do not exist.

On the other hand these objects exist objectively, as they are in immediate experience. The relation of objects making up an environment to the plants and the animals in no sense

[From *The Journal of Philosophy,* XIX (1922), 157–163. Reprinted by permission.]

renders these objects subjective. What are termed the natures of objects are in the objects, as are their so-called sensuous qualities, but these natures are not in the objects either as external or internal relations, they are of the very essence of the objects, and become relations only in the thought process. The so-called sensuous qualities exist also in the objects, but only in their relations to the sensitive organisms whose environments they form.

The causal effect of the living organisms on their environment in creating objects is as genuine as the effect of the environment upon the living organism. A digestive tract creates food as truly as the advance of a glacial cap wipes out some animals or selects others which can grow warm coats of hair. An animal's sensitiveness to a particular character in an object gives the object in its relation to the animal a peculiar nature. Where there is sensitiveness to two or more different characters of the object, answering to reactions that conflict and thus inhibit each other, the object is insofar analyzed. Thus the width of a stream would be isolated from the other characters of the stream through the inhibition of the animal's tendency to jump over it. In the immediate experience in which the animal organism and its environment are involved, these characters of the objects and the inhibited reactions that answer to them are there or exist, as characters, though as yet they have no significance nor are they located in minds or consciousnesses.

Among objects in the immediate experience of animals are the different parts of their own organisms, which have different characters from those of other objects—especially hedonic characters, and those of stresses and excitements—but characters not referred to selves until selves arise in experience. They are only accidentally private, i.e., necessarily confined to the experience of single individuals. If—after the fashion of the Siamese Twins—two organisms were so joined that the same organ were connected with the central nervous system of each, each would have the same painful or pleasurable object in experience. A toothache or a pleased palate are objects for a single individual for reasons that are not essentially different from those which make the flame of a match scratched in a room in which there is only one individual an object only for that individual. It is not the exclusion of an object from the experience in which others are involved which renders it subjective; it is rendered subjective by being referred by an individual to his self, when selves have arisen in the development of conduct. Exclusive experiences are peculiarly favorable for such reference, but characteristics of objects for everyone may be so referred in mental processes.

Among objects that exist only for separate individuals are so-called images. They are *there,* but are not necessarily *located* in space. They do enter into the structure of things, as notably on the printed page, or in the hardness of a distant object; and in hallucinations they may be spatially located. They are dependent for their existence upon conditions in the organism—especially those of the central nervous system—as are other objects in experience such as mountains and chairs. When referred to the self they become memory images, or those of a creative imagination, but they are not mental or spiritual stuff.

Conduct is the sum of the reactions of living beings to their environments, especially to the objects which their relation to the environment has "cut out of it," to use a Bergsonian phrase.[1] Among these objects are certain which are of peculiar importance to which I wish to refer, viz., other living forms which belong to the same group. The attitudes and early indications of actions of these forms are peculiarly important stimuli, and to extend a Wundtian term may be called "gestures." These other living forms in the group to which the organism belongs may be called social objects and exist as such before selves come into existence. These gestures call out definite, and in all highly organized forms, partially predetermined reactions, such as those of sex, of parenthood, of hostil-

[1] [Henri Bergson (1859–1941), French philosopher, author of *Time and Free Will* (1888), *Matter and Memory* (1896), *Creative Evolution* (1907), and other works.]

ity, and possibly others, such as the so-called herd instincts. Insofar as these specialized reactions are present in the nature of individuals, they tend to arise whenever the appropriate stimulus, or gesture calls them out. If an individual uses such a gesture, and he is affected by it as another individual is affected by it, he responds or tends to respond to his own social stimulus, as another individual would respond. A notable instance of this is in the song, or vocal gesture of birds. The vocal gesture is of peculiar importance because it reacts upon the individual who makes it in the same fashion that it reacts upon another, but this is also true in a less degree of those of one's own gestures that he can see or feel.

The self arises in conduct, when the individual becomes a social object in experience to himself. This takes place when the individual assumes the attitude or uses the gesture which another individual would use and responds to it himself, or tends so to respond. It is a development that arises gradually in the life of the infant and presumably arose gradually in the life of the race. It arises in the life of the infant through what is unfortunately called imitation, and finds its expression in the normal play life of young children. In the process the child gradually becomes a social being in his own experience, and he acts toward himself in a manner analogous to that in which he acts toward others. Especially he talks to himself as he talks to others and in keeping up this conversation in the inner forum constitutes the field which is called that of mind. Then those objects and experiences which belong to his own body, those images which belong to his own past, become part of this self.

In the behavior of forms lower than man, we find one individual indicating objects to other forms, though without what we term signification. The hen that pecks at the angleworm is directly though without intention indicating it to the chicks. The animal in a herd that scents danger, in moving away indicates to the other members of the herd the direction of safety and puts them in the attitude of scenting the same danger. The hunting dog points to the hidden bird. The lost lamb that bleats, and the child that cries each points himself out to his mother. All of these gestures, to the intelligent observer, are significant symbols, but they are none of them significant to the forms that make them.

In what does this significance consist in terms of a behavioristic psychology? A summary answer would be that the gesture not only actually brings the stimulus-object into the range of the reactions of other forms, but that the nature of the object is also indicated; especially do we imply in the term significance that the individual who points out indicates the nature to *himself*. But it is not enough that he should indicate this meaning—whatever meaning is—as it exists for himself alone, but that he should indicate that meaning as it exists for the other to whom he is pointing it out. The widest use of the term implies that he indicates the meaning to any other individual to whom it might be pointed out in the same situation. Insofar then as the individual takes the attitude of another toward himself, and in some sense arouses in himself the tendency to the action, which his conduct calls out in the other individual, he will have indicated to himself the meaning of the gesture. This implies a definition of meaning—that it is an indicated reaction which the object may call out. When we find that we have adjusted ourselves to a comprehensive set of reactions toward an object we feel that the meaning of the object is ours. But that the meaning may be ours, it is necessary that we should be able to regard ourselves as taking this attitude of adjustment to response. We must indicate to ourselves not only the object but also the readiness to respond in certain ways to the object, and this indication must be made in the attitude or role of the other individual to whom it is pointed out or to whom it may be pointed out. If this is not the case it has not that common property which is involved in significance. It is through the ability to be the other at the same time that he is himself that the symbol becomes significant. The common statement of this is that we have in mind, what we indicate to another that he shall do. In giving directions, we give the direction to ourselves at the same time that we give it to another. We assume also his attitude of response to our requests, as an individual to whom the direction has the same signification in his conduct that it has to ourselves.

But signification is not confined to the particular situation within which an indication is given. It acquires universal meaning. Even if the two are the only ones involved, the form in which it is given is universal—it would have the same meaning to any other who might find himself in the same position. How does this generalization arise? From the behavioristic standpoint it must take place through the individual generalizing himself in his attitude of the other. We are familiar enough with the undertaking, in social and moral instruction to children and to those who are not children. A child acquires the sense of property through taking what may be called the attitude of the generalized other. Those attitudes which all assume in given conditions and over against the same objects, become for him attitudes which everyone assumes. In taking the role which is common to all, he finds himself speaking to himself and to others with the authority of the group. These attitudes become axiomatic. The generalization is simply the result of the identity of responses. Indeed it is only as he has in some sense amalgamated the attitudes of the different roles in which he has addressed himself that he acquires the unity of personality. The "me" that he addresses is constantly varied. It answers to the changing play of impulse, but the group solidarity, especially in its uniform restrictions, gives him the unity of universality. This I take to be the sole source of the universal. It quickly passes the bounds of the specific group. It is the *vox populi, vox dei,* the "voice of men and of angels." Education and varied experience refine out of it what is provincial, and leave "what is true for all men at all times." From the first, its form is universal, for differences of the different attitudes of others wear their peculiarities away. In the play period, however, before the child has reached that of competitive games—in which he seeks to pit his own acquired self against others—in the play period this process is not fully carried out and the child is as varied as his varying moods; but in the game he sees himself in terms of the group or the gang and speaks with a passion for rules and standards. Its social advantage and even necessity makes this approach to himself imperative. He must see himself as the whole group sees him. This again has passed under the head of passive imitation. But it is not in uniform attitudes that universality appears as a recognized factor in either inner or outer behavior. It is found rightly in thought and thought is the conversation of this generalized other with the self.

The significant symbol is then the gesture, the sign, the word which is addressed to the self when it is addressed to another individual, and is addressed to another, in form to all other individuals, when it is addressed to the self.

Signification has, as we have seen, two references, one to the thing indicated, and the other to the response, to the instance and to the meaning or idea. It denotes and connotes. When the symbol is used for the one, it is a name. When it is used for the other, it is a concept. But it neither denotes nor connotes except, when in form at least, denotation and connotation are addressed both to a self and to others, when it is in a universe of discourse that is oriented with reference to a self. If the gesture simply indicates the object to another, it has no meaning to the individual who makes it, nor does the response which the other individual carries out become a meaning to him, unless he assumes the attitude of having his attention directed by an individual to whom it has a meaning. Then he takes his own response to be the meaning of the indication. Through this sympathetic placing of themselves in each other's roles, and finding thus in their own experiences the responses of the others, what would otherwise be an unintelligent gesture, acquires just the value which is connoted by signification, both in its specific application and in its universality.

It should be added that insofar as thought—that inner conversation in which objects as stimuli are both separated from and related to their responses—is identified with consciousness, that is insofar as consciousness is identified with awareness, it is the result of this development of the self in experience. The other prevalent signification of consciousness is found simply in the presence of objects in experience. With the eyes shut we can say we are no longer conscious of visual objects. If the condition of the nervous system or certain tracts in it, cancels the relation of individual and his environment, he may be said to lose consciousness or some portion of it; i.e., some objects or all of them pass out of experience for this individual. Of peculiar interest is the disappearance of a painful object, e.g., an aching tooth under a local anesthetic. A general anesthetic shuts out all objects.

As above indicated analysis takes place through the conflict of responses which isolates separate features of the object and both separates them from and relates them to their responses, i.e., their meanings. The response becomes a meaning, when it is indicated by a generalized attitude both to the self and to others. Mind, which is a process within which this analysis and its indications take place, lies in a field of conduct between a specific individual and the environment, in which the individual is able, through the generalized attitude he assumes, to make use of symbolic gestures, i.e., terms, which are significant to all including himself.

While the conflict of reactions takes place within the individual, the analysis takes place in the object. Mind is then a field that is not confined to the individual, much less is located in a brain. Significance belongs to things in their relations to individuals. It does not lie in mental processes which are enclosed within individuals.

XVII

SCIENTIFIC METHOD AND
THE MORAL SCIENCES

It had become a commonplace of the psychologist that there
is a structure in our experience which runs out beyond what
we ordinarily term our consciousness; that this structure of
idea determines to a degree not generally recognized the very
manner of our perception as well as that of our thinking, and
yet that the structure itself is generally not in the focus of
our attention and passes unnoticed in our thought and perceiving. It was this dependence of our field of direct experience upon such an unrecognized part of what we call mind
that Freud [1] has made the theme of his doctrines, in a realm
that lies on the border of the abnormal or just over it. It is
one of the valuable by-products of the Freudian psychology
that it has brought many people to recognize that we do not
only our thinking but also our perceiving with minds that
have already an organized structure which determines in no
small degree what the world of our immediate and reflective
experience shall be. It is possible to recognize other censors
beside those dramatically placed by Freud at the door of so-
called consciousness to pass upon the figures that enter our
dreams.

It is to one of these that I wish to call attention. It is that
the intelligible order of the world implies a determined moral
order—and for a moral order we may substitute a social order,
for morality has to do with the relations of intelligent beings

[From the *International Journal of Ethics,* XXXIII (1923), 229–
247.]

[1] [Sigmund Freud (1856–1939), Austrian psychiatrist who invented psychoanalysis. See his *General Introduction to Psychoanalysis* (1910).]

with each other—and that this determined moral or social order is a world as it should be and will be. We may express this as Kant expressed it as a world in which happiness will be proportioned to worth, or as the Utilitarians expressed it by saying that it will be one in which there will be realized the greatest happiness of the greatest number, or we may give it more concreteness by looking to a New Jerusalem that religious doctrine pictures, or we may find it in a perfect Absolute of which we and our finite universe are but imperfect and inadequate parts and expressions. Whatever the conception of this moral order, definite or vague, it always has implied that the process of the universe in which we live in a real sense is akin to and favorable to the most admirable order in human society.

The most definite form which this belief or faith has taken in the western world is that of the plan of salvation as presented in Christian doctrine. The import of this doctrine was that whatever further purposes a divine providence might have in the conduct of the universe, man's moral regeneration and the growth of a society which this made possible was an end which was always involved in the physical world which was man's habitat. This was most succinctly expressed by St. Augustine,[2] and passed into the form which is perhaps most familiar to us in Milton's "Paradise Lost" and "Paradise Regained." The sharpness of outline of the Plan has faded with the entirely new heavens and new earth which natural science, since the time of Galileo, has unfolded before men's eyes and minds, but the idea that the universe is in some way geared to the intelligence and excellence of our social and moral order has not disappeared from the back of men's minds. Scientists such as Huxley [3] have pointed out the incongruities that lie between this conception and the findings of a physical

[2] [St. Augustine (A.D. 354–430), one of the four Latin Fathers of the Church, Bishop of Hippo. His *Confessions* (*ca.* 400) demonstrates Divine Providence in his own life; his *City of God* (*ca.* 412) does so on the large scale of human history.]

[3] [See T. H. Huxley's Romanes Lectures, *Evolution and Ethics* (1893).]

science, that sees in the whole life of the human race but an inconsiderable moment on an inconsiderable speck within the physical universe, that finds in a civilized moral society an aberration from a biological nature that is red in tooth and claw, and subject to a ruthless law of the survival of the fittest. And yet men, even in moods which were not emotional nor mystical, have rarely regarded their habitat as hostile or indifferent to what was best in their social life and structure.

However, it is very evident that the aspect of this kinship between human society and its secular habitat which belongs to our present scientific age is and must be profoundly different from that of St. Augustine, or St. Thomas Aquinas,[4] or Luther,[5] or Milton. In no one respect is this perhaps more evident than in our attitude toward the evils which the catastrophes of nature, disease and physical suffering entail upon us.

The view that the ordering of the world was primarily for the greater glory of God in the salvation of man, made of every event that affected men a direct action of providence with reference to the members of the human race, and there could be but one intelligent as well as but one pious attitude over against the action of providence, that of acceptance with thanksgiving or with resignation. Suffering and evil came as discipline.

It is hardly necessary to rehearse the steps in the development of the insistent curiosity of recent science, which has refused to accept any given order of nature as final, or to believe that seemingly inevitable events may not conceivably become quite different if we only comprehend what the manner of their happening is, or to forgo the hope that human ingenuity may avert misfortunes if we can only understand their causes and conditions.

4 [St. Thomas Aquinas (1225–1274), medieval Italian philosopher and Doctor of the Roman Catholic Church. His *Summa Theologica* (1267–1273) is a scholastic exposition of philosophy and theology.]

5 [Martin Luther (1483–1546), a monk who led the German Reformation.]

Here are two quite fundamentally opposed attitudes toward the kinship of the intelligence of men and the order of the world they live in. It is customary to call the one teleological and the other mechanical, to call the one spiritual and the other materialistic. The first attitude takes it pretty definitely for granted that we know what is right and what is wrong, that in certain definite respects we know what the social order should be; that the intelligent man in his moral conduct, and this is social conduct, starts off with certain truths given in his nature or by revelation, and shows his intelligence by shaping his action to these truths; that the path of righteousness is one that he who runs may read and a man though a fool need not err therein. If the moral order, of which these truths are an essential part, is given, then the kinship of men's intelligence to the order of the physical universe will show itself in the triumph of this moral or social order, and men can themselves start off with this order as a presupposition in their conduct in the world. The end is given in advance, this is the meaning of teleology, and if we are confident that the universe is so constituted as to achieve this end, we will be intelligent in acting on this assumption.

We have seen that Huxley quite frankly denies, in the name of science, any justification for this faith. He saw nothing in nature that was akin to the social or moral order. In fact he regarded what he called altruistic conduct as an abandonment of the road along which nature was going. This view of Huxley arose in part out of an interpretation of biological evolution that is seen to be inadequate. Kropotkin [6] could point out that social organization, with just that sort of conduct which Huxley called altruistic, is as legitimately to be considered an outcome of an evolutionary process as is the survival of the fittest individual in the struggle for existence. But Huxley's position is of interest because it so ingenuously assumes that a moral order must be an order which is given in advance, while our knowledge of nature is all drawn from what has

[6] [Peter Kropotkin (1842–1921), Russian anarchist, author of *Mutual Aid, a Factor in Evolution* (1902).]

happened. In our acquaintance with nature we can never assume a determining idea that fixes the result before it happens, as is the case when our ideas determine what the results of our conduct will be. So we speak of nature as mechanical or materialistic. This is just where the break seems to come between what we consider men's intelligence in moral and social conduct, and in men's understanding of nature. We can still believe, of course, that in the end the process of the universe will further ideals of a morally ordered society, and probably most men who are conversant with the findings of science and committed to its methods of research, still in the back of their minds carry this faith, or attitude of mind, but this attitude can be of no service in understanding objects about us in the everyday life of the scientifically minded. It is reserved for religious moods, when we try to bring together what are in their logic incompatible.

Let us state this incompatibility in its simplest form. In our moral conduct we control our actions in considerable degree, i.e., in proportion as we are intelligent, by our purposes, by the ideas of results not yet attained, that is, our conduct is teleological. In our comprehension of nature the result is controlled entirely by antecedent causes, that is nature proceeds mechanically, and there seems to be no kinship between such a nature and the intelligence of men seeking for a better social order.

I have no intention of broaching the metaphysical problem of the relation of a mind that is spiritual and a nature that is material. The question that I want to ask is this: Can the world of natural science provide objects for the world of social and moral conduct?

If we drop back two or three centuries, whether we measure them historically or in present attitudes of mind, we find a view of the physical world which furnished the objects that purposive social and moral conduct demanded. In the first place the physical cosmos as a whole appeared simply as the stage on which the plans of a divine providence were being enacted. In the second place the separate objects with which men's conduct was engaged found their meaning in this providential plan and led to conduct which this plan for human society demanded. Men's attitudes toward disease, toward events which in present legal phraseology are denominated "acts of God," were those of supplication and resignation. In general those things which engaged human personal interest most acutely and which still had to be regarded from the standpoint of the community to which men belonged could always be conceived of as existing to fulfill the destinies of men in human society. In essence these physical things and occurrences were identical with their import for the success or failure of men's undertakings. They were as physical things and occurrences just what they meant for human conduct. Today a disease is the history of a bacillus, an earthquake is a shift in surface strata due to gravitational forces, while the incredible vastness of the spread of matter and its inconceivable temporal stretches in comparison with the inconsequential minuteness of humanity and its momentary duration rob the physical universe of any seeming relevancy to the fortunes of our race.

This is the more striking because the period within which this shift of cosmical values has taken place is that within which physical things and their forces have become subservient to men's purposes, to an extent that would have been beyond the imaginational stretch of the medieval or ancient world. The physical universe which by its enormity has crushed the human insect into disappearing insignificance has like a jinn in the Arabian tale shown itself infinitely complaisant in magnifying man's mechanical capacity. In accepting his negligible crevice in the physical whole man has found access to the minute structure of things and by this route has reached both the storehouse and powerhouse of nature. The heraldic device of man's conquering intelligence should be a design blending differential x, the bacillus, and the electron. If humanity has fled shivering from the starry spaces, it has become minutely at home in the interstices of the speck that it inhabits for an instant.

But if we have succeeded in applying science to our mechanical task, and in this have accomplished prodigies, we do not seem to have succeeded in applying scientific method to the formulation of our ends and purposes. Consider the Great War. The ideas that plunged Europe and then dragged the rest of the world into that catastrophe, the imperialisms, national, militaristic and economic, are roughly identical with those that embroiled Christendom in the seventeenth century. It was only the weapons that crashed through those four years that belonged to the intellect of the twentieth century. There attaches to it the grotesquerie of a Yankee at the Court of King Arthur. Or consider the government of a cosmopolitan city, or of a great nation. There is at the disposal of the community for the carrying out of its policies the apparatus of a hundred sciences, but to secure the bare formulation of a policy we are forced to involve ourselves in the factional interests of parties that are psychologically closely parallel to the turbulent politics of an ancient or a medieval commonweath. We are enormously clever at fashioning our means, but we are still in no small measure dependent for conceiving our ends upon outworn mental structures that our very science has invalidated.

But it would be a mistake to assume that scientific method is applicable only in the fashioning and selection of means, and may not be used where the problem involves conflicting social ends or values. The advance of scientific medicine in dealing with public health amply substantiates this.

In this advance numerous social values embodied or championed by various institutions, government, the church, the school and the family, have sought to maintain themselves against scientific procedure in combating disease and safeguarding health. Individual rights, religious dogmas and cults, family control of children, the economic advantage of cheap child labor for business, and many other accepted social values have been set up as absolute, across the path of progress of scientific public health conservation. But the demonstrated results of the hospital, vaccination, quarantine, and other means of medical service to the health of the community have forced men to bring these values into the field of other public goods and restate them so that public health could be the better preserved.

I imagine that the scientific advance of medicine presents as enlightening an illustration as could be found of the issue that seems to exist between scientific method and our conduct in social and moral affairs. The human community did not wait for a medical science to convince it that health is a community good. Combating disease by its medicine men has been one of the chief common concerns even in primitive societies whose technique was entirely magical. We do not turn to scientific method to determine what is a common good, though we have learned to avail ourselves of it in some of our common efforts and practices in pursuit of the good. However, scientific method is not an agent foreign to the mind, that may be called in and dismissed at will. It is an integral part of human intelligence, and when it has once been set at work it can only be dismissed by dismissing the intelligence itself. Unfortunately men have committed this sin against their intelligence again and again. They have incontinently rejected the very method which human intelligence has learned to employ because its results came in conflict with other social goods which they were unwilling to either sacrifice or restate. But again and again when they have undertaken to use their minds thereafter, they have found that their minds had become committed to the method they had rejected. The past history of and the present struggle with venereal disease illustrate this, chapter for chapter. Scientific method does not undertake to say what the good is, but when it has been employed, it is uncompromising in its demand that that good is no less a good because the scientific pursuit of it brings us within the taboos of institutions that we have regarded as inviolable. Nor does scientific method assert that the family and the church are not goods because its pursuit of public health has trenched upon conceptions of them which men have held to be practically absolute. What scientific method does require, if it is to be consistently used, is that all the conflicting ends, the institutions and their hitherto inviolable values, be brought together and so restated and reconstructed that intelligent conduct may be possible, with reference to *all* of them. Scientific method requires this because it is nothing but a highly developed form of impartial intelligence.

Here, then, is the issue, so far as an issue exists, between scientific method and social and moral conduct. If the community is seeking an end by the intelligent method of science and in doing this runs counter to its habits in attaining and maintaining other ends, these ends are just as subject to restatement and reconstruction as are the means themselves. Nor does science pretend to say what this restatement or reconstruction must be. Its one insistent demand is that all the ends, all the valuable objects, institutions, and practices which are involved, must be taken into account. In other words, its attitude toward conflicting ends is the same as its attitude toward conflicting facts and theories in the field of research. It does not state what hypothesis must be adopted. It does insist that any acceptable hypothesis must take into account all the facts involved.

Now such a method can be in conflict with social conduct only if that conduct sets up certain ends, institutions and their values, which are to be considered as inviolable in the form in which they have been received and are now accepted. There is no issue between scientific method and moral and social conduct that springs from the fact that science deals with the relation of past facts to each other while conduct deals with future ends.

Science does not attempt to formulate the end which social and moral conduct ought to pursue, any more than it pretends to announce what hypothesis will be found by the research scientist to solve his problem. It only insists that the object of our conduct must take into account and do justice to all of the values that prove to be involved in the enterprise, just as it insists that every fact involved in the research problem must be taken into account in an acceptable hypothesis. Scientific method is at war with dogmatism whether it appears in doctrine, or cult, or in social practice. Scientific method is not teleological in the sense of setting up a final cause that should determine our action, but it is as categorical in insisting upon our considering all factors in problems of conduct, as it is in demanding the recognition of all of the data that constitute the research problem.

Scientific method does not ensure the satisfactory solution of the problem of conduct, any more than it ensures the construction of an adequate hypothesis for the research problem. It is restricted to formulating rigorously the conditions for the solution. And here appears a profound difference between the two situations, that of moral and social conduct, and that of so-called scientific research. In problems of conduct we must act, however inadequate our plan of action may be. The research problem may be left because of our inability to find a satisfactory hypothesis. Furthermore, there are many values involved in our problems of social conduct to which we feel that we are unable to do justice in their whole import, and yet when they are once envisaged they appear too precious to be ignored, so that in our action we do homage to them. We do not do justice to them. They constitute our ideals. They abide in our conduct as prophecies of the day in which we can do them the justice they claim. They take on the form of institutions that presuppose situations which we admit are not realized, but which *demand* realization.

Such an ideal is democracy written into our governmental institutions. It implies a social situation so highly organized that the import of a protective tariff, a minimum wage, or of a League of Nations, to all individuals in the community may be sufficiently evident to them all, to permit the formation of an intelligent public sentiment that will in the end pass decisively upon the issue before the country. This is what democratic government means, for the issue does not actually exist as such, until the members of the community realize something of what it means to them individually and collectively. There cannot be self-government until there can be an intelligent will expressed in the community, growing out of the intelligent attitudes of the individuals and groups in whose experience the community exists. Our institutions are insofar democratic that when a public sentiment is definitely formed and expressed it is authoritative. But an authoritative public sentiment upon a public issue is very infrequent. My guess is that the number of instances of that in the history of the United States of America could be told upon the fingers of two hands, perhaps upon the fingers of one hand. In the meantime, as the then President Taft [7] assured us on a historic occasion, we are governed by minorities, and the relatively intelligent minorities are swayed by the import of the issue to these minorities.

However, we are unwilling to surrender the ideal of such a government, if only for the sake of the exceptional occasions upon which it is realized, but more profoundly because we cherish the hope that the form of the institution in some way helps toward the realization of what it promises. The most grandiose of these community ideals is that which lies behind the structure of what was called Christendom, and found its historic expression in the Sermon on the Mount, in the parable of the Good Samaritan, and in the Golden Rule. These affirm that the interests of all men are so identical, that the man who acts in the interest of his neighbors will act in his own interest. Actually the history of Christendom has been a history of war and strife, and we are forced to admit that in these wars dynastic, national, and civil has arisen the intensive consciousness of the larger communities. It was the horror of the Great War that aroused, perhaps for the first time in the human race, a public sentiment passing all national bounds and demanding some organization that could express this sentiment and avert a still more terrible horror. The history of Christianity is the history of men's refusal to surrender this ideal.

To indicate in what concrete ways, psychological, social, and

[7] [William Howard Taft (1857–1930), 26th President of the United States (1909–1913) and Chief Justice of the Supreme Court (1921–1930).]

technological, the presence of these ideals in men's minds may have directly or indirectly favored their realization lies beyond the scope of this paper. What must be indicated is that they have only been kept in men's minds by institutions set up for this specific purpose. An institution should arise and be kept alive by its own function, but insofar as it does not function, the ideal of it can be kept alive only by some cult, whose aim is not the functioning of the institution, but the continued presence of the idea of it in the minds of those that cherish it.

The church is the outstanding illustration of such an institution. Its most important function has been the preservation in the minds of the community of the faith in a social order which did not exist. At the other end of the scale may be placed certain economic institutions, notably that of exchange. The economic man may be an abstraction, but he certainly exists and functions, and we need no cult to keep alive the faith in the functioning of money, though there is hardly an agency that has had more profound effects in bringing all men into association with each other. Between these lie our various institutions. We feel from time to time the necessity of arousing in our souls an emotional appreciation of the value of the family, of democracy, of the common school, of the university, because in their actual operation they do not express that value adequately.

The psychological technique of maintaining such a cult is the presentation by the imagination of a social situation free from the obstacles which forbid the institution being what it should be, and we organize social occasions which in every way favor such a frame of mind. We gather together in a place of worship, where we meet on the single common basis of all being worshipers of one God, or gather at a Thanksgiving, where all the differences and indifferences of family life are ignored, or we turn with affectionate regard to the Little Red School House where all the children were found studying the same books and immersed in the same common school life. Now the emotional and intellectual attitude of these occasions is essentially different from that of any common undertaking to make the institution more effective, to reform it. The attitude implied in the cult of an institution is frankly hostile toward that which seeks its reform. The mental attitude attending a cult is always conservative, and if we are undertaking its reform we consider it reactionary. The emotional attitude in the cult of an institution flows from the very obstacles that defeat its proper functioning. We may become profoundly interested in the reform of an institution for better service, but if we wish to appraise it emotionally we envisage the wrongs, the vice, the ignorance, the selfishness, which the ideal of the institution condemns, and which frustrate its operation.

Now it is just these factors in social and moral conduct which render the application of scientific method, in that field, so profoundly different from its application in the field of the natural sciences. The formula is simple enough. Your conduct must take into account all of the values which are involved in the social or moral problem. But how are we to define these values? They ought to be defined by the conflict out of which the problem has arisen. In many cases they are sufficiently defined to enable us to act intelligently. If it is a question of visiting distant friends we find out how valuable it is to us, by the sacrifice of other things for which we wish to spend the money which the journey would cost. When we have counted up the cost, we may conclude that it isn't worth what we should have to forgo. Of course the mere surrender of the contemplated visit is not the whole result. We have found out how much we want it, and have probably prepared to bring it about under more favorable conditions. For purposes of conduct, values define themselves definitely enough when they are brought into conflict with each other. So facts define themselves in scientific problems. The facts in the problem of the prevention of arteriosclerosis are the observations which indicate that none of the causes that have been supposed to conduce to it do actually account for it. The facts in the hunt for a pneumonia serum are that none of those constructed after the fashion of other successful sera give the desired immunity. The facts are determined by conflict.

But see how different the situation becomes when the problem is not the prevention of a disease, but the prevention of crime. If the problem were simply the determination of the values involved in terms of loss to the victims and to the community, over against the effort and expense involved in catching and punishing the criminal, the problem would not be a difficult one. No civilized community has ever hesitated to take steps in view of the danger which the existence of crime entails. The difficulties arise over the methods of so-called criminal justice. It is supposed to prevent crime, but it does not prevent it. At least it does not prevent it as vaccination prevents smallpox epidemics. It has some preventive effect. It is a palliative. But we cannot simply surrender criminal justice as inefficient, to use some other method, nor even to reform it simply from the standpoint of rendering it more efficient. For criminal justice has a cult value. We cherish the attitude of public reprobation of crime, or rather let us say of public vengeance upon the criminal, because of the emotional sanction it gives to a community ordered by a common law. We overlook the fact that we cannot keep up this emotional attitude without branding the criminal as an outcast, without in some sense preserving a criminal class or caste, and we are quite unwilling to estimate the value of this branding simply in terms of its preventive power. It has an absolute value too precious to be surrendered. If our social problem were simply that of prevention, we should have a standard by which we could fairly measure the values involved. We could never treat leprosy scientifically if we retained the older attitude of regarding the leper as unclean. The relatively recent history of the scientific treatment of the mentally diseased is one of passing out of a cult attitude toward the insane. Or consider nationalism. We cannot simply set about the elimination of war by methods which history has amply justified, because of the cult value of patriotism. The time-honored and simplest method of arousing the emotional consciousness of national unity is presentation of the common enemy. It is confessedly most difficult if not impossible to arouse this emotional consciousness out of the common life within the community itself. And at times patriotism seems to have an almost infinite value. The cult values are incommensurable.

And yet these problems are not only real problems, they are insistent problems, and as I have before observed, we cannot defer action with reference to them, although these and most of the other social and moral problems are shot through with these incommensurable cult values. Nor can we take the attitude of the superior person, and affect the pose of one whose higher intelligence has raised himself above these incommensurables. They and what they represent are the most precious part of social heritage. But it is not their incommensurability that constitutes their value, nor should we hesitate to abandon the cult estimate of these institutions if their values can be stated in terms of their functions. The cult value of the institution is legitimate only when the social order for which it stands is hopelessly ideal. Insofar as it approaches realization, its functional value must supersede its ideal value in our conduct.

It is to this task that a scientifically trained intelligence must insistently devote itself, that of stating, just as far as possible, our institutions, our social habits and customs, in terms of what they are to do, in terms of their functions. There are no absolute values. There are only values which, on account of incomplete social organization, we cannot as yet estimate, and in face of these the first enterprise should be to complete the organization if only in thought so that some rough sort of estimate in terms of the other values involved becomes conceivable. And there is only one field within which the estimation can be made, and that is within the actual problem. The field within which we can advance our theory of states is that of the effort to avert war. The advance in our doctrine of criminal justice will be found in the undertaking of intelligent crime prevention. The problems of social theory must be research problems. It is to one group of these problems which I wish particularly to refer. These are the problems of practical politics in the nation and especially in our municipalities.

I have already called attention to the chasm that separates the theory and practice of our democracy. The theory calls for the development of an intelligent public sentiment upon the issues before the community. In practice we depend not upon these to bring the voters to polls, but upon the spirit of party politics. The interest in the issues is so slight that any machine in a great city, that can ensure by party organization and patronage a relatively small group of partisans who will always vote with the machine, can continue its hold on the city government for a considerable period no matter how corrupt its administration may be. It is perhaps this situation that leads us to overestimate the somewhat rough and clumsy method of registering public sentiment which the ballot box affords in a democracy. And in our heated efforts to reform corrupt administrations we accept the shibboleths of the professional politician that the essence of democracy is in voting on one side or the other. We attach a cult value to these somewhat crude methods of keeping a government of some sort going. The real hope of democracy, of course, lies in making the issues so immediate and practical that they can appear in the minds of the voter as his own problem. The wide spread of the manager instead of the manger or feed box form of city government is perhaps the most heartening sign of the times that this is beginning to take place. It does not seem to be an impossible task to get the average voter to see that the bulk of the administration of his municipality consists in carrying on a set of operations of vital importance to himself in an efficient businesslike fashion, that the question of public ownership of public utilities is simply a phase of this efficient administration, and that it is perfectly possible for a community to get such an efficient administration. The advance in the practice and theory of democracy depends upon the successful translation of questions of public policy into the immediate problems of the citizens. It is the intensive growth of social interrelations and intercommunications that alone renders possible the recognition by the individual of the import for his social life of the corporate activity of the whole community. The task of intelligence is to use this growing consciousness of interdependence to formulate the problems of all, in terms of the problem of everyone. Insofar as this can be accomplished cult values will pass over into functional values.

Finally I wish to recur to the dictum to which I referred at the opening of this paper: That the intelligible order of the world implies a moral or social order, i.e., a world as it should be and may be. What form does this take if we apply scientific method to social conduct?

We have seen that the earliest formulation of it by Christian theology was that the intelligence of the creator and ruler of the world must show itself in bringing about in this world or the next the perfect society which man's moral and social nature implied and that our intelligence consists in accepting the inspired statement of this order. Scientific method has no vision, given in the mount, of a perfected order of society, but it does carry with it the assumption that the intelligence which exhibits itself in the solution of problems in natural science is of the same character as that which we apply or should apply in dealing with our social and moral problems; that the intelligible order of the world is akin to its moral and social order because it is the same intelligence which enters into and controls the physical order and which deals with the problems of human society. Not only is man as an animal and as an inquirer into nature at home in the world, but the society of men is equally a part of the order of the universe. What is called for in the perfection of this society is the same intelligence which he uses in becoming more completely a part of his physical environment and so controlling that environment. It is this frank acceptance of human society as a part of the natural order that scientific method demands when it is applied to the solution of social problems, and with it comes the demand, that just as far as possible we substitute functional values for cult values in formulating and undertaking to solve our social problems.

The difference in the pictures of the universe presented by these two attitudes is striking enough. The one contemplates a physical world in which man and the society of men are but pilgrims and strangers, seeking an abiding city not made with hands, eternal in the heavens. The goal toward which all creation moves was to be attained through the individual members of the human community becoming good, i.e., living by certain absolute and incommensurable values housed and hallowed by social institutions. This morality or social *dressur* calls for only so much intelligence as is required to recognize these institutions and the claims which their ideals make upon us. Anyone can be good, though but a few can be clever. There is hardly any kinship between this attitude and the agelong struggle of the human community to make itself intelligently at home in the physical habitat in which it finds itself. Man has domesticated the animals now these many centuries. He is but slowly advancing with painful effort in the domestication of the germ, though it is at present much more essential to community life.

The scientific attitude contemplates our physical habitat as primarily the environment of man who is the first cousin once removed of the arboreal anthropoid ape, but it views it as being transformed first through unreflective intelligence and then by reflective intelligence into the environment of a human society, the latest species to appear on the earth. This human society, made up of social individuals that are selves, has been intermittently and slowly digging itself in, burrowing into matter to get to the immediate environment of our cellular structure, and contracting distances and collapsing times to acquire the environment that a self-conscious society of men needs for its distinctive conduct. It is a great secular adventure, that has reached some measure of success, but is still far from accomplishment. The important character of this adventure is that society gets ahead, not by fastening its vision upon a clearly outlined distant goal, but by bringing about the immediate adjustment of itself to its surroundings, which the immediate problem demands. It is the only way in which it can proceed, for with every adjustment the environment has changed, and the society and its individuals have changed in like degree. By its own struggles with its insistent difficulties, the human mind is constantly emerging from one chrysalis after another into constantly new worlds which it could not possibly previse. But there is a heartening feature of this social or moral intelligence. It is entirely the same as the intelligence evidenced in the whole upward struggle of life on the earth, with this difference, that the human social animal has acquired a mind, and can bring to bear upon the problem his own past experiences and that of others, and can test the solution that arises in his conduct. He does not know what the solution will be, but he does know the method of the solution. We, none of us, know where we are going, but we do know that we are on the way.

The order of the universe that we live in *is* the moral order. It has become the moral order by becoming the self-conscious method of the members of a human society. We are not pilgrims and strangers. We are at home in our own world, but it is not ours by inheritance but by conquest. The world that comes to us from the past possesses and controls us. We possess and control the world that we discover and invent. And this is the world of the moral order. It is a splendid adventure if we can rise to it.

XVIII

THE GENESIS OF THE SELF
AND SOCIAL CONTROL

It is my desire to present an account of the appearance of the self in social behavior, and then to advert to some implications of such an account in their bearings upon social control.

The term "behavior" indicates the standpoint of what follows, that of a behavioristic psychology. There is an aspect of this psychology that calls for an emphasis which I think has not been sufficiently given it. It is not simply the objectivity of this psychology which has commended it. All recent psychology, insofar as it lays claim to a scientific approach, considers itself objective. But behavioristic psychology, coming in by the door of the study of animals lower than man, has perforce shifted its interest from psychical states to external conduct. Even when this conduct is followed into the central nervous system, it is not to find the correlate of the neurosis in a psychosis, but to complete the act, however distant this may be in space and time. This doctrine finds itself in sympathetic accord with recent realism and pragmatism, which places the so-called sensa and the significances of things in the object. While psychology has been turning to the act as a process, philosophic thought has been transferring contents that had been the subject-matter of earlier psychology from the field of states of consciousness to the objective world. Prebehavioristic psychology had a foot in two worlds. Its material was found in consciousness and in the world of physiology and physics. As long, however, as psychology was occupied with states of consciousness which constituted objects, there was an inevitable duplication. The whole physiological and physical appa-

[From the *International Journal of Ethics,* XXXV (1924–1925), 251–277.]

ratus could be stated in terms of states of consciousness, and solipsism hovered in the background. A psychology that is called upon to analyze the object into the states of consciousness which it is studying may conceivably be an empirical science, but insofar its world is not the world of the other sciences. A behavioristic psychology, on the other hand, that is not responsible for the content of the object, becomes a science that is cognate with physiology and dynamics, and escapes the trail of the epistemological serpent.

I am not concerned with the philosophical justification of this attitude of behavioristic psychology; I merely wish to emphasize its inevitable tendency to deal with processes, that is, with acts, and to find its objects given in the world with which all science deals. From Descartes'[1] time on, it has been a border state, lying between philosophy and the natural sciences, and has suffered the inconveniences which attend buffer states. Descartes' unambiguous and uncompromising division between an extended physical world, and an unextended world of thought, when it reached the pineal gland found itself in ambiguous territory, and only avoided compromise by leaving the relations of mind and body to the infinite power of his *deus ex machina*. The difficulties which have attended psychology's regulation of these relations have been only in part metaphysical. More fundamentally they have been logical. The natural sciences start pragmatically with a world that is there, within which a problem has arisen, and introduce hypothetical reconstructions only insofar as its solution demands them. They always have their feet upon the solid ground of unquestioned objects of observation and experiment, where Samuel Johnson placed his in his summary refutation of Berkeley's idealism.[2] Speculative philosophy, beset with the problem of epistemology, found its problem in the

1 [René Descartes (1596–1650), French philosopher and scientist. His works, including the *Discourse on Method* (1637) and the *Meditations* (1641), have earned for him the title "father of modern philosophy."]

2 [Samuel Johnson (1709–1784), English author. He "refuted" Berkeley's subjective idealism by kicking a stone.]

nature and very existence of the world inside which the problems of the natural sciences appeared, and which furnished the
test of its hypotheses. Thus psychology as a philosophic discipline carried the epistemological problem into the experience
of the individual, but as a science located the problem in a
given world which its epistemological problem could not accept as given. Between the two, its sympathies have always
been with the presuppositions and method of the natural sciences. On the one hand, as empirical science it has sought to
regard the so-called consciousness of the individual as merely
given in the sense of the objects of the natural sciences, but
as states of consciousness were still regarded as cognitive, they
had inevitably inherited the epistemological diathesis. On the
other hand, as experimental science it was forced to place
states of consciousness within or without the processes it was
studying. Placing them in interactionism within the natural
processes ran counter to the presuppositions of its scientific
procedure, so that the prevailing attitude has been that of
epiphenomenalism, an adaptation of Leibnitz' preestablished
harmony and Spinoza's parallel attributes. They ran as harmless conscious shadows beside the physical and physiological
processes with which science could come to immediate terms.
But this proved but an unstable compromise. The conscious
streak that accompanied the neuroses could answer only to
sensing and thinking as processes; as qualities and significance
of things, states of consciousness became hardly tolerable re-
duplications of things, except in the case of the secondary
qualities. The molecular structure of things seemed to remove
these from the hypothetical objects of physical science, and
consciousness proved a welcome dumping ground for them.
This bifurcation of nature proves equally unsatisfactory. The
horns and the hoofs go with the hide. States of contact experience have no better right to objective existence than those of
distance experience. Psychology, however, has not been interested in these epistemological and metaphysical riddles, it has
been simply irritated by them. It has shifted its interest to the
processes, where phenomenalism is most harmless, appearing

as physiological psychology, as functional psychology, as dynamic psychology, and has ignored the problems for which it had no care. The effect of this has been to give the central nervous system a logical preeminence in the procedure and textbooks of psychology which is utterly unwarranted in the analysis of the experience of the individual. The central nervous system has been unwittingly assimilated to the logical position of consciousness. It occupies only an important stage in the act, but we find ourselves locating the whole environment of the individual in its convolutions. It is small wonder, then, that behaviorism has been welcomed with unmistakable relief, for it has studied the conduct of animals in necessary ignoration of consciousness, and it has been occupied with the act as a whole, not as a nervous arc.

But the relief with which one turns to conduct and away from states of consciousness has not disposed of the problems involved in the ambiguous term "consciousness," even for the psychologist. Bergson's theory of perception [3] was at least a step toward the clarification of this ambiguity. It recognizes that insofar as the content of the percept can be termed consciousness, it indicates a diminution of the reality of the object rather than an addition, and this diminution answers to the active interests of the organism, which are represented in the central nervous system by paths of possible response. These coordinated paths in some sense cut out the object of perception. The percept is relative to the perceiving individual, but relative to his active interest, not relative in the sense that its content is a state of his consciousness. It is at least meaningless to lodge the so-called sensuous characters of things in the cortex. When, however, Bergson suggests that certain of these qualities may be the condensation of vibrations, we seem again to be in the presence of qualities that are states of consciousness. Presumably the condensations, e.g., the actual quality of color, do not exist in the object, but in the condensing mind. How-

[3] [Henri Bergson, *Matter and Memory*, translated by N. M. Paul and W. S. Palmer (London and New York: George Allen & Co., Ltd., and The Macmillan Company, 1911), especially pp. 22–35.]

ever, Bergson's statement at least placed the central nervous system in the world of things, of percepts, on the one hand, and on the other placed the characters of things in pure perception in the things themselves; but the divorce of duration, as psychical, from a static intellectualized spatial world left a dichotomy which was functional only from the standpoint of a Bergsonian metaphysics. Neo-realism undertook to return all the qualities of things to the things, over against a mind which was simply aware of the sensa. This simple, radical procedure left problems of a perception which was still cognitive in its nature, which a Critical Realism sought to solve by retreating to representative perception again. It remained for pragmatism to take the still more radical position that in immediate experience the percept stands over against the individual, not in a relation of awareness, but simply in that of conduct. Cognition is a process of finding out something that is problematical, not of entering into relation with a world that is there.

There is an ambiguity in the word "consciousness." We use it in the sense of "awareness," "consciousness of," and are apt to assume that in this sense it is coextensive with experience, that it covers the relation of the sentient organism to its environment insofar as the environment exists for the organism. We thus predicate of this existence of the environment for the organism the attitude of cognition on the part of the organism. The other use of consciousness to which I refer is in the sense of certain contents, to wit, the sense qualities of things, more especially the so-called secondary qualities, the affections of the body of the sentient organism, especially those that are pleasurable and painful, the contents of the images of memory and imagination, and of the activities of the organism, so far as they appear in its experience. There is another field, that of self-consciousness, to which I am not as yet referring. There is a common character which in varying degree belongs to all of these contents, that is, that these contents could not appear at all, or exactly as they do appear, in the experience of any other organism. They are in this sense private, though this privacy does not imply necessarily anything more than difference of access or of perspective on the part of the different organisms. If we take the pragmatic attitude, referred to above, consciousness in the first sense, that of awareness, would disappear from immediate experience, while the world that is there for the organism would still be there. A particular organism would become conscious from this standpoint, that is, there would be a world that would exist for the organism, when the organism marked or plotted or, to use Bergson's term, canalized its environment in terms of its future conduct. For Bergson, a percept is an object of possible action for an organism, and it is the active relationship of the organism to the distant object that constitutes it an object. Bergson meets the difficulty that the organism can exercise no physical influence upon the distant object by his assumption that consciousness in this sense is in reality not an addition to the object, but an abstraction from all in the relation of the organism to the object which does not bear upon this action. There arises, then, a selected series of objects, determined by the active interests of the organism.

An environment thus arises for an organism through the selective power of an attention that is determined by its impulses that are seeking expression. This peculiar environment does not exist in the consciousness of the form as a separate milieu, but the consciousness of the organism consists in the fact that its future conduct outlines and defines its objects. Insofar as the organization of one individual differs from that of others, it will have a private environment, though these differences may be called those of standpoint. They are objective differences. They exist in nature. The most fundamental phase of these differences is found in the determination of what the relativist calls a "consentient set," i.e., the selection of those objects which may all be considered as "here" with reference to the individual. It is this set, which is co-gredient with the individual, that constitutes an environment within which motion may take place. These perspectives of nature exist in nature, not in the consciousness of the organism as a stuff. In this relation of a peculiar environment for an individual, there is no implication of an awareness. All that is implied is that the ongoing activity of the individual form marks and defines its world for the form, which thus exists for it as it does not for any other form. If this is called consciousness, a behavioristic psychology can state it in terms of conduct.

Consciousness in the second sense, that of a peculiar content or contents, implies relativity in another sense, in the sense of emergence, as this has been defined by Alexander, in *Space Time and the Deity*,[4] and accepted by Lloyd Morgan, in *Emergent Evolution*.[5] In evolution not only have new forms appeared, but new qualities or contents in experience. It is the sensitivities of forms that are the occasions for the appearance, in the worlds of these forms, of new characters of things, answering to all the senses, and new meanings answering to their new capacities for conduct. And these new characters and new meanings exist in nature as do the forms of physical objects, though they are relative to the sensitivities and capacities of the individual forms. If we drop awareness from immediate experience, Alexander's distinction between perception and enjoyment may be also dropped. This distinction lies between the awareness of perception of external objects and that of the experience of the individual in perception and his other processes. Pleased palates and irritated or suffering members are there in the same sense as other percepts or objects. And this is true also of straining muscles, of fearful objects, or a turned stomach, or an attractive thing, nor can we deny this sort of objectivity to imagery, because access to it is confined to the individual in whose world it appears. Part of this imagery fits into the world that is there, and is with great difficulty analyzed out. That which will not fit in becomes located in our pasts or in futures of varying degrees of definiteness.

4 [Samuel Alexander, *Space, Time, and Deity* (London: Macmillan and Co., 1920), II, 14.]
5 [C. Lloyd Morgan, *Emergent Evolution* (New York: H. Holt, 1923), p. 9.]

If my friend enters the room, and I catch a glimpse of his face, the imagery of his face fills out the countenance, and I see him with his whole complement of features. The same imagery might have figured in my memory of last meeting him. Or it might have figured in the plan I entertained of calling, on the following evening. It belongs either to the passing present, or to the irrevocable past, or to the contingent future. This imagery is for the percipient as objective as the so-called sense object. It may enter that object and be indistinguishable from it. Where it can be distinguished, however, it is recognized as having this private character; that is, while we assume that the color of the object perceived, even if it vary from eye to eye, is in some respects identical for all eyes insofar as the organs are alike, it is not assumed that the image which one has is there for other eyes, or imaginations. While this sole accessibility of imagery to the individual does not in itself render it less objective, it places it at the disposal of the individual, when he attains to a mind which it can furnish. The same is true of the other class of objects which in his experience is accessible only to him. I refer to the objects which the individual possesses from the inside, so to speak, the parts of his organism, especially as they are painful or pleasurable. In the so-called lower animals, there is no evidence that this private field is organized and used as the possession of a self. The passing present is neither extended into a memory series, nor into an anticipated future.

Imagery is but one phase of the presence of the past in the passing present. In the living form it appears as facility in the response, and in the selection of the stimulus, in selective discrimination, in the stimulus. Imagery emerges, in the sense of Alexander, as the content of the past in the stimulus, and as meaning in the response. Imagery and meaning are there in the objects as contents, before they become material for the mind, before the mind appears in conduct.

I have referred to the doctrine of relativity. More specifically, my reference was to formulation of the doctrine given in Professor Whitehead's three books, *The Principles of Natural*

Knowledge [1919], *The Concept of Nature* [1920], and *The Principle of Relativity* [1922]. What I have had particularly in mind is Whitehead's recognition, as over against current Einsteinian doctrine, that if motion is to be accepted as an objective fact, we must also accept the existence in nature of so-called consentient sets at rest, determined by their relation to so-called percipient events. The same events in nature appear in different consentient sets, as these events are ordered in different time systems, and this ordering in different time systems is dependent upon their relations to different percipient events. Motion in nature implies rest in nature. Rest in nature implies co-gredience, i.e., a persistent relation of here and there with reference to some individual, and it is this that determines the time system in accordance with which events are ordered. If rest is a fact in nature, we must conceive of it as stratified, to use Whitehead's term, by the different temporal perspectives of different individuals, though a group of individuals may have the same perspective; we must, however, remember that this is a stratification of nature not in a static space, but a nature whose extension is affected with a time dimension.

It is this conception of the existence in nature of consentient sets determined by their relations to percipient events that I wish to generalize so that it will cover the environment in relation to the living form, and the experienced world with reference to the experiencing individual. This is evidently only possible if we conceive life as a process and not a series of static physicochemical situations, and if we regard experience as conduct or behavior, not as a series of conscious states. This I take to be the essence of Bergson's philosophy of change, in accordance with which our perceptual world is determined by the actions that are taking place. Conduct does cut out and fashion the objects upon which action is directed. It is only with reference to life as an ongoing process that the animal determines his habitat. The most convincing illustration can be found in the different presentation of the life of a community, in terms of a social statics, the statistical data of population and occupations and the like, or in terms of the actual lives of the different individuals who make up the community. In the latter case we realize that each individual has a world that differs in some degree from that of any other member of the same community, that he slices the events of the community life that are common to all from a different angle from that of any other individual. In Whitehead's phrase, each individual stratifies the common life in a different manner, and the life of the community is the sum of all these stratifications, and all of these stratifications exist in nature. It is this recognition that takes psychology out of its isolation, as a science that deals with what is found in the mind of an individual, and makes of it the standpoint from which to approach reality as it is going on.

It is evident that a statement of the life of each individual in terms of the results of an analysis of that which is immediately experienced would offer a common plane of events, in which the experience of each would differ from the experiences of others only in their extent, and the completeness or incompleteness of their connections. These differences disappear in the generalized formulations of the social sciences. The experiences of the same individuals, insofar as each faces a world in which objects are plans of action, would implicate in each a different succession of events. In the simplest illustration, two persons approach a passing automobile. To one it is a moving object that he will pass before it reaches the portion of the street that is the meeting place of their two paths. The other sees an object that will pass this meeting point before he reaches it. Each slices the world from the standpoint of a different time system. Objects which in a thousand ways are identical for the two individuals, are yet fundamentally different through their location in one spatiotemporal plane, involving a certain succession of events, or in another. Eliminate the temporal dimension, and bring all events back to an instant that is timeless, and the individuality of these objects which belongs to them in behavior is lost, except insofar as they can represent the results of past conduct. But taking time seriously, we realize that the seemingly timeless character of our spatial world and its permanent objects is due to the consentient set which each one of us selects. We abstract time from this space for the purposes of our conduct. Certain objects cease to be events, cease to pass as they are in reality passing and in their permanence become the conditions of our action, and events take place with reference to them. Because a whole community selects the same consentient set does not make the selection less the attitude of each one of them. The life-process takes place in individual organisms, so that the psychology which studies that process in its creative determining function becomes a science of the objective world.

Looked at from the standpoint of an evolutionary history, not only have new forms with their different spatiotemporal environments and their objects arisen, but new characters have arisen answering to the sensitivities and capacities for response. In the terms of Alexander, they have become differently qualitied. It is as impossible to transfer these characters of the habitats to the consciousness of the forms as it is to transfer the spatiotemporal structure of the things to such a so-called consciousness. If we introduce a fictitious instantaneousness into a passing universe, things fall to pieces. Things that are spatiotemporally distant from us can be brought into this instant only in terms of our immediate contact experience. They are what they would be if we were there and had our hands upon them. They take on the character of tangible matter. This is the price of their being located at the moment of our bodies' existence. But this instantaneous view has the great advantage of giving to us a picture of what the contact experience will be when we reach the distant object, and of determining conditions under which the distance characters arise. If the world existed at an instant in experience, we should be forced to find some realm such as consciousness into which to transport the distance or so-called secondary qualities of things. If consciousness in evolutionary history, then, has an unambiguous significance, it refers to that stage in the development of life in which the conduct of the individual marks out and defines the future field and objects which make up its environment, and in which emerge characters in the objects and sensitivities in the individuals that answer to each other. There is a relativity of the living individual and its environment, both as to form and content.

What I wish to trace is the fashion in which [the] self and the mind [have] arisen within this conduct.

It is the implication of this undertaking that only selves have minds, that is, that cognition only belongs to selves, even in the simplest expression of awareness. This, of course, does not imply that below the stage of self-consciousness sense characters and sensitivity do not exist. This obtains in our own immediate experience insofar as we are not self-conscious. It is further implied that this development has taken place only in a social group, for selves exist only in relation to other selves, as the organism as a physical object exists only in its relation to other physical objects. There have been two fields within which social groups have arisen which have determined their environment together with that of their members, and the individuality of its members. These lie in the realm of the invertebrates and in that of the vertebrates. Among the Hymenoptera and termites there are societies whose interests determine for the individuals their stimuli and habitats, and so differentiate the individuals themselves, mainly through the sexual and alimentary processes, that the individual is what he is because of his membership within those societies. In the complex life of the group, the acts of the individuals are completed only through the acts of other individuals, but the mediation of this complex conduct is found in the physiological differentiation of the different members of the society. As Bergson has remarked of the instincts, the implements by which a complex act is carried out are found in the differentiated structure of the form. There is no convincing evidence that an ant or a bee is obliged to anticipate the act of another ant or bee, by tending to respond in the fashion of the other, in order that it may integrate its activity into the common act. And by the same mark there is no evidence of the existence of any language in their societies. Nor do we need to go to the invertebrates to discover this type of social conduct. If one picks up a little child who has fallen, he adapts his arms and attitude to the attitude of the child, and the child adapts himself to the attitude of the other; or in boxing or fencing one responds to stimulus of the other, by acquired physiological adjustment.

Among the vertebrates, apart from the differentiation of the sexes and the nurture and care of infant forms, there is little or no inherited physiological differentiation to mediate the complexities of social conduct. If we are to cooperate successfully with others, we must in some manner get their ongoing acts into ourselves to make the common act come off. As I have just indicated, there is a small range of social activity in which this is not necessary. The suckling of an infant form, or a dog fight, if this may be called a social activity, does not call for more than inherited physiological adjustment. Perhaps the so-called herding instinct should be added, but it hardly comes to more than the tendency of the herd to stick together in their various activities. The wooing and mating of forms, the care of the infant form, the bunching of animals in migrations, and fighting, about exhaust vertebrate social conduct, and beyond these seasonal processes vertebrate societies hardly exist till we reach man. They exhaust the possibilities in vertebrate structure of the mediation of social conduct, for the vertebrate organism has shown no such astonishing plasticity in physiological differentiation as that which we can trace among the insects, from isolated forms to members of the societies of the termites, the ants, and the bees.

A social act may be defined as one in which the occasion or stimulus which sets free an impulse is found in the character or conduct of a living form that belongs to the proper environment of the living form whose impulse it is. I wish, however, to restrict the social act to the class of acts which involve the cooperation of more than one individual, and whose object as defined by the act, in the sense of Bergson, is a social object. I mean by a social object one that answers to all the parts of the complex act, though these parts are found in the conduct of different individuals. The objective of the act is then found in the life-process of the group, not in those of the separate individuals alone. The full social object would not exist in the environments of the separate individuals of the societies of the Hymenoptera and termites, nor in the restricted societies of the vertebrates whose basis is found alone in physiological adjustment. A cow that licks the skin of a calf stuffed with hay, until the skin is worn away, and then eats the hay, or a woman who expends her parental impulse upon a poodle, cannot be said to have the full social object involved in the entire act in their environments. It would be necessary to piece together the environments of the different individuals or superimpose them upon each other to reach the environment and objects of the societies in question.

Where forms such as those of the Hymenoptera and the termites exhibit great plasticity in development, social acts based on physiological adjustment, and corresponding societies, have reached astonishing complexity. But when the limit of that plasticity is reached, the limit of the social act and the society is reached also. Where, as among the vertebrates, that physiological adjustment which mediates a social act is limited and fixed, the societies of this type are correspondingly insignificant. But another type of social act, and its corresponding society and object, has been at least suggested by the description of the social act based upon physiological adjustment. Such an act would be one in which the different parts of the act which belong to different individuals should appear in the act of each individual. This cannot mean, however, that the single individual could carry out the entire act, for then, even if it were possible, it would cease to be a social act, nor could the stimulus which calls out his own part of the complex act be that which calls out the other parts of the act insofar as they appear in his conduct. If the social object is to appear in his experience, it must be that the stimuli which set free the responses of the others involved in the act should be present in his experience, not as stimuli to his response, but as stimuli for the responses of others; and this implies that the social situation which arises after the completion of one phase of the act, which serves as the stimulus for the next participant in the complex procedure, shall in some sense be in the experience of the first actor, tending to call out, not his own response, but that of the succeeding actor. Let us make the impossible assumption that the wasp, in stinging a spider which it stores with its egg, finds in the spider a social object in the sense which I have specified. The spider would have to exist in the experience of the wasp as live but quiescent food for the larva when it emerges from the egg. In order that the paralyzed spider should so appear to the wasp, the wasp would need to be subject to the same stimulus as that which sets free the response of the larva; in other words, the wasp would need to be able to respond in some degree as the larva. And of course the wasp would have to view the spider under the time dimension, grafting a hypothetical future onto its passing present, but the occasion for this would have to lie in the wasp's tending to respond in role of larva to the appropriate food which it is placing in storage. This, then, presents another possible principle of social organization, as distinguished from that of physiological differentiation. If the objects that answer to the complex social act can exist spatiotemporally in the experience of the different members of the society, as stimuli that set free not only their own responses, but also as stimuli to the responses of those who share in the composite act, a principle of coordination might be found which would not depend upon physiological differentiation. And one necessary psychological condition for this would be that the individual should have in some fashion present in his organism the tendencies to respond as the other participants in the act will respond. Much more than this would be involved, but this at least would be a necessary precondition. A social object answering to the responses of different individuals in a society could be conceived of as existing in the experiences of individuals in that society, if the different responses of these individuals in the complex acts could be found in sufficient degree in the natures of separate individuals to render them sensitive to the different values of the object answering to the parts of the act.

The cortex of the vertebrate central nervous system provides at least a part of the mechanism which might make this possible. The nervous currents from the column and the stem of the brain to the cortex can there bring the acts that go out from these lower centers into relation with each other so that more complex processes and adjustments can arise. The centers and paths of the cortex represent an indefinite number of possible actions; particularly they represent acts which, being in competition with each other, inhibit each other, and present the problem of organization and adjustment so that overt conduct may proceed. In the currents and crosscurrents in the gray matter and its association fibers, there exist the tendencies to an indefinite number of responses. Answering to these adjustments are the objects organized into a field of action, not only spatially but temporally; for the tendency to grasp the distant object, while already excited, is so linked with the processes of approach that it does not get its overt expression till the intervening stretch is passed. In this vertebrate apparatus of conduct, then, the already excited predispositions to thousands of acts, that far transcend the outward accomplishments, furnish the inner attitudes implicating objects that are not immediate objectives of the individual's act.

But the cortex is not simply a mechanism. It is an organ that exists in fulfilling its function. If these tendencies to action which do not get immediate expression appear and persist, it is because they belong to the act that is going on. If, for example, property is a social object in the experience of men, as distinguished from the nut which the squirrel stores, it is because features of the food that one buys innervate the whole complex of responses by which property is not only acquired, but respected and protected, and this complex so innervated is an essential part of the act by which the man buys and stores his food. The point is not that buying food is a more complicated affair than picking it up from the ground, but that exchange is an act in which a man excites himself to give by making an offer. An offer is what it is because the presentation is a stimulus to give. One cannot exchange otherwise than by putting one's self in the attitude of the other party to the bargain. Property becomes a tangible object, because all essential phases of property appear in the actions of all those involved in exchange, and appear as essential features of the individual's action.

The individual in such an act is a self. If the cortex has become an organ of social conduct, and has made possible the appearance of social objects, it is because the individual has become a self, that is, an individual who organizes his own response by the tendencies on the part of others to respond to his act. He can do this because the mechanism of the vertebrate brain enables the individual to take these different attitudes in the formation of the act. But selves have appeared late in vertebrate evolution. The structure of the central nervous system is too minute to enable us to show the corresponding structural changes in the paths of the brain. It is only in the behavior of the human animal that we can trace this evolution. It has been customary to mark this stage in development by endowing man with a mind, or at least with a certain sort of mind. As long as consciousness is regarded as a sort of spiritual stuff out of which are fashioned sensations and affections and images and ideas or significances, a mind as a locus of these entities is an almost necessary assumption, but when these contents have been returned to things, the necessity of quarters for this furniture has disappeared also.

It lies beyond the bounds of this paper to follow out the implications of this shift for logic and epistemology, but there is one phase of all so-called mental processes which is central to this discussion, and that is self-consciousness. If the suggestions which I have made above should prove tenable, the self that is central to all so-called mental experience has appeared only in the social conduct of human vertebrates. It is just because the individual finds himself taking the attitudes of the others who are involved in his conduct that he becomes an object for himself. It is only by taking the roles of others that we have been able to come back to ourselves. We have seen above that the social object can exist for the individual only if the various parts of the whole social act carried out by other members of the society are in some fashion present in the conduct of the individual. It is further true that the self can exist for the individual only if he assumes the roles of the others. The presence in the conduct of the individual of the tendencies to act as others act may be, then, responsible for the appearance in the experience of the individual of a social object, i.e., an object answering to complex reactions of a number of individuals, and also for the appearance of the self. Indeed, these two appearances are correlative. Property can appear as an object only insofar as the individual stimulates himself to buy by a prospective offer to sell. Buying and selling are involved in each other. Something that can be exchanged can exist in the experience of the individual only insofar as he has in his own makeup the tendency to sell when he has also the tendency to buy. And he becomes a self in his experience only insofar as one attitude on his own part calls out the corresponding attitude in the social undertaking.

This is just what we imply in "self-consciousness." We appear as selves in our conduct insofar as we ourselves take the attitude that others take toward us, in these correlative activities. Perhaps as good an illustration of this as can be found is in a "right." Over against the protection of our lives or property, we assume the attitude of assent of all members in the community. We take the role of what may be called the "generalized other." And in doing this we appear as social objects, as selves. It is interesting to note that in the development of the individual child, there are two stages which present the two essential steps in attaining self-consciousness. The first stage is that of play, and the second that of the game, where these two are distinguished from each other. In play in this sense, the child is continually acting as a parent, a teacher, a preacher, a grocery man, a policeman, a pirate, or an Indian. It is the period of childish existence which Wordsworth has described as that of "endless imitation." [6] It is the period of Froe-bel's kindergarten plays. In it, as Froebel recognized, the child is acquiring the roles of those who belong to his society.[7] This takes place because the child is continually exciting in himself the responses to his own social acts. In his infant dependence upon the responses of others to his own social stimuli, he is peculiarly sensitive to this relation. Having in his own nature the beginning of the parental response, he calls it out by his own appeals. The doll is the universal type of this, but before he plays with a doll, he responds in tone of voice and in atti-tude as his parents respond to his own cries and chortles. This has been denominated imitation, but the psychologist now recognizes that one imitates only insofar as the so-called imi-tated act can be called out in the individual by his appropri-ate stimulation. That is, one calls or tends to call out in him-self the same response that he calls out in the other.

The play antedates the game. For in a game there is a regu-lated procedure, and rules. The child must not only take the role of the other, as he does in the play, but he must assume the various roles of all the participants in the game, and gov-ern his action accordingly. If he plays first base, it is as the one to whom the ball will be thrown from the field or from the catcher. Their organized reactions to him he has embedded in his own playing of the different positions, and this organized reaction becomes what I have called the "generalized other" that accompanies and controls his conduct. And it is this gen-eralized other in his experience which provides him with a self. I can only refer to the bearing of this childish play atti-tude upon so-called sympathetic magic. Primitive men call out in their own activity some simulacrum of the response which they are seeking from the world about. They are chil-dren crying in the night.

[6] [William Wordsworth (1770–1850), English poet. On Mead's point, see Wordsworth's "Ode: Intimations of Immortality" (1807).]

[7] [F. W. A. Froebel (1782–1852), German educator who instituted the kindergarten system. His *Mutter—und Rose—Lidder* (1844) was translated by Susan Bow as *Mother Play* (1895).]

The mechanism of this implies that the individual who is stimulating others to response is at the same time arousing in himself the tendencies to the same reactions. Now, that in a complex social act which serves as the stimulus to another individual to his response is not as a rule fitted to call out the tendency to the same response in the individual himself. The hostile demeanor of one animal does not frighten the animal himself, presumably. Especially in the complex social reactions of the ants or termites or the bees, the part of the act of one form which does call out the appropriate reaction of another can hardly be conceived of as arousing a like reaction in the form in question, for here the complex social act is dependent upon physiological differentiation, such an unlikeness in structure exists that the same stimulus could not call out like responses. For such a mechanism as has been suggested, it is necessary to find first of all some stimulus in the social conduct of the members of an authentic group that can call out in the individual, that is responsible for it, the same response that it calls out in the other; and in the second place, the individuals in the group must be of such like structure that the stimulus will have the same value for one form that it has for the other. Such a type of social stimulus is found in the vocal gesture in a human society. The term "gesture" I am using to refer to that part of the act or attitude of one individual engaged in a social act which serves as the stimulus to another individual to carry out his part of the whole act. Illustrations of gestures, so defined, may be found in the attitudes and movements of others to which we respond in passing them in a crowd, in the turning of the head toward the glance of another's eye, in the hostile attitude assumed over against a threatening gesture, in the thousand and one different attitudes which we assume toward different modulations of the human voice, or in the attitudes and suggestions of movements in boxers or fencers, to which responses are so nicely adjusted. It is to be noted that the attitudes to which I have referred are but stages in the act as they appear to others, and include expressions of countenance, positions of the body, changes in breathing rhythm, outward evidence of circulatory changes, and vocal sounds. In general these so-called gestures belong to the beginning of the overt act, for the adjustments of others to the social process are best made early in the act. Gestures are, then, the early stages in the overt social act to which other forms involved in the same act respond. Our interest is in finding gestures which can affect the individual that is responsible for them in the same manner as that in which they affect other individuals. The vocal gesture is at least one that assails our ears who make it in the same physiological fashion as that in which it affects others. We hear our own vocal gestures as others hear them. We may see or feel movements of our hands as others see or feel them, and these sights and feels have served in the place of the vocal gestures in the case of those who are congenitally deaf or deaf and blind. But it has been the vocal gesture that has preeminently provided the medium of social organization in human society. It belongs historically to the beginning of the act, for it arises out of the change in breathing rhythm that accompanies the preparation for sudden action, those actions to which other forms must be nicely adjusted.

If, then, a vocal gesture arouses in the individual who makes it a tendency to the same response that it arouses in another, and this beginning of an act of the other in himself enters into his experience, he will find himself tending to act toward himself as the other acts toward him. In our self-conscious experience we understand what he does or says. The possibility of this entering into his experience we have found in the cortex of the human brain. There the coordinations answering to an indefinite number of acts may be excited, and while holding each other in check enter into the neural process of adjustment which leads to the final overt conduct. If one pronounces and hears himself pronounce the word "table," he has aroused in himself the organized attitudes of his response to that object, in the same fashion as that in which he has aroused it in another. We commonly call such an aroused organized attitude an idea, and the ideas of what we are saying accompany all of our significant speech. If we may trust to the statement in one of St. Paul's epistles, some of the saints spoke with tongues which had no significance to them. They made sounds which called out no response in those that made them. The sounds were without meaning. Where a vocal gesture uttered by one individual leads to a certain response in another, we may call it a symbol of that act; where it arouses in the man who makes it the tendency to the same response, we may call it a significant symbol. These organized attitudes which we arouse in ourselves when we talk to others are, then, the ideas which we say are in our minds, and insofar as they arouse the same attitudes in others, they are in their minds, insofar as they are self-conscious in the sense in which I have used that term. But it is not necessary that we should talk to another to have these ideas. We can talk to ourselves, and this we do in the inner forum of what we call thought. We are in possession of selves just insofar as we can and do take the attitudes of others toward ourselves and respond to those attitudes. We approve of ourselves and condemn ourselves. We pat ourselves upon the back and in blind fury attack ourselves. We assume the generalized attitude of the group, in the censor that stands at the door of our imagery and inner conversations, and in the affirmation of the laws and axioms of the universe of discourse. *Quod semper, quod ubique.*[8] Our thinking is an inner conversation in which we may be taking the roles of specific acquaintances over against ourselves, but usually it is with what I have termed the "generalized other" that we converse, and so attain to the levels of abstract thinking, and that impersonality, that so-called objectivity that we cherish. In this fashion, I conceive, have selves arisen in human behavior and with the selves their minds. It is an interesting study, that of the manner in which the self and its mind arise in every child, and the indications of the corresponding manner in which it arose in primitive man. I cannot enter into a discussion of this. I do wish, however, to refer to some of the impli-

---

8 ["What always, what everywhere (has been believed)."]

cations of this conception of the self for the theory of social control.

I wish to recur to the position, taken earlier in this paper, that, if we recognize that experience is a process continually passing into the future, objects exist in nature as the patterns of our actions. If we reduce the world to a fictitious instantaneous present, all objects fall to pieces. There is no reason to be found, except in an equally fictitious mind, why any lines should be drawn about any group of physical particles, constituting them objects. However, no such knife-edge present exists. Even in the so-called specious present there is a passage, in which there is succession, and both past and future are there, and the present is only that section in which, from the standpoint of action, both are involved. When we take this passage of nature seriously, we see that the object of perception is the existent future of the act. The food is what the animal will eat, and his refuge is the burrow where he will escape from his pursuer. Of course the future is, as future, contingent. He may not escape, but in nature it exists there as the counterpart of his act. So far as there are fixed relations there, they are of the past, and the object involves both, but the form that it has arises from the ongoing act. Evolutionary biology, insofar as it is not mere physics and chemistry, proceeds perhaps unwittingly upon this assumption, and so does social science insofar as it is not static. Its objects are in terms of the habitat, the environment. They are fashioned by reactions. I am merely affirming the existence of these objects, affirming them as existent in a passing universe answering to acts.

Insofar as there are social acts, there are social objects, and I take it that social control is bringing the act of the individual into relation with this social object. With the control of the object over the act, we are abundantly familiar. Just because the object is the form of the act, in this character it controls the expression of the act. The vision of the distant object is not only the stimulus to movement toward it. It is also, in its changing distance values, a continual control of the act of approach. The contours of the object determine the organ-

ization of the act of its seizure, but in this case the whole act
is in the individual and the object is in his field of experience.
Barring a breakdown in the structure or function, the very
existence of the object ensures its control of the act. In the
social act, however, the act is distributed among a number of
individuals. While there is or may be an object answering to
each part of the act, existing in the experience of each individual, in the case of societies dependent upon physiological
differentiation the whole object does not exist in the experience of any individual. The control may be exercised through
the survival of those physiological differentiations that still
carry out the life-process involved in the complex act. No
complication of the act which did not mediate this could survive. Or we may take refuge in a controlling factor in the act,
as does Bergson, but this is not the situation that interests us.
The human societies in which we are interested are societies
of selves. The human individual is a self only insofar as he
takes the attitude of another toward himself. Insofar as this
attitude is that of a number of others, and insofar as he can
assume the organized attitudes of a number that are cooperating in a common activity, he takes the attitudes of the group
toward himself, and in taking this or these attitudes he is defining the object of the group, that which defines and controls
the response. Social control, then, will depend upon the degree to which the individual does assume the attitudes of those
in the group who are involved with him in his social activities.
In the illustration already used, the man who buys controls his
purchase from the standpoint of a value in the object that
exists for him only insofar as he takes the attitude of a seller as
well as a buyer. Value exists as an object only for individuals
within whose acts in exchange are present those attitudes
which belong to the acts of the others who are essential to the
exchange.

The act of exchange becomes very complicated; the degree
to which all the essential acts involved in it enter into the acts
of all those engaged therein varies enormously, and the control
which the object, i.e., the value, exercises over the acts varies

proportionately. The Marxian theory of state ownership of capital, i.e., of exclusive state production, is a striking illustration of the breakdown of such control.[9] The social object, successful economic production, as presented in this theory, fails to assume the attitudes of individual initiative which successful economic production implies. Democratic government, on the theory of action through universal interest in the issues of a campaign, breaks down as a control, and surrenders the government largely to the political machine, whose object more nearly answers to the attitudes of the voters and the nonvoters.

Social control depends, then, upon the degree to which the individuals in society are able to assume the attitudes of the others who are involved with them in common endeavor. For the social object will always answer to the act developing itself in self-consciousness. Besides property, all of the institutions are such objects, and serve to control individuals who find in them the organization of their own social responses.

The individual does not, of course, assume the attitudes of the numberless others who are in one way or another implicated in his social conduct, except insofar as the attitudes of others are uniform under like circumstances. One assumes, as I have said, the attitudes of generalized others. But even with this advantage of the universal over the multiplicity of its numberless instances, the number of different responses that enter into our social conduct seems to defy any capacity of any individual to assume the roles which would be essential to define our social objects. And yet, though modern life has become indefinitely more complex than it was in earlier periods of human history, it is far easier for the modern man than for his predecessor to put himself in the place of those who contribute to his necessities, who share with him the functions of government, or join with him in determining prices. It is not the number of participants, or even the number of different functions, that is of primary importance. The impor-

9 [Karl Marx (1818–1883), German social philosopher and socialist leader. His *Das Kapital*, 3 vols. (1867–1909), is a classic of modern socialism and communism.]

tant question is whether these various forms of activities belong so naturally to the member of a human society that, in
taking the role of another, his activities are found to belong to
one's own nature. As long as the complexities of human society
do not exceed those of the central nervous system, the problem
of an adequate social object, which is identical with that of an
adequate self-consciousness, is not that of becoming acquainted with the indefinite number of acts that are involved
in social behavior, but that of so overcoming the distances in
space and time, and the barriers of language and convention
and social status, that we can converse with ourselves in the
roles of those who are involved with us in the common undertaking of life. A journalism that is insatiably curious about
the human attitudes of all of us is the sign of the times. The
other curiosities as to the conditions under which other people live, and work, and fight each other, and love each other,
follow from the fundamental curiosity which is the passion of
self-consciousness. We must be others if we are to be ourselves.
The modern realistic novel has done more than technical
education in fashioning the social object that spells social control. If we can bring people together so that they can enter
into each other's lives, they will inevitably have a common
object, which will control their common conduct.

The task, however, is enormous enough, for it involves not
simply breaking down passive barriers such as those of distance
in space and time and vernacular, but those fixed attitudes of
custom and status in which our selves are embedded. Any self
is a social self, but it is restricted to the group whose roles it
assumes, and it will never abandon this self until it finds itself
entering into the larger society and maintaining itself there.
The whole history of warfare between societies and within societies shows how much more readily and with how much
greater emotional thrill we realize our selves in opposition to
common enemies than in collaboration with them. All over
Europe, and more specifically at Geneva, we see nationals
with great distrust and constant rebounds trying to put
themselves in each other's places and still preserve the selves

that have existed upon enmities, that they may reach the common ground where they may avoid the horror of war, and meliorate unendurable economic conditions. A Dawes Plan [10] is such a social object, coming painfully into existence, that may control the conflicting interests of hostile communities, but only if each can in some degree put himself in the other's place in operating it. The World Court and the League of Nations are other such social objects that sketch out common plans of action if there are national selves that can realize themselves in the collaborating attitudes of others.

[10] [Charles Gates Dawes (1865–1951), American statesman and banker who served as Vice-President of the United States in the administration of Calvin Coolidge (1925–1929). In 1924 he submitted a plan which reduced German payments of reparations and stabilized German finances.]

✺ XIX ✺

THE NATURE OF AESTHETIC EXPERIENCE

Man lives in a world of Meaning. What he sees and hears means what he will or might handle. The proximate goal of all perception is what we can get our hands upon. If we traverse the distance that separates us from that which we see or hear and find nothing for the hand to manipulate, the experience is an illusion or a hallucination. The world of perceptual reality, the world of physical things, is the world of our contacts and our manipulations, and the distance experience of the eye and the ear means first of all these physical things.

Physical things are not only the meaning of what we see and hear; they are also the means we employ to accomplish our ends. They are mediate in both senses. They constitute a meaning of all that lies between us and our most distant horizons, and they are the means and instruments of our consummations. They lie in this mediate fashion between the distant stimuli that initiate our acts and the enjoyments or disappointments that terminate them. They are the proximate goal of our sights and sounds, and they are the instrumental stuff in which we embody our ends and purposes.

Thus on the one hand they constitute the hard physical realities of science, and on the other the material out of which to build the world of our heart's desire, the stuff that dreams are made of.

It is perhaps the most striking characterization which one can make of the thinking of the Western world since the Ren-

[From the *International Journal of Ethics,* XXXVI (1925–1926), 382–393.] I have not made specific acknowledgments in the article to Professor Dewey, but the reader who is familiar with his *Experience and Nature* will realize that it was written under the influence of that treatise.

aissance, that it has separated these two essential aspects of the world, has indeed made them incommensurable. Science informs us with increasing exactness of the ultimate elements of stuff or energy out of which the universe is made, and how they change. The world that rewards or defeats us, that entices or repels us, our remunerations and frustrations, our delights and distresses, what is finally significant and worthy of our effort, the beauty, the glory, and the dream, cannot be formulated in the language of exact science, nor have we found any common vernacular in which we can speak of the world of physical things and the values which after all they subtend.

This break between the definition of the things that constitute the means and the ends and values which they embody is not confined to the description of physical instruments and their uses, for it bisects the field of the social sciences as well. It has made economics the dismal science. It has mechanized and anatomized psychology. It has made ethics utilitarian, and aesthetics an affair of esoteric formulae.

It is not a break that can be healed by a new philosophic formula, though insight that is profound enough can exorcise metaphysical oppositions that have hardened into accepted realities, and exhibit the break as that which lies between the generalized technique of life and the ends and purposes which we have been able to formulate.

We are all of us engaged in complicated social activities whose accomplishments lie hopelessly beyond our appreciation. History later will lift out the ramifications of the unnumbered cooperative acts which have led up to what will be significant and desirable in human experience, but the individual experiences that have gone to make the achievement will never share in this significance. Closer at hand we see the routine and drudgery of countless uninterested hands and minds fashion in factories and mines the goods for which men give their wealth and themselves, and in the enjoyment of which men may be bound together in common interests which were quite divorced from their manufacture. Indeed, this is the definition of drudgery, the blind production of goods, cut off from all the interpretation and inspiration of their common enjoyment. It is the tragedy of industrial society that division of labor can interrelate and exploit the social nature of men's technical production so far in advance of their common fruitions, that all the earned significance of the work of our hands is foreign to its elaborate technique.

It has been the inspiration of universal religions, of political democracy, and later of industrial democracy to bring something of the universal achievement, of the solemn festival, of common delight into the isolated and dreary activities which all together make possible the blessed community, the state, the cooperative society, and all those meanings which we vaguely call social and spiritual.

In this intersection of what Professor Dewey has called the technical and the final, this attempted grasping of the consummation of the complex efforts of men in society to infuse meaning into the detail of existence, aesthetic experience may be isolated as a separate phase. What is peculiar to it is its power to catch the enjoyment that belongs to the consummation, the outcome, of an undertaking, and to give to the implements, the objects that are instrumental in the undertaking, and to the acts that compose it something of the joy and satisfaction that suffuse its successful accomplishment.

The beatitude that permeates the common striving of men after an infinite God of their salvation, belongs to the cathedral. The delight which follows upon successful adjustment of one's body to the varied reactions to the elements of a landscape flows over into the landscape itself. The pleasure that imbues our bodily and social balance of reaction to a human form inspires the statue. The felicity that animates harmonious movements of men runs through the dance. To so construct the object that it shall catch this joy of consummation is the achievement of the artist. To so enter into it in nature and art that the enjoyed meanings of life may become a part of living is the attitude of aesthetic appreciation.

I have presented aesthetic experience as a part of the attempt to interpret complex social life in terms of the goals toward which our efforts run. The other parts are the religious, political, educational, hygienic, technical undertakings among others, which attempt to look into the future of our common doings, and so select and fashion the ends we want that we can direct and interpret our immediate conduct. These endeavors do not carry with them the satisfactions that belong to finalities. They are infected by the interest which belongs to the fashioning of means into ends, to the shaping and testing of hypotheses, to invention and discovery, to the exercise of artisanship, and to the excitement of adventure in every field. It is the province of action, not that of appreciation. Our affective experience, that of emotion, of interest, of pleasure and pain, of satisfaction and dissatisfaction, may be roughly divided between that of doing and enjoying, and their opposites, and it is that which attaches to finalities that characterizes aesthetic experience.

And the intellectual attitudes are as markedly different. In the fashioning of means into ends, in the use of tools, and the nice adjustment of people and things to the accomplishment of purposes, we give attention only to that which forwards the undertaking; we see and hear only enough to recognize and use, and pass from the recognition to the operation; while in appreciation we contemplate, and abide, and rest in our presentations. The artisan who stops to sense the nice perfection of a tool or a machine has interrupted its use to appreciate it, and is in an aesthetic mood. He is not interested in its employment, he is enjoying it. The statesman who turns from the construction of his speeches, the ordering of his statistics, the meeting of political opposition, the whole technique of putting across his projects for bettering conditions and life of children, to the picture of their healthful and joyous life, is for the time being no longer in action. He is savoring the end that he is fashioning into practicable politics. When one stops in his common labor and effort to feel the surety of his colleagues, the loyalty of his supporters, the response of his public, to enjoy the community of life in family, or profession, or party, or church, or country, to taste in Whitmanesque manner [1] the commonalty of existence, his attitude is aesthetic. In the arts it appears in appropriate decoration, that which infuses the spirit of the meaning of the instrument into its structure and adornment, that which informs our equipment and mediate efforts with the significance and splendor of their accomplishments. It adds distinction to utility, and poetry to action, "the joy of elevated thoughts, the sense sublime of something far more deeply interfused" to our best and finest efforts. It comes in healthful pulses in the most strenuous enterprises, as we stop in climbing great mountains to gather not only breath and refreshment, but the charm and magnificence that each fresh *étape* reveals. From time immemorial men have dedicated them as festivals, and solemn concourses.

While this aesthetic attitude which accompanies, inspires, and dedicates common action finds its moment of ideal finality in future achievement, the material in which its significance and beauty is fashioned is historic. All the stuff with which the most creative imagination works is drawn from the storehouses and quarries of the past. All history is the interpretation of the present, that is, it gives us not only the direction and trend of events, the reliable uniformities and laws of affairs, but it offers us the irrevocableness of the pattern of what has occurred, in which to embody the still uncertain and unsubstantial objects we would achieve. We import the finalities of past victories and defeats into the finalities of the uncertain future. The solidity and definiteness and clarity of our undertakings are the donation of the past.

All this is healthful and normal. In its perfection it reaches the field of the fine arts, but it involves the creative imagination and aesthetic appreciation of the least artistically endowed of those who are fortunately engaged in the rewarding undertakings of life. But those that can import the aesthetic experience into activity must be fortunately engaged and engaged in rewarding undertakings. And this means more than

1 [Walt Whitman (1818–1892), American poet who celebrated ordinary things and common people.]

the mere adaptation of means to end, the mere successful co-operative fashioning of the goods which are enjoyed in common. The enjoyment of its ultimate use must be suggested by the intermediate steps in its production, and flow naturally into the skill which constructs it. It is this which gives joy to creation, and belongs to the work of the artist, the research scientist, and the skilled artisan who can follow his article through to its completion. It belongs to coordinated efforts of many, when the role of the other in the production is aroused in each worker at the common task, when the sense of team play, *esprit de corps,* inspires interrelated activities. In these situations something of the delight of consummation can crown all intermediate processes.

It is unfortunately absent from most labor in a modern competitive industrial society. But the thirst for enjoyment is still there, and the imagination, deprived of its normal function. When the goal is too far removed in time and method of approach, the imagination leaps to the ultimate satisfactions which cannot be fused with the uninteresting detail of preparation, and daydreaming supervenes and cuts the nerve of action. Normal aesthetic delight in creation is the recovery of the sense of the final outcome in the partial achievement, and gives assurance to the interest of creation. In daydreaming it is the very lack of connection between means and the end that leads one to the Barmecide feast of an end that is not expressed in terms of means. In the aesthetic appreciation of the works of great artists, what we are doing is capturing values of enjoyment there, which fill out and interpret our own interests in living and doing. They have permanent value because they are the language of delight into which men can translate the meaning of their own existence. But prerogative fine art has never been the dominant language of men's hearts, and even before the industrial revolution and the introduction of machine production, drudgery occupied most men's hands, and reverie—the field of the daydream—was the ever-present escape from its ennui. It is silly and inept to offer hopeless counsels of perfection, to undertake by the spread of so-called culture to replace the consummatory objects in men's reveries by the imagery of great artists, or to replace machine production by medieval artisanship. To be sure no one does baldly offer such programs, but so far as the aesthetic character of the reverie has been considered, and insofar as men have inveighed against machine industry as crushing out the artistic impulse such programs would be fair implications. From the standpoint of pathology, Freudian psychology has at least recognized the serious importance of the reverie as a field of escape, while organized labor has at least made evident that the factory organization of drudgery has put a social value into it which lifts it out of the field of mere painful effort.

Under the most favorable conditions, one cannot say under normal conditions, a man's work would be in itself interesting, and apart from the immediate interest in the operation, the sense of the whole that he is completing would grow with the advancing production, and give him aesthetic delight. The imagery which would provide this comes from the stream of reverie, but in the absence of these fortunate conditions, agreeable pictures of satisfied longings are apt to flood his mind, and they are likely to answer to the so-called inferiority complexes. It is true that just insofar as we can endow men with the gift of artisanship, creative impulse in any direction, and provide them with the opportunity of expressing it, insofar we will give them opportunity for aesthetic delight in the midst of their labor, but with humanity as it is and society as it is this is frankly impossible, though just in the degree to which it is possible to add creative interest to work, will aesthetic delight be added to labor.

On the other hand, in the words of Professor Dewey "shared experience is the greatest of human goods," and if out of the drudgery that men put through together there arises a social end in which they are interested, achieving this end will have its delight, and insofar as this end can involve the tasks themselves, the dignity and delight of the social realization will suffuse the tasks. The socializing of industry, of which the Guild Socialists have presented a rather impossible program, offers the ultimate escape from unaesthetic toil. Every invention that brings men closer together, so that they realize their interdependence, and increase their shared experience, which makes it more possible for them to put themselves in each other's places, every form of communication which enables them to participate in each other's minds, brings us nearer this goal. While we marvel at the new inventions which enable us to pass into the experiences of others, we perhaps fail to realize the unrecognized, unconscious pressure of the isolated individual in modern society. The isolated man is the one who belongs to a whole that he yet fails to realize. We have become bound up in a vast society, all of which is essential to the existence of each one, but we are without the shared experience which this should entail. The pressure upon the inventor will not cease until the isolation of man within society has passed.

Two of these mechanisms have spread the pattern of men's reveries before our outward eyes, the daily press and the movie film. With marvelous exactness they have copied the type of happening, and the sort of imagery, that run behind the average man's eyes and fill up the interstices of overt conduct, and they emphasize and expand what is needed to render the reverie vivid and concrete.

The newspaper has, of course, other functions. The most important of these is purveying the news. The theory of an acquisitive society is that news is valuable. One is willing to pay for it. Its value varies with its truth. Theoretically the newspaper which comes into the market with guaranteed goods will outsell its competitors, but this is to reckon without the host, or in this case without the reverie. There are certain limited fields, such as the stock market, and the results of the last election, in which the truth value of news holds absolutely. Outside of these fields, and the farther one gets away from them, the more does the enjoyability, the consummatory value, of the news bulk in value on the market. The reporter is generally sent out to get a story, not the facts. Furthermore, newspapers are organs—organs of certain fairly defined groups. They demand that the news shall take the forms which conform as far as possible to the results desired by these groups. It is this realm of the reverie—of imagined enjoyable results—which dictates the policy of the daily press.

Whether this form of the enjoyed result has an aesthetic function or not depends upon whether the story of the news, after being thrown into this acceptable form, serves to interpret to the reader his experience as the shared experience of the community of which he feels himself to be a part. The enjoyable imagery may hardly rise above unsatisfied animal impulses of gain, sex, or hate, but insofar as it has what is called the human appeal, or that of nation, town, or class, it serves to give the man the gratification of his experience as shared by the community to which he belongs. These forms are after all the determining forms which interpret his social experience.

It is evident that these forms will change and, if you like, improve, as the group to which the paper appeals realizes itself in the larger interests and undertakings of the community. It does not necessarily lose its peculiar individuality, but it becomes functional in the greater society in a creative sense. In this sense an intelligent newspaper management may lead its readers, but it can never get far away from the form of the news which their reveries demand.

The movie externalizes the reverie even more vividly than the daily press. It was foreshadowed by the picture sections of the press. And it has come with a peculiar appeal, for it intensifies a certain type of enjoyment of which the reverie is at best parsimonious. Our visual images are slight, incomplete, and not readily controlled. We do our thinking in the form of conversation, and depend upon the imagery of words for our meanings. It is only at favored moments that vivid pictures of the past throng the imagination. Visual imagery operates largely in filling out perception, as in reading or in the recognition of seen objects, rather than in satisfying the inward eye, which was the bliss of Wordsworth's solitude. When motion was added to the stereopticon, a certain sort of widely craved delight was flung at the community with open hands. But while this delight, of which nature has been somewhat penurious with us, is greatly exalted in the movie, the significant value of the imagery is minimized. It does not lend itself readily to shared experience. The movie has no creative audiences such as have been the inspiration of the moving speeches of great actors. Under the power of an orator one is in the perspective of the whole community. He sees the "picture" in his own perspective. The isolation of the members of a compact audience in a movie theater is in crying contrast with the shared response of those that, each at his own breakfast table, read the morning press.

It is reasonable, therefore, that it should be that which is more private and particular in the reverie that dominates the movie, that is, the escape values. For while the reverie provides us with the imagery of common values, the common consummatory experiences, it provides us also with the compensations for our defeats, our inferiorities, and our unconfessed failures. And what the average film brings to light is that the hidden unsatisfied longings of the average man and woman are very immediate, rather simple, and fairly primitive. And this is not without its consolations. The thus unwittingly confessed defeats of men are not of the wide and generous impulses. It is that which is rather primitive in us that is repulsed in modern society. At least, judged by this standard, it may be guessed that whatever defeats meet men's efforts to reach the larger social goods, the efforts themselves in their shared experiences have been rewarding. They do not give rise to inferiority complexes. The compensatory and escape values are not the only ones that find expression in the movie, but I think they are the dominating values, and in large measure fix the public's taste and, therefore, select the themes for most of the films.

One cannot without vivid curiosity watch the effect which the sudden release of this function of the reverie will have on the community. The man who finds sidesplitting humor in the near-disasters of Charlie Chaplin [2] is presumably finding compensation for some repressed primitive tendencies to inflict suffering and pains upon his enemies. Does this discovery of a situation in which one may enjoy unreproved the terrors and fright of another quicken the old impulse and render him callous to the sufferings of others? I think not. I think the experience is rather a catharsis, in an Aristotelian phrase, than a reversion. Nor does the physically timid man become more courageous from watching with compensatory delight Doug Fairbanks [3] annihilate a nest of bandits. But there should be a certain release, and relief from restraint, which comes from the fulfillment of the escape reaction with a richness of imagery which the inner imagination can never offer. If these escape reactions play any legitimate part in the economy of keeping house with one's self, and I think they do, the elaboration of them at just the point where the imagination fails should emphasize that function, and the enjoyed imagery is genuinely aesthetic.

Whether or not the escape reaction is a dominant interest in the movie public in determining the type of film, there is a vast number of them that do not answer to that motive. Some of them appeal simply to interest in a story vividly told in pictures, to a sympathetic love of adventure, and to the response to beauty in nature and to delight in picturesque and distant scenes. One captures something of the same values that he seizes in travel and adventurous outings. A genuine aesthetic effect is produced if the pleasure in that which is seen serves to bring out the values of the life that one lives.

In pictures whose attraction is their salaciousness there can be no aesthetic effect. They are sensual rather than sensuous. They are not the cause of finding meaning and pleasure in other things, nor are they informed with the meaning of

2 [Motion-picture comedian, born 1889.]

3 [Douglas Fairbanks (1883–1939), American motion-picture actor who specialized in adventure roles.]

that which leads up to their own enjoyment. They blot out all but the immediate response.

In closing I wish to refer again to this inchoate phenomenon of the human reverie, which the press and the movie have projected before us.

We are apt to consider it as a purely private affair with each individual, his desultory meanderings of idea and purpose and imagery, perhaps more gruesomely presented in James Joyce's *Ulysses*,[4] than elsewhere in literature. It is, indeed, infected with privacy and therefore subject to disintegration. But it passes into the universal meanings of common discourse and cooperative effort, and out of it arise the forms of universal beauty, the intuitions of the inventor, the hypotheses of the scientist, and the creations of the artist. It is that part of the inner life of man which cannot be given its implicated meaning because of the incompleteness of social organization. It marks man's isolation within society. We have decried its vulgarity when the daily press and the movie films have stripped off its privacy. It is better, however, to live with our problems than to ignore them.

[4] [James Joyce (1882–1941), Irish novelist. His *Ulysses* (1922) is one of the controversial masterpieces of modern literature.]

THE OBJECTIVE REALITY OF PERSPECTIVES

The grandiose undertaking of Absolute Idealism to bring the whole of reality within experience failed. It failed because it left the perspective of the finite ego hopelessly infected with subjectivity and consequently unreal. From its point of view the theoretical and practical life of the individual had no part in the creative advance of nature. It failed also because scientific method, with its achievements of discovery and invention, could find no adequate statement in its dialectic. It recognized the two dominant forces of modern life, the creative individual and creative science, only to abrogate them as falsifications of the experience of the absolute ego. The task remained unfulfilled, the task of restoring to nature the characters and qualities which a metaphysics of mind and a science of matter and motion had concurred in relegating to consciousness, and of finding such a place for mind in nature that nature could appear in experience. A constructive restatement of the problem was presented by a physiological and experimental psychology that fastened mind inextricably in an organic nature which both science and philosophy recognized. The dividend which philosophy declared upon this restatement is indicated in William James's reasoned query "Does 'Consciousness' Exist?" [1] The metaphysical assault upon

[From the *Proceedings of the Sixth International Congress of Philosophy*, edited by Edgar Sheffield Brightman (New York: Longmans, Green and Co., 1927), pp. 75–85. Reprinted in *The Philosophy of the Present* (LaSalle, Ill.: The Open Court Publishing Co., 1932). Reprinted by permission of The Open Court Publishing Co.]

1 [William James, "Does 'Consciousness' Exist?" *The Journal of Philosophy, Psychology, and Scientific Methods*, I (1904). Reprinted in William James, *Essays in Radical Empiricism*, edited by R. B. Perry (New York: Longmans, Green, and Co., 1912), pp. 1–38.]

the dualism of mind and nature, that has been becoming every day more intolerable, has been made in regular formation by Bergson's evolutionary philosophy, by neo-idealism, by neo-realism, and by pragmatism. And no one can say as yet that the position has been successfully carried.

I wish to call attention to two unconnected movements which seem to me to be approaching a strategic position of great importance—which may be called the objectivity of perspectives. These two movements are, first, that phase of behavioristic psychology which is planting communication, thinking, and substantive meanings as inextricably within nature as biological psychology has placed general animal and human intelligence; and secondly, an aspect of the philosophy of relativism which Professor Whitehead has presented.

Professor Whitehead interprets relativity in terms of events passing in a four-dimensional Minkowski world.[2] The order in which they pass, however, is relative to a consentient set. The consentient set is determined by its relation to a percipient event or organism. The percipient event establishes a lasting character of here and there, of now and then, and is itself an enduring pattern. The pattern repeats itself in the passage of events. These recurrent patterns are grasped together or prehended into a unity, which must have as great a temporal spread as the organism requires to be what it is, whether this period is found in the revolutions of the electrons in an iron atom or in the specious present of a human being. Such a percipient event or organism establishes a consentient set of patterns of events that endure in the relations of here and there, of now and then, through such periods or essential epochs, constituting thus slabs of nature, and differentiating space from time. This perspective of the organism is then there in nature. What in the perspective does not preserve the enduring character of here and there, is in motion. From the standpoint of some other organism these moving objects

2 [Hermann Minkowski (1864–1909), Lithuanian mathematician who developed a four-dimensional geometry which influenced the formulation of the general theory of relativity.]

may be at rest, and what is here at rest will be, in the time system of this other perspective, in motion. In Professor Whitehead's phrase, insofar as nature is patient of an organism, it is stratified into perspectives, whose intersections constitute the creative advance of nature. Professor Whitehead has with entire success stated the physical theory of relativity in terms of intersecting time systems.

What I wish to pick out of Professor Whitehead's philosophy of nature is this conception of nature as an organization of perspectives, which are there in nature. The conception of the perspective as there in nature is in a sense an unexpected donation by the most abstruse physical science to philosophy. They are not distorted perspectives of some perfect patterns, nor do they lie in consciousnesses as selections among things whose reality is to be found in a noumenal world. They are in their interrelationship the nature that science knows. Biology has dealt with them in terms of forms and their environments, and in ecology deals with the organization of environments, but it has conceded a world of physical particles in absolute space and time that is there in independence of any environment of an organism, of any perspective. Professor Whitehead generalizes the conception of organism to include any unitary structure, whose nature demands a period within which to be itself, which is therefore not only a spatial but also a temporal structure, or a process. Any such structure stratifies nature by its intersection into its perspective, and differentiates its own permanent space and time from the general passage of events. Thus the world of the physical sciences is swept into the domain of organic environments, and there is no world of independent physical entities out of which the perspectives are merely selections. In the place of such a world appear all of the perspectives in their interrelationship to each other.

I do not wish to consider Professor Whitehead's Bergsonian edition of Spinoza's underlying substance that individualizes itself in the structure of the events, nor his Platonic heaven of eternal objects where lie the hierarchies of patterns, that are there envisaged as possibilities and have ingression into events, but rather his Leibnitzian filiation, as it appears in his conception of the perspective as the mirroring in the event of all other events. Leibnitz made a psychological process central in his philosophy of nature. The contents of his monads were psychical states, perceptions, and *petites perceptions*,[3] which were inevitably representative of the rest of the reality of the universe of which they were but partially developed expressions. The represented content of all monads was identical, insofar as it was clear and distinct, so that the organization of these perspectives was a harmony preestablished in an identity of rational content. Professor Whitehead's principle of organization of perspectives is not the representation of an identical content, but the intersection by different time systems of the same body of events. It is, of course, the abandonment of simple location as the principle of physical existence, i.e., that the existence of a physical object is found in its occupancy of a certain volume of absolute space in an instant of absolute time; and the taking of time seriously, i.e., the recognition that there are an indefinite number of possible simultaneities of any event with other events, and consequently an indefinite number of possible temporal orders of the same events, that make it possible to conceive of the same body of events as organized into an indefinite number of different perspectives.

Without undertaking to discuss Professor Whitehead's doctrine of the prehension into the unity of the event of the aspects of other events, which I am unable to work out satisfactorily, from the summary statements I have found in his writings, I wish to consider the conception of a body of events as the organization of different perspectives of these events, from the standpoint of the field of social science, and that of behavioristic psychology.

In the first place, this seems to be exactly the subject-matter of any social science. The human experience with which social

---

[3] [Leibnitz' notion of "minute (unconscious) perceptions."]

science occupies itself is primarily that of individuals. It is only so far as the happenings, the environmental conditions, the values, their uniformities and laws enter into the experience of individuals as individuals that they become the subject of consideration by these sciences. Environmental conditions, for example, exist only insofar as they affect actual individuals, and only as they affect these individuals. The laws of these happenings are but the statistical uniformities of the happenings to and in the experiences of A, B, C, and D. Furthermore the import of these happenings and these values must be found in the experiences of these individuals if they are to exist for these sciences at all.

In the second place, it is only insofar as the individual acts not only in his own perspective but also in the perspective of others, especially in the common perspective of a group, that a society arises and its affairs become the object of scientific inquiry. The limitation of social organization is found in the inability of individuals to place themselves in the perspectives of others, to take their points of view. I do not wish to belabor the point, which is commonplace enough, but to suggest that we find here an actual organization of perspectives, and that the principle of it is fairly evident. This principle is that the individual enters into the perspectives of others, insofar as he is able to take their attitudes, or occupy their points of view.

But while the principle is a commonplace for social conduct, its implications are very serious if one accepts the objectivity of perspectives, and recognizes that these perspectives are made up of other selves with minds; that here is no nature that can be closed to mind. The social perspective exists in the experience of the individual insofar as it is intelligible, and it is its intelligibility that is the condition of the individual entering into the perspectives of others, especially of the group. In the field of any social science the objective data are those experiences of the individuals in which they take the attitude of the community, i.e., in which they enter into the perspectives of the other members of the community. Of course the social scientist may generalize from the standpoint of his universe of discourse what remains hopelessly subjective in the experiences of another community, as the psychologist can interpret what for the individual is an unintelligible feeling. I am speaking not from the standpoint of the epistemologist, nor that of the metaphysician. I am asking simply what is objective for the social scientist, what is the subject-matter of his science, and I wish to point out that the critical scientist is only replacing the narrower social perspectives of other communities by that of a more highly organized and hence more universal community.

It is instructive to note that never has the character of that common perspective changed more rapidly than since we have gained further control over the technique by which the individual perspective becomes the perspective of the most universal community, that of thinking men, that is, the technique of the experimental method. We are deluded, by the ease with which we can, by what may be fairly called transformation formulae, translate the experience of other communities into that of our own, into giving finality to the perspective of our own thought; but a glance at the bewildering rapidity with which different histories, i.e., different pasts have succeeded each other, and new physical universes have arisen, is sufficient to assure us that no generation has been so uncertain as to what will be the common perspective of the next. We have never been so uncertain as to what are the values which economics undertakes to define, what are the political rights and obligations of citizens, what are the community values of friendship, of passion, of parenthood, of amusement, of beauty, of social solidarity in its unnumbered forms, or of those values which have been gathered under the relations of man to the highest community or to God. On the other hand there has never been a time at which men could determine so readily the conditions under which values, whatever they are, can be secured. In terms of common conditions, by transformation formulae, we can pass from one value field to another, and thus come nearer finding out which is more valuable, or rather how to conserve each. The common perspective is comprehensibility, and comprehensibility is the statement in terms of common social conditions.

It is the relation of the individual perspective to the common perspective that is of importance. To the biologist there is a common environment of an anthill or of a beehive, which is rendered possible by the intricate social relationships of the ants and the bees. It is entirely improbable that this perspective exists in the perspectives of individual ants or bees, for there is no evidence of communication. Communication is a social process whose natural history shows that it arises out of cooperative activities, such as those involved in sex, parenthood, fighting, herding, and the like, in which some phase of the act of one form, which may be called a gesture, acts as a stimulus to others to carry on their parts of the social act. It does not become communication in the full sense, i.e., the stimulus does not become a significant symbol, until the gesture tends to arouse the same response in the individual who makes it that it arouses in the others. The history of the growth of language shows that in its earlier stages the vocal gesture addressed to another awakens in the individual who makes the gesture not simply the tendency to the response which it calls forth in the other, such as the seizing of a weapon or the avoiding of a danger, but primarily the social role which the other plays in the cooperative act. This is indicated in the early play period in the development of the child, and in the richness in social implication of language structures in the speech of primitive peoples.

In the process of communication the individual is an other before he is a self. It is in addressing himself in the role of an other that his self arises in experience. The growth of the organized game out of simple play in the experience of the child, and of organized group activities in human society, placed the individual then in a variety of roles, insofar as these were parts of the social act, and the very organization of these in the whole act gave them a common character in indicating what he had to do. He is able then to become a generalized other in addressing himself in the attitude of the group or the community. In this situation he has become a definite self over against the social whole to which he belongs. This is the common perspective. It exists in the organisms of all the members of the community, because the physiological differentiation of human forms belongs largely to the consummatory phase of the act.

The overt phase within which social organization takes place is occupied with things, physical things or implements. In the societies of the invertebrates, which have indeed a complexity comparable with human societies, the organization is largely dependent upon physiological differentiation. In such a society, evidently, there is no phase of the act of the individual in which he can find himself taking the attitude of the other. Physiological differentiation, apart from the direct relations of sex and parenthood, plays no part in the organization of human society. The mechanism of human society is that of bodily selves who assist or hinder each other in their cooperative acts by the manipulation of physical things. In the earliest forms of society these physical things are treated as selves, i.e., those social responses, which we can all detect in ourselves to inanimate things which aid or hinder us, are dominant among primitive peoples in the social organization that depends on the use of physical means. The primitive man keeps *en rapport* with implements and weapons by conversation in the form of magic rites and ceremonies. On the other hand the bodily selves of members of the social group are as clearly implemental as the implements are social. Social beings are things as definitely as physical things are social.

The key to the genetic development of human intelligence is found in the recognition of these two aspects. It arises in those early stages of communication in which the organism arouses in itself the attitude of the other and so addresses itself and thus becomes an object to itself, becomes in other words a self, while the same sort of content in the act constitutes the other that constitutes the self. Out of this process thought arises, i.e., conversation with one's self, in the role of the specific other and then in the role of the generalized other, in the fashion I indicated above. It is important to recognize that the self does not project itself into the other. The others and the self arise in the social act together. The content of the act may be said to lie within the organism but it is projected into the other only in the sense in which it is projected into the self, a fact upon which the whole of psychoanalysis rests. We pinch ourselves to be sure that we are awake as we grasp an object to be sure that it is there. The other phase of human intelligence is that it is occupied with physical things. Physical things are perceptual things. They also arise within the act. This is initiated by a distant stimulus and leads through approximation or withdrawal to contact or the avoidance of contact. The outcome of the act is in consummation, e.g., as in eating, but in the behavior of the human animal a mediate stage of manipulation intervenes. The hand fashions the physical or perceptual thing. The perceptual thing is fully there in the manipulatory area, where it is both seen and felt, where is found both the promise of the contact and its fulfillment, for it is characteristic of the distant stimulation and the act that it initiates that there are already aroused the attitudes of manipulation,—what I will call terminal attitudes of the perceptual act, that readiness to grasp, to come into effective contact, which in some sense control the approach to the distant stimulation. It is in the operation with these perceptual or physical things which lie within the physiological act short of consummation that the peculiar human intelligence is found. Man is an implemental animal. It is mediate to consummation. The hand carries the food to the mouth, or the child to the breast, but in the social act this mediation becomes indefinitely complicated, and the task arises of stating the consummation, or the end, in terms of means. There are two conditions for this: one is the inhibition, which takes place when conflicting ways of completing the act check the expression of any one way, and the other is the operation of the social mechanism, which I have described, by which the individual can indicate to others and to himself the perceptual things that can be seized and manipulated and combined. It is within this field of implemental things picked out by the significant symbols of gesture, not in that of physiological differentiation, that the complexities of human society have developed. And, to recur to my former statement, in this field selves are implemental physical things just as among primitive peoples physical things are selves.

My suggestion was that we find in society and social experience, interpreted in terms of a behavioristic psychology, an instance of that organization of perspectives, which is for me at least the most obscure phase of Professor Whitehead's philosophy. In his objective statement of relativity the existence of motion in the passage of events depends not upon what is taking place in an absolute space and time, but upon the relation of a consentient set to a percipient event. Such a relation stratifies nature. These stratifications are not only there in nature but they are the only forms of nature that are there. This dependence of nature upon the percipient event is not a reflection of nature into consciousness. Permanent spaces and times, which are successions of these strata, rest and motion, are there, but they are there only in their relationship to percipient events or organisms. We can then go further and say that the sensuous qualities of nature are there in nature, but there in their relationship to animal organisms. We can advance to the other values which have been regarded as dependent upon appetence, appreciation, and affection, and thus restore to nature all that a dualistic doctrine has relegated to consciousness, since the spatiotemporal structure of the world and the motion with which exact physical science is occupied is found to exist in nature only in its relationship to percipient events or organisms.

But rest and motion no more imply each other than do objectivity and subjectivity. There are perspectives which cease to be objective, such as the Ptolemaic order, since it does not select those consentient sets with the proper dynamical axes, and there are those behind the mirror and those of an alcoholic brain. What has happened in all of these instances, from the most universal to the most particular, is that the rejected perspective fails to agree with that common perspective which the individual finds himself occupying as a member of the community of minds, which is constitutive of his self. This is not a case of the surrender to a vote of the majority, but the development of another self through its intercourse with others and hence with himself.

What I am suggesting is that this process, in which a perspective ceases to be objective, becomes if you like subjective, and in which new common minds and new common perspectives arise, is an instance of the organization of perspectives in nature, of the creative advance of nature. This amounts to the affirmation that mind as it appears in the mechanism of social conduct is the organization of perspectives in nature and at least a phase of the creative advance of nature. Nature in its relationship to the organism, and including the organism, is a perspective that is there. A state of mind of the organism is the establishment of simultaneity between the organism and a group of events, through the arrest of action under inhibition as above described. This arrest of action means the tendencies within the organism to act in conflicting ways in the completion of the whole act. The attitude of the organism calls out or tends to call out responses in other organisms, which responses, in the case of human gesture, the organism calls out in itself, and thus excites itself to respond to these responses. It is the identification of these responses with the distant stimuli that establishes simultaneity, that gives insides to these distant stimuli, and a self to the organism. Without such an establishment of simultaneity, these stimuli are spatiotemporally distant from the organism, and their reality lies in the future of passage. The establishment of simultaneity wrenches this future reality into a possible present, for all our presents beyond the manipulatory area are only possibilities, as respects their perceptual reality. We are acting toward the future realization of the act, as if it were present, because the organism is taking the role of the other. In the perceptual inanimate object the organic content that survives is the resistance that the organism both feels and exerts in the manipulatory area. The actual spatiotemporal structure of passing events with those characters which answer to the susceptibilities of the organism are there in nature, but they are temporally as well as spatially away from the organism. The reality awaits upon the success of the act. Present reality is a possibility. It is what would be if we were there instead of here. Through the social mechanism of significant symbols the organism places itself there as a possibility, which acquires increasing probability as it fits into the spatiotemporal structure and the demands of the whole complex act of which its conduct is a part. But the possibility is there in nature, for it is made up of actual structures of events and their contents, and the possible realizations of the acts in the form of adjustments and readjustments of the processes involved. When we view them as possibilities we call them mental or working hypotheses.

I submit that the only instance we have of prehension in experience is this holding together of future and past as possibilities—for all pasts are as essentially subject to revision as the futures, and are, therefore, only possibilities—and the common content which endures is that which is common to the organism and environment in the perspective. This in the organism is identified with the spatiotemporally distant stimuli as a possibly real present, past, and future. The unity lies in the act or process, the prehension is the exercise of this unity, when the process has been checked through conflicting tendencies, and the conditions and results of these tendencies are held as possibilities in a specious present.

Thus the social and psychological process is but an instance of what takes place in nature, if nature is an evolution, i.e., if it proceeds by reconstruction in the presence of conflicts, and if, therefore, possibilities of different reconstructions are present, reconstructing its pasts as well as its futures. It is the relativity of time, that is, an indefinite number of possible orders of events, that introduces possibility in nature. When there was but one recognized order of nature, possibility had no other place than in the mental constructions of the future or the incompletely known past. But the reality of a spatiotemporally distant situation lies ahead, and any present existence of it, beyond the manipulatory area, can be only a possibility. Certain characters are there, but what *things* they are can only be realized when the acts these distant stimulations arouse are completed. What they are now is represented by a set of possible spatiotemporal structures. That these future realizations appear as present possibilities is due to the arrest of the act of the organism, and its ability to indicate these possibilities.

That these possibilities have varying degrees of probability is due to the relation of the various inhibited tendencies in the organism to the whole act. The organization of this whole act the human social organism can indicate to others and to itself. It has the pattern which determines other selves and physical things, and the organism as a self and a thing, and the meanings which are indicated have the universality of the whole community to which the organism belongs. They constitute a universe of discourse. It is the fitting in of the particular tendencies into this larger pattern of the whole process that constitutes the probability of the present existence of the things which any one act implies. Its full reality is still dependent upon the accomplishment of the act, upon experimental evidence. It is then such a coincidence of the perspective of the individual organism with the pattern of the whole act in which it is so involved that the organism can act within it, that constitutes the objectivity of the perspective.

The pattern of the whole social act can lie in the individual organism because it is carried out through implemental things to which any organism can react, and because indications of these reactions to others and the organism itself can be made by significant symbols. The reconstruction of the pattern can take place in the organism, and does take place in the so-called conscious process of mind. The psychological process is an instance of the creative advance of nature.

In living forms lower than man the distant perspective may

through sensitivity exist in the experience of the form and the grasping of this in the adjustments of conduct answer to the formation of the stratification of nature, but the reconstruction of the pattern within which the life of the organism lies does not fall within the experience of the organism. In inanimate organisms the maintenance of a temporal structure, i.e., of a process, still stratifies nature, and gives rise to spaces and times, but neither they nor the entities that occupy them enter as experiential facts into the processes of the organisms. The distinction of objectivity and subjectivity can only arise where the pattern of the larger process, within which lies the process of the individual organism, falls in some degree within the experience of the individual organism, i.e., it belongs only to the experience of the social organism.

A PRAGMATIC THEORY OF TRUTH

As far back in time and in cultural epochs as we can trace human society we can find there something that answers to philosophy and something that answers to science. They are the myth and the cult. In early social conditions they stand vaguely for theory and practice. In terms closer to the ideas and activities to which they refer they may be called "rationalizations" and "habits." It is clear that the habit comes before the rationalization or explanation. The cult is not any habit. It is one that is social not only in its origin and expression but also in its function and valuation. It belongs to the group and it serves to relate this primitive society to its habitat and to its past and future. The myth supervenes upon the cult. The cult rapidly became archaic, not simply in the sense of old, but in the sense of having outlived the situations out of which it had arisen. Whatever reasons we find for this or however we label them, the fact made them strange as habits. They could not be understood entirely through the situations within which they were practiced, and the myth was the explanation. The myth gave preeminently the explanation that did not arise naturally out of the original situation. It was the explanation of a habit, that just as a habit was inexplicable. It is a reason for action when the reason does not lie in the actual situation within which the action is going on. This is, however, in one respect not a correct statement of what takes place, for it says that some *reason* existed in the situation before a reason had to be sought, whereas only things existed there. Our cautious ancestors, when yawning, blocked

[From *Studies in the Nature of Truth*, "University of California Publications in Philosophy," XI (1929), 65–88. Reprinted by permission of the University of California Press.]

the way to the entrance of evil spirits by putting their hands before their mouths. *We* find a *reason* for the gesture in the delicacy of manner which forbids an indecent exposure. But evil spirits were spirits that one warded off. The parry is simply the obverse side of the thrust. If we insist on taking analysis into conduct in which it had no place, we must find the correlate to the later reason in the sufficient definition of earlier things. We do this when we replace the evil spirit by the microbe and form new and better habits instead of rationalizing the old ones.

Perhaps I am myself indecorous in suggesting an analogy between a certain sort of philosophic analysis and a guarded yawn, but I will venture it for it opens a door to a distinction worth making. I refer to the distinction between a scientific approach to nature and that of a philosophy that has ensnarled itself in a hopeless epistemological problem. While science has been discovering and hypothetically constructing things that lead to new and fortunate responses to the world, this philosophy has rationalized the discarded attitudes toward nature. Those discarded attitudes were the relations of a soul or mind to a world whose *raison d'être* was its being the habitat of man. The philosophic rationalizations of these attitudes have consisted in presenting the world in the guise of men's sensations and ideas, in a word, in his states of consciousness. The primary reference of nature to mind which obsessed Renaissance philosophy was the rationalization of the medieval cult. Treading close upon its heels came the task of getting back to external things from a world described in states of mind. Science, Galileo like, cared for none of these things. It was occupied in replacing the furniture of earth and heaven with masses, velocities, accelerations, chemical elements, and living cells to which predictable responses could be secured. While science has been interested solely in getting new and reliable things, and in its mental processes only as means to this end, philosophy has not only made the thought process its field but has insisted on so analyzing it that new things and old can both be stated in the same mental terms. It has not given to the thing its value of a thing before the problem arose and after the solution, but has kept it in terms of logical and metaphysical speculation. It has not only explained the old and so rationalized it, but has as well forced the new into the same dress. My thesis is that the object that tells its own tale has no longer a place in the field of analysis, but is simply there, until it breaks down and propounds some other problem for thought.

Professor Whitehead in *Science and the Modern World* [1] displays the entire adequacy of medieval doctrine in its explanation of all that happened. There was a reason to be found for everything either in Heaven or on Earth or if need be in Hell. But Professor Whitehead did not point out that this perfect fit between doctrine and the course of events in the world reflected rather the nice adjustment of the cult to men's needs. In the face of every exigency the cult presented men with something to do. They were not called upon to think. The cry was not, how shall I understand? but what shall I do to be saved? Granted the ineradicable guilt of man and the incomprehensibility of an infinite perfect God, and explanation was almost too easy. There was abundant occupation for scholastic thought in the adjustment of such incongruous ingredients, as Greek philosophy, the Pauline doctrine, and the administrative theory of the Roman hierarchy. But these speculations did not touch the world of things within which men lived and moved and had their being. Things were not analyzed. They were what they were, what aroused men to action and satisfied their needs or drove them to the refuge of the Church. I think Professor Whitehead is wrong in calling this a rationalistic mind. Rationalization set in with the Renaissance; and while Renaissance science set about the discovery of new things, philosophy set about the task of restating the new world in the terms of the old. Leibnitz' deity was not only the God of the Theodicy but the supreme mathematician as well. The world was a mechanism,

1 [Alfred North Whitehead, *Science and the Modern World* (New York: The Macmillan Company, 1925), pp. 16–19.]

but the work of a supreme mechanic to serve his ends. Descartes' anxious effort to avoid quarrels with the Holy Office was not simply an escape complex. However, this attitude of philosophy must not be accounted to it for unrighteousness. Science was quite incompetent to present society with a complete new world. It offered only ultimate physical and dynamical elements and a powerful apparatus of analysis.

This may seem to some, perhaps in an invidious sense, a long way from truth. Its relation to my theme is this: Science set out from a world which was there but which presented new problems. Science analyzed the world and put it together again in a Newtonian system and left the material universe there. Problems fortunately continued to abound, but a system of masses moving according to Newton's laws was the presupposition of the solution of these problems.[2] Truth had nothing to do with the world insofar as it was not involved in the problem. But philosophy's problem was to bring this world of science both in its analysis and synthesis into accord with the world men believed they were living in. It had to find a way of stating the world that was there for science—the mechanical world—in terms of the objects that men sense and want and fear. I mean that philosophy's task of rationalization compelled it to make a problem out of the world which for science was simply there, as the presupposition of the problem science was undertaking to solve. Rationalization, if I may repeat, is giving an explanation for attitudes and responses, when the situation which originally called them out has passed away. It provides another situation which will still arouse these responses. The Newtonian mechanical universe in a considerable measure removed the situations which called out naturally the responses due to man's central position in the world. Philosophy in rationalizing this new situation sought so to restate the world which science did not call in question that human experience would remain central. Philosophy had then to restate the world

2 [Sir Isaac Newton (1642–1727), English physicist whose law of gravity and laws of motion became the foundation of modern classical physics.]

which for science was unshaken, and the success of science compelled it to use the results of scientific analysis. When it sought for its own $\pi o\hat{v}$ $\sigma\tau\hat{\omega}$,[3] that world within which its problem lay, it could find it only in the mind of the individual—*cogito ergo sum*[4]—and Hume shattered that. For science, truth is the accord of its hypothetical construction with the world within which the problem has appeared. For philosophy this world has also been made a problem, and we can therefore exclaim with Pontius Pilate, What is truth?

My proposition is that every problem presupposes what is not involved in that problem, and which is insofar valid. The truth of the judgment which represents the solution of the problem rests upon the harmony of its dictum with that whose validity is not problematic. There are various implications of this proposition. One is that there is no such thing as Truth at large. It is always relative to the problematic situation. What is not involved in the problem is not true nor is it false; it is simply there, though there is no suggestion that a problem may not break out anywhere within it. Confessedly the world of science presents the evident illustration of this. Research is ready to find a problem at any point in the structure of scientific doctrine, a problem which may invalidate any theory. Indeed it welcomes such outbreaks, and lives its exciting life in their midst. What arrests the philosopher's attention is that this attitude carries with it no sense of insecurity. The philosopher still has the Medievalist's yearning to rest in the arms of finality. Whether idealist or realist or neo-Kantian phenomenalist, he seeks repose for his perturbed spirit in the everlasting arms of an absolute of one sort or another. His philosophic mind is attuned to the present French political mind; it cannot conceive of security of method, it must have security of structure.

It is true that the scientist philosophizes; and who does not? And then he is prone to lead a double life, to seek repose from the excitements of research in the restful arms of an ul-

3 ["Standpoint" or "starting-point."]
4 [Descartes' principle, "I think; therefore, I am."]

timate doctrine that in some fashion envelopes him. He assures himself and us that Newton's laws were but first approximations; that however theories effloresce and wither, the data of science remain unchanged—or at least that it is always possible to so restate them that they take on the form of eternity, and with this view *sub specie aeternitatis* he is assured that his philosophic God is in his heaven. But this is not his scientific attitude. In this attitude, data do not implicate persistent structure. They appear first of all as exceptions—the phenomena of the heavens which Greek astronomy from the time of Pythagoras on sought to "save"—but when the saving theory has rescued them, they are no longer exceptions, they have become instances. In a sense we can identify, "sprinkled along the waste of years," the observations of the Mesopotamian Magi, of Hipparchus, of Ptolemy, of Tycho Brahe, and of our own astronomical tables; but, when so isolated, they have no being in any system independent of those within which they have appeared. They are building stones which had their places in many "transitory structures high," but "it nought avails their architects now to have built high in heaven towers" for they have no final place in any abiding edifice. The datum must seek its meaning either in its opposition to the doctrine which it invalidates, or in that which the genius of the scientist constructs to give it again a local habitation and a name, or in the theory of the historic process by which it has passed through many "fabrics huge" which have risen like exhalations and vanished like the cloud-capped towers of skyey landscapes, but there is no ultimate structure in which their final meaning reposes. Nor does the scientist, when he is not crowning his lifework with Gifford lectures, endow his data with the logical form of such final meanings. They are pertinent solely to the experiences within which they arise. Still less can the data be identified with the building material of the world within which the problem appears. The evidence for this is found in the presupposition of this world as the conditions for the appearance of the data. Whether the datum appears as an exception or as an experimental finding in support of a hypothesis, its existence involves things that cannot by definition be stated in terms of the given world. This speaks out of the very nature of the exception, and it is heard equally clearly in the nature of a conclusive experiment. The experimental finding must take place under conditions which rigorously exclude the theory which the findings will support—otherwise there is an *argumentum in circulo*.[5] You must be able to prove that your guinea pig has the disease, which appears after inoculation with the hypothetical germ, by means of clinical evidence other than presence of the germ. You cannot by the same findings prove (a) that the guinea pig contracted the disease through the germ and (b) that the disease which the guinea pig contracted is the disease in question. Now it is of course true that we continue to talk about the disease in terms of the germ that was identified in the experiment, but it has become a very different affair. Then it was something foreign to the life-process of the guinea pig; now it has become a parasite that has a natural habitat within that process. You describe the life-process of host and parasite in a single biochemical formula.

The truth that your experiment establishes is that the world—an ongoing intelligible concern—within which a problem has arisen, continues to exhibit itself as the same ongoing intelligible concern under conditions which alone can be stated in terms of the hypothesis you have presented. The new predicate with which you are qualifying this subject cannot already be implied in the subject. The copula which triumphantly connects them is the experiment, so constructed as rigorously to exclude the new character from the subject that was there and at the same time to jockey the world into such a situation that it inevitably exhibits this character.

But how can it inevitably exhibit this character unless there was already present in the subject that which implies the

5 ["Circular argument"—one that assumes what it sets out to demonstrate.]

predicate? That is, how can we make a universal proposition out of the mere juxtaposition of two experiences—unless there is in advance in the subject, as it appears in the judgment, the connection which the copula has merely exhibited? The answer is found in the form of the problem that appears in the subject of the judgment. Back of any such experiment as that to which I referred above, lies the breakdown of medical description and treatment of the disease. Instances appear which negative this description and practice. One cannot describe and treat the disease as the disease has been described and treated; which means that other characters which call out different responses, and which did not enter into the former picture of the disease, are now a part of the picture. The solution of the difficulty is found, if it is found, in a reconstruction of the picture that enables the conflicting tendencies to find expression—that is, which enables the inhibited action to go on. There is a meaning in the old accounts and methods and there is a meaning in the new experiences which invalidate them. Truth is found in such a formulation of meaning that the conduct which these meanings have implied may be made possible. We never simply throw away values which have been there. They are allotted to their proper spheres, within which they give rise to appropriate responses. The subject of the *judgment,* as distinct from that of the final *proposition,* is the situation within which this conflict lies, and the final predicate which the experiment justifies, is the reconstructed picture which gives to the conflicting values their own functions. We are not in the judgment simply associating two experiences with each other. We are making possible the experience which the conflicting elements in the subject situation call for. The reconstructed picture of the disease gives to the former conflicting characters of the subject an organization which admits of intelligent response. The subject so characterized is then insofar true, but the organization of meanings was not in the former subject. Insofar as the reorganization is carried out consistently with these meanings, the result necessarily follows, but the reason for the connection between the reconstructed picture and the appropriate consequences was not present in the former subject.

But it was in nature, was it not? It was not in that phase of nature which appeared in the experience of the men who recognized the problem and solved it. The judgment is a natural process taking place in the experience of human organisms, and its truth is a natural condition that attends upon the success of these organisms in solving their problem. The word "success" I do not entirely like, because of the implications which are apt to go with it. It is associated with satisfactions and the agreeable experiences which attend upon satisfactions. The test of truth which I have presented is the ongoing of conduct, which has been stopped by a conflict of meanings—and in meanings I refer to responses or conduct which the characters of things lead up to. The truth is not the *achievement* of the solution, still less the gratification of him who has achieved it. There is something of the old hedonistic fallacy in this. Pleasure undoubtedly attends upon the object of one's desire, but one does not therefore desire the pleasure. One is generally gratified by the solution of one's problem, but the test is the ability to act where action was formerly estopped. The action may be a very sorry affair and afflicted with gloom, but if the road now lies open to the meanings which had nullified each other, this road is the true road. I hope I have made evident that in this doctrine the data are not in the world out of which the problem has arisen, but belong to the statement of the problem; and that in the solution of the problem, they pass in new forms into the reconstructed meanings which experiment shows to fit into the world, insofar as it was not involved in this problem.

Truth is then synonymous with the solution of the problem. But judgment must be either true or false, for the problem is either solved or is not solved. In this sense a judgment becomes a proposition. The proposition is a presentation in symbolic form of the copula stage of the judgment. In the subject stage lies the conflict between different responses. You call up James Brown by telephone at his office, and are informed that Mr. Brown is not in the city. This means to you the postponement of your interview. But a friend tells you that a short time ago he saw James Brown, and this means a possible holding of the interview. You may catch him before he leaves, and you call up his house. The subject of the judgment is a man whom you will meet later in the week and a man whom you will meet today. The undertakings inhibit each other. The predicate stage of the judgment, the hypothesis that he is leaving but has not yet left, presents a different James Brown, who so organizes your responses to see him later and to see him today, that they are no longer in conflict, and the reply from the house establishes the truth of the proposition that you can see him, if you can reach the house within an hour, and thus reports the copula stage of the judgment, which has tested the hypothesis. This lies within the field of conduct and the truth of the proposition characterizes that conduct, but it also sets up an affirmation which transcends that hastily accomplished interview. It is eternally true that James Brown was at his house on that day and on that hour. The established judgments precipitate propositions which seem to belong to another realm—"truths which wake to perish never."

My guess is that we can best come to terms with these truths in their last retreat, the propositional function. *If* the telephonic conversation spoke truly, and *if* James Brown is a man of his word, it is to all eternity true that James Brown was at his house on that day and on that hour. But a truth that—only making and supposing—wakes to perish never is affected with an eternity that has lost its impressiveness. I do not mean that it has lost its usefulness. This propositional function may establish an alibi that will save James Brown from the electric chair. But its translation into a timeless realm has a string tied to it that must sadly disturb its enjoyment of that rarified atmosphere, and the shadowless landscapes of that Platonic heaven. What has happened to the judgment in its precipitation into a proposition is that it has so purified itself from the empirical event out of which it arose that it can now enter into relational symbiosis with an indefinite number of other propositions. And the advantage of this is enormous. It connects James Brown's spatiotemporal location with the entire complex of his city's life and for that matter with all history and may in future time make it the firmly supporting datum of some historian's fabric of the past. But its truth is hypothetical, and draws its lifeblood from the realm out of which it emerged into the realm "in which we never know what we are talking about nor whether what we are saying is true," if I may follow Professor Mackay [6] in quoting Bertrand Russell, unless we can get some nourishment out of the insubstantial tissues of that logical symbiosis. But the number of those who can subsist on this subsistent diet becomes smaller and smaller as we climb up toward its infinite classes and the letters of the Hebraic alphabet. The fact is that we do not want the "all"; we want the "anys." We are interested in the possible combinations of propositions which will organize our conduct and the world within which that conduct takes its course and which gives to that conduct its interpretation and its import. The truth of any relational complex that inhabits this realm of eternal objects or universals or ideals will be found in its effectual employment in the construction of working hypotheses. They must themselves be coherent to be effectually employed, but coherency is not truth. It is not the coherence of doctrine but its cogency that implicates truth and cogency resides ever in the field of activity.

In one aspect of Professor Loewenberg's paradox of the judgment, the judgment is shown to include in its description both the "what" within the judgment and the "that" which must inevitably transcend the judgment.[7] My simple-minded

---

[6] [D. S. Mackay, "Esthetic and Experimental Truth," *University of California Publications in Philosophy*, X (1928), 68.]

[7] [Jacob Loewenberg, "The Paradox of Judgment," *The Journal of Philosophy*, XXV (1928), 197–205.]

escape from this paradox is found in regarding the truth of the judgment to lie in such a construction of the "what" that it becomes a "that"; and further in the assumption that when this takes place it is no longer a judgment, but something that is there. When the hypothesis works it ceases to be a hypothesis; it is reality, not eternal, indefeasible reality, but the only reality with which we are acquainted, which we fear or hope will break down to be again reconstructed.

I am positing here moments of problematic reflection and moments of unreflective reality; but is not reflective experience coterminous with life, is not life a continuous solution of problems? Pragmatic doctrine identifies thought with the solution of problems, and thinking is what raises human experience above that of the beasts that perish. There is, of course, here an ambiguity in the word "thought." It includes commonly our consummations, our aesthetic experiences, our possessions, our enjoyments and our sufferings, but I will for the moment put aside this ambiguity, and turn to the question of the relations of the different problems to one another. Have they not an essential connection among themselves, so essential a connection that a man's life seems to be the attempted solution of the single problem of his intelligent existence? Is not this the implication of the unity of his personality, and does it not become evident in the most thoroughgoing undertaking of life? Can we not fairly say, that what we call our conscious life turns out to be one concatenated enterprise of thought, within which we become now intermittently and now steadily aware of the interwoven tissue of our seemingly discrete problems? Especially is it not true that the solution of no one problem can be achieved without that of many others and perhaps without the solution of all of them? This is beyond doubt what we are apt to imply when we undertake to grasp the world as a whole, and bring into vital unity the presentations of many sciences, and get out to our view the involvements of each in each other. It is genuine thinking because it leaves nothing out. It has the entire history of philosophy behind it and it is peculiarly the attitude of the religions. If we recognize such a genuine grappling with the universe as the problem of the mind, the problem of the whole self, and further recognize the present insolubility of the problem, except as partial solutions exhibit an approach toward the intelligibility of the universe, does not this pragmatic doctrine itself sweep us into the current of Idealism? What is the world but a continued working hypothesis, a thought structure which is continually completing itself, as the problem breaks out now here and now there? From this standpoint does not the coherency, not simply of ideas but of the problems among themselves, become the very test, not of a final truth, but of the approach toward truth? Is the universe in thought anything but the judgment in the process of ceaseless predication?

Now there are many points from which I could attack, however successfully, this account of experience, commencing with the ambiguity which I suggested above in the term "thought," but there is, I think, an appeal in the idealistic doctrine that is of a more profound importance. It is found on the one side in the constructive and integrative character of scientific thought and on the other in the demand so insistently made that the world must be an intelligible whole. Our problem is the attainment of an intelligible universe, and we advance toward it by processes of scientific hypothesis, which are never out of the range of possible attack and which are generally but provisionally adopted; and this advance toward a goal at infinity, so far as our minute endeavors are concerned, takes place by continual reconstructions in many fields that confessedly implicate one another. The goal of experience lies indefinitely beyond experience, and the method of approach is by a thought construction which can have no criterion but the growing coherency of their objectives and their partial attainments.

Now insofar as *scientific* procedure is concerned, a test of truth, to be found in the organic interrelation of problems and their partial solutions, we can without more ado incon-

tinently dismiss. Both Schelling [8] and Hegel were committed
to it by their philosophies of nature, but their grandiose undertakings awakened no sympathetic interest in experimental
science. I do not mean that the scientist does not recognize
that the solution of one problem may wait upon the solution
of another or of many other problems. I am calling attention
to the fact that the experimental method can only be applied
where a reality which is not called in question sets the conditions to which any hypothetical solution must conform. The
scientist puts a question to nature, and so far as the answer to
that question is concerned, nature cannot herself be problematical. The scientist's technique consists largely in distinguishing that which is in doubt from that which is indubitable. You may deny the truth of his solutions, but you cannot
by any possibility persuade him to regard his problem as lying
inside of another larger problem, for then he has nothing by
which to test his own hypothesis. Survey the almost inextrica-
ble maze of scientific hypotheses which have been called out
by Relativity, the quantum postulate, the seeming corpuscu-
lar nature of light, the Compton shift,[9] the evidences for different diameters and forms of the electron, the rate of radia-
tion of the stars, and the presence of high voltage short rays
reaching our atmosphere from stellar space, and note what,
in all this confusion, is stable and unquestioned; what it is to
which each hypothesis must accord if it is to enter into a scientific doctrine of nature. It is the experimental finding which
has been obtained in complete abstraction from any and all hypotheses. These for the scientist are firm reality, and these
findings are simply certain happenings, determined within the
limit of the error of observation, in a world which is not in-

[8] [Friedrich W. J. von Schelling (1775–1854), German philosopher. His
Ideen zu einer Philosophie der Natur (1799) argued that nature is not
inferior to mind, but manifests mind in various degrees.]

[9] [Compton effect: the lengthening of X-ray waves produced by a dis-
persion of the energy quanta of these rays when they collide with electrons of atoms of elements with low atomic weights. Named after its
discoverer, the American physicist, Arthur Holly Compton (b. 1892).]

volved in the problems which engage the intense interest of science. If the Pragmatic doctrine is a logical generalization of scientific method, it cannot merge the problem that engages thought with a larger problem which denies validity to the conditions that are the necessary tests of the solution which thought is seeking.

Realists and Pragmatists alike have agreed that the perceptual knowledge to which the expert in knowledge, I mean the scientist, ties up, must be recognized as valid, though they have fallen out sadly among themselves over the definition of the percept. In reference to these civil strifes, I should like to point out that the scientist's findings are always in terms of things, never in terms of sensa or percepts, and that the legitimate analysis of perception by scientific psychology also always presupposes things. The psychologist has his own laboratories, and comes back to his own indubitable findings in terms of his own apparatus and *Versuchstiere*.[10] It is by means of what happens to these things in observation that any theory of observation must be tested. To reverse the order of testing lands us in Bertrand Russell's world inside of his brain. In the nature of the case it is not an observable brain, but one which we can only adumbrate by the probable correspondences of logical patterns. It affords however an heroic example of "following the argument" even when it leads the dialectician not only into a hole, but also into pulling the hole in after him. One afflicted with claustrophobia may prefer the heroic leap of Santayana's Animal Faith.[11]

There is, however, no question that there is a profound meaning in seeing the world whole, but the most enlightening approach to its meaning is to be found in bounding it, that is in discovering what it is not. We never mean by the expression, if we are using it profitably, what the world is going to

10 ["Guinea pigs."]

11 [Animal faith is the belief in existence which, although it cannot be known intuitively or rationally demonstrated, is operative in man in his efforts to survive in nature. See George Santayana, *Scepticism and Animal Faith* (New York: C. Scribner & Sons, 1923).]

be. Seeing the world whole will include undoubtedly the sort of wisdom which carries us sagaciously from the past into the future; but this is wisdom, it is not knowledge. The future is really future, it is not merely what we do not see, and no acuity of prophetic vision could bring the morrow in its essential character into our experience. Every morrow emerges. Again, seeing the world whole does not connote any exhaustive resumption of the past. Every generation rewrites and so in a sense relives the past. The histories that we have transcribed would have been as impossible to the pens of our fathers as the world we live in would have been inaccessible to their eyes and to their minds—and that not because we have richer sources than they. History is the interpretation of the past in terms of the present as truly as it is the interpretation of the present in terms of the past. Another Socrates has fascinated Athenian youths, another Caesar has crossed the Rubicon, another Jesus has lived in Galilee since any of us were children. And we know that our children will inhabit a different world from ours and will inevitably rewrite the annals we have so laboriously composed. But this does not disturb us, nor do we feel that seeing our world whole involves the vision of their future nor its attendant past. Past and future are actually oriented in the present. It is the import of the present that we desire, and we can find it only in the past that the present's own unique quality demands and in that future to which it alone can lead. In a sense every unexampled present creates the past that is logically demanded for its explanation. It is the fathomless wealth of the perceptual present that was veiled to Hegel's eyes. Seeing the world whole is gathering that import so far as in us lies. All experimental findings are lodged in perceptual presents and they are the final touchstones of all theories, and it is from the unpredictable solutions of its problems that the ineffable future flowers out. There is another sense in seeing the world whole that we have already touched upon, in the phrase, the logical symbiosis of propositions. But there abstraction lodged them in a subsistent world, where they had the bloodless being of unimaginable entities that could be characterized only by empty symbols. Symbols are in truth the appropriate stimuli of our attitudes. Attitudes are the responses which are present in our behavior either in advance of the stimulation of things, or, already aroused, yet await the occasion for their full expression. In the first case they may appear as ideas or concepts, in the second as the meanings which constitute things. The concept of a book is the organization of attitudes, which, given the stimulus, will express themselves in reading, writing, borrowing, drawing, buying or selling the book. They are all there in the dispositions of men, as forms of conduct which await the appropriate spring to call them out. Given the symbolic stimulus whether in articulate speech or in imagery, and the responses are there in the conduct which is organized by them. In the second case the book is there as an adequate stimulus to the response and has the meaning which was implied in the so-called concept. The book can acquire that meaning only in a situation within which the implications of that which happens can be actually present in the happening. The rush of the torrent carries death to the man who rashly ventures into it. It has not that *meaning* unless in advance of his fatal plunge this outcome was present in its nature, and it is only in the organized conduct of men that the bare relatedness of events and things can pass over into meaning, that meaning can invest events and things. This investiture takes place through the value which the symbol attains when the indication to another becomes also an indication to him who gives it to his fellow. The torrent is not only the blind power which sweeps the victim to his death, but in the community of those who communicate with each other, the force of the torrent has taken on a meaning insofar as each is wont to indicate this to others and so to himself. It has become something more than the succession of masses of water with their overwhelming momentum. In the experience of the community this force is something to be avoided or perhaps made use of for the production of industrial power. Entering into relation with the community, the torrent has acquired a meaning, which apart from that relationship it did not formerly possess. Through communication men have become able by symbols to organize their innumerable attitudes of possible conduct. The very relationship of the symbols to one another is the outward evidence of the relationship of possible acts which these attitudes express in conduct. Woven together into structures of symbols they excite in men the related processes which they make possible; and things, becoming the world or environment of such a society, acquire the meanings which this conduct connotes.

Now seeing the world whole is response in the widest scope of such common conduct. It means entering into the most highly organized logical, ethical, and aesthetic attitudes of the community, those attitudes which involve all that organized thinking, acting, and artistic creation and appreciation imply. It involves being at home in the universe of discourse, in the kingdom of ends, and in the world of beauty and significance. Seeing the world whole is the recognition of the most extensive set of interwoven conditions that may determine thought, practice, and our fixation and enjoyment of values. The truth of such vision is found in its competent evocation of the meanings with which society has endowed its world, insofar as it successfully interprets our ends and our appreciations. Both the ideas and the meanings which they connote lie within conduct and are only pertinent to the exigencies within which they appear, but they bring to bear upon these incidents which make up our lives the full rational, social, and cultured nature of citizens of an organized world. Coherency here spells applicability, but it does not spell truth. Seven nights ago, I followed, delightedly, Professor Adams as he led the way through the intricacies of the metaphysical landscape of existence and meaning.[12] Thanks to his competence we did not finally come upon truth in a valley of dry bones of bare existence, nor in a tempting mirage of meanings, but we found truth in the content which meaning gives

[12] [George P. Adams, "Truths of Existence and of Meaning," *University of California Publications in Philosophy*, XI (1929), 35–61.]

to existence and the reality which existence gives to meaning.
The formula by which he infused life into these dry bones
and concreted these values I cannot employ. Mine is not the
mastermind for which it will work.

Thought is indeed constructive in the hypothesis, but I cannot find that the structure of reality within which her reconstructive work goes on is also hers. She indeed presents
this structure in her blueprints, but it has not arisen out of
her thinking. Thinking pushes on this structure into the emergent future, but to my mind she lays no claim to the world
which she thinks and aids in building out.

Truth expresses a relationship between the judgment and
reality. In the formula of this paper the relationship lies between the reconstruction, which enables conduct to continue,
and the reality within which conduct advances. The judgment comes with healing in its wings. It might be called a
reparations theory, for, as we all know, a reparations commission requires first of all a formula, a healing formula. Most
reparations commissions are no sooner organized than they
adjourn, to be called together when a committee, appointed
to discover such a formula, can report. Such a formula is a
judgment. Its relationship is not so much that of correspondence as of agreement. The judgmental reconstruction fits into
organized reality. Of course a formula may fit and still be
ineffectual. That is, many so-called truths are insignificant
and trivial, but this overlooks the character of the judgment,
which is one of reconstruction and does not attain truth until experience can proceed where it was inhibited. If coherence means such a dovetailing of the hypothetical reconstruction with given reality, we might call the relationship that of
coherence. But coherence theories of truth have in view rather
the coherence of the structure of the judgment, assuming that
as a thought structure it must be consonant with a thought
constructed universe, if only it be correctly thought. That is,
coherence refers to the formation of the hypothesis rather
than to its agreement with the given conditions of further
conduct.

Now it is evident that theories of truths will vary with their corresponding theories of reality. As I have just indicated, an idealistic doctrine which sees in the universe a thought structure that is the product of a timeless judgment, will find its criterion of truth in the adequacy of the thought process, an adequacy which will be revealed in the coherence of the judgment. For it is only in that inner coherence that a finite judgment can show its harmony with the infinite process of which it is a part. The whole universe is not there to enable the mind to estimate its coherence with its entire structure, but the process is identical with that of the absolute and insofar as this process reveals its identity by its inner coherence it possesses the only standard of truth possible. All idealisms are not Hegelian nor neo-Hegelian, in the common usage of that term, but what I take to be common to them all is the approach to reality from the standpoint of thought. We can approach the noumenal nature of reality only through the noumenal nature of thought; the perceptual dress of nature is transient, contingent, and particular. It is only by thought that we can get inside of it to its uniformities, its abiding structure, and its inherent necessities. Such an approach will inevitably look for its test of truth in the competency of the thinking that reveals it.

A realism whose method is that of analysis sees in reality ultimate elements and the relations which they subtend. Having anatomized reality into relata and the relations, truth of the judgment is found in a correlation between these and the cognitions which answer to them in the mind. We find a new set of relations and relata, that lying between things and the awareness of the mind. If these relations offer the same pattern of structure as that which they answer to in nature, we have the test of the truth of the logical pattern as it appears in the judgment. It is confessedly a truth of logical correspondence. It becomes incumbent then upon any doctrine of the truth of the judgment to present so much of its view of reality as is involved in its own criterion.

So much of a doctrine of reality is, I think, evident from

what has gone before in this paper; that the experience in which human beings are involved is a constituent part of the reality which they judge; that the problems do not arise in minds which regard nature from without but within nature itself, because these human beings are phases of nature. In other words the doctrine is behavioristic not only in a psychological sense but also in a metaphysical sense—using metaphysics as Professor Dewey has undertaken to present it in *Experience and Nature* [1925]. This implies in particular that the so-called triadic relation holds between organisms and nature; that nature exists in varied aspects in its relation to the organisms of which it is patient, in Professor Whitehead's phrase. I do not agree with what I take to be Professor Broad's interpretation of Professor Whitehead's doctrine,[13] that the so-called sensa exist in the immediate proximity of the organisms and are, as it were, projected into an absolute space-time of events. I see no reason for questioning the adjectives of things as actually qualifying them, where they are in experience in their relations with organisms endowed with sense processes. The crux of such a doctrine, of course, lies in the common world. There are dark hints of a theory of this common world in Professor Whitehead's publications, in exiguous phrases and appended notes. I presume it has been given in his Gifford Lectures, and will be accessible to us in their publication.[14]

The logical extension of the view of nature existing in perspectives is that societies are organisms in Professor Whitehead's definition of an organism and that there is a common nature that is there in its relationship to such a social organism. The problem is then shifted to the nature of the experience of the members of these societies. For this experience is both private and public. I have my own doctrine for this social character of experience which I have elsewhere pre-

[13] [C. D. Broad, *Scientific Thought* (London: Kegan Paul, Trench Trubner & Co., Ltd., 1923), Pt. II.]

[14] [Whitehead's Gifford Lectures were published as *Process and Reality* (1929).]

sented [15] and at which I have hinted above. What it amounts to in a very summary formulation is that society exists in the social nature of its members, and the social nature of its members exists in their assumption of the organized attitudes of others who are involved with them in cooperative activities, and that this assumption of organized attitudes has arisen through communication. That is, communication makes participation possible, to use Professor Dewey's phrase. There are then aspects of nature which exist only for each organism. For example, the experience of what goes on within a man's body is accessible only to himself. He can share his experiences of his own headaches with others only by appealing to private experiences of their own, but he does immediately put himself in the place of others in their common undertakings in the world and observes things spatiotemporally and meaningfully as they observe them. Answering to these common experiences there lies before them a common world, the world of the group. This common world is continually breaking down. Problems arise in it and demand solution. They appear as the exceptions to which I have referred above. The exceptions appear first of all in the experience of individuals and while they have the form of common experiences they run counter to the structure of the common world. The experience of the individual is precious because it preserves these exceptions. But the individual preserves them in such form that others can experience them, that they may become common experience. They are the data of science. If they have been put in the form of common experiences, the task appears of reconstructing the common world so that they may have their place and become instances instead of exceptions. Now the only test that can be offered of the truth of the reconstruction lies in the fitting in of the hypothesis into the common world insofar as it is not affected by the problem, which appeared in the exception.

If experience must accord with a reality beyond itself, the

[15] *The Journal of Philosophy*, XIX, 157–163. [Essay XVI in the present volume: "A Behavioristic Account of the Significant Symbol."]

test of truth will be a correspondence of its structure with the structure of external reality; or if reality is an absolute of which experience is an incomplete phase, then truth will lie in the congruence of the process of experience with that of the absolute. In both these alternatives, experience itself constitutes an epistemological problem of which other problems are only separate instances, a problem which is given in the assumed cognitive reference of experience to something beyond itself. In the doctrine I have undertaken to present, experience is not itself a problem. It is simply there. The problems arise within it. The criterion of truth does not then transcend experience, but simply regards the conditions of ongoing experience which has become problematic through the inhibitions of the natural processes of men. The solution of the problem lies entirely within experience and is found in the resolution of the inhibitions. Furthermore, the rational solution of problems takes place through minds which have arisen in social evolution. The criterion, then, of the truth of the solutions will involve the aspect of nature that answers to the society which is the habitat of these minds. The criterion calls for the continuance of a common world. It excludes for example a possible irrational or arational aspect of reality. But it does not exclude the appearance of the novel, the emergent. I take it that this is the negative reflection of the propositional function, and the field of modern logical theory. Our experience can only be open to that which is novel if the forms are empty. This is another way of saying that the problem can appear anywhere in experience. The view of reality which belongs to this statement of the doctrine does in a considerable degree determine the theory of truth and its criterion.

In conclusion allow me to recur to rationalization. We rationalize when we so restate and interpret a new order of things that old habits and attitudes find objects to arouse and sustain them. The familiar illustration is the aesthetic conservation of outworn religious cults. As another illustration, I suggested the conservation in Renaissance philosophy of the old central position of man in the universe by the resolution of the world into states of mind. Evidently the impelling but often unconscious motive is the salvation of the values which still attach to the old responses. Any successful formulation must excite consecrated emotional attitudes. Philosophically the salvation of mind replaced the salvation of the soul, but back of the epistemology lay the sense of the supreme value of human experience. I am entirely agreed that the conservation of the value of human experience lies as a liability upon philosophic doctrine, but I make bold to say that in the passage of time since Descartes, Spinoza, and Leibnitz the preservation of these values through the cognitive relation of mind to the universe has become more and more precarious. Let me offer as evidences such divergent findings as those of Bradley's *Appearance and Reality*,[16] Bertrand Russell's "A Free Man's Worship" [17] and Santayana's *The Realm of Essence*.[18] In the dominant philosophic current since the Renaissance lies the implication of some structure of reality which the structure of thought undertakes to reflect or sets up as a postulate, a structure, whatever it may be, that has the immutability and irrevocability of the past. And it is in this immutable and irrevocable order that philosophies have sought the firm foundation of their values, insofar as they have not despaired of them. Thus they have rationalized new orders to find in them the implications of the old. Science, in the meantime, in its practice, has cheerfully not to say joyfully scrapped its old structures and only preserved its method. Of course science has never accepted the responsibility for the preservation of values, though an honorable exception should be made in recognizing the responsibility which science is taking upon

16 [F. H. Bradley, *Appearance and Reality* (London and New York: S. Sonnenschein and Co., and The Macmillan Co., 1893; 2nd edn., rev., 1906).]

17 [Bertrand Russell, "A Free Man's Worship," *Mysticism and Logic* (New York: W. W. Norton & Co., 1929), pp. 46–57.]

18 [George Santayana, *The Realm of Essence* (New York: C. Scribner's Sons, 1927).]

itself for the physiological and psychical health of the community. Philosophy, on the other hand, in its conspectus of reality and in its ethical doctrine, can never evade the responsibility for the values of the community.

Now I take it that the most distinctive mark of the Pragmatic movement is the frank acceptance of actual ongoing experience, experimentally controlled, as the standpoint from which to interpret the past and anticipate the future. So far as I can see this acceptance must recognize as ruled out any absolute order within which is to be placed a final concatenation of events past, present, and future. For in such an ultimate framework there is no place for an emergent future with its implicated new past, nor is there any allowance for different orders of different aspects of the universe. The problem, then, which Pragmatism faces is the maintenance of values by methods, in the place of structure. It is not the revival of emotional response by the assimilation of the new to the old, upon which we can depend. On the contrary it becomes necessary to recast the old as that which leads up to the new situation. This we readily carry out in our rapidly changing accounts of the past of the physical world and of its inhabitants. Can we as readily apply it to the pressing problems of social reconstruction with their profound implications of the values that are involved in possession, in national and personal rights, in the family and in the church?

❦❧ XXII ❦❧

THE NATURE OF THE PAST

The present is not the past and the future. The distinction which we make between them is evidently fundamental. If we spread a specious present so that it covers more events, as Whitehead suggests, taking in some of the past and conceivably some of the future, the events so included would belong, not to the past and the future, but to the present. It is true that in this present there is something going on. There is passage within the duration, but that is a present passage. The past arises with memory. We attach to the backward limit of the present the memory images of what has just taken place. In the same fashion we have images of the words which we are going to speak. We build out at both limits. But the images are in the present. Whitehead's suggestion that rendering these images sufficiently vivid would spread the specious present is quite beside the mark.[1] No memory image, however vivid, would be anything but a memory image, which is a surrogate merely for what was or will be spoken.

The actual passage of reality is in the passage of one present into another, where alone is reality, and a present which has merged in another is not a past. Its reality is always that of a present. The past as it appears is in terms of representations of various sorts, typically in memory images, which are themselves present. It is not true that what has passed is in the past,

[1] [Alfred North Whitehead, *The Concept of Nature* (London: Cambridge University Press, 1920), chap. 3.]

for the early stages of a motion lying within a specious present are not past. They belong to something that is going on. The distinction between the present and the past evidently involves more than passage. An essential condition is its inclusion in some present in this representational form. Passage as it takes place in experience is an overlapping of one specious present by another. There is continuity of experience, which is a continuity of presents. In this continuity of experience there is distinction of happening. There is direction. There is dependence or conditioning. What is taking place flows out of that which is taking place. Not only does succession take place, but there is a succession of contents. What is going on would be otherwise if the earlier stage of the occurrence had been of a different character. It is always a passage of something. There is always a character which connects different phases of the passage, and the earlier stage of the happening is the condition of the later stage. Otherwise there would be no passage. Mere juxtaposition of events, if this is conceivable, would not constitute passage. The connection involves both identity and difference, and it involves that in the identiy which makes the condition for that which follows. The immediate position of a moving body is conditioned by that which preceded it. Continuity is involved as a presupposition in passage in experience.

Although apparently sudden dislocations take place, back of these we imply continuities within which these dislocations could be resolved into continuities. The spatiotemporal connections which these continuities express involve the conditioning of any spatiotemporal position by a previous set of positions. This conditioning is not complete determination, but the conditions that are involved in the continuity of passage are necessary. That which is novel can emerge, but conditions of the emergence are there. It is this conditioning which is the qualitative character of the past as distinguished from mere passage. Mere passage signifies disappearance and is negative. The conditioning, spatiotemporally considered, is the necessity of continuity of relationship in space-time and of characters which are dependent upon space and time, such as velocities and momenta. The discontinuous is the novel. When a force is applied which is responsible for an acceleration, the moment at which that force is applied may be as respects its appearance an emergence from a continuous past, but the spatiotemporal continuities set conditions for the accelerations which result from the application of the force.

There are other continuities which we look for besides those of space-time. These are those of the so-called uniformities of nature. The embedding of any two successive events and their characters, however fortuitous they may seem, within a continuity of happening registers itself as carrying some conditioning of their happening in the succession within which they have appeared. The physical sciences push this conditioning into spatiotemporal form as far as it is possible. They attempt so to state the two happenings that the mere fact that one occurs at a certain place and time determines in some degree that which follows upon it. The ideal of this presentation is an equation between a situation at one moment and that at the next. We seek such a statement that the mere passage of experience will determine that which takes place. Where this can rigorously be carried out we reach what Whitehead calls the Aristotelian adjectives of events, but where it is impossible to so present the happenings that the continuity of passage determines what will take place we have in his terms pseudo-adjectives of events. But that the continuities of space-time do carry with them conditions of that which takes place is a fundamental presupposition of experience. The order within which things happen and appear conditions that which will happen and appear.

It is here that we find the function of the past as it arises in memory and the records of the past. Imagery is not past but present. It rests with what we call our mental processes to place these images in a temporal order. We are engaged in spreading backward what is going on so that the steps we are taking will be a continuity in the advance to the goals of our conduct. That memory imagery has in it characters which tend to identify it as belonging to the past is undoubtedly true, and these characters seem to be frequently independent of its place in a continuous order. A face or a landscape may flash upon the inward eye with seemingly intrinsic evidence of past experience, although we may have great difficulty in placing them. The evidence is not necessarily of an immediate character. There are certain sorts of images which belong to our pasts and we are confident of them because they fit in. And there are sorts of images which betray the operation of the imagination. A memory may be recognized as such by a method of exclusion, because it has not the fashion of the fancy—because we cannot otherwise account for it. The assurances which we give to a remembered occurrence come from the structures with which they accord.

What is, then, the immediate occasion for this building out of specious presents into a past? These presents themselves pass into each other by an overlapping process. There is no break except under what may be called pathological conditions. We do not build out into the past to preserve mere continuity, i.e., to fill out breaks in reality. But it is evident that we need to complete something that is lacking in that which is going on. The span of that which occupies us is greater than the span of the specious present. The "what it is" has a temporal spread which transcends our experience. This is very evident in the pasts which we carry around with us. They are in great part thought constructs of what the present by its nature involves, into which very slight material of memory imagery is fitted. This memory in a manner tests and verifies the structure. We must have arisen and eaten our breakfasts and taken the car, to be where we are. The sense of this past is there as in implication and bits of imperfect scenes come in at call—and sometimes refuse to arise. But even in this latter case we do not feel that the past is lost.

It may be said that the existence in experience of affairs that transcend our presents is the very past under discussion, and this is true, and what I am endeavoring to make evident. The past is an overflow of the present. It is oriented from the present. It is akin on the one side to our escape fancies, those in which we rebuild the world according to our hearts' desires, and on the other to the selection of what is significant in the immediate situation, the significant that must be held and reconstructed, but its decisive character is the pushing back of the conditioning continuities of the present. The past is what must have been before it is present in experience as a past. A past triumph is indefinitely superior to an escape fancy, and will be worn threadbare before we take refuge in the realm of the imagination, but more particularly the past is the sure extension which the continuities of the present demand.

The picture which Bergson gives of it seems to me to belie both its character in experience and its functional character—the picture of an enormous incessantly accreting accumulation of "images" against which our nervous systems defend us by their selective mechanisms.[2] The present does not carry any such burden with it. It passes into another present with the effects of the past in its textures, not with the burden of its events upon its back. And whatever account we give of our exiguous imagery, it is marked by what Bergson has himself emphasized, its function of filling out present perceptions. It bears no evidence of the richness of material which Bergson predicates. It is hard to recover and disappointing in its detail. Imagery plays the same role in the past that it plays in the present, that of supplying some element of detail that makes the construction possible.

The inevitability of existence is betrayed in its continuity. What follows flows from what was. If there is continuity, then what follows is conditioned by what was. A complete break between events would remove the character of inevitability. The elimination of continuity is the gist of Hume's attack upon causality. While the recovery of continuity in passage is the gist of Kant's second deduction of the categories. If there were bare replacement of one experience by another, the experience would not be that of passage. They would be different

<hr />

[2] [Henri Bergson, *Matter and Memory*, translated by N. M. Paul and W. S. Palmer (London and New York: George Allen & Co., Ltd., and The Macmillan Co., 1911), pp. 76–77.]

experiences, each wrapped up in itself, but with no connection, no way of passing from one to the other. Even a geometrical demonstration involves passage from situation to situation. The final structure is a timeless affair in the sense that it is a completed structure which is now irrelevant to the passage by which it has arisen. Any passage is insofar inevitable as earlier stages condition later achievements, and the demonstration is the exhibition of the continuity of the passage. One route when it is once taken is as inevitable as another. The child's whimsical movements of the men upon the chessboard is as inevitable as the play of the expert. In the one case its inevitability is displayed by the psychologist and in the other by the logician. Continuity in the passage of events is what we mean by the inevitable.

But bare continuity could not be experienced. There is a tang of novelty in each moment of experience. Kant reached this by the *Mannigfaltigkeit der Empfindungen*,[3] an unordered sensuous content which becomes experience when it is placed within the forms of the understanding. Without this break within continuity, continuity would be inexperienceable. The content alone is blind, and the form alone is empty, and experience in either case is impossible. Still Kant's chasm between the two is illusory. The continuity is always of some quality, but as present passes into present there is always some break in the continuity—within the continuity, not of the continuity. The break reveals the continuity, while the continuity is the background for the novelty.

The memory of the unexpected appearance of a supposedly far distant friend, or the memory of an earthquake can never recover the peculiar tang of the experience. I remember that there was a break which is now connected with just the phases of the experience which were unconnected. We recall the joy or the terror, but it is over against a background of a continuum whose discontinuity has been healed. Something was going on—the rising anger of a titan or the adjustment of the

---

3 ["Manifold of sense presentations."]

earth's internal pressures which resulted in that which was unexpected, but this was not the original experience, when there was no connection between the events before the occurrence and the sudden emergence. Even if no qualitative causal connection appears in the memory, the spatiotemporal connection is there to be developed as thought or imagination may refashion it. Redintegration of the past can never bring back the unexpected. This is just the character of the past as distinguished from the passage of presents into each other. The primal break of novelty in passage is gone and the problem of bridging the contingent factors is before the mind, though it may go no further than the oppressive sense of chance or fate. The character of the past is that it connects what is unconnected in the merging of one present into another.

The corresponding character of the future is still more evident. The novel is already there in the present and introduced breaks into the continuity which we must repair to attain an approach to certainty in the future. The emergent future has therefore a hypothetical character. We can trace the spatio-temporal continuities into it and the less rigorous continuities of other uniformities, but the particular aspects they will assume depend upon the adjustments which the present with its novelties will call out. Imagery from past continuities, such as the concluding words in the sentence we are speaking, or the house around the corner which we are nearing, approach the inevitable, but we may break the discourse and an explosion may send us down another road. The inevitable continuities belong to the structure of the hypothetical plans of action before us.

What is now to be said of these pasts and futures, when we seek them outside of human experience in terms of which we have been considering them? In the first place we can say that the only pasts and futures of which we are cognizant arise in human experience. They have also the extreme variability which attaches to human undertakings. Every generation rewrites its history—and its history is the only history it has of the world. While scientific data maintain a certain uniformity within these histories, so that we can identify them as data, their meaning is dependent upon the structure of the history as each generation writes it. There is no texture of data. Data are abstractions from things and must be given their places in the constructive pasts of human communities before they can become events. It is tempting to illustrate this in the shifting histories which our present generation has constructed of its habitat—including the whole universe, so far as it has been able to survey it, but the phenomenon is too evident and striking to call for illustration. Every advance in the interpretation of spectroscopic observations of the stars, every advance in the theory of the atoms opens the door to new accounts of the millenia of stellar history. They rival at present the rapidly changing histories of human communities. The immutable and incorruptible heavens exist only in rhetoric. Minute shifts in the lines of the spectrum or the readings of the spectroscope may add or subtract billions of years to the life of the stars.

The validity of these pasts depend upon the continuities which constitute their structure. These continuities in passage are the essence of inevitability, and when we feel the continuity we have reached the security we seek. It is an error to assume that the security depends upon the form of the continuity. For the Psalmist the only form of continuity that gave security was that of the Everlasting Hills and for the Greeks it was the Unchangeable Heavens. We find greater security in the laws of stellar evolution because it knits the continuities of the atoms with the continuities of the stars. The continuities of process are more universal than those of structure. More particularly we have swept away the cosmical and metaphysical chasm between the changeless heavens and the contingent earth. Ancient metaphysics divorced the two inseparable components of passage—the continuous and the emergent. The doctrine of evolution has obliterated the scandal from the union out of which arise all objects in experience. There is no more striking contrast in the history of thought than the gathering security with which we control events by rapidly reconstructing our histories, which reveal our dependable continuities when we stretch them out into their implied pasts; and the helplessness of ancient and medieval thought that found continuity only in a changeless order and an irrevocable past.

The conclusion is that there is no history of presents that merge into each other with their emergent novelties. The past which we construct from the standpoint of the new problem of today is based upon continuities which we discover in that which has arisen, and its serves us until the rising novelty of tomorrow necessitates a new history which interprets the new future. All that emerges has continuity, but not until it does so emerge. If we could string together the presents as presents we would present the conditions under which the novel could arise but we would not deduce that which arose. Out of the discovered continuities of that which has arisen with all that has gone before we can reconstruct it—in the future, and we obtain the field for this reconstruction by stretching backward in history the newfound continuities. Within our narrow presents our histories give us the elbowroom to cope with the ever-changing stream of reality.

If the novel emerges, there can be no history of a continuity of which it is a constituent part, though when it has emerged the continuities which it exhibits may enable us to state a succession of events within which it appears. Let us assume that life has emerged. In a genuine sense the conditions which allow of this emergence determine its appearance. It could not have appeared earlier than these events. The history of life will relate it to these events, which have now become its conditions, but previously were not its conditions, for there was no life to constitute those events the conditions of life. The setting up of the relation between the events which have become conditions and the emerging life is an establishment of continuity between the world before life and life itself, which was inconceivable before life appeared, as one establishes in his memory a continuity between the moment before the earthquake happened and the earthquake, which in its unexpectedness permitted in its happening no such connection. The past thus belongs to a generalized form of experience. It is the arising of relations between an emergent and a conditioning world. Any organism, taken in its widest Whiteheadean sense, maintains itself by means of relationships which, extended backward as well as forward, constitute a history of the world, but evidently it arises only after the appearance of that which gives to the world this value. The past consists of the relations of the earlier world to an emergent affair—relations which have therefore emerged with the affair.

NATIONAL-MINDEDNESS AND
INTERNATIONAL-MINDEDNESS

. . . . War on occasions makes the good of the community the supreme good of the individual. What has the pacifist who would abolish war to put in its place?

In a word we make the public good our immediate interest when it arouses the fighting spirit. Otherwise it is apt to be a philanthropic good, to reach which we must put [to] one side our private interests. To be interested in the public good we must be disinterested, that is, not interested in goods in which our personal selves are wrapped up. In wartime we identify ourselves with the nation, and its interests are the interests of our primal selves. And in the fighting mood we find that we are in sympathetic accord with all others who are fighting for the same cause. Then we experience the thrill of marching in common enthusiasm with all those who in daily life are our competitors, our possible rivals, and opponents. The barriers are down which we erect against our neighbors and business associates. In daily life they may be hostile to our interests. We proceed warily. We protect ourselves even against our partners, associates, and employees with contracts and agreements defended with penalties. Even our good manners are means of keeping possible bores at a distance. It is sound sense to regard everyone as a possible enemy. In wartime these barriers are down. We need to feel the support of our fellows in the struggle and we grapple them to ourselves. The great issue itself is hallowed by the sense of at-oneness of a vast multitude.

It is easy to study this in everyday situations. Gather ten

[From the *International Journal of Ethics,* XXXIX (1929), 392–407.]

or fifteen of your acquaintances and make the subject of your conversation the admirable qualities and services of someone known to all. Then change the subject of converse to someone for whom all have a common dislike, and note how much warmer is the sense of at-oneness of those who are engaged in common disparagement than in encomium. The hostile attitude is peculiarly favorable to social cohesion. The solid South is the product of common hostility to the Negro as a social equal. The Ku Klux Klan is a deliberate manufacture of compact groups by the use of racial and religious antipathies. I think it is worth our while to make some inquiry into this cohesive power, which the hostile impulse in human nature exercises with such absolute authority.

We have long known that behind the spiritual exaltation of wartime patriotism and the irresponsibility of mob-consciousness lies the same psychological mechanism. And this fact is a ground neither for extolling it nor for damning it. It is just a psychological mechanism which like other mechanisms has served both fine and ignoble ends. It is equally inept to define, with Dr. Johnson, patriotism as the last refuge of the scoundrel, and to exalt Judge Lynch as the embodiment of social justice. But it is both apt and obligatory upon us to examine this mechanism when we are not caught in its meshes, and are free to comprehend it; for when we are involved in it, it is next to impossible to approach it with impartial consideration. Neither the patriot in his moment of exaltation nor the member of the blind mob in his unrestrained ferocity is capable of following the dictum: Know thyself. He may conceivably get outside of his intoxication, but he is then engaged in controlling his passionate impulses. He is in no mood to understand them.

I have already indicated the character of this mechanism. The hostile impulse unites us against the common enemy, because it has force enough to break down customary social textures, by which we hold others at a distance from our inexpugnable selves. But it was this social structure by which we realized ourselves. Our rights and our privileges, our distinctions of capacity and skill, our superiorities and our inferiorities, our social positions and prestige, our manners and our foibles not only distinguish and separate us from others but they constitute us what we are to ourselves. They constitute our individualities, the selves that we recognize, when we thank God that we are not as other men are, and when we determine upon what terms we can live and work with members of our families, with our neighbors and our countrymen. If these are in any degree broken down we are no longer the same individuals that we were. To join ourselves with others in the common assault upon the common foe we have become more than allies, we have joined a clan, have different souls, and have the exuberant feeling of being at one with this community.

There lie in all of us both of these attitudes. It is only in our common interests and our identities with others that there is found the stuff out of which social selves are made—and it is only in distinguishing and protecting these selves from others that we exercise the self-consciousness that makes us responsible and rational beings.

But even the apparatus of this self-consciousness we have borrowed from the community. What are our rights in which we defend ourselves against all comers, but the rights which we recognize in others, that ours may be recognized by others? What are our peculiar powers and capacities but the facilities by which we perform our parts in common undertakings, and where would they be if others did not recognize them and depend upon them? The proudest assertion of independent selfhood is but the affirmation of a unique capacity to fill some social role. Even the man who haughtily withdraws himself from the crowd, thinks of himself in terms of an ideal community which is but a refinement of the world in which he lives. It is by assuming the common attitudes to each other, which an organized community makes possible, that we are able to address ourselves in the inner forum of our thoughts and private purposes. A self is a composite or interaction of these two parts of our natures—the fundamental impulses which make us cooperating neighbors and friends, lovers and parents and children, and rivals, competitors, and enemies; on the other side the evocation of this self which we achieve when we address ourselves in the language which is the common speech of those about us. We talk to ourselves, ask ourselves what we will do under certain conditions, criticize and approve of our own suggestions and ideas, and in taking the organized attitudes of those engaged in common undertakings we direct our own impulses. These two parts are the matter and the form of the self, if I may use Aristotelian phraseology. The one is the stuff of social impulses and the other is the power which language has conferred upon us, of not only seeing ourselves as others see us but also of addressing ourselves in terms of the common ideas and functions which an organized society makes possible. We import the conversation of the group into our inner sessions and debate with ourselves. But the concatenated concepts which we use are ours because we are speaking in the language of the outer universe of discourse, the organized human world to which we belong.

In the sophisticated field of self-consciousness we control our conduct. We place ourselves over against other selves and determine what we want to do, what we have a right to do, and what other people may do. Here we assert ourselves and maintain ourselves by recognized rights and accorded privileges. In the field of the stuff—the matter—of personality we have no such power. We are born with our fundamental impulses. We choose our business associates and the members of our clubs and the guests at our dinner parties, but we *fall in* love, and whatever action we take upon this primal premiss, it is not a matter of our own choice. We say that we instinctively help a child who has fallen down, and our immediate attitudes toward puppies, kittens, and little pigs are different from those we take toward dogs, cats, and hogs, and the impulse to helpfulness is just as much an endowment as the impulse of hostility. This primal stuff of which we are made up is not under our direct control. The primitive sexual, parental, hostile, and cooperative impulses out of which our social selves are built up are few—but they get an almost infinite field of varied application in society, and with every development of means of intercourse, with every invention they find new opportunities of expression. Here by taking thought we can add to our social stature. But we have no direct control over our loves and our hates, our likes and our dislikes, and for this reason we are relatively helpless when a common enemy fuses us all into a common patriotic pack or stampedes us under the influence of sympathetic terror.

This, then, is the stuff out of which human social selves are made up, their primal stuff or matter of social impulses, and the form of sophisticated self-consciousness. But society is the interaction of these selves, and an interaction that is only possible if out of their diversity unity arises. We are indefinitely different from each other, but our differences make interaction possible. Society is unity in diversity. However there is always present the danger of its miscarriage. There are the two sources of its unity—the unity arising from the interconnection of all the different selves in their self-conscious diversity and that arising from the identity of common impulses; the unity, for example, of the members of a great highly organized industrial concern or of the faculties and the students of a great university and the unity of a crowd that rushes to save a child in danger of its life. By these two principles of unity society is maintained; but there is an ever present risk of failure. Every society has it at the back of its mind. We want security and we distrust it. Society in every period of its history has presented to itself that danger in one form or another. Today we dread the Bolsheviki. At another time it has been the "interests"; at times the mob, and at other times the arbitrary power of a monarch.

We come back to our original question, How shall we get and maintain that unity of society in which alone we can exist? The ever present method of creating cohesion from below, from the impulses, is found in the common hostile impulse. The criticisms which are exercised upon the civil motives are but illustrations of this. Government is by partisanship. We can bring the voters to the polls only through their hostility to opposite parties. A campaign for a community chest is quickened by competitive teams. The great days of the religions have been the days of hostility, between the religions, between the Church and the sects, or between different churches. The fight with the devil and all his angels united men whom a common hope of salvation left untouched. More evident still is the need of the fighting attitude when a large community with varied groups and opposing interests is to be brought into a self-conscious whole. The antagonism of the Chinese to the Japanese and the English did more than anything else to awaken a Chinese national spirit. In our Civil War slavery was the issue, because it divided the nation. Men of the North fought for the Union and in fighting for it they felt it. The readiest way of arousing an emotional appreciation of a common issue is to fight together for that issue, and until we have other means of attaining it we can hardly abandon war.

It is not a question of thrills nor of satisfying a deep-seated bellicosity in the human animal. It is a question of making ourselves actually feel the values that are wrapped up in the community. While war was still a possible national adventure, there was a certain rough psychological justification for the dictum, that at least one war in a generation was essential for the spiritual hygiene of the nation. The toleration of secret diplomacy, the cherishing of national honor and peculiar interests as lying outside the field of negotiation had behind it an obscure but profound feeling that in national honor and in these peculiar interests were symbolized a national unity which could be made precious by the arbitrament of war.

What better illustration of this can be found than in the Monroe Doctrine? None are agreed upon what the doctrine is. The nations of South and Central America in whose interests it was inaugurated with one voice denounce it. It is absurd to say that we can find an issue in the threatened neighborhood on this hemisphere of European powers, when our continent-wide, unfortified Canadian frontier, within the century and more since it was established, is almost the only frontier in the whole wide world that has not been crossed by belligerent forces. No, it is something—no matter what it is—for which we will *fight*. To think of it in these terms is to feel that there is a nation back of it. The more unintelligible the issue is, the more it emphasizes the unanimity of the community. It is an issue that cannot be discussed for we cannot in cold blood find out what the issue is. We must be of one mind about it, for it is impossible to have different minds about that which no one can comprehend. The only issue involved in the Monroe Doctrine is this, are you a patriot, are you a red-blooded American, or are you a mollycoddle? Let us get down to real reasons and abandon good reasons. Even when we hope that there may be no future wars, we feel that we should keep certain issues which can arouse the fighting spirit, for the sake of their effect in drawing men together in a fashion which cannot be achieved by public interests, which are after all so divisive.

I take it that this is the real question that is put up to us by Professor James's moral equivalent of war.[1] Can we find outside of the fighting spirit that unifying power which presents a supreme issue to which all others are subordinated, which will harden us to undergo everything, and unite us in the enthusiasm of a common end?

> When I have borne in memory what has tamed
> Great Nations, how ennobling thoughts depart
> When men change swords for ledgers, and desert
> The student's bower for gold, some fears unnamed
> I had, my Country—am I to be blamed?[2]

There is nothing in the history of human society nor in

---

[1] [Mead's discussion of James is directed to the latter's pamphlet, *The Moral Equivalent of War* (1910), reprinted in William James, *Memories and Studies,* ed. Henry James, Jr. (New York: Longmans, Green and Co., 1911), pp. 265–296.]

[2] [William Wordsworth, *Poems Dedicated to Independence and Liberty,* XVII.]

present-day experience which encourages us to look to the primal impulse of neighborliness for such cohesive power. The love of one's neighbor cannot be made into a common consuming passion. The great religions that have sought to embody it when they have dominated society have appeared as the Church militant. Auguste Comte, the great French sociologist and philosopher, sought to fashion a universal religion out of it. It gathered a handful of great souls into its communion. How widespread was its sweep of the community may be indicated by the tale that, in London, a gathering of the Comtists took place within which a schism arose. For even in this church sects appeared. A London wag reported that the members of the convention gathered in one cab and came away in two. There is, to be sure, no falling off in numbers of those who identify themselves with different Christian sects in the Western world, but there never was a time when the churches have had less power in organizing the community into common action. We can unite with common zeal to aid the victims of famines, of earthquakes, and of conflagrations, but we do not go into nor come out of such common undertakings with a sense of the supremacy of the nation or society that holds us together. The passion of love between the sexes isolates those whom it consumes, and family life segregates us. The positive social impulses exhibit no forces that bind us immediately together in conscious devotion to the complex community out of which our sophisticated selves arise. They have their place in the cults, mores, and customs that form the tissue of human society, but they do not flame out into a patriotism that can fuse men in the devotion to the fatherland.

The Great War has presented not a theory but a condition. If war were a possible measure of public policy, it might be kept for the sake of social cohesion, even if the ends for which wars are ostensibly fought were illusory and inadequate. But the Great War has made this no longer possible. Every war if allowed to go the accustomed way of wars will become a world war, and every war pursued uncompromisingly and intelligently must take as its objective the destruction not of hostile forces but of enemy nations in their entirety. It has become unthinkable as a policy for adjudicating national differences. It has become logically impossible. This is not to say that it may not arise. Another catastrophe may be necessary before we have cast off the cult of warfare, but we cannot any longer *think* our international life in terms of warfare. It follows that if we do *think* our national and international life, we can no longer depend upon war for the fusion of disparate and opposing elements in the nation. We are compelled to reach a sense of being a nation by means of rational self-consciousness. We must *think* ourselves in terms of the great community to which we belong. We cannot depend upon feeling ourselves at one with our compatriots, because the only effective feeling of unity springs from our common response against the common enemy. No other social emotion will melt us into one. Instead of depending upon a national soul we must achieve national-mindedness.

Professor James seems to have thought that we might substitute some other cult for the cult of warfare and reach the same emotional result—the cult of youth conscripted to necessary social labor. But cults are not deliberately created in this fashion. Plato admitted this. He needed a set of cults for his ideal state, but he was compelled to postulate them as already in being. Even his philosopher king could not legislate cults into existence. Mussolini refuses to recognize the logic of the situation.[3] He is depending upon the hostile impulse to fuse his Fascist state, and he is compelled to talk in terms of wars. He has to quicken imaginations with pictures of Roman conquests, and the threat of full panoplied legions. He is undertaking to arouse an Italian soul, not to fashion an Italian mind. He is, undoubtedly, very far from wanting the wars whose threat helps to hold this society together, for nothing would more certainly shatter it than the operation of a modern war; but he can safely threaten for a while, in a Europe

[3] [Benito Mussolini (1883–1945), Italian dictator and founder of Fascism.]

whose surrounding populations have had a surfeit of fighting. The task of becoming nationally minded is then that which the outcome of the Great War is imposing upon us.

We enter upon our civil conflicts with the comfortable sense of a sovereign state behind us endowed with supreme and ultimate force to compel adherence to law and order. This state can if necessary call out the national troops to enforce the unity of the community which conflicting interests may have threatened. Can we keep this sort of state unless it is endowed with an army trained to fight the country's wars? A police force, even a national police force, is not an army. The dread sovereignty of the state is evidenced in troops trained to the unthinking obedience which warfare enforces. If we are compelled to surrender war with the blind military obedience which it puts into the hands of the state, we will be compelled to think out rational solutions of our civil quarrels and think them out a good deal more quickly. It is a great deal easier to feel than it is to think. It is a great deal easier to be angry with one's enemy than to sift the grounds of one's quarrel and find the basis for a reasonable solution. And if you can find grounds for making your enemy the enemy of the community—a Bolshevik, for example—the procedure is still easier. To use the mind with which the community has endowed you to compass the common interests rather than as a means of pursuing your own interest is a strenuous affair, and this is what it means to become nationally minded. Let me repeat if we surrender war there is no way of maintaining national unity except in discovering that unity in the midst of the diversity of individual concerns. There *is* a common good in which we are involved, and if society is still to exist we must discover it with our heads. We cannot depend upon our diaphragms and the visceral responses which a fight sets in operation.

There is something profoundly pathetic in the situation of great peoples, that have been struggling up through long centuries of fighting and its attendant miseries, coming closer and closer to each other in their daily life, fashioning unwittingly larger racial, lingual, liturgical, confessional, political, and economic communities, and realizing only intermittently the spiritual life which this larger community confers upon them, and realizing it only when they could fight for it. The pathos comes out most vividly in the nationalisms of the nineteenth and twentieth centuries. These nationalisms have meant the sudden realization that men belonged to communities that transcended their groups, families, and clans. They had attained selves through which they entered into relation with their common nationals, and the only way in which they could seize upon and enjoy this new spiritual experience was in the fight for its symbols, their common language and literature, and their common political organizations. The pathos lies in the inability to feel the new unity with the nation except in the union of arms. It is not that men love fighting for its own sake, but they undergo its rigors for the sake of conjunction with all those who are fighting in the same cause. There is only one solution for the problem and that is in finding the intelligible common objects, the objects of industry and commerce, the common values in literature, art, and science, the common human interests which political mechanisms define and protect and foster. But all these values are at first divisive. They appear at first as individual and class interests and at first one fights for them and against others who threaten them. The rational attitude is to find what common values lie back of the divisions and competitions. Within our communities the process of civilization is the discovery of these common ends which are the bases of social organizations. In social organization they come to mean not opposition but diverse occupations and activities. Difference of function takes the place of hostility of interest. The hard task is the realization of the common value in the experience of conflicting groups and individuals. It is the only substitute. In civilized communities while individuals and classes continue to contend, as they do, with each other, it is with the consciousness of common interests that are the bases both for their contentions and their solutions. The state is the guardian of these common interests, and its authority lies in the universal interest of all in their maintenance. The measure of civilization is found in the intelligence and will of the community in making these common interests the means and the reason for converting diversities into social organization.

The Great War has posed the problem before contending nations of carrying civilization into the community of nations; that is, it has left us with the demand for international-mindedness. The moral equivalent of war is found in the intelligence and the will both to discover these common interests between contending nations and to make them the basis for the solution of the existing differences and for the common life which they will make possible.

This is the moral equivalent of war if the office of war is to adjust international differences. As an adjudicator war is utterly discredited since, as I have said, if war is logically pursued it leaves nothing to be adjudicated, not even the enemy nations themselves. However, it has not been the peace treaties after hostilities have ceased that have been the valuable contributions which warfare has made to human history. Professor James has indicated them—the spiritual heritage of devotions and heroisms and the consecrations of national values which occupy the most precious pages in history, and the emotional exaltation which accompanies the merging of a crowd of discrete individuals into a living union of men with a single purpose. These are the by-products of war which are in themselves invaluable, but to compass which no people would deliberately undertake war. This constitutes the paradox with which Professor James opened the discussion of his theme. It is a paradox the full depth of which he did not sound. The lying secret diplomacies, the exasperations of suppressed minorities, the profiteering of individuals and combines, the underhand conservation of selfish interests, which men have allowed in the past and still in a measure allow because they keep war as a valued possibility to hold the nation together—this is a stranger paradox. Must we simply sur-render the values which we dare not directly invoke?

It is a question that concerns both ethics and psychology. The answer of ethics has already been given. The spiritual losses of war in prospect enormously outweigh any estimate we dare put upon these by-products. The psychological solu-tion Professor James sought in a somewhat fantastic cult of youth conscripted for social labor. He would substitute a harmless cult for one that is extremely hazardous. We have seen that cults cannot be manufactured to order. The willing-ness of the communities of the world to keep up the apparatus of fighting and the threat of war is an advertisement both of the supreme value of the larger national self and the extreme difficulty of bringing the citizen to realize it. What Professor James saw was that it was only in war that public interests do not leave men cold. The war taxes are the only taxes that are willingly paid. It is still so much easier to revert to the old dispensation and chant with the Psalmist that our God is a man of war.

What I am seeking to bring out is that the chief difficulty in attaining international-mindedness does not lie in the clash of international interests but in the deep-seated need which nations feel of being ready to fight, not for ostensible ends but for the sake of the sense of national unity, of self-deter-mination, of national self-respect that they can achieve in no other way so easily as in the readiness to fight.

National-mindedness and international-mindedness are in-extricably involved in each other. Stable nations do not feel the need in any such degree as those that are seeking stability. It was the militaristic fusing of the German nation out of separate German states by Bismarck's policy of blood and iron [4] and the fusion of a vast backward community of Rus-sian peasants by a Czardom with a pan-Slavic battle-cry that played a great part in the origins of the Great War. When the French are convinced that the German nation no longer needs

[4] [Otto von Bismarck (1815–1898), German statesman whose policies unified Germany under Prussia.]

to threaten her neighbors in order that she may feel her own national self, the fears of France will subside. Bismarck's proud sentence—Germany fears God and no one else on earth —was the challenge of a nation that dared not disarm because it feared internal disintegration. Bismarck's God was a man of war, that was the reflex of an international inferiority complex.

The outlawry of war as proclaimed in the Peace Pact goes then only halfway toward its great goal. It will be presumably approved by the nations of the world. So far as ostensible international differences are concerned, the peoples of the Western world are agreed that they should be settled by some method of negotiation, and that war to this end is no longer a policy which civilized nations may pursue. Self-defense remains a permissible ground for fighting, but with no war of offense there would be none of defense, and wars would vanish with the development of adequate means of negotiation, but we are not willing to have the readiness to fight disappear. So we retain national honor and peculiar interests. Why cannot these be adjudicated as well? Because these touch the sense of national self-respect. As long as we have these provisos, we have the proud sense of being willing to fight—to stake everything upon the assertion of national selfhood. It was this sense which President Wilson's [5] unfortunate phrase offended—being too proud to fight. It was seemingly a phrase that contained a contradiction in terms. Pride predicates a fighting spirit.

Now, if I am not mistaken such an attitude at the present period in human history is a revelation of an uncertainty of national selfhood and a grasping after the approved means of securing it—the wartime spirit. For at this period of the world's history there is no point of national honor and peculiar interest which is not as open to reasonable negotiation in a community of self-respecting nations as any of the so-called

[5] [Woodrow Wilson (1856–1924), 27th President of the United States (1913–1921).]

justiciable and negotiable issues, if we were sure of ourselves. But we are not sure of our national selves, and a certain amount of national psychoanalysis would be very valuable if not very probable. One thing, however, is clear, that we cannot attain international-mindedness until we have attained a higher degree of national-mindedness than we possess at present; and a rough gauge of it will be found in the necessity of retaining national honor and peculiar interests as *causae belli*.[6]

Such a formulation seems to imply that if we were willing to get down to real reasons and abandon good reasons, if we were willing to be really reasonable we could immediately banish the threat of war from our international and our national life. I do not believe that this is the case. Civilization is not an affair of reasonableness; it is an affair of social organization. The selfhood of a community depends upon such an organization that common goods do become the ends of the individuals of the community. We know that these common goods are there, and in some considerable degree we can and do make them our individual ends and purposes, to such a degree that we have largely banished private warfare from the recognized methods of maintaining self-respect in civil conflicts. But there are still great gaps in our social organization, notably between our producers and the social service which they perform. Here there are groups that have to assure themselves of their self-respect by fighting on occasions. The labor unions and the employers as well preserve their solidarity, that is their sense of common selfhood, by the mechanism of hostility, that is by the threats of strikes and lockouts. Back of it lies the inability of the laborer to realize himself in the social process in which he is engaged. Where such a situation becomes acute, men, if they can, will always bind themselves together by hostile organizations to realize their common purposes and ends and thus assure themselves the selfhood which

[6] ["Causes of war."]

society denies them. Men will always jealously maintain and guard this mechanism to assure themselves to themselves. We will get rid of the mechanism of warfare only as our common life permits the individual to identify his own ends and purposes with those of the community of which he is a part and which has endowed him with a self.

THE PHILOSOPHIES OF ROYCE, JAMES, AND DEWEY IN THEIR AMERICAN SETTING

That part of North America to which our forefathers came, the Atlantic Coast from Maine to Florida, and that ever receding frontier of which they progressively took possession, that frontier that was at last arrested by the Pacific stretching from Washington to southern California, this far-stretching country defines in geography and history the community of the United States of America. But while historical geography thus draws its boundaries and marks out the set of its vast adventure, it does not define and exhibit the mind that was formed within this American community and that informed and shaped the course of that adventure.

It was a mind that brought with it from Europe habits already formed of ecclesiastical and political self-government. The dominant habits were those of Puritanism and the democracy of the town meeting. The philosophy of the Puritanism is indicated in the phrase "thrift and righteousness." Calvinism had found a place for business within its spiritual economy. It could find the blessing of God in what the medieval church had called usury. It opened the door to a capitalistic regime. God had given men property and blessed them in its increase, and punished the unprofitable steward by taking away even that which he had. In England, the Puritans and their successors from whom the American colonists came remained after the restoration a subordinate part of the nation. The monarchy, parliament, and the courts, and the social hierarchy from which their functionaries were drawn, bore

[From the *International Journal of Ethics,* XL (1929–1930), 211–231.]

witness to old feudal habits that still controlled the national
life, set the standards of conduct, gave form to social values,
and furnished their emotional resonance. The culture of England's ruling class, sprung from an unbroken history, dominated the spiritual life of the community. When the colonies
threw off their allegiance to the English crown and entered
the family of independent nations, they had brought about a
change which was even more profound than their political
revolution. They had changed the character of the state which
gave the former colonists their political consciousness. When
they recognized themselves as citizens it was no longer as
members of the English social hierarchy. For this they had substituted a political national structure which was a logical development of the town meeting. The state has never impressed itself upon the American citizen. It is nothing but the
extension in representative form of the political habits of the
town meeting. The caucus and the political boss stand so
largely for its *modus operandi* that it commands little weight
of inherited respect. It was not until the national state became
a practical necessity in the administration and distribution of
public lands that it became an essential part of the political
consciousness of the community west of the Alleghenies. Then
it could be appealed to for the development of roads, canals,
and railways. Apart from these the pioneers continued to gov-
ern themselves in the fashion of town meetings. Any man was
qualified for an office if he could secure the votes for his election. And the astonishing thing was that it worked so well.
Thinly spread over a vast continent, this nexus of town meetings not only governed themselves in rough-and-ready fashion
but organized states which were organic parts of the United
States, and the fundamental reality of it in men's consciousness was baptized in blood. But the reality of it grew out the
solution of their problems. It was a union that had to be
achieved, not one that could be brought out like an invisible
writing in men's ancient inherited experience. The habit of
self-government in local affairs was an inherited English
method, but the creation of a national state out of these

habits was purely American. Despite two revolutions English society had preserved the outward form of a state which symbolized its unity in the forms of feudal loyalties, while the power had been shifted to a parliament within which the representatives of new groups were given a voice in governmental control. But these representatives belonged to a hereditary ruling class who fused their representation of a rising democracy with the historical traditions of the English gentleman—the essence of English liberalism. Within the community the men whom commerce and industry had clothed with new demands placed these demands in the keeping of those who had the historic tradition and training. So the as yet unfranchised voters and the nonconformists could find their articulate spokesman in so typical an English gentleman and so vivid a churchman as Gladstone.[1] The education and social training which we call culture was in the minds of Englishmen an essential part of the consciousness of the state. Carlyle [2] wanted to deepen it into a religion and Disraeli [3] saw in it not only the opportunity of Tory democracy but of a farflung imperialism. The state could be realized not only in the symbolic person of the monarch but also in the dependence of the masses upon those whose training and social position gifted their representatives with the right to fight their battles within the ancient structure of the state. It was not only the military victories of England that were won on the fields of her public schools. The historical and functional universality of the state could be still incarnated in a social feudal structure. The training, the culture, and the ideas of its upper classes were essential factors even in the political struggles which democratized its government.

It is, I think, necessary to recall this fundamental difference

1 [William Gladstone (1809–1898), British statesman who led the Liberal Party from 1868 to 1894.]

2 [Thomas Carlyle (1795–1881), British philosopher, historian, and man of letters.]

3 [Benjamin Disraeli (1804–1881), British statesman and author who became leader of the Tory Party.]

between the American and English communities, if we are to understand the part played in our life by a culture which in one sense is as much English as American.

These differences of attitude in the corresponding groups in the English and American communities stand out most sharply, if we recognize that in England they were dominant elements in the middle class which was fighting its way to a controlling political position, a middle class which stood between a lower class of tenants, farm laborers, and the industrial proletariat of the manufacturing cities, on the one side, and the upper class of gentility, nobility, and the crown above them, on the other. In American society there was nothing below them and nothing above them. They did not have to convince a community of ancient tradition that their control would not sacrifice the values woven into its social structure and hallowed by its history. If the American Puritan was freed from the opposition of his English fellow, he was freed also from the necessity of deepening his philosophy to meet the demands of a more varied community. He had problems enough, but these did not include that of justifying his way of life and the principles underlying his view of the world to powerful hostile parts of his own community. This type of English individualism was set free to propagate itself in a great continent without its natural enemies.

It was an individualism which placed the soul over against his Maker, the pioneer over against society, and the economic man over against his market. The relations were largely contractual. Behind it lay a simplified religious philosophy, a theology, in which dogmatic answers were given to questionings as to the purpose of the world, the future of the human soul, moral obligations, and social institutions. Its Calvinism had separated church and state. It had come to terms with the Newtonian revolution and eighteenth-century enlightenment. Popular education and economic opportunity sprang naturally from its social attitude and its geographical situation. It was the distillation of the democracy inherent in Calvinism and the Industrial Revolution at liberty to expand and proliferate for a century without the social problems which beset it in Europe. The American pioneer was spiritually stripped for the material conquest of a continent and the formation of a democratic community.

It has not been, therefore, either in the fields of philosophic reflection and aesthetic appreciation or in that of historic retrospect that the American has sought for the import of his political activity. His most comprehensive institutions of social control and organization have found their reason for existence in the immediate problems of the community. The same is true of the economic life of the community. Success in business has not meant entrance into time-honored ruling classes. In no country in the world has striking success in business been so occupied with the economic organization and development in the economic processes themselves. Those larger communities which political and economic activities have always implied and involved, and which the historic relations of members of the European nations have in some sort expressed, have had little or no existence in the retrospect and historic structure of the American mind, with which to dignify and build out the import of activities which transcend their immediate field.

It has followed that the values of these social processes have been found in the achievements they have immediately secured or in the interest in the activities themselves, and as the immediate ends in politics and business are inadequate expressions of their values in the community the ideal phase of politics and business has been found in the process rather than in their objectives. This implicit philosophy has been inarticulate. That it is there is evidenced in the social values which have permeated and controlled political and economic life in America, values which have transcended our politics and our business. The advance which has been achieved in our society has in the main been due neither to leadership nor to ideas. There have been a few outstanding exceptions, but by and large I think this is true of the history of the community, of the United States. And yet we have inherited the literature, the philosophy, and the art of the Europe from which we separated ourselves in our political and economic undertakings. It was a culture which did not root in the active life of the community. The colleges which were the natural habitats of this culture, which should therefore have endowed with this culture those who were going out into the active life of the community, were not the centers from which the politicians and businessmen of the community were drawn. In the earlier years of our history they trained a larger percentage of the clergymen than of any other calling, but the separation of church and state was too profound not only in our institutions but also in our social attitudes to allow the church to be a dominant force in the direction of the onward life of the community.

It is this break between the culture and the directive forces in the community that was characteristic of the century and a quarter of the history of the mind of America. It stands out in all expressions of this culture, but it is to its import in philosophy that I wish to draw attention.

In eighteenth-century thought, science had discovered laws in nature and assumed them to exist in social processes. As God enacted them in nature, let the monarch enact them in society; and personal obligation to these monarchs would ensure their operation in church and state. It was the undertaking of the romantic philosophies to fuse these two principles of social control into one. Nature was rational and society was rational. The principle of control was reason, but this controlling reason could be found only in an inclusive self that contained nature and society. Contrariety, the irrational, contradiction, evil, and sin, in nature and men, could only be overcome by the wider experience within which these disappear in the rational. What the romantic philosophy undertook was to find this process, in which the contradictions disappear in the higher synthesis, within the experience of the individual mind; but as the solution must be already achieved in the timeless process of the infinite, the finite mind could find no direction for its conduct within its own reason.

It could only realize itself in taking its place within so much of the transcendent whole as was evident in its experience. As that experience widened we could realize more and more of that infinite whole, but we had no such intelligent process within ourselves as would enable us to take the helm into our own hands and direct the course of our own conduct, either in thought or action. Still it was a romantic philosophy that was warm with the inner life of the self, and it vivified the past by reliving it. It brought romance into history and philosophy.

This romantic philosophy was reflected in America in Emerson and the members of the Concord School,[4] but in America it answered neither to the program of the Absolute Idealists that sought to sweep all activities of the spirit, scientific, aesthetic, religious, and political, within the logic of the development of the self, nor to the undertaking of Carlyle to find within the depths of the self a principle of feudal leadership that could guide English society out of the wastes of the Industrial Revolution. It was allied in America to the clerical revolt against Calvinism and brought with it a romantic discovery of a self that could interpret nature and history by identifying itself with their processes, but it was worked out neither in the logic of thought and social organization nor with regard to the demands of immediate social problems. It was a part of American culture, a culture which was fundamentally European. But the American became self-conscious in his belief that he had broken with the structure of European society. He felt himself to be hostile to the society from which his culture sprang. Nor was this break between culture and social activities mended by the literature of the New England group. This was shot through with a nostalgia for the richer and profounder spiritual experience across the Atlantic. It followed from this situation that culture in America was not an interpretation of American life. And yet the

4 [Ralph Waldo Emerson (1803–1882), American poet, essayist, and lecturer. He formed a discussion group at his home in Concord; transcendentalism was the topic of concentrated interest.]

need for interpretation was present in American consciousness, and the lack of a competent native culture was recognized. I believe that there is no more striking character of
American consciousness than this division between the two
great currents of activity, those of politics and business on the
one side, and the history, literature, and speculation which
should interpret them on the other.

This culture appeared then in the curricula of American
schools and colleges. There was no other to put in its place.
America's native culture accepted the forms and standards of
European culture, was frankly imitative. It was confessedly
inferior, not different. It was not indigenous. The cultivated
American was a tourist even if he never left American shores.
When the American felt the inadequacy of the philosophy
and art native to the Puritan tradition, his revolt took him
abroad in spirit if not in person, but he was still at home for
he was an exponent of the only culture the community
possessed.

When the great speculative mind of Josiah Royce appeared
in a California mining camp and faced the problem of good
and evil and examined the current judgments and the presuppositions back of them, he inevitably turned to the great
philosophies of outremer,[5] in his dissatisfaction with the shal-
low dogmatism of the church and college of the pioneer. In
all European philosophies since the time of Descartes the
problem of knowledge had been central, the problem of relating the cognitive experience of the individual mind to the
great structures of the physical universe which Newtonian
science presented, and to the moral universe which western
society in its states and churches predicated. Some of these
structures were new and some were old, and at various points
they clashed with each other. The scientific presentations demanded acceptance on the basis of objective evidence. When
they clashed with inherited dogma the individual had to find
within himself, if he attempted to think out his problem, the

[5] ["Across the sea," "abroad."]

reason for acceptance or rejection. If the clash came between scientific doctrines evidence could be obtained from the findings. The scientist was not thrown back upon his own mind. But if the conflict arose between the dogmas in social institutions and scientific doctrine no such appeal could be made to accept findings. Western thought presupposed an ordered, intelligible, moral universe. Its ordered intelligible character, that is, its uniformity, enabled the mind to test its scientific findings, but its moral order presupposed a supreme end or purpose in which the purposes of voluntary individuals could appear as elements of an organized whole. However, no such ordered moral whole is given by which one may test his individual purpose. The same might be said of intelligible nature. No complete universe is given by which the scientist may test his hypothesis. But the scientist is quite willing to accept the experimental test of his hypothesis. His experience thus becomes a part of the objective world of science. For no modern scientist has skepticism been a practical problem. But the Western world has been obsessed with the conception of a given moral order with which the individual will must accord if the individual is to be moral. The scientist is not the less scientific because the hypothesis which he has brought to the experimental test is later proved to be incorrect. But the moral individual is good or bad as he has or has not conformed to the given moral order, and yet his judgment is fallible. Only Kant's rigorous but empty categorical imperative offers a seemingly logical escape from the dilemma. As it proved in the case of Kant and his idealistic successors, the established institutions of society offer the only palpable expressions of such a given moral order. Here skepticism is a practical problem. And it was out of attempted solution of the relation of the individual will and its purpose to a given all-inclusive aim of the absolute will that Royce's idealism arose.

Such skepticism has had its place in the American community, but it has belonged mainly to the adolescent over against the claims of the dogma of the church. It was not reflected in the general attitude of a community engaged in the reconstruction of its institutions. A striking difference between the spiritual lives of Europe and America, since the American revolution, is that a continuous process of revolution and reconstruction was going on in Europe while American institutions have been subject to no conscious reconstruction. The values embodied in the institutions of the European communities were felt to be profoundly threatened, or revolutionary parties sought to restate them in their own programs, or political and social reformers insisted that the changes they sought would not imperil them. In the background of all thought lay these values, and it is this sense of them in the face of the profound changes that were going on that gave to Europe in the nineteenth century its peculiar character. This same culture brought to American shores lacked this background of social reconstruction. It was foreign and yet it was our only culture. The dominance of middle-class ideals of contractual freedom, of political democracy, of freedom of the school from the church, these were commonplaces in American consciousness. The insurgence of these concepts and attitudes into an old feudally ordered society gave a rich setting for novelist, poet, and historian. The cultured American had to become a European to catch the flavor. He had to get another soul as does the man who has learned a new vernacular or who has traveled in foreign parts. Our own bitter struggle to abolish slavery that the country might remain a united community found little to illuminate and interpret it in this culture. The problem was not a European problem. Skepticism had a profound social import in Europe. The freethinker was not simply one who criticized theological dogma. He was a libertarian in a political sense and was thought to be endangering all institutions. It is only necessary to reflect upon socialism in Europe, and to think of the meaninglessness of it in the American community during the nineteenth century, to bring vividly to consciousness the profound difference between the European and the American minds. The result of this was that while there was a cultured group in the community, and while culture was sought vividly in institutions of learning, in lyceums and clubs, it did not reflect the political and economic activities which were fundamental in American life. We realize that Kant, Fichte,[6] Schelling, and Hegel each stood for a phase of the reconstruction that was going on in the German community; and we realize that this romantic idealism was not so foreign to the English community that Green could not draw from this idealism a new and living sense of the individual in the community and the social reality that expressed itself in the individual. But one cannot dream of that philosophy interpreting the relation of the American individual to society. And yet the American philosopher had to acquire his detachment of thought, his sense of the philosophic problem, and his training in philosophic disciplines in these European philosophies. They were, of course, as much his as were the Medieval doctrines of Thomas and Scotus,[7] or the philosophies of Greece. But Royce did not present the problems of American consciousness in the terms of the older philosophies. They were recognizedly distant in history, but he did present the problem of the relation of the American individual to his universe, physical and moral, in terms of the absolute idealism that was at home in a German, almost a Prussian soil. It is only in a community in which personal subordination is sublimated into identification of the self with the larger social whole, where feudal social organization still persists, that romantic idealism can interpret the immediate problem of the individual to the world. It was the passionate struggle of Royce's great mind to fashion, in his philosophy of Loyalty, an expression of this idealism which would fit the problem of American thought. He was obliged to take it into the vernacular of the church, where alone skepticism had a meaning, to seek for reverberations from Calvinistic and Pauline conceptions. His individual

[6] [Johann Gottlieb Fichte (1762–1814), German philosopher who elaborated a system of moral idealism.]

[7] [Duns Scotus (*ca.* 1266–1308), a scholastic philosopher noted for the subtlety of his thought.]

was voluntaristic; the judgment was an expression of purpose. His individual is American in his attitude, but he calls upon this American to realize himself in an intellectual organization of conflicting ends that is already attained in the absolute self, and there is nothing in the relation of the American to his society that provides any mechanism that even by sublimation can accomplish such a realization. Not even in the Blessed Community, with Royce's social analysis of the self, does Royce lay hands upon an American social attitude that will express his undertaking. Causes, loyalty to which unites the man to the group, so far from fusing themselves with higher causes till loyalty reaches an ultimate loyalty to loyalty, remain particular and seek specific ends in practical conduct, not resolution in an attained harmony of disparate causes at infinity. Nor does Royce's stroke of genius—the infinite series involved in self-representation—reflect the self-consciousness of the American individual. The same remark may be made upon Royce's doctrine of interpretation. In each of these conceptions Royce points out that the individual reaches the self only by a process that implies still another self for its existence and thought. If the structure of reality that is organized about the self in the social process is already there, the concept affords a striking picture of its infinity. The logical implication, empty in itself, can interpret a structure if the structure is there and reveal its character. But the American even in his religious moments did not make use of his individualism—his self-consciousness—to discover the texture of reality. He did not think of himself as arising out of a society, so that by retiring into himself he could seize the nature of that society. On the contrary, the pioneer was creating communities and ceaselessly legislating changes within them. The communities came from him, not he from the community. And it followed that he did not hold the community in reverent respect.

We are not likely to exaggerate the critical importance of religion, as the carrier of the fundamental standards of social conduct, in the building up of the great American community; but it belonged to the character of the pioneer that his religious principles and doctrines like his political principles and doctrines were put into such shape that he could carry them about with him. They were part of the limited baggage with which he could trek into the unpeopled west. He was not interested in their origins or the implications of those origins, but in the practical uses to which they could be put. And no American, in his philosophical moments, regarding the sectarian meetinghouses of a western community would have felt himself at home in [the] spiritual landscape of Royce's Blessed Community. Notwithstanding Royce's intense moral sense and his passionate love of the community from which he came and to which he continued to belong, his philosophy belonged, in spite of himself, to culture and to a culture which did not spring from the controlling habits and attitudes of American society. I can remember very vividly the fascination of the idealisms in Royce's luminous presentations. They were a part of that great world of outremer and exalted my imagination as did its cathedrals, its castles, and all its romantic history. It was part of the escape from the crudity of American life, not an interpretation of it.

In the psychological philosophy of William James, on the other hand, we find purpose explaining and elucidating our cognition, rather than setting up a metaphysical problem which can only be solved by positing an infinite intellect. James's chapter on the concept is the source of his later pragmatism, and of the pregnant ideas which both Royce and Dewey confess that they owe to him. The passage from the percept to the concept is by way of attentive selection and the source of this attentive selection must be found in the act. Knowledge predicates conduct, and conduct sets the process within which it must be understood. Royce admits it, and considers the judgment an act, and then proceeds to draw metaphysical conclusions, if the universe is a moral universe. But for James the act is a living physiological affair, and must be placed in the struggle for existence, which Darwinian evolution had set up as the background of life. Knowledge is an expression of the intelligence by which animals meet the problems with which life surrounds them. The orientation of knowledge is changed. Its efficacy can be determined not by its agreement with a preexistent reality but by its solution of the difficulty within which the act finds itself. Here we have the soil from which pragmatism sprang. Both Royce and James were influenced by the science of their period. Royce was affected by mathematical science at the point at which mathematics and logic coalesce, and he was a considerable figure in the development of symbolic logic. James's medical training brought him under the influence of the biological sciences. But back of this lay James's own individual problem—the skepticism of adolescence set in a long period of illness that sickened both body and mind. What could he believe that would give him the assurance with which to face life? He demanded the right to believe that he might live. There must be a meaning in life that transcended the mechanistic conception of it which the biological sciences presented. Renouvier fortified him in his refusal to surrender the will to mechanism.[8] The mechanistic doctrine could not be proved, and his own will to believe pulled him out the pit.

James, though born in New York, was a New Englander. New England was the seat of the Puritan tradition and also the seat of culture, both that of the Old World and that which had continued to flourish in America. He had the keenest aesthetic response and had even tentatively addressed himself to the artist's life. Residence abroad had equipped him with European languages and made him at home in Europe, as he was at home in Boston and at Harvard, but his mental and moral citizenship was in America, as that of his brother Henry [9] was not. In his own experience he was not aware of the break between the profound processes of American life and its culture. He was not of pioneer stock. He condemned

---

[8] [Charles Bernard Renouvier (1815–1903), French philosopher whose writings on freedom influenced William James at a crucial point in the latter's intellectual development.]

[9] [Henry James (1843–1916), famous novelist, brother of William James.]

the crudity, the political corruption, the materialism of American life, but he condemned it as an American. It was perhaps because the solution that he sought for his own problems did not take him to foreign systems, that it was out of his own physiology and psychology, that he felt his way to an intellectual and moral world within which he could live, that the cleavage between life and culture did not appear in his philosophy. His philosophy was a native American growth. The adolescent skepticism with which his mental struggles began was common to American youth who thought at all, and he found and fashioned within himself the weapons with which to defeat it. He lived and thought freely. If any man's culture has been a part of himself, this was true of James. He carried no burden of learning or critical apparatus, and he was instinctively responsive to what was native to other people. Like Goethe [10] he was at home in any circle, but without Goethe's sophistication. And yet he remained a New Englander, as far as American life was concerned. The principle of his solution was found in the individual soul. His was a lofty individualism. He was ready to go to the help of the Lord against the mighty, and called on others to go with him, but it was as individuals they were to go, to bring more moral order into a pluralistic unfinished universe.

He heralded the scientific method in philosophy. The test of the hypothesis was in its working, and all ideas were hypotheses. Thinking was but a part of action, and action found its completion and its standards in consequences. He adopted Peirce's laboratory habit of mind. But what were the consequences? In the laboratory of the scientist the hypothesis—the idea—is fashioned in terms of anticipated consequences. The experiment must be adjusted to certain prevised events, if the experiment is to say anything. The control of conduct is as essential in the formation of ideas as in the culmination of the act which tests them. And here lies the whole case of pragmatism in its interpretation of knowledge, for if the

[10] [Johann Wolfgang von Goethe (1749–1832), German poet and dramatist, author of *Faust*.]

idea comes into the act, without becoming a part of the apparatus for intelligent control in this situation, the consequences will not test the truth of the idea. They will reveal nothing but the attitude of the individual. Now from the early days in which James was fighting for a foothold of assurance in living, through the poignant thought brought to expression in the will to believe, in his profoundly sympathetic analysis of types of religious experience, and in the lectures on pragmatism, James faced ideas of freedom of the will, of God, and the moral order of the universe, which demanded acceptance of the individual, at the peril of the loss of the values they subtend. And James fought to make the attitude of the individual in these crises pragmatic evidence of the truth of these ideas. This led to the ambiguous term "satisfaction" as the test of truth. This predisposition inevitably blurred his analysis of knowledge in conduct and the nature of the idea. For all of his analysis of the self, James's individual remained a soul in his article on the moral philosopher, and even in his celebrated chapter on habit. It entered in advance of the situation it helped to determine. It carried standards and criteria within itself. It was still the American individual that had fashioned the ecclesiastical and political community within which it lived, though James was a New Englander and no pioneer and lived in a community old enough to have its own culture, though it was a culture that was in great measure sterile in the development of the larger American community. His individual had that in him which was not fashioned in the living process in which his intelligence arose.

John Dewey was also a New Englander like James, and like Royce he was intellectually bred in the idealisms of Kant, Fichte, Schelling, and Hegel, and can say today that

> If there be a synthesis in ultimate Being of the realities which can be cognitively substantiated and of meanings which should command our highest admiration and approval, then concrete phenomena,—ought to be capable of being exhibited as definite manifestations of the eternal union of the real-ideal,

though today this is for Dewey a condition contrary to fact. But while Royce went to Harvard, Dewey went to the University of Michigan. Both Dewey and Royce published psychologies, though Dewey's came earlier in the development of his thought, and constituted in its treatment of the will and the emotions an early step in the formulation of conduct as the field of experience. Like Royce, Dewey was profoundly influenced by James's psychology, though as I have already indicated it suggested to him a method of interpretation of knowledge rather than a metaphysical problem to be worked out in Hegelian fashion. As in the case of James, it was biological science with its dominant conception of evolution that offered him a process within which to analyze and place intelligence.

It would, however, be an error to ascribe to James's *Psychology* the starting-point of Dewey's independent thought. In his *Outline of Ethics* (1891), in which are to be found the essential positions of his ethical doctrine, among his many acknowledgments to English idealistic and naturalistic writers, he makes no reference to James; and yet here we find him denouncing the "fallacy that moral action means something more than action itself." Here we find the "one moral reality—the full free play of human life," the "analysis of individuality into function including capacity and environment," and the "idea of desire as the ideal activity in contrast with actual possession." How far he had traveled from his earlier position appears from the following passage from an article printed in 1884. He there

> declares that God, as the perfect Personality or Will, is the only Reality, and the source of all activity. It is therefore the source of all activity of the individual personality. The Perfect Will is the motive, source, and realization of the life of the individual. He has renounced his own particular life as an unreality; he has asserted that the sole reality is the universal Will, and in that reality all his actions take place.[11]

[11] I am indebted for this quotation to the thesis of Dr. Maurice Baum, entitled "A Comparative Study of the Philosophies of William James and John Dewey."

In the *Outline of Ethics* we find the will, the idea, and the consequences all placed inside of the act, and the act itself placed only within the larger activity of the individual in society.

All reference of knowledge to a preexistent ideal reality has disappeared. Knowledge refers to consequences imagined or experienced. Dewey passed out of his idealistic position by the way of the psychological analysis of the moral act. He occupied himself with the function of knowledge in doing. Instead of finding in the conflict of aims a problem, that knowledge can solve only in an absolute will, it becomes the immediate moral problem of the individual within the act. And his next step was by way of the school, in which he subjected his philosophy to the more severe test of actual accomplishments in education. He accepted the headship of the Department of Philosophy at the University of Chicago upon the condition that it should include that of Education; and his earliest steps in the new field were in the establishment of the Experimental School, in which the education of the children was worked out upon the principle that knowing is a part of doing.

Now Pragmatism is recognized as a part of a current of thought which has had other expressions in other communities. Elsewhere in particular it has been allied with an anti-intellectualism, as for example in Bergson's philosophy. Two characteristics of this phase of modern thought may be noted, one the reference of thought to conduct, and the other the inclusion of intelligence within the sweep of biologic evolution. That these should lead to anti-intellectualism implies that intelligence and thought are not so native to human conduct and behavior even in their most elaborate social expressions, but that they deform experience. In other words, it is assumed that thought has the function not only of facilitating conduct but also of presenting reality as well. Even a theory of knowledge cannot serve two masters, and it was the task of freeing cognition from the shackles of a divided allegiance which Dewey accomplished in his *Essays in Experimen-*

tal Logic. Here Peirce's laboratory habit of mind follows through the whole process of knowing. In particular it is exhibited in elaboration of the problem from which it starts upon its experimental undertaking. In isolating the sense data, and the relations which the conflicts of experience have shaken out, in sharp logical distinction from the nonproblematic world within which it arises, Dewey exempts the logical process that is seeking knowledge from any responsibility for the world that has set the problem. It frees having, enjoying, and suffering and the percept, as the statement of the object that is simply there, from a consciousness *of,* and the way is open for the more complete analysis of consciousness in *Experience and Nature.* The gist of it is that what had been already achieved for the moral act was now established for the act of knowing, and if cognition is not responsible for the world that sets the problem still less is it called upon to read back into a preexistent reality its accomplishment in the solution of its problem, the "fallacy of conversion of eventual functions into antecedent existence." In *Experience and Nature* the parallelism between the analysis of the moral act and the cognitive act is completed. As it is shown in the former that it is in social participation that the peculiar character of the moral appears, so in the latter it is through the participation that is involved in communication, and hence in thought itself, that meaning arises. There is a grand simplicity in the advance from the *Syllabus* and *Outline of Ethics* in 1891 to *Experience and Nature* and *The Quest for Certainty* in 1929. As Whitehead has admonished us, "Seek for simplicity and then distrust it." It is a wise admonition, but before we address ourselves to the subtle problems and the difficult readjustments which any great reconstruction brings with it, we may stop to enjoy the sense of enormous relief with which one completes *The Quest for Certainty.* That baffled sense of the philosophic squirrel running a ceaseless dialectical round within his cage, that despairing sense of the philosophic Sisyphus vainly striving to roll the heavily weighted world of his reflection up into a preexistent reality—these drop away and the philosopher can face about toward the future and join in the scientist's adventure. Not the eagerness to grapple with a dialectical opponent, not the sense of escape into a city not built with hands, but the sense of freedom for action—it is a novel attitude in which to lay down a profound philosophic treatise.

It has been a term of opprobrium that has been cast upon Dewey's doctrine that it is the philosophy of American practicality. But now that the world has become somewhat more respectful of us and more curious about us it may not, perhaps, be opprobrious to recognize the relation of Dewey's habitat to his philosophic output. In the first place it was beyond the Alleghenies that he formulated his problem and worked out the essentials of his doctrine. Though Hegelianism flourished in a small and somewhat Teutonic group in St. Louis, which was not without its repercussions in America, as witness both Royce and Dewey, it was Royce who established the absolute idealisms in American thought by making them a part of culture. There was no sublimation of the individual in the structure of society in America which could make absolute idealism an outgrowth of American consciousness; but as a part of culture it took its place, and the center of gravity of this culture was in New England. I have indicated what seems to me the important characteristic of American life, the freedom, within certain rather rigid but very wide boundaries, to work out immediate politics and business with no reverential sense of a preexisting social order within which they must take their place and whose values they must preserve. We refer to this as individualism, perhaps uncouth, but unafraid. In its finest form it was embodied in William James, for it was in him refined by a genuine native culture. Now there is only one way in which such an individualism can be brought under constructive criticism, and that is by bringing the individual to state his ends and purposes in terms of the social means he is using. You cannot get at him with an ethics from above, you *can* reach him by an ethics that is simply the development of the intelligence implicit in his act. I take it that it is such an implicit intelligence that has been responsible for the steady development and social integration that has taken place in the American community, with little leadership and almost entirely without ideas. It is hardly necessary to point out that John Dewey's philosophy, with its insistence upon the statement of the end in the terms of the means, is the developed method of that implicit intelligence in the mind of the American community. And for such an implicit intelligence there is no other test of moral and intellectual hypotheses except that they work. In the profoundest sense John Dewey is the philosopher of America.

✙✙ XXV ✙✙

PHILANTHROPY FROM THE POINT
OF VIEW OF ETHICS

In its current use charity implies both an attitude and a type of conduct which may not be demanded of him who exercises it. Whatever the donor's inner obligation may be, the recipient on his side can make no claim upon it. Yet the inner obligation exists and in part limits the charity itself, for the donor cannot fail in his other commitments because he has answered the appeals of charity with too great a generosity. Within the appeal itself, however, lies a positive claim upon the donor which he recognizes, though he may be at a loss to estimate its force or to establish a criterion by which to judge between rival claims upon his bounty.

Back of the obligation of the donor lies the human impulse to help those in distress. It is an impulse which we can trace back to animals lower than man. There it is most evident in the parental care of the young, but the impulse may be called out by other relations. It may extend to adult members of the herd or pack to which the animal belongs. It is nicely interwoven with the hostile impulses in animal play. Its strength in humankind is at times deprecated by charity organizations, which desire to bring the impulse under rational control. The kindliness that expresses itself in charity is as fundamental an element in human nature as are any in our original endowment. The man without a generous impulse is abnormal and abhorrent.

Obligation arises only with choice: not only when impulses

[From *Intelligent Philanthropy*, edited by Ellsworth Faris, Ferris Laune, and Arthur J. Todd (Chicago: University of Chicago Press, 1930), pp. 133–148. Reprinted by permission.]

are in conflict with each other, but when within this conflict they are valued in terms of their anticipated results. We act impulsively when the mere strength of the impulse decides; when the anticipated results of action either are not present in the volitional experience or do not affect the onward march of the impulse to its expression. We may condemn such impulsive action, but the condemnation is based upon the fact that a sense of values, with the consequent possibility of reasoned choice, did not play its proper part in the action.

It is evident that here is a field within which there may be no clear-cut moral judgments. How much influence should I allow to a dislike which I find that I have for an acquaintance? In certain situations this may be quite clear. I must pay what is due him. If the dislike is not justified by defects in character or ability, it should not influence my voting for him at an election. But I will not make him a companion on a journey or an associate in social undertakings in which temperamental agreement is of importance. Between these extremes there may lie a multitude of situations in which the impulsive attitude plays a questionable part in our decisions. Falling in love, and the conduct that grows out of it, are shot through with actions which are determined by impulses that are not and perhaps cannot be estimated in terms of consequences.

The kindly impulses that lead us to help those in distress lie within this field—so much so that they may breed beggars —while organized charity has arisen to bring reason into their exercise. Bringing reason into charity consists, on the one hand, in definitely tracing out the consequences of impulsive giving, and, on the other hand, of so marking out the distress and misery of the community that constructive remedial work may take the place of haphazard giving. Organized charity, however, covers but a small part of the field within which these kindly impulses express themselves. Among our own kith and kin, among our friends, in those undertakings that seek to advance human welfare and lessen its suffering in numberless ways, in "the little nameless unremembered acts of kindness and of love," these impulses are called out, and in few of them could we justify their exercise by a reasoned statement of consequences. Indeed, in many of them, such a rationalization of the impulse would diminish if not extinguish its worth and beauty. In kindness, the genuineness and strength of the impulse weigh heavily in our estimate of its worth and that of its author.

So far I have regarded these kindly impulses as if they stood upon the same moral level as hostility, sex, or hunger. And yet, in common parlance, kindness is nearly synonymous with goodness. That this is not merely a eulogistic approval of kindness by those that profit by it is evidenced by that sense of inner obligation which, as I have above indicated, is a part of our charitable attitudes. It is, of course, difficult if not impossible to isolate the fundamental impulses of our natures. Those which I have referred to as the kindly impulses are normally present to some degree however slight in our attitudes to all those about us; but the hostile impulse may quite completely banish them when it seeks the suffering and death of an enemy, and when our dislikes and resentments render us unsympathetic with their objects. In these situations we experience little or no impulse to assist them in their misfortunes, nor do our attitudes carry with them a sense of obligation to act as Good Samaritans. Nevertheless, the sense of obligation which is entailed by our social relations is present: economic relations obtain and persist; we must pay our debts and meet other obligations. In these economic and other social situations we do not simply respond to the stimuli which others embody—paying debts is not merely succumbing to pressure. We speak to ourselves, however unwillingly, with the voice of the creditor and of the community, assessing ourselves with the obligation. Our moral self-consciousness implies our own action as stimulus to our own response, and this action as stimulus appears in a comprehending assumption of the role of those who exact payment from us.

That the recognition of an obligation is at the same time the assertion of a right is tantamount to the individual's identifying himself with those who make the claim upon him.

For an obligation is always a demand made by another or by others. When the obligation seems to involve only one's self or an impersonal landscape, the impulse to action assumes obligatory form only when the individual speaks to himself in the role of another. In obligation the values involved always assume a personal form. Thus in the expression of impulses in which those of kindliness are not dominant or from which they may seem to be entirely absent a man identifies himself sufficiently with the community to lay upon himself those obligations which he in turn exacts from others toward himself. In these situations, as I have said, the obligation does not attach to the impulse. The obligation lies in that response of the community to the individual's action with which he identifies himself. And it is these demands of others upon him with which he identifies himself that are the carriers of the values involved in the act. The impulse to strike or to help, for instance, is as yet unvalued. It is in the result that the value appears. When the impulses come into conflict with each other, the conflict announces itself in the incongruence of the ends which the impulses reach. One may not strike a man when he is down. And it is not the mere incongruence of the ends that carries with it the moral judgment. It is that voice of others in which we join that conveys the moral import of the conflicting values. Both must be there: the voice of the community and our own; the ordered community that endows us with its rights and its obligations, and ourselves that approve or dissent.

There is a definite movement within the field of organized charity toward the assessment of wealth for those purposes which organized charity seeks to fulfill. There is a certain amount of misery which the community should meet in its own interests as well as in the interests of those who are succored. A community chest presents a budget that appeals not simply to the charitable impulses, but to the sense of justice as well. In a word, charity carries a certain burden that ought in any case to be met. Those whose incomes include a surplus above the necessities, whether their souls are stirred by the suffering or not, may well recognize a responsibility to bear their part in meeting this community obligation. When this point has been reached there arises a logical demand that this should be met by the community in the same manner in which it meets its other obligations, through taxation.

Illustrations of this are found in compulsory insurance of employees against the disabilities of old age, sickness, and unemployment. In these situations the responsibility of the community for the disabilities, and the loss which the community suffers through them, takes them out of the field of charity. The appeal is no longer made to charity, but to the sense of justice. The obligation comes from the social values involved upon the individual as an integral part of the community. The morality of paying taxes for these purposes is in no sense lodged in a kindly impulse to relieve the misery which such systems of insurance undertake to meet. What I desire to maintain is that, when the charitable impulse does carry a sense of obligation with it, we always imply a desirable social order within which the goods which our charity confers would come to the recipients as their due or as part of their proper equipment for life in the community. It may be regarded as an unimportant truism to state that the moral standard of charity is to be found in the social value of the benefit to the recipient. In its commonest definition charity is doing good to others—especially to those who are most in need of it. But the ethics of charity is not exhausted by the recognition of the good that accrues to those who receive it. There is first of all the problem which I have already presented, the sense of obligation of the charitable person, even though that obligation cannot be enforced against him by society. The second problem is the standard which is implied in the appeals of different objects of charity.

The position stated above comes to this: that when a man feels not simply an impulse to assist another in distress, but also an obligation, he always implies a social order in which this distress would make a claim upon the community that could be morally enforced, as, for example, in a community where employees in industry are insured, the distresses incident to old age, sickness, and unemployment must be relieved. In contrast with this may be placed a conception that has obtained and still obtains in some circles, namely, that suffering and misery are part of the divine order, where they serve the purposes of punishment and discipline. Under this doctrine charity is a duty laid by God upon man for his own good, and which may accrue to him as a merit. I would still maintain that back of these legalistic conceptions has lain the assumption of the parable of the Good Samaritan that we are neighbors of those in distress; back of the eschatology of the church has always lain the thesis of the Sermon on the Mount that men are all brethren in one family. In immediate sympathy with distress we have already identified ourselves with its victims. In this the human kindly impulse stands above the impulse in lower animals from which it developed. In man even the immediate impulse that lies above the automatisms is the response of a self, and a self-experience is possible only insofar as the individual has already taken the attitude of the other. The very word "sympathy" announced this, as does the plea to "put yourself in his place," made in the effort to stimulate charity.

We characterize this sympathetic attitude of man as humane, as being human, thus distinguishing it from the impulse of the lower animal, for it involves participation in some sense in the suffering of the other. The participation exhibits itself in the experience of him who sympathizes, not so much in the sharing of the suffering as in the incipient attitudes of reaction against and withdrawal from the suffering object. We feel ourselves shrinking from or tending to push away the evil, and these attitudes stimulate our kindly impulse to relieve the sufferer. This is all, however, on the impulsive level. A sense of obligation has not yet arisen, for obligation arises only in the conflict of values. Even the immediate identification of the self with the other does not in itself take us beyond the impulsive attitude of relieving suffering. When, however, these values in terms of sympathetic identification with the others in distress are presented, they have a peculiar immediacy and poignancy; while, on the other hand, their very immediacy and poignancy militate against their statement in terms of rational means. It is difficult to carry over the interest in helping the immediate sufferer into long-distant plans for removing the social causes of the suffering. A man who is ready enough to put his hand into his pocket to assist a starving man who is out of work will hardly identify this impulse with a political campaign for insurance against unemployment.

These two situations present the *terminus a quo* [1] and the *terminus ad quem* [2] of reflective judgment in a certain field of charity. At first the act is hardly above the impulsive level— an almost unreflective push to relieve distress, the strength of which is largely dependent on the degree to which one "puts himself in the other man's place," or the completeness of the sympathy aroused. This very attitude, however, of putting one's self in the other man's shoes brings with it not only the stimulus to assist him, but also a judgment upon that situation. Distress is conceivably remediable, or at the worst can be alleviated. The charitable response which we find in ourselves is one which can and should be called out in others, or more logically still the evil should so far as possible have been obviated. One cannot assume the role of the wretched without considering under what conditions the wretchedness can or may be avoided. As I have already indicated, the immediate effect of sympathetic identification with the other is to call out the other's response in attempting to ward off or alleviate suffering, and this calls out at once resentment or criticism against the individuals or institutions which may seem to be responsible for it. The step from this attitude to the idea of social conditions under which this evil would not exist is inevitable. Out of these ideas arise plans, possibly

1 ["Starting-point"; literally, "end (or limit) from which."]
2 ["Terminal point"; literally, "end (or limit) to which."]

practical, for remedying at the source the misfortunes of those in distress.

This highly schematized path from impulsive charity to social reconstruction serves to indicate, on the one hand, a definite development which has taken place in many instances, and, on the other hand, that structural background of attitude and behavior which lies behind our humane impulses and out of which their ethics and philosophy arise. The very sympathetic identification with those we want to assist is in the logic of our nature the espousal of a cause. Universal religions have issued from their frustration—New Jerusalems where all tears are wiped away, Nirvanas where all wants have ceased. In any case it must be in our reactions against evils, and with its victims with whom we sympathize, that the ethics of charity must lie. The bare impulse to help is on the same level with that of the dogs that licked the sores on Lazarus' body. The identification of ourselves with Lazarus puts in motion those immediate defensive reactions which give rise not only to efforts of amelioration but also to judgments of value and plans for social reform.

It is a mistake, however, to assume that putting one's self in the place of the other is confined to the kindly or charitable attitude. Even in a hostile attack one feels in his own muscles the response of the other, but this only arouses still further one's own attack and directs the response to the attack of the opponent; and in the consciousness of one's rights one places himself in the attitude of others who acknowledge that right in so far as he recognizes this right as inhering in them. These identifications with others lead to self-assertion and a sense of individuality, which eventuate in the maintenance of self-interest and, at a further remove, in a sense of justice. They do not involve that sympathetic identification with the other which belongs to the kindly impulses. In the latter, one expresses himself in assistance and protection. Insofar as the impulse is dominant, the interest of the other has become his own, which he now champions. That one champions the interests of others, with which he has identified himself, implies a social order within which the removal of these evils would make the same claim upon all that they make upon the charitable individual. It is in the feel of this implication that there inheres the sense of obligation which we experience in the presence of distress and disability, though the social order in which we find ourselves may make no explicit claim upon us to alleviate it. The feel of this obligation may be very vague, a mere affirmation that such misery ought not to be. It may be formulated in the belief in another world, a world to come, or in another golden age that lies behind.

In taking the attitude of the other who appeals to our sympathy, the conduct called out tends to maintain the other rather than the self. There is, then, a fundamental difference in the organization of this behavior from that which characterizes behavior either in the attitude of hostility or in the cooperative acts in which the responses of others determine our own. In the latter the interest may be said to lie in the structure and maintenance of the self through his comprehending participation in the other or others. The sympathetic identification with the individual in distress, however, calls out in us the incipient reactions of warding off, of defense, which the distress arouses in the sufferer, and these reactions become dominant in the response of the one who assists. He places himself in the service of the other. We speak of this attitude as that of the unselfishness or self-effacement of the charitable individual. But even this attitude of devotion to the interest of the other is not that of obligation, though it is likely to be so considered in an ethical doctrine which makes morality synonymous with self-sacrifice. The earliest appearance of the feel of obligation is found in the appraisal of the relief to the distressed person in terms of the donor's effort and expenditure. The good of the man with whom we sympathetically identify ourselves is greater than that which would arise if we expended the effort and means on the ends of a self that refused to respond to his extremity. What I give up is slight in comparison with his need. This is but an early stage in the development of the moral judgment, and in the case of the generous individual may appear rather as a defense of an act under strong impulsion than as a motive to the act. But even in the immediacy of the situation that seemingly involves only the giver and the recipient, there is the implication of a community in which the good has a universal value—"which of them was neighbor to him that fell among thieves?" It is, however, an implication that can become explicit only when the social structure and the ideas behind it make it possible to regard the others as neighbors. The generalization of the prophetic message, its conception of the community as the children of Jehovah, made this possible. In the Greek city-state it was only in political and economic relations that the citizen could realize himself over against the others in the community. The generalization of these relations was indeed possible, but only in terms of a reason which could be the experience of a few, and a reason which defined and fixed existing relationships rather than obliterated them. With the decadence of the city-state and under the empire the philosopher, whether slave or emperor, could regard himself as a citizen of the world only so far as he had thought his way out of the structure of social relations, rather than by feeling his way into them.

The moralizing of the impulse to identify one's own interest with that of the other evidently depends upon making this attitude functional in the society in which the individual has reached his self-consciousness and whose structure is essential to the maintenance of his own self. Religion in its ecclesiastical organization may make a place for a particular group who have sold all that they had and have given it to the poor. Such ascetic groups are in a sense samples of the social order that should exist. On the other hand, their restriction to cloistered groups is a confession that the attitude cannot be made the principle of society in this world. And this fixation of the attitude leaves the charity of the layman outside of any program of social reconstruction. Its value is a personal one, an act of piety, an expression of otherworldliness, and the acquirement of merit; or it may be regarded as engendering and cultivating worthy traits of character, consideration for others, kindliness—in a word, humaneness. Over against a too legalistic or vengeful justice it appears as mercy. Then there remain the countless instances in which a sympathetic charity informed with wisdom may rescue others from social shipwreck, from suffering and distress, and help them to better social and physical conditions of life. It is in these instances that charity shines by its own light and becomes almost synonymous with goodness. Here are values which can be intelligently weighed against each other when they come into conflict, and within the social order as it exists reconstruction of the lives and fortunes of individuals can be accomplished. It is indeed in this remedial activity, this salvaging of otherwise unavoidable losses in the community as it is, this amelioration of the existence of the "poor whom ye have always with you," that we generally conceive of charity. It found its place in feudal conditions which have obtained socially long after feudalism was politically defunct. *Noblesse oblige* was a sense of some sort of responsibility for dependents. It was, in a way, institutionalized in chivalry. Because of the close genetic relation between the kindly impulses and the parental impulses it has always been peculiarly vivid in its response to the misfortunes of children.

And still the evils which charity has thus corrected or assuaged have been part of the order of society, and the obligation felt by the charitable did not arise from the duties which were inherent in that order. We return again to the implication of an order within this sense of obligation. The close relation which has existed between religion and charity, as we have seen, has given form to this implication; but human experience, especially in recent times, has abundantly proved that the implication lies in social attitudes, which religious doctrines have formulated but for which they are not responsible. If we undertake to give it its simplest and most immediate expression, it would take this form: that the need to which we respond is one which would be met if the intelligence which informs our social order and its institutions could reach the development which is implicit within them. That is, the moral appeal lying behind the obligation to charity is drawn not from the distress that is to be alleviated or the deficient goods which are to be supplied, but from the sort of conduct and experience and the sort of selves which society implies though it does not make them possible. For example, the moral appeal to charitable endowment of education lies not in the darkened minds of the uneducated but in the fact that there is a wealth of meaning in life and profound values which would interpret it to all members of the community if our social order gave to all the cultural background and the training which would bring out these hidden implications.

The compulsion of the appeal lies first in the location of these values in the relations of men to one another and to the nature that forms the environment of human society. Science, art, religion, and the techniques of living simply bring out, render serviceable and effective, these meanings and values. They are the realization of the wealth which belongs implicitly to all members of society. Cultured classes in some sense have an access to this wealth, which is denied to masses in the community whose social experiences and relationships, nevertheless, constitute this wealth. And, secondly, the means of furnishing this access to continuously wider groups is not found in simply enlarging the capacity and functions of institutions which already belong to social intercourse and control. The present order of society does not make enlargement of cultural means possible, and our immediate duties are formulated in terms of the order within which we live. Those who have advantages cannot share them with the rest of the community. This could only be possible in a community more highly organized, otherwise bred and trained. So far as this community is concerned, we can morally enjoy what from one standpoint is an exploitation of those whose submerged life has given us economic and spiritual wealth which our peculiar situations have enabled us to inherit. To sell all we have and give to the poor would not change this situation.

But we feel the adventitious nature of our advantages, and still more do we feel that the intelligence which makes society possible carries within itself the demand for further development in order that the implications of life may be realized.

It is this feel for a social structure which is implicit in what is present that haunts the generous nature, and carries a sense of obligation which transcends any claim that his actual social order fastens upon him. It is an ideal world that lays the claim upon him, but it is an ideal world which grows out of this world and its undeniable implications.

It is possible to specify the claims of this ideal world in certain respects. A human being is a member of a community and is thereby an expression of its customs and the carrier of its values. These customs appear in the individual as habits, and the values appear as his goods, and these habits and goods come into conflict with each other. Out of the conflict arise in human social experience the meanings of things and the rational solution of the conflicts. The rational solution of the conflicts, however, calls for the reconstruction of both habits and values, and this involves transcending the order of the community. A hypothetically different order suggests itself and becomes the end in conduct. It is a social end and must appeal to others in the community. In logical terms there is established a universe of discourse which transcends the specific order within which the members of the community may, in a specific conflict, place themselves outside of the community order as it exists, and agree upon changed habits of action and a restatement of values. Rational procedure, therefore, sets up an order within which thought operates; that abstracts in varying degrees from the actual structure of society. It is a social order, for its function is a common action on the basis of commonly recognized conditions of conduct and common ends. Its claims are the claims of reason. It is a social order that includes any rational being who is or may be in any way implicated in the situation with which thought deals. It sets up an ideal world, not of substantive things but of proper method. Its claim is that all the conditions of conduct and all the values which are involved in the conflict must be taken into account in abstraction from the fixed forms of habits and goods which have clashed with each other. It is evident that a man cannot act as a rational member of society, except as he constitutes himself a member of this wider commonwealth of rational beings. But the ethical problem is always a specific one, and belongs only to those habits and values which have come into conflict with each other. About this problem lies the ordered community with its other standards and customs unimpaired, and the duties it prescribes unquestioned.

The claims of the ideal world are that the individual shall take into account all of the values which have been abstracted from their customary settings by the conflict and fashion his reconstruction in recognition of them all. Thus, the otherwise unquestioned right of a man to expend his own wealth in his business, family, and personal interests comes into conflict with the needs of youths in impoverished classes for enlightened and adequate training. The claims of reason are that these values shall be regarded apart from their character as private property and the social restrictions which limit the development of children of poorer classes. Whatever he ultimately does, the charitable man feels it incumbent upon him to consider what could be accomplished with a portion of his wealth if it were devoted intelligently to increasing opportunities for education. So much money, in abstraction from the interests that seek it, would spell the enlightenment of many and a raised standard of public education. It is only by stepping into this field in which the possible accomplishments of this wealth can be impartially contemplated that the owner of the wealth feels himself able to decide to give or not to give.

It is clear, however, that reason would operate in a vacuum, unless these values of enlightenment—of science, aesthetic appreciation, and human associations—can take on forms which are freed from the social restrictions placed upon them by the groups which have possessed them. The phrase "republic of letters" has signified this freeing of culture from its class connotation. In a sense it constitutes an ideal world, which does not mean that these values exist in a world by themselves, but that the products of science, art, and human association can and should take on forms which would bring them within the province of any mind and nature able to respond to them. Now the claims of such ideal values lie not simply or primarily in the widening of the community that enjoys them, but in the superiority and efficiency of the science, art, and human relations which are so freed. It is not until science has become a discipline to which the research ability of any mind from any class in society can be attracted that it can become rigorously scientific, and it is not until its results can be so formulated that they must appeal to any enlightened mind that they can have universal value. Artistic creation and aesthetic appreciation must attain forms which have the same universality of objectivity; human relations should become such that their full social import interprets them. Reason is then a medium within which values may be brought into comparisons with each other, in abstraction from the situations within which they have come into conflict with each other; and within this impartial medium it becomes possible to reconstruct values and our conduct growing out of them.

Furthermore, certain of these values, such as those of science and art, have been given a form in which they become accessible to all minds with adequate training and social background. That is, they have been given a form which abstracts them from the restrictions which economic, feudal, and cultural class distinctions lay upon great numbers in the community. This sets up what may be called the "democratic ideal" of removing such restrictions. Now it is within this field that charity is so largely active, not in setting in motion great schemes of social reconstruction, but in bringing about or helping to bring about in specific cases just such a removal of restrictions; and, I take it, the obligation which the charitable individual feels is the demand that these restrictions should be removed. It is not a demand which society as it is now organized can enforce against him. It is a part of the growing consciousness that society is responsible for the ordering of its own processes and structure so that what are common goods in their very nature should be accessible to common enjoyment. We vaguely call it "progress." The charitable man sees and feels in an immediate situation the opportunity of an advance in this direction, and the opportunity may become a duty which he lays upon himself.

INDEX

Abbott, Edith, lxvii
Act, 79–81, 91, 129, 316, 395; dialectic within, 7–8; phases of, xx–xxii, li–liii *(see also* Perception, Manipulation, Consummation); philosophy of, xvi, xix–xxii, xliii–xliv, xlvii, l–li, lxi; as process, 267, 268. *See also* Activity, Conduct, Social act
Activity, xvii, xviii, 7, 38, 39, 43–45, 85; conflict in, 7, 13, 14, 23
Adams, G. P., 337
Addams, Jane, lxvii
Adrastus of Aphrodisias, 180
Aesthetic experience, 294–305
Aesthetics, xix, 7, 23, 295
Alexander, Samuel, xlv, 273, 277
Alexander the Great, 168
Allen, Wm. H., xxxv, lxv
Alleyne, S. F., 185
Ames, Van Meter, lxii
Anderson, B. M., Jr., lxvii
Angell, James Rowland, xvii, xviii, 14, 96, 111
Animal faith, 334
Animal perception, xx, 73–81
Apollonius of Perga, 180
Appearance and Reality, 343
Apperceptionsmasse, 115–116
Aquinas, St. Thomas, 250, 381
Archimedes, 176
Areopagitica, 157
Aristarchus of Samos, 207
Aristotle, 161, 171–172, 179, 184, 197
Association, 74, 76, 128
Astronomy, 174–181, 183
Atkinson, E., 70
Attention, 6, 14–15, 20, 36, 45, 49, 58, 79, 117, 118, 120, 121, 148, 272
Augustine, St., 249, 250
Austin, John, 162

Bacon, Sir Francis, 208
Baldwin, James Mark, xix, 47, 48, 95, 97, 99, 102, 116, 143
Baum, Maurice, 387
Behavior, 267. *See also* Act, Conduct, Experience
Behaviorism, xxv–xxvi. *See also* Psychology
Bentham, Jeremy, 162
Bentley, Arthur F., xliv
Berkeley, George, lxvi, 186, 268
Bergson, Henri, xxi, xlv, xlviii, lx, 242, 270–272, 275, 278, 290, 307, 349
Berry, G. G., 68
Bismarck, Otto, 367
Bosanquet, Bernard, 27, 28, 46
Bow, Susan, 285
Bradley, A. C., 46
Bradley, F. H., 27, 28, 343
Breckinridge, Sophonisba P., lxvii
Brewster, John M., xiv, lxiii
Brightman, E. S., lxvi, 306
Broad, C. D., 340
Buber, Martin, lxi

Caird, Edward, 46
California, University of, xxiii
Carlyle, Thomas, 373, 377
Carr, Harvey, xvii
Chaplin, Charlie, 304
Charity, xliii, 233, 392, 393, 395, 396, 397, 398, 399, 401, 402, 403
Chicago, City Club of, xxvi
Chicago, University of, xiii, xvii, xxiv, xxv, xxxiii, xxxiv, lxi, 388
Communication, 97, 101, 312, 313, 341
Community, 311, 355, 357, 363, 393, 394, 395, 403, 404
Compton, A. H., 333

The Library of Liberal Arts

The American Heritage Series

. . . .

The Library of Literature

· ·

CRANE, STEPHEN, *The Red Badge of Courage*, ed. Frederick C. Crews, 6

DICKENS, CHARLES, *Great Expectations*, ed. Louis Crompton, 2

HAWTHORNE, NATHANIEL, *The Scarlet Letter*, ed. Larzer Ziff, 1

MELVILLE, HERMAN, *Moby Dick*, ed. Charles Feidelson, 5

One Hundred Middle English Lyrics, ed. Robert D. Stevick, 7

SWIFT, JONATHAN, *Gulliver's Travels*, ed. Martin Price, 3

TWAIN, MARK, *The Adventures of Huckleberry Finn*, ed. Leo Marx, 4